Corpora in Cognitive Linguistics

Corpora in Cognitive Linguistics

Corpus-Based Approaches
to Syntax and Lexis

edited by
Stefan Th. Gries
Anatol Stefanowitsch

Mouton de Gruyter
Berlin · New York

Mouton de Gruyter (formerly Mouton, The Hague)
is a Division of Walter de Gruyter GmbH & Co. KG, Berlin.

The hardcover edition was published in 2006 as volume 172
of the series *Trends in Linguistics. Studies and Monographs*.

♾ Printed on acid-free paper which falls within the guidelines
of the ANSI to ensure permanence and durability.

The Library of Congress has cataloged the hardcover edition as follows:

Corpora in cognitive linguistics : corpus-based approaches to syntax
and lexis / edited by Stefan Th. Gries, Anatol Stefanowitsch.
    p. cm. − (Trends in linguistics. Studies and monographs ; 172)
    Includes bibliographical references and index.
    ISBN-13: 978-3-11-018605-5 (hardcover : alk. paper)
    ISBN-10: 3-11-018605-5 (hardcover : alk. paper)
    1. Cognitive grammar − Data processing.   I. Gries, Stefan Thomas, 1970−   II. Stefanowitsch, Anatol, 1970−   III. Series.
    P165.C67 2006
    415.0285−dc22
                                                                    2006006477

ISBN 978-3-11-019826-3

Bibliographic information published by the Deutsche Nationalbibliothek

The Deutsche Nationalbibliothek lists this publication in the Deutsche
Nationalbibliografie; detailed bibliographic data are available in the Internet
at http://dnb.d-nb.de.

© Copyright 2006, 2007 by Walter de Gruyter GmbH & Co. KG, D-10785 Berlin
All rights reserved, including those of translation into foreign languages. No part of this
book may be reproduced or transmitted in any form or by any means, electronic or mechanical, including photocopy, recording or any information storage and retrieval system, without permission in writing from the publisher.
Cover design: Martin Zech, Bremen.
Printed in Germany.

Contents

Introduction *Stefan Th. Gries*	1
Ways of intending: Delineating and structuring near-synonyms *Dagmar Divjak*	19
Corpus-based methods and cognitive semantics: The many senses of *to run* *Stefan Th. Gries*	57
Go-V vs. *go-and*-V in English: A case of constructional synonymy? *Stefanie Wulff*	101
Syntactic leaps or lexical variation? – More on "Creative Syntax" *Beate Hampe and Doris Schönefeld*	127
The place of prototypicality in corpus linguistics: Causation in the hot seat *Gaëtanelle Gilquin*	159
Passivisability of English periphrastic causatives *Willem Hollmann*	193
Transitivity schemas of English EAT and DRINK in the BNC *John Newman and Sally Rice*	225
Caused posture: Experiential patterns emerging from corpus research *Maarten Lemmens*	261
From conceptualization to linguistic expression: Where languages diversify *Doris Schönefeld*	297
Name index	345
Subject index	349

Introduction*

Stefan Th. Gries

1. Cognitive Linguistics and Functional Linguistics: Common assumptions and methods

In two widely received publications, Lakoff (1990, 1991) argues in favor of what he calls "empirical linguistics", a branch of linguistics governed by the so-called Generalization Commitment, the "commitment to characterize the general principles governing all aspects of human language" (Lakoff 1990: 53). Two particular branches of empirical linguistics as he sees it are Cognitive Linguistics and Functional Linguistics. According to Lakoff (1991: 54), Cognitive Linguistics is governed by the cognitive commitment to "make one's account of human language accord with what is generally known about the mind and brain from disciplines other than linguistics". Functional Linguistics, he continues, is "a branch of cognitive linguistics that primarily studies the more limited area of how communicative function plays a role" (1991: 55). If we simply accept this distinction for the sake of the argument (without necessarily subscribing to the way the distinction is made given the historical primacy of functional approaches), then the next natural questions are: what are the assumptions held by cognitive and functional linguists?, and what do they investigate?

A recent introduction to Cognitive Linguistics (Croft and Cruse 2004: Chapter 1) discusses several assumptions shared by many, if not most, cognitive linguists. Two such assumptions are those in (i) and (ii).

(i) Language is not an autonomous cognitive faculty.
(ii) Knowledge of language emerges from language use (Croft and Cruse 2004: 1).

The first assumption resonates with Lakoff's characterization quoted above and emphasizes that cognitive and functional linguists often bring findings from other behavioral sciences to bear on the investigation of language and linguistic structure. A particularly prominent role among these other sciences is certainly played by cognitive psychology, as is evidenced by the impact that psychological research into categorization and prototypicality has had on Cognitive Linguistics; in addition, work in Cognitive Linguistics often makes reference to the way in which humans perceive, and interact with, the world, an approach that will recur in most of the papers of this volume.

The second assumption is concerned with the fact that, rather than assuming that knowledge of language is best conceived of as categorical and determined by discrete either-or parameter settings, linguistic knowledge is ultimately shaped by how language is actually put to use and the ways in which language use influences the representation and the processing of linguistic categories; as will become obvious below, each article in this volume embraces this assumption.

A third assumption which permeates most cognitive-linguistic work and which is also worth pointing out in the present context, is that there is no categorical difference between syntax and the lexicon. Contrary to most mainstream linguistics of the 20th century, syntactic structures at various levels of schematicity are considered meaningful in their own right and, thus, do not differ in kind from words or morphemes (cf. Langacker 1987; Croft and Cruse 2004: Chapter 9).

On the basis of these and other assumptions less relevant to our present purposes, cognitive and functional linguists have investigated a wide variety of issues, although the domains of semantics and syntax have probably enjoyed some prominence over most of the other core disciplines of linguistics, which is also reflected in the present volume. Within semantics, much work was concerned with offering and elaborating new approaches towards notorious issues in lexical semantics such as the characterization of word meanings in general as well as (the relations holding between) word senses of polysemous words and constructions. Within syntax, much work was concerned with the identification of meaningful syntactic structures, so-called constructions, and characterization and explanation of their semantic and distributional properties. However, given the assumed close connection between syntax and lexis, many studies in this field routinely use syntactic arguments to support semantic claims and vice versa, a characteristic that will surface in each of the contributions below.

So far, we have been concerned, at a very general level though, with the kinds of assumptions cognitive and functional linguists hold and with the kinds of issues cognitive and functional linguists have often turned to. In addition, however, we can now also ask what the methodological orientation of these kinds of empirical linguistics has looked like.

It may come as a surprise that – in spite of the commitments cited above and the prominence of the term *usage-based* in recent years – with relatively few exceptions corpus-based approaches have not enjoyed a particular prominence. In addition, the methodological orientation of Cognitive Linguistics and Cognitive Grammar (as well as related disciplines such as Construction Grammar) has so far been relatively qualitative. However, when compared to a large body of research in other paradigms within 20th century mainstream theoretical linguistics, much work within Cognitive Linguistics has already adopted a much broader and more balanced empirical perspective, one that did not solely rely on acceptability judgments of isolated or and/or made-up sentences but also incorporated many other kinds of evidence. Given the overall cognitive orientation in general and the second fundamental assumption in particular, it comes as no surprise that this empirical perspective also included various experimental paradigms such as sorting (e.g., Jorgensen [1990], Sandra and Rice [1995], Bencini and Goldberg [2000]), elicitation tasks (e.g. Rice [1996], Raukko [1999]), priming and reaction time studies (cf., e.g., Rosch and Mervis [1975] for an early study from cognitive psychology or, within Cognitive Linguistics, Hare and Goldberg [1999] and Gries and Wulff [to appear]) and various different paradigms on research on metaphor and idiom comprehension (cf. Gibbs [1995] for a comprehensive overview).

In Functional Linguistics, by contrast, approaches based on performance data from natural settings, i.e. usage data, have a longer tradition. For example, much linguistic research originating in Eastern Europe has been already strongly quantitative and text-based (cf., e.g., John Benjamins's book series LLSEE), and later work by, to name just one prominent example, Givón has relied on text counts from, say, literary sources (cf., e.g., Givón [1983]).

While these functional approaches were based on counts of phenomena within texts, it is often not appreciated that corpus linguistics has actually been around for much longer than is commonly assumed: Early corpus-based work even includes work from the 19th century (e.g. Käding [1897]), but corpus linguistic methods also underlie the pedagogically motivated studies of Thorndike [1921] as well as Thorndike and Lorge [1944] and Fries [1952]. After the compilation of the first corpora aiming at representativity (e.g., the Survey of English Usage founded in 1959) and during the past few decades, corpus linguistics has rapidly become an autonomous methodological paradigm within linguistics. During the general upsurge of corpus-based work especially in Northern Europe, the text-based orientation of much work within Functional Linguistics has also carried over to Cognitive Linguistics where, especially with reference to the notion of usage-based approaches, many studies are now also based on the analysis of naturally-occurring language in the form of electronic corpora.

2. Corpus Linguistics: Common assumptions and methods

At a first superficial glance, corpus linguistics, the analysis of naturally-occurring data, may appear to be a relatively homogeneous methodology. However, a closer look reveals that this assessment is mistaken. Rather, corpus linguistics rather seems to be a category with a prototype structure: there are a few criteria that are – though not individually necessary – shared by much, if not most, work within corpus linguistics, and there is a variety of criteria which are less central to the work of many corpus linguists. It is probably fair to say that the set of the former criteria comprises, among other things, those listed below:

- the analysis is based on a corpus or corpora of naturally-occurring language which are machine-readable so that the retrieval of the search patterns is computerized;
- the corpus is intended or taken to be balanced and/or representative of the modality/register/variety the study is aimed at;
- the analysis is, or at least attempts to be, systematic and exhaustive, meaning that the corpus does not simply serve as a database of examples from which some can be chosen *ad libitum* and others neglected, but that the whole (sample of the) corpus is taken into consideration so that even less frequent patterns must somehow be integrated or at least addressed;
- the analysis aims at more than just accounting for categorical either-or phenomena, but uses statistical data (frequencies, percentages/probabilities, statistical methods) to also cover the middle ground between what is possible/grammatical and what is not;
- the analysis proceeds on the basis of frequency lists (of words, morphemes, grammatical patterns, etc.), concordance lines in which the word of interest is shown in its natural context, and collocations, i.e. lists or tables in which for the word of interest the (most frequent) neighboring words are given.

In addition to these probably relatively uncontroversial criteria, there are some other parameters along which corpus-based studies can be distinguished; I will focus on two of these.

The first important parameter to be singled out here is the level of granularity at which an analysis proceeds. For example, some studies take lemmas as their central focus in order to, for instance, be able to collapse individual word forms and, thus, make more general statements (cf. Atkins, Kegl, and Levin [1988], Atkins and Levin [1995], Hanks [1996], Stefanowitsch and Gries [2003]). Other studies just take one individual word form as their starting point, leaving aside – largely for reasons of computational convenience – other inflected forms. Finally, there are (considerably fewer) studies that have chosen a finer resolution by distinguishing between different inflectional forms of a lemma in order to be able to identify systematic correlations between individual word forms and, say, the preferred constructional patterns these forms occur in or the range of sense with which the forms are associated (examples are Biber [1986], Atkins [1987], Berglund [1991] and several papers from this volume). It is worth pointing out here that neither of these approaches is *a priori* superior over the others – rather, the methodological choice is of course determined by one's research question and, not to forget, unfortunately also by more pragmatic factors such as retrievability, considerations of data sparseness etc.

The second important parameter is qualitativity/quantitativity. This parameter can play a role in two different respects. One the one hand, corpus-based work often makes it necessary to operationalize subjective qualitative phenomena on the basis of quantification, i.e. by using frequency data from corpora. On the other hand, and this is the more important interpretation here, corpus-based studies differ as to the role quantitativity plays in the evaluation of the results. For example, some corpus-linguistic studies are rather qualitative in the sense that their contribution is mainly based on which categories are observed and which are not and what this implies. Most studies are somewhere in the middle between the very qualitative and the very quantitative endpoints of the scale. This majority of studies restricts themselves to reporting frequency data and (usually) attribute some importance to the different frequencies with which particular categories are attested in the data and the consequences this has for the phenomenon under investigation. However, these studies do not adopt a statistically-informed perspective; well-known examples include Meyer (1991), Oostdijk and de Haan (1994), Berglund (1997), Oh (2000), Stubbs (2002, 2003). In the domain of Cognitive/Functional Linguistics, the prominence of this intermediately quantitative perspective is even more prominent; examples include Bybee and Scheibman (1999), Boas (2003), Mukherjee (2003), Barlow and Kemmer (2004), Davidse and Vanden Eynde (2004) etc.

The third and final kind of approach is comparatively quantitative and statistical in nature and still rather infrequent in Cognitive Linguistics. Studies belonging to this approach may not only exhibit the methodological rigor found in, say, psychology and/or psycholinguistics, but they are also often methodologically similar to work commonly counted as belonging to the domains of computational linguistics and/or information retrieval. Two main strands can be identified. On the one hand, such studies may adopt a hypothesis-testing approach, which is why they also consider important the observed frequencies of whatever categories the study is concerned with, but the key characteristic setting them apart from the intermediately quantitative studies is that they also aim at determining (i) to which extent the observed data deviate from data one would expect on the basis of chance alone and/or (ii) to which extent one part of the data significantly differs from some other part of the data. Usually, such studies assess the degree of deviation in terms of monofactorial or multifactorial significance testing and maybe even effect sizes. On the other hand, such studies may rely on quantitative exploratory techniques such as clustering (cf., e.g., Biber [1986, 1993] for well-known examples in quantitative corpus linguistics).

3. Overview of the present volume

All of the papers in this volume are central corpus-linguistic papers in the sense that they subscribe to all of the central corpus-linguistic tenets outlines above. Methodologically, most of them lean towards the rather quantitative end of the spectrum, but they differ with respect to their granularity and the questions they address – all of them, however, deal with topics that have long been central to the cognitive-linguistic enterprise as mentioned above and sometimes even overlap, but they all introduce fresh data, ideas, and methods within this still rapidly evolving discipline.

The nine papers can be classified into groups on the basis of both the topics that are addressed and the methods that have been employed. The first four papers are all concerned with semantic similarity, namely semantic similarity of (i) different words, (ii) different senses of a single word, and (iii) words and different syntactic structures. Divjak explores how patterns and the cluster analysis of a fine-grained characterization of usage events allow for distinguishing between lexical near synonyms in Russian. Gries conducts a detailed study of the English verb *to run* and demonstrates how correlational and multifactorial statistics can answer several notoriously difficult issues in the area of polysemy research. Wulff uses the recently established technique of collostructional analysis to differentiate constructional near synonyms in English. Finally, Hampe and Schönefeld's contribution explores the degree of schematicity of constructions, analyzing the creative use of verbs in English resultative constructions. They illustrate that, contrary to what might be assumed on the basis of the introspective data used by many authors, strong collocational restrictions set an upper limit for the currently predominant fusion model of argument structure constructions. Methodologically, these four papers are not only all situated at the quantitative end of the qualitativity/quantitativity continuum, but they also all show how linguistic analysis can benefit – both in terms of objectivity and replicability as well as coverage – from precise corpus-based operationalizations and they outline how statistical techniques can illuminate issues otherwise difficult to address.

Another group consists of the papers by Gilquin, Hollmann, and Newman and Rice, which are concerned with how different aspects of causation and transitivity are manifested linguistically. More specifically, Gilquin explores the much underestimated theoretical issue of how to determine the (degree of) prototypicality of linguistic elements by testing how different definitions of prototypical causation are reflected in authentic data from English. Hollmann's paper is concerned with the typological question of transitivity of periphrastic causatives and suggests possibly universal implicational hierarchies on the basis of his (English) data. Newman and Rice investigate different degrees of transitivity and their patternings with different inflectional forms on the basis of the verbs *to eat* and *to drink* in the British National Corpus.

Last but not least, a final small group consists of papers on the role of image schemas in cognitive linguistics and their corpus-based exploration. Lemmens analyzes causative posture verbs in Dutch in terms of their patterns and image-schematic variations while Schönefeld uses multifactorial statistics to look into image schematic patterns of posture verbs in German, English, and Russian. The papers show clearly how the analysis of large corpora allows for the discovery, analysis, and motivation of experientially based patterns and how their construals differ across languages. In what follows, the papers will be surveyed in more detail.

Divjak is concerned with near synonymous Russian verbs from the semantic field of INTENDING TO CARRY OUT AN ACTION, namely *xotet'* 'want, intend', *dumat'* 'intend, think of', *sobirat'sja* 'intend, be about', and *namerevat'sja* 'intend, mean'. First, Divjak adopts the relatively coarse-grained perspective of which constructional alternations these verbs – which all share the pattern [V_{finite} $V_{infinitive}$] – license and what this tells about their argument structure and event structure; this part of the investigation is based on elicited data.

Second, Divjak investigates the similarities and dissimilarities of these verbs' usage patterns in a 10m word corpus of literary data. In contrast to the first part of her study, this case study is based on a strongly quantitative analysis of very fine-grained descriptions of how these verbs are used to probe beyond the coarse-grained differences of complementation: Each instance of a verb in her 793 sentences sample has been coded for a variety of what Atkins (1987: 24) has referred to as ID tags, i.e. "syntactic or lexical markers in the citations which point to a particular dictionary sense of the word". Taking together all 47 ID tags of all occurrences of a search word in a sample, one arrives at a so-called behavioral profile (cf. Hanks 1996: 75ff.) of a word, as precise a measure of a word's patterns as one can get. The enormous amount of data yielded by this empirical procedure (more than 37,000 data points) is then submitted to a hierarchical agglomerative cluster analysis to detect patterns of association not visible to the naked eye. Discussing cluster results based on formal as well as semantic ID tags, Divjak demonstrates how these translate into, or correlate with, radial network representations, supporting this hitherto largely intuitive method with robust empirical and objective evidence.

The study by Gries consists of two different parts. In the first part, Gries present a comprehensive analysis of all 815 occurrences of the verb *to run* in the British component of the International Corpus of English and the (American English) Brown corpus. The result is a network-like representation of more than 40 senses and their cognitive-linguistically motivated interrelations which is, however, non-committal with respect to issues of mental representation and processing. However, the main points of the paper are made in its second part. Just like Divjak in her paper, Gries first develops a behavioral profile of *to run* by coding all occurrences with respect to a large number of formal characteristics of the verb phrase with *to run* and the clause in which it occurs as well lexical and semantic characteristics of all of *to run*'s arguments and adjuncts, yielding an overall number of approximately 200,000 data points. On the basis of this behavioral profile, Gries proposes a variety of corpus-linguistic methods to address several notorious problems cognitive linguists face; his study can therefore be categorized as fine-grained and quantitative in nature.

In one case study, he shows how the identification of the prototypical sense of *to run* – a problematic question since many different subjective and conflicting criteria can be brought to bear on this issue – can be aided and made more objective by investigating the markedness of the candidate senses' behavioral profiles. In another, he demonstrates how the behavioral profile can also help resolving the notorious problem of lumping vs. splitting senses, an issue that has plagued (cognitive) semanticists and lexicographers alike, by determining the degree of distributional overlap of senses that may be lumped; the same technique can be used to determine the most useful points where a sense may be connected to a semantic network. Other case studies explore the correlation between clusters of senses and the degree to which verb senses can be identified automatically on the basis of a few ID tags of occurrences. Gries concludes by proposing additional multifactorial techniques for sense identification and arguing that such corpus-based techniques have much more to offer to tackling such central problems of cognitive linguistics than most cognitive linguists have so far considered possible.

The paper by Wulff investigates the semantics of two partially lexically filled clause-level constructions, namely the *go-and*-V construction (*I go and check the drinks*) and the *go*-V construction (*Go find the books and show me*). Previous approaches to these patterns have sometimes considered the latter construction a derivative of the former. Wulff conducts a thoroughly quantitative and relatively coarse-grained analysis of the two patterns from a Construction Grammar perspective. On the basis of 5,320 instances of *go-and*-V construction and 454 instances of the *go*-V construction culled from the BNC, Wulff investigates the verbs filling the V slot in terms of their attracted and repelled collexemes (i.e. verbs that prefer or disprefer to occur with one construction; cf. Stefanowitsch and Gries [2003] for details), Vendlerian situation types, Levin's (1993) scheme of verb classification, and distinctive collexemes (i.e., verbs that exhibit a strong preference to occur in one of the constructions as opposed to the other; cf. Gries and Stefanowitsch [2004] for details). She finds, among other things, that the range of observed verbs contradicts observations formulated in previous, less empirical approaches and that, while the constructions are semantically similar, the number of differences between the constructions on every level of her analysis is so large that the two patterns should rather be considered independent constructions in their own right.

Hampe und Schönefeld's study explores creative uses of verbs in argument structures. They argue against the Construction Grammar account of such cases, promoting an item-specific, verb-based approach instead in which the novel use of a verb V in some construction C triggers the retrieval of another verb, or other verbs, and schemas at different levels of abstraction, which are much more strongly associated with C. On the basis of data from the British component of the International Corpus of English and the British National Corpus, they analyze collocations and collostructions of four verbs (*bore, encourage, fear,* and *support*) in complex-transitive constructions, namely the caused-motion construction and the resultative construction.

Hampe and Schönefeld find, among other things, that the motivations for novel uses of these verbs in syntactic patterns differ considerably from cases where the novel structure revives uses that were grammaticalized earlier (e.g., the use of *encourage* in the pattern [V DO PP$_{adverbial}$]) while other uses exhibit more radical departures (e.g., the instances of *support* in the caused-motion construction). In addition, while syntactic creativity has been at the center of interest so far, Hampe and Schönefeld point out that the creativity of verbal use is also strongly constrained by lexical collocational preferences; accordingly the authors attribute a higher degree of importance to abstractions at a lower level than that of argument structure constructions.

The study by Gilquin is devoted to exploring the relationship between a central notion within cognitive linguistics, prototypicality, and (corpus) frequency. After a brief survey of the notion of prototypicality, Gilquin starts out by reviewing three models of prototypical periphrastic causation in the cognitive-linguistic literature. With respect to the ordering of the elements making up a causative construction, the iconically most typical type of causation is that of the action chain, where energy is transmitted from the causer to the cause (if present) to the patient. The second model Gilquin addresses is Langacker's (1991) billiard-ball model of causation with its emphasis of causing motion, and the third one is Lakoff and Johnson's (1980) model of direct manipulation, where prototypical causation is defined on the basis of a number of interactional properties.

After a brief discussion of how prototypicality relates to salience and frequency, Gilquin then turns to an analysis of 3,574 constructions with the main periphrastic causative verbs (*cause, get, have,* and *make*) in 10m words from the British National Corpus (BNC). Her approach can be classified as (i) of intermediate granularity since she is mainly interested in the verbs as instantiations of the respective lemmas, but also takes into consideration variants such as active and passive, and (ii) as moderately quantitative, since most of her results are based on frequency data and their implications.

Her first result is that – while there is considerable variation across verbs – the theoretical models are not readily reflected in the corpus data. While the obtained differences concerning the iconically motivated orders could also be attributed to different complementation patterns of the verb, the discrepancies concerning the other two models cannot be explained away as easily. Upon relaxing her definition of prototypicality, however, Gilquin obtains results conforming more closely with the theoretically motivated expectations; for example, some individual parameters of causation are more frequent. Gilquin arrives at the conclusion that prototypicality is a much less straightforward notion than has often been implicitly assumed and, thus, requires more in-depth investigation and, ideally, multiple kinds of converging evidence.

Just like Gilquin, Hollmann investigates periphrastic causatives. His focus is on their passivizability. Hollmann studies 400 examples of periphrastic causatives with *make* from the written part of the BNC (90m words) with respect to how transitivity parameters are significantly (in the statistical sense of the term) associated with passives and, thus, presumably (crosslinguistically) relevant to transitivity/passivizability. As a first step, Hollmann modifies and extends Hopper and Thompson's (1980) well-known approach to transitivity in a way that makes it more adequate for dealing with causatives; these modifications involve refining or omitting parameters (e.g., the individuation of objects) as well as adding semantic parameters (e.g., the assumption of a frame of control or Rice's [1987] criterion of the specificity of events).

Hollmann then codes his causatives with respect to the parameters causality, aspect and directness, sphere of control and specifity. He finds significant associations for nearly all of these parameters; his study can therefore be situated among the fine-granularity and quantitative approaches. On the basis of the associations obtained, Hollmann formulates several possibly universal implicational hierarchies of transitivity/passivizability of causatives; to this, he adds other implicational hierarchies that concern his refined parameters on the basis of his own earlier work. Interestingly, while the main point of the proposed hierarchies based on the periphrastic causative with *make* is a typological one, they also make it possible to formulate intralinguistic predictions concerning, for example, the ways different English causative verbs passivize. Hollmann concludes by emphasizing the role quantitative studies can play for analyses in which several factors have to be taken into consideration simultaneously.

Newman and Rice's paper is – like Hollmann's – concerned with transitivity. More specifically, they investigate diathesis alternations in a sample of more than 7,500 instances of the verb lemmas *to eat* and *to drink* in spoken and written parts of the BNC. At the same time, the study is an in-depth description of how these alternations are tied to TAM marking, a variety of other formal properties of the verbs under consideration, their arguments, and the modality (spoken vs. written); Newman and Rice's paper can therefore be considered an analysis at a relatively fine-grained level (when it comes to verb forms) and moderately quantitative.

For example, Newman and Rice observe a preponderance of *to eat* over *to drink*, but, more interestingly, they also obtain results that contrast with previous results on transitive clauses such that (i) the uses of the two verbs in transitive and intransitive clauses are not identical across modalities and (ii) transitive uses outnumber intransitives in spoken language. In addition, they also find that this difference is at least partially contingent on modalities and subject choices.

With respect to some quantifiable parameters underlying transitivity, Newman and Rice focus on the degrees of individuation and affectedness of the direct objects, again obtaining results that, among other things, contradict those previous works that associated low transitivity with spoken language and provide a wealth of data relevant to lexicographers and descriptive linguists alike. Their main conclusion, however, is that different inflectional forms do often have their own preferences of patterning, a finding that is in line with the results presented by Divjak and Gries, whose behavioral-profile analysis came to the same conclusion at even finer levels of granularity.

Lemmens investigates the causative variants of the three cardinal posture verbs *zitten* 'sit', *liggen* 'lie', and *staan* 'stand' in Dutch by relating them to their non-causative counterparts. His study is based on 7,550 instances of caused posture verbs from a selection of a 65m words corpus of Dutch journalese; it is a coarse-grained approach and, in spite of the sample size, largely qualitative in nature. Building on his own earlier work on the topic, he starts out from the assumption that posture verbs are prototype categories and discusses uses of the three cardinal posture verbs and their

Introduction 13

causative counterparts with reference to a variety of experiential patterns and image-schematic properties including (in)activity, functionality, and control and resistance. In addition, he points out several instances of mismatch between the causative and the non-causative verbs regarding, for example, the readiness with which metaphorical uses are found. He concludes by emphasizing how the large-scale corpus approach adopted makes it possible to identify the large degree of productivity manifested by the semantic network instantiated by the posture verbs and by proposing promising future research strategies following from his findings.

Last but not least, the study by Schönefeld is concerned with the fact that, while many of the scenarios humans talk about are identical, the collocations used to talk about these events are language-specific to a considerable degree. She attributes part of this variation to different strategies of conceptualization and investigates construal operations of visual image schemas governing the posture verbs *sit*, *stand*, and *lie*. In a first step, following earlier work by Gibbs, Schönefeld associates each of these posture verbs with a set of image schemas, a so-called image-schematic profile, which for *stand* comprises the image schemas BALANCE, CENTRE-PERIPHERY, COMPULSION, (COUNTER)FORCE, RESISTANCE, CONTACT, LINKAGE, SUPPORT, and VERTICALITY. Her data consist of several thousand examples of English *sit*, *stand*, and *lie* as well as their translation equivalents in German (*sitzen*, *stehen*, and *liegen*) and Russian (*sidet'*, *stojat'*, and *ležat'*) from journalese corpora of 3m words each. While the overall frequencies of the canonical posture verbs themselves differ considerably, the more instructive results are based on the frequency distributions of semantic classes of the trajectors to which the verbs belong (such as humans, abstract/concrete objects, etc.) and the prepositions co-occurring with the three verbs focused on. Given the multifactorial data set (OBJECT TYPES × POSTURE VERB × LANGUAGE and PREPOSITION× POSTURE VERB × LANGUAGE), Schönefeld reports the results of several hierarchical configural frequency analyses, a multifactorial technique for the analysis of large multidimensional frequency tables; her study is therefore strongly quantitative and formally coarse-grained.

As was mentioned at the outset, in spite of the ever increasing importance of the notion of "usage-based approaches", corpus-linguistic approaches are still not very frequent let alone standard in Cognitive Linguistics. I hope, however, that the short presentations of the papers have stimulated some interest in the papers that follow and the kind of looking at language they represent. In addition, I also hope that the methods and results introduced in this volume – many of them fairly new to the cognitive-linguistic community – will (i) stimulate new research questions and studies and (ii) help to set the stage for a major methodological paradigm shift in the direction of corpus work, which will hopefully yield increasingly objective and usage-based results.

Note

*   I thank Dagmar Divjak for comments and discussion.

Corpora

British National Corpus: ⟨http://www.natcorp.ox.ac.uk/⟩.
International Corpus of English: British Component: ⟨http://www.ucl.ac.uk/english-usage/ice-gb/⟩.
Dutch newspaper corpora of the Instituut voor Nedelandse Lexicologie: ⟨http://www.inl.nl⟩.

References

Atkins, Beryl T. Sue
   1987   Semantic ID tags: Corpus evidence for dictionary senses. *Proceedings of the Third Annual Conference of the UW Centre for the New Oxford English Dictionary*, 17–36.
Atkins, Beryl T. Sue, Judy Kegl, and Beth Levin
   1988   Anatomy of a verb entry: From linguistic theory to lexicographic practice. *International Journal of Lexicography* 1 (2): 84–126.
Atkins, Beryl T. Sue and Beth Levin
   1995   Building on a corpus: A linguistic and lexicographical look at some near synonyms. *International Journal of Lexicography* 8 (2): 86–114.
Barlow, Michael and Suzanne Kemmer
   2004   Usage and frequency: Input vs. output and implications for grammatical analysis. Paper presented at Conceptual Structure, Discourse, and Language, Edmonton, Alberta, Canada.
Bencini, Giulia. and Adele E. Goldberg
   2000   The contribution of argument structure constructions to sentence meaning. *Journal of Memory and Language* 43 (4): 640–651.

Berglund, Ylva
    1997   Future in present-day English: Corpus-based evidence on the rivalry of expressions. *ICAME Journal* 21: 7–20.

Biber, Douglas
    1986   Spoken and written textual dimensions in English: resolving the contradictory findings. *Language* 62 (2): 384–414.
    1993   Co-occurrence patterns among collocations: A tool for corpus-based lexical knowledge acquisition. *Computational Linguistics* 19 (3): 531–538.

Boas, Hans C.
    2003   *A Constructional Approach to Resultatives.* Stanford, CA: CSLI Publications.

Bybee, Joan and Joanne Scheibman
    1999   The effect of usage on degrees of constituency: The reduction of *don't* in English". *Linguistics* 37 (4): 575–596.

Croft, William and D. Alan Cruse
    2004   *Cognitive Linguistics.* Cambridge: Cambridge University Press.

Davidse, Kristin and Martine Vanden Eynde
    2004   Analysing the grammaticalization of EDGE noun-expressions: a data-driven approach. Paper presented at Conceptual Structure, Discourse, and Language, Edmonton, Alberta, Canada.

Fries, Charles C.
    1952   *The Structure of English: An Introduction to the Construction of Sentences.* New York: Harcourt Brace.

Gibbs, Raymond W. Jr.
    1995   *The Poetics of Mind: Figurative Thought, Language, and Understanding.* Cambridge: Cambridge University Press.

Givón, Talmy (ed.)
    1983   *Topic Continuity in Discourse: Quantitative Cross-Language Studies.* Amsterdam/Philadelphia: John Benjamins.

Gries, Stefan Th. and Anatol Stefanowitsch
    2004   Extending collostructional analysis: A corpus-based perspective on 'alternations'". *International Journal of Corpus Linguistics* 9 (1): 97–129.

Gries, Stefan Th. and Stefanie Wulff
    2005   Do foreign language learners also have constructions? Evidence from priming, sorting, and corpora. *Annual Review of Cognitive Linguistics* 3: 182–200.

Hanks, Patrick
    1996   Contextual dependency and lexical sets. *International Journal of Corpus Linguistics* 1 (1): 75–98.

Hare, Mary L. and Adele E. Goldberg
   1999   Structural priming: purely syntactic? In: M. Hahn and S.C. Stones (eds.), *Proceedings of the 21st Annual Meeting of the Cognitive Science Society*, 208–211. Mahwah, NJ: Lawrence Erlbaum.

Hopper, Paul and Sandra A. Thompson
   1980   Transitivity in grammar and discourse. *Language* 56 (2): 251–299.

Käding, Wilhelm
   1897   *Häufigkeitswörterbuch der deutschen Sprache*. Steglitz: privately published.

Jorgensen, Julia C.
   1990   The psychological reality of word senses. *Journal of Psycholinguistic Research* 19 (3): 167–190.

Lakoff, George
   1987   *Women, Fire, and Dangerous Things*. Chicago, IL: The University of Chicago Press.
   1990   The invariance hypothesis: Is abstract reason based in image schemas? *Cognitive Linguistics* 1 (1): 39–74.
   1991   Cognitive linguistics versus generative linguistics: How commitments influence results. *Language and Communication* 11 (1/2): 53–62.

Lakoff, George and Mark Johnson
   1980   *Metaphors We Live By*. Chicago, IL: The University of Chicago Press.

Langacker, Ronald W.
   1987   *Foundations of Cognitive Grammar. Vol. I. Theoretical Prerequisites*. Stanford, CA: Stanford University Press.
   1991   *Foundations of Cognitive Grammar. Vol. II. Descriptive Application*. Stanford, CA: Stanford University Press.

Levin, Beth
   1993   *English Verb Classes and Alterations: A Preliminary Investigation*. Chicago, IL: The University of Chicago Press.

Meyer, Christian
   1991   A corpus-based study of apposition in English. In: Karin Aijmer and Bengt Altenberg (eds.), *English Corpus Linguistics*, 166–181. London: Longman.

Mukherjee, Joybrato
   2003   Corpus data in a usage-based cognitive grammar. In: Karin Aijmer and Bengt Altenberg (eds.), *The theory and use of corpora*, 85–100. Amsterdam: Rodopi.

Oh, Sun-Y.
   2000   *Actually* and *in fact* in American English: A data-based analysis. *English Language and Linguistics* 4 (2): 243–268.

Oostdijk, Nelleke and Pieter de Haan
    1994   Clause patterns in Modern British: A corpus-based quantitative study. *ICAME Journal* 18: 41–79.

Raukko, Jarno
    1999   An "intersubjective" method for cognitive-semantic research on polysemy: The case of *get*. In: Masako K. Hiraga, Chris Sinha and Sherman Wilcox (eds.), *Cultural, psychological and typological issues in cognitive linguistics*, 87–105. Amsterdam/Philadelphia: John Benjamins.

Rice, Sally
    1996   Prepositional prototypes. In: Martin Pütz and Rene Dirven (eds.), *The Construal of Space in Language and Thought*, 135–165. Berlin/New York: Mouton de Gruyter.

Rosch, Eleanor and Catherine B. Mervis
    1975   Family resemblances: Studies in the internal structure of categories. *Cognitive Psychology* 7: 573–605.

Sandra, Dominiek and Sally Rice
    1995   Network analyses of prepositional meaning: Mirroring whose mind – the linguist's or the language user's? *Cognitive Linguistics* 6 (1): 89–130.

Stefanowitsch, Anatol and Stefan Th. Gries
    2003   Collostructions: Investigating the interaction between words and constructions. *International Journal of Corpus Linguistics* 8 (2): 209–243.

Stubbs, Michael
    2002   Two quantitative methods of studying phraseology in English. *International Journal of Corpus Linguistics* 7 (2): 215–44.

Stubbs, Michael and Isabel Barth
    2003   Using recurrent phrases as text-type discriminators. *Functions of Language* 10 (1): 61–104.

Thorndike, Edward L.
    1921   *A Teacher's Wordbook*. New York: Columbia Teachers College.

Thorndike, Edward L. and Irving Lorge
    1944   *The Teacher's Word Book of 30,000 Words*. New York: Columbia University Press.

Ways of intending: Delineating and structuring near-synonyms[*]

Dagmar Divjak

Abstract

This paper presents research into five Russian near-synonymous verbs that, in combination with an infinitive, express the concept INTEND TO CARRY OUT AN ACTION.

After a short outline of the distribution-based approach advocated in this paper (Section 1) I lay the basis for providing a verifiable solution to three major problems of synonym research. First, I will pursue the question of how to delineate a series of near-synonyms and to distinguish near-synonyms from semantically closely related verbs (Section 2). To this end, I will use elicited data on the networks of constructions that characterize intentional verbs. Next, I will consider two interrelated problems, i.e. how to structure and describe a series of near-synonyms (Section 3). Here, I will rely on corpus-data to set up a behavioral profile for each verb; on the basis of these profiles a data structuring technique, cluster analysis, will be used to determine the degree of similarity between the verbs. The results do not only shed light on the internal structure of a series of near synonyms and provide an objective basis for drawing a network representation; in addition, the clusters facilitate singling out the major properties along which the verbs in a series of near-synonyms differ.

Keywords: verb classification; argument and event structure; distribution-based behavioral profiles; cluster analysis; radial network representations.

1. Near-synonyms: Between grammar and lexicon?

In cognitively inspired approaches to language, grammar and lexicon are seen as forming a continuum and encoding meaning on different levels that are progressively characterized by a higher degree of specificity (Goldberg 1995: 32). The meaning conveyed by both types of structures is considered to be conceptual, i.e. "it represents a way of conceptualizing experience in the process of encoding it and expressing it in language" (Croft 1999: 77).

If both constructions and lexemes have (conceptual) meaning, it seems reasonable to assume that these meanings must interact when they are put in contact, i.e. the meaning of the lexeme has to be compatible with the meaning assigned by the construction to the slot the lexeme occupies (Goldberg 1995: 24, 50; Lemmens 1998: 232; Stefanowitsch and Gries 2003: 213). Hence, all verbs that are compatible with a given construction share the meaning component – however abstract – that facilitates this combination. Fisher et al. (1991: 331) assume that "the closer any two verbs [are] in their semantic structure, the greater the overlap should be in their licensed syntactic structures". Differences in networks of constructions for (groups of) verbs can thus be expected to reveal systematic meaning differences between the (groups of) verbs that do share constructional characteristics and verbs that do not have any of these properties (Atkins and Levin 1995: 96). In other words, lexemes or lemmas that share membership in a network of constructions share a fair amount of meaning at the coarse-grained constructional level. Network-information can therefore be used to delineate semantically coherent verb classes (for an application see Apresjan 1967 for Russian and Levin 1993 for English), as I will illustrate in Section 2. Yet, the meaning encoded in "grammatical" constructions and the networks they form for a given lexeme or lemma is insufficient for a detailed "lexical" semantic analysis, as Section 3 will show. Networks of constructions do not directly yield an exhaustive meaning description (cf. Smessaert et al. 2005). Fisher et al. (1991: 382) hypothesize that "the meaning of verbs in sentences is parceled out (sometimes redundantly) between the clausal structure and the lexicon".

It is the aim of this paper to elucidate, on the one hand, how the semantic information contained in the concept INTEND is divided over grammar and lexicon (as Section 4 will show), and, on the other hand, to describe which aspects of lexeme-specific meaning are encoded in the form of constructional slots and which reside in lexical collocational preferences (as Section 3 will make clear). To this end, I will study the distribution of Russian verbs that express INTEND on two levels. Both the grammatical and the lexical level contain types of form-meaning pairings speakers of a language have at their disposal to express a specific phenomenon of "ceived" reality (Talmy 2000: 139ff), to present different perspectives on a situation (cf. Wierzbicka 1985: 327; Apresjan [1974] 1995b: 251–255; Taylor 2003: 268). Yet, there is a limit to the alternate grammatical and lexical coding options available per situation. Data on restrictions and preferences can be used to both delineate and discover the structure of the Intentional category (cf. Croft 1999: 69–74). Given that the meaning of grammatical constructions is more schematic than the meaning of lexical structures it seems efficient to start a meaning description of lexemes from the coarse-grained, constructional level. In the constructional part of the case study (presented in Section 2) I have opted for elicitation tests with 15 native speakers of Russian to delineate a group of near-synonyms, the main reason being that, strictly speaking, a corpus can never provide negative evidence (Hanks 1996: 78) and negative evidence is what the first part of this paper builds on.[1] At the fine-grained level of lexical meaning description (Section 3), however, the analysis relies on the precise formal make-up as well as the exact content of the slots in a construction and on the relative frequency with which the formal make-up and lexical-semantic contents of these slots appear in a random representative sample of the language. In the corpus-based part of this paper, cluster analysis will be used to discover the structure of the data.

2. Delineating series of near-synonyms

Synonymy has received relatively little attention in Western linguistics. It is said to "waste" the limited lexical resources on one and the same semantic unit, and therefore it shouldn't exist. But, even if synonyms name one and the same situation, they name it in different ways; they present it from different perspectives. Near-synonyms are neither in free variation, nor in complementary distribution. And this fact provides interesting information about the structure of a particular semantic and related conceptual space.

The research presented in this paper concentrates on what Cruse (2000: 158–160) would classify as plesionyms or near-synonyms, and Apresjan ([1974] 1995: 219) would label non-exact or quasi-synonyms, i.e. lexemes that are characterized by high similarity and low contrastivity in meaning. Generalizing it can be said that Western studies on synonymy make use of diagnostic frames of the type *He was killed but I can assure you that he was not murdered* to decide on the near-synonymous status of two items, here *kill* and *murder* (Cruse 2000: 158–160). Russian research on this topic relies on a metalanguage made up of primitives to delineate groups of near-synonyms. Once translated into the metalanguage, lexemes can be compared. To qualify as near-synonyms the overlap in the translation has to be bigger than the sum of the differences for two lexemes, or at least equal to the sum of the differences in case of three or more lexemes. Apart from that, the overlap has to relate to the assertion of the definition that contains "genera proxima", the syntactic main words of which coincide (Apresjan et al. 1995: 60, 62, 64, 70, Apresjan et al. 2000: XL).

These methods for delineating near-synonyms rely on introspection, however, and the results they produce are therefore unlikely to replicate. Within Natural Language Processing more objective and thus verifiable measures are used to approximate semantic relatedness and similarity (cf. Rubenstein and Goodenough [1965] for an early application and Mohammad and Hirst [submitted] for an extensive overview and discussion of the measures available to date). Most of these distributional measures are typically applied to enormous collections of texts from which collocation information is extracted. Some measures incorporate basic dependency information, e.g. the verb/object relationship, in the word features on the basis of which the similarities are computed. I will argue that precise syntactic and semantic data on the distribution of the potentially near-synonymous lexemes over constructions and of their collocates over the slots of those constructions can be used to measure the degree of similarity between lexemes even in a limited dataset objectively.[2] To assess the validity of the results, I will contrast the most extensive dictionary treatment available for the group of near-synonyms expressing INTEND with the series as it is delineated by the composition of the network of constructions intentional verbs are part of. On the basis of a paraphrase into semantic metalanguage the Dictionary of Synonyms (Levontina in Apresjan et al. 1999[2]: 385–390) selects four intentional verbs i.e. *planirovat'* 'plan', *dumat'* 'intend, think (of)', *namerevat'sja* 'intend, mean' and *sobirat'sja* 'intend, be about' and defines them as 'want to do something and be prepared to put in effort in order to do that'. The group as defined by elicited data[3] on the network of constructions each verb is part of comprises six verbs, i.e., *namerevat'sja* 'intend, mean' *sobirat'sja* 'intend, be about', *predpolagat'* 'intend, propose', *dumat'* 'intend, think (of)' and *xotet'* 'want, intend'.

2.1. Puzzling constructional differences

In Russian, approximately 300 verbs occur in the [V_{FIN} V_{INF}] pattern, i.e. combine with an infinitive. On a motivational iconic view this pattern signals a high degree of interrelatedness of the events expressed; hence all verbs that take part in it share at least the meaning component that facilitates this combination. Yet, there seem to be three main parameters along which verbs that combine with an infinitive vary. The parameters focus on different facets of events or situations. First, the main participants of events or situations are encoded in the verb's argument structure that is the basis of the simplex sentence. Next, if two (or more) events are being reported on, the most usual way to link the two verbs expressing these events is by means of two coordinated main clauses or complex sentences consisting of a main clause and a subordinate clause (cf. Talmy 2000: Ch. 6; Cristofaro 2003: Ch. 5–7). Finally, the events these verbs express take place at a specific moment in time and have a specific temporal contour, i.e. an imperfective and/or perfective aspect (cf. Pustejovsky 1991). These syntactic parameters have cognitive-semantic dimensions (cf. Tsai et al. 1998) that can be interpreted as encoding the degree of integration between the finite verb event and the infinitive event. In the following three subsections I will briefly sketch how these parameters differentiate between the four verbs studied. For more elaborate justification and discussion I refer to Divjak (2004: 48–108).

2.1.1. On things and processes

The first parameter is concerned with the cognitive status of the event expressed by the infinitive, seen from the point of view of the finite verb event (cf. Cristofaro 2003: 256). In other words, this diagnostic measures the direction of integration between two verbs used in a simplex sentence, as I will illustrate shortly in examples (1) through (4).

Verbs are relational predications that profile interconnections and are in this respect "conceptually dependent", i.e. "one cannot conceptualize interconnections without also conceptualizing the entities that they interconnect" (Langacker 1987: 215). Within the confines of a simplex sentence, the majority of verbs can link up with nouns [V_{FIN} N], a minority with another verb [V_{FIN} V_{INF}]. Nouns and verbs differ as to how the entities they designate are conceptualized (Langacker 1987: Ch. 5 and 7); verbs are relational entities that express processes and are "scanned sequentially over conceived time", whereas nouns or non-relational things are a-temporal, "scanned as a unitary whole, unrelated to time". Bonding with both kinds of entities or only with one of them reveals the conceptualization-type typical of a verb.

The verb *planirovat'* 'plan' from example (1) (taken from Apresjan and Pall 1982, 2: 58) combines both with nouns or non-relational things and with infinitives, i.e. entities that likewise express a process and thus have their own relational profile. A difference in construction is always accompanied by a difference in meaning (Langacker 1987: 294): different constructions represent different ways of construing an event. Yet, combining with nouns or verbs does not affect the meaning of *planirovat'* 'plan' itself; this can be witnessed from dictionaries that list both the combination with noun and verb as instantiating one and the same sense.

(1)   Он **планирует поехать** в Москву.
      'He$_{NOM}$ is **planning**$_{IP\ FIN}$ **to travel**$_{PF\ INF}$ to Moscow$_{ACC\ F\ SG}$.'[4]

(1)' Он **планирует поездку** в Москву.
      'He$_{NOM}$ is **planning**$_{IP\ FIN}$ **a trip**$_{ACC\ F\ SG}$ to Moscow$_{ACC\ F\ SG}$.'

Evidence for this claim can be found at the more abstract level illustrated in example (2): with *planirovat'* 'plan' a pro-noun *èto* 'this' that abstracts over nouns, thus including *poezdka* 'trip' in (1)', can be used to refer to the verb *zaderživat'* 'arrest' (cf. Smessaert et al. 2005 and references therein).

(2)   [...] и нам пришлось **задерживать** вас раньше, чем мы **это планировали**. [А. Маринина. Стилист.]
      '[...] and we had to **arrest**$_{IP\ INF}$ you earlier, than we$_{NOM}$ had **planned**$_{IP\ FIN}$ **that**$_{ACC\ N\ SG}$'

In the majority of cases, it is sufficient to have one entity that is "scanned sequentially over conceived time" and "profiles interconnections" to build a full-fledged clause; that verb typically is (the) finite (verb). Verbs like *planirovat'* 'plan' do not need another relational temporal process: the infinitive *zaderživat'* 'arrest' can be subsumed under a pro-noun *èto* 'this'. Thus, *planirovat'* 'plan' treats the infinitive or relational entity as any other non-relational entity it combines with. This reification possibility may be interpreted as signaling that the arguments are mapped iconically: the infinitive process is treated as a thing, conceptually subordinate to the process expressed by *planirovat'* 'plan'. The infinitive *zaderživat'* 'arrest' is mainly considered for the role of object it plays in the argument structure of *planirovat'* 'plan'.

The situation is quite different with *dumat'* 'intend, think (of)', *namerevat'sja* 'intend, mean' and *sobirat'sja* 'intend, be about'. *Namerevat'sja* 'intend, mean' lacks the possibility of combining with non-verbal entities altogether, thus being restricted to combinations with an infinitive. For *dumat'* 'intend, think (of)' and *sobirat'sja* 'intend, be about' a difference in construction, i.e. a combination with an infinitive or with a noun, goes together with a sharp difference in the meaning of *dumat'* and *sobirat'sja* themselves. Take the example of *dumat'* (taken from Apresjan and Pall [1982, 1: 389–390]). With a preposition and a nominal object *dumat'* roughly means 'think', as is exemplified in (3); in this sense, *dumat'* has a perfective counterpart *podumat'*. The other lemma, illustrated in (4), is restricted to combinations with an infinitive, and can be translated 'intend'. In this sense, *dumat'* does not have a perfective.

(3) Он/она/они [...]   (по)думал/а/и [...]   о   будущем
     He/she/they$_{NOM}$ think$_{IP (P) PAST M 3SG/F 3SG/3PL}$ about$_{PREP}$ future$_{PREP N SG}$

(4) Он/она/они ... думал/а/и [...]   остаться   дома.
     He/she/they$_{NOM}$ intend$_{IP PAST M 3SG/F 3SG/3PL}$ to stay$_{PF INF}$ home$_{ADV}$

In contrast to *planirovat'* 'plan' in (2), referring to the infinitive by means of a pro-noun that abstracts over the noun *buduščee* 'future' in (3) causes a change in the meaning of *dumat'*; in (3)' *dumat'* translates as 'think', in (3)'' as 'intend'.

(3)' ?[...] и нам пришлось задерживать вас раньше, чем мы об этом думали.
      '[...] and we had to **arrest**$_{IP INF}$ you earlier, than we$_{NOM}$ had been **thinking**$_{IP PAST 3PL}$ **about**$_{PREP}$ **that**$_{ACC N SG}$'

(3)'' [...] и нам пришлось задерживать вас раньше, чем мы думали это сделать.
       '[...] and we had to **arrest**$_{IP INF}$ you earlier, than we$_{NOM}$ had **intended**$_{IP FIN}$ **to do**$_{PF INF}$ **that**$_{ACC N SG}$'

In other words, in their intentional sense *namerevat'sja* 'intend, mean', *dumat'* 'intend, think (of)' and *sobirat'sja* 'intend, be about' necessarily evoke the idea of another process, i.e. an entity with a relational profile. The relational profile of the infinitive cannot be backgrounded or made conceptually subordinate to the finite verb; the situation these finite verbs express is such that it cannot exist without a second process.[5] The balance between the events expressed by the finite and infinite verb in (4) differs from the balance between the verbs in example (1). Only a minority of verbs – for Russian typically modals, intentionals, tentatives (verbs that express *try*), resultatives and phasals – displays this behavior. These categories are cross-linguistically attested (compare Dixon's [1996: 176–179] "Secondary verbs" and Givón's [1990: 517, 533] "Modality verbs"). For Russian, it can be claimed that the anchor point of a [V_{FIN} V_{INF}] construction with one of these verbs as finite verb is being moved from the finite verb onto the infinitive. As a result, the arguments are mapped non-iconically (cf. Croft 2001: 216–220, 254–259), a phenomenon typical of verbs that are on the way towards grammaticalization. Interestingly, in non-Indo-European languages similar concepts as the ones just named are not necessarily expressed as verbs but are found as affixes or adverbs instead (Dixon 1996: 178).

Obviously, the meaning of the [V_{FIN} V_{INF}] construction interacts in non-trivial ways with the meaning (components) of the lexeme that occupies its finite verb slot. Some concepts seem to be more prone to semantic shifts than others. In the next sections I will lay stress on constructions that make explicit properties of the finite verb that remain implicit in [V_{FIN} V_{INF}] structures. More specifically, I will explore how "close" the second verb process needs to be to the finite verb, "spatially" and temporally; this will shed light on the strength and independence of the (finite) verb and the concept it expresses. In Section 2.1.2, I will concentrate on "spatial" distance. In order to do this, I will check which verbs that combine with an infinitive are restricted to the [V_{FIN} V_{INF}] pattern and which finite verbs can appear in other constructions as well.

2.1.2. Clausal remnants?

Planirovat' 'plan' can introduce *that*-complement clauses and can use these complement constructions to express the infinitive content alternatively: example (5) can be partially paraphrased using the pattern of (6). Both examples are presented in the form they were taken from the Internet.

(5) *BMW планирует продать в 2003 году 190 тыс. автомобилей 5-й серии.* [http://www.autoizvestia.ru/news/?id=2826]
'BMW$_{NOM}$ *plans*$_{IP\ PRES\ 3SG}$ to sell$_{PF\ INF}$ in 2003 190 000 series 5-cars.'

(6) *SiS планирует, что продаст на $90 млн. за второй квартал.* [http://sns.yaroslavl.ru/news/index.php?show=mon&in_mon=01.05.3] (lit.)
'SiS$_{NOM}$ *plans*$_{IP\ PRES\ 3SG}$, that$_{COMP}$ it will sell$_{PF\ FUT\ 3SG}$ for $90 million in the second quarter.'

Langacker's (1991 Ch. 10) description of English complementation in terms of conceptual subordination to and dependence on the main clause can be transposed to Russian. Construing the second, infinitive verb's content (*prodat'* 'sell' in [5]) as a full-fledged complement clause (as is done by *čto prodast* 'that it will sell' in [6]) equals considering the second verb event for the role it plays within the superordinate relationship expressed by the main clause and implies imposing a nominal construal on the second verb. Similar conclusions on the status of the infinitive have been drawn for *planirovat'* 'plan' in Section 2.1.1. Yet, complement clause constructions are not only a (complementary) diagnostic for the status of finite verb and infinitive. In addition *that*-complementation is an explicit measure for the degree of integration between the two verbs of the construction as it requires detaching the second verb structure conceptually from the finite verb. *That*-complementation signals both distance and objectivity (Wierzbicka 1988: 132 ff; Langacker 1991: 446–449). Indeed, in the same "plan"-sense, *planirovat'* 'plan' could introduce a *that*-complement clause with non-coreferential subject; the action that is being planned is not necessarily carried out by the person who is planning it, as illustrated in (7).

(7) **Нижегородский Минфин планирует, что** в *2005 году* **область** получить [sic] *доходы от деятельности госпредприятий в размере 13,125 млн. рублей*
[8312.ru/0-889-9289-0/20041026-20041026/709404--48/]
'The [...] ministry of finances plans that in 2005 the province will receive income (from ...) in the amount of 13.125 million rubles.'

Unlike *planirovat'* 'plan', the verbs *dumat'* 'intend, think (of)', *namerevat'sja* 'intend, mean' and *sobirat'sja* 'intend, be about' cannot be used in their *intend* sense with a *that*-complement construction. Although *dumat'* and *sobirat'sja* can subordinate a construction (Apresjan and Pall [1982, 1: 389–390, 1982, 2: 427–429]) the intentions reported on are restricted to occurrence in the [V_{FIN} V_{INF}] sequence. *Dumat'* can take a *that*-clause in its 'think' sense exemplified in (3). The English translations of the Russian examples in (8) illustrate that for *sobirat'sja* as well a difference in construction goes together with a sharp difference in meaning. Note in passing that native speakers suggested an aspectual change from imperfective to perfective for both finite and infinitive verb between examples (8) and (8)'.

(8) […] *воры вовсе не* **собирались предпринимать** *следующую попытку обчистить вашу квартиру.* [А. Маринина. Я умер вчера.]
'The thieves$_{NOM\,M\,PL}$ did not at all ***intend***$_{IP\,PAST\,3PL}$ ***to undertake***$_{IP\,INF}$ a next attempt to clean out your apartment.'

(8)' […] *воры не* **собрались** *[там],* **чтобы предпринять** *следующую попытку обчистить вашу квартиру.*
'The thieves$_{NOM\,M\,PL}$ did not ***gather/assemble***$_{PF\,PAST\,3PL}$ [there$_{ADV}$], ***in order to***$_{ADV\,COMP}$ ***undertake***$_{PF\,INF}$ a next attempt to clean out your apartment.'

Givón (1990 Ch. 13 and Ch. 21) proposes a cross-linguistically supported account of complementation that explicitly refers to the degree of integration or binding between two verbs. According to Givón, the degree of morphosyntactic integration between finite and infinite verb can be seen as iconically coding the degree of semantic integration of two single events into a single complex event structure. The meaning of the verbs *dumat'* 'intend, think (of)', *namerevat'sja* 'intend, mean' and *sobirat'sja* 'intend, be about' is exclusive to co-referential constructions that contain an infinitive: they are restricted to the highest degree of binding and are most susceptible to semantic integration as a single event.

Apart from morphosyntactic integration, Givón (1990: 520) identifies a necessary cognitive pre-condition for considering two events a single complex event, i.e. co-temporality. Cristofaro (2003a: 120) takes the comparable "degree to which the boundaries between these SoAs [States of Affairs] are eroded or kept intact" as the basic component of semantic integration. In Section 2.1.3 I will explore the (im)possibility of modifying both verbs in a [V$_{FIN}$ V$_{INF}$] structure with conflicting time adverbials and relate the findings to the aspectual behavior of the verbs, aspect being the most natural way to impose boundaries on events in Russian. In so doing I obtain a second measure for the degree of integration between these four finite verbs and the infinitive, that is moreover independent of the verb's argument structure and conceptual subordination of one event to the other.

2.1.3. On time

The verb *planirovat'* 'plan', could be used in a construction that localizes the finite verb and the infinitive in two different and not necessarily tightly sequential moments in time. More concretely, the finite verb *'plan'*, illustrated in (1) and (5), could take a specification as to when exactly the management of BMW undertook the act of setting the sales targets, as (9) shows.

(9) *На собрании акционеров **21ого декабря 2002ого года** BMW **запланировал продать** в **2003 году** 190 тыс. автомобилей.*
'At the shareholders meeting **on December 21st 2002** BMW$_{NOM}$ **planned**$_{PF\ PAST\ M\ 3SG}$ **to sell**$_{PF\ INF}$ 190 000 cars **in 2003**.'

The occurrence of temporal distance between two events entails their conceptual distance: in (9) the finite verb and the infinitive express distinct though related events (cf. Langacker 1991: 299 ftn. 11 and references therein; Lemmens 1998: 152). Inspection of the data for all 300 Russian verbs that combine with an infinitive reveals that if both finite verb and infinitive can be modified with separate time adverbials, the finite verb has a perfective counterpart, as imperfective *planirovat'* 'plan' from (1) and (5) has *zaplanirovat'* 'plan' in (9): without having the perfective to rely on, it is impossible to ascertain whether a particular event, expressed by the finite verb, has ended before the second event, expressed by the infinitive, starts unfolding. However, not all verbs that combine with an infinitive and have both imperfective and perfective forms can be used in a construction in which the finite verb and the infinitive are modified with conflicting time adverbials. Having a perfective counterpart is a necessary but not a sufficient condition.

The verbs *dumat'* 'intend, think (of)', *namerevat'sja* 'intend, mean' and *sobirat'sja* 'intend, be about', show another pattern. In their intentional sense these verbs do not have perfective counterparts and demand overlap in or tight sequentiality of time, "a necessary cognitive pre-condition for considering two events a single though complex event" (Givón 1990: 520). As opposed to PLANNING, INTENDING cannot occur at a time different from the intended action. This requirement is illustrated in (10).

(10) */??***Вчера офицер намеревался завтра применить решительные меры.**
'*Yesterday*$_{ADV}$ the officer$_{NOM\ M\ SG}$ ***intended***$_{IP\ PAST\ M\ 3SG}$ ***to take***$_{PF\ INF}$ decisive measures ***tomorrow***$_{ADV}$.'

On the interpretation that the occurrence of temporal distance between two verbs entails the conceptual distance between the events expressed, the verbs *dumat'* 'intend, think (of)', *namerevat'sja* 'intend, mean' and *sobirat'sja* 'intend, be about' fulfill the cognitive requirement for being considered one complex event.

In sum, I have illustrated that the verbs *dumat'* 'intend, think (of)', *namerevat'sja* 'intend, mean' and *sobirat'sja* 'intend, be about' on the one hand, and *planirovat'* 'plan' on the other hand, take part in fundamentally distinct networks of constructions that directly relate to the argument and event structure of the verbs. Systematic cognitive-semantic differences between verbs can be uncovered by referring to the differences in the networks they are part of. In Section 2.2 I will interrelate these structural findings and infer from them meaning differences between the verbs studied (cf. Tsai et al. 1998).

2.2. Interpreting constructional differences

About 27% of the approximately 300 verbs that combine with an infinitive in Russian have the same three properties as *planirovat'* 'plan'. When the case marking that comes with the finite verb is taken into account additionally, *planirovat'* 'plan' is aligned with *proektirovat'* 'plan, project', *namečat'* 'plan' and *predložit'* 'propose, suggest', a group the constructional potential of which strongly resembles *postanovit'* 'decide, resolve', *rešit'* 'decide' and *opredelit'* 'define, determine'. Intuitively, it is clear that these verbs express in themselves full-fledged events that thus do not need to be close to another event, not within the confines of one sentence (see 2.1.2), and not in time (see 2.1.3). Thus, *planirovat'* 'plan' can be seen as a prototypical main verb whereas *dumat'* 'intend, think (of)', *namerevat'sja* 'intend, mean', *sobirat'sja* 'intend, be about', *predpolagat'* 'intend, propose' and *xotet'* 'want, intend' are integrated with the infinitive to an extent that they can no longer be considered prototypical construction kernels by themselves. The latter three verbs belong to a class containing about 22% of all verbs that combine with an infinitive; the three verbs mainly differ from the other verbs in the category with respect to implication relations and aspectual behavior.[6]

Taking the four verbs through the stativity tests that apply for Russian (Flank 1995: 27, 33–38) shows that they do not classify for the same situation type: native speakers accept *planirovat'* 'plan' as a concretization of 'doing something', whereas *dumat'* 'intend, think (of)', *namerevat'sja* 'intend, mean' and *sobirat'sja* 'intend, be about' clearly do not relate to such an activity-primitive. Apart from that, as the corpus sample (see Section 3.1) confirms, only *planirovat'* 'plan' occurs with aspectualizers and recent time adverbs and reacts positively in imperative and adverbial tests. In other words, in combination with an infinitive, *planirovat'* 'plan' qualifies as an activity verb, whereas the other three qualify as states. Stative finite verbs cannot be pinned down to a moment in time that would be completed before the infinitive event starts taking place (see also Section 2.1.3). This distinction is confirmed by the aspectual behavior of the verbs (cf. Pustejovsky 1991: 55): *planirovat'* 'plan' is the only[7] verb that has a perfective, *zaplanirovat'*, and, as the corpus sample reveals, is also used in the perfective in combination with an infinitive, a fact denied by Levontina (in Apresjan et al. 1999[2]: 388).

A comparison of the present analysis to the description of these four verbs as presented in Levontina (Apresjan et al. 1999[2]: 385–390) shows that the argument- and event-structure possibilities and restrictions reveal the major semantic break between the four verbs, viz. the break between the concept expressed by *sobirat'sja* 'intend, be about', *namerevat'sja* 'intend, mean' and *dumat'* 'intend, think (of)' on the one hand, and by *planirovat'* 'plan' on the other hand. PLANNING refers to the full-fledged, independent activity of plotting future actions on a timeline whereas INTENDING is merely a (preparatory) state referring to the impulse to carry out an action that cannot exist independently of the action the subject intends to carry out (compare Levontina in Apresjan et al. [1999[2]: 385–390]). In sum, the coarse-grained formal and related meaning differences that characterize the two groups of verbs provide the foundation to divide the group *planirovat'* 'plan', *dumat'* 'intend, think (of)', *namerevat'sja* 'intend, mean' and *sobirat'sja* 'intend, be about' listed in (Apresjan et al. 1999[2]: 385–390) up in two.

On the basis of these findings I propose to reserve the term "near-synonym" for lexemes that show constructional similarity, i.e. I will exclude *planirovat'* 'plan', but I will consider as near-synonyms *dumat'* 'intend, think (of)', *namerevat'sja* 'intend, mean', *sobirat'sja* 'intend, be about' and also *predpolagat'* 'intend, propose' and *xotet'* 'want, intend' that display identical behavior. A similar delineation is suggested in Evgen'eva (2001², 1: 590–591); in addition, the proposed division does not go against the treatment presented in (Apresjan et al. 1999²: 390). *Xotet'* 'want, intend' is listed in the "analogi" section for Intentional verbs, together with *predpolagat'* 'intend, propose' and other verbs that are semantically similar, but "not to such an extent that they can be considered near-synonyms" (Apresjan et al. 1995: 102). At the same time, the possible 'Intentional' use of *xotet'* 'want, intend' is explicitly mentioned in the discussion of near-synonyms that express wish or desire (Apresjan et al. 1999²: 458), because it differentiates *xotet'* 'want, intend' from *želat'* 'wish (for), desire', *mečtat'* 'dream (of, about)' and *žaždat* 'thirst (for, after)'. Meaning-based methodologies seem to lack a precise enough measure to determine the degree of similarity; the proposed solutions may thus be influenced by the authors' opinion on what an intention should be as well as by prototype effects typical of human categorization. An approach that builds on distribution of parameters from argument- and event-structure offers a viable alternative; language has delineated categories in a more rigid way, yet without erasing all traces of center-periphery structuring, as I will illustrate in Section 3. Recent publications differ on the question of whether syntactic similarity is required for semantically similar verbs. Atkins and Levin (1995: 96) contend that syntactic differences are possible because "the linguistic conceptualization of the event each verb represents is different in a way that affects syntactic behavior". Plungjan and Raxilina (1998: 109–111) maintain that "often, semantic differences between near-synonyms provide the differences in their syntactic behavior". Yet, is it necessary to consider such verbs near-synonyms? Wouldn't it be more revealing to consider constructionally divergent verbs as "semantically close verbs", as Atkins and Levin (1995) now and then label the "near-synonyms" they are analyzing? Being denied the status of near-synonyms does of course not imply that *planirovat'* 'plan' is semantically unrelated to *dumat'* 'intend, think (of)', *namerevat'sja* 'intend, mean' and *sobirat'sja* 'intend, be about'. Yet, more precise insights into lexical knowledge can be gained from working with a layered structuring for traditional semantic categories. The differences in distribution can be interpreted as pointing in the direction of two adjacent positions on a scale of degree (cf. Cruse 1986: 285–286). Givón (1990: 535) does indeed rank similar verbs in terms of the "strength of intent" with roughly the order: WANT > INTEND > PLAN > CAN. If an agent displays stronger intent, the probability of accomplishing the intended task increases. And, of course, if the subject is undertaking action, as is the case with *planirovat'* 'plan', the likelihood of achieving results rises proportionally. This adjacency might be another reason why some dictionaries do include *planirovat'* 'plan' as a near-synonym of verbs expressing INTENT (Apresjan et al. 1999[2]: 385–390) whereas others do not (Evgen'eva 2001[2], 1: 590–591).

On the view of near-synonyms I propose, minor dissimilarities between verbs are allowed: what lexemes "prefer" inside constructions reveals the variation between *dumat'* 'intend, think (of)', *namerevat'sja* 'intend, mean', *sobirat'sja* 'intend, be about', *predpolagat'* 'intend, propose' and *xotet'* 'want, intend'. This variation can best be modeled at the subconceptual level, however (cf. Edmonds and Hirst 2002: 115). The question for Section 3 is then: how much variation is there at the lexical level and how can it be measured? To determine the degree of variation and elucidate the relation between the lexemes, I will investigate their distribution at a more fine-grained level; for each lexeme I will establish the frequency with which all slots in every [V_{FIN} V_{INF}] construction in the sample occur in a particular syntactic form and with a particular semantic content.

3. Structuring series of near-synonyms

Delineating groups of near-synonyms on the basis of constructional (dis)similarities results in larger groups of near-synonyms than usual: in analyses, synonyms tend to be treated in pairs (cf. Taylor 2003). Therefore, the internal structure of a group of near-synonyms is an issue that has hitherto remained largely undiscussed in the literature (with the notable exceptions of Edmonds and Hirst [2002] and Divjak and Gries [to appear]). Investigating the internal structure of a category requires a description of each of its elements. To maximize verifiability, the basis for a description should be as objective as possible. Recent computational and corpus-linguistic approaches to the lexicon make use of the assumed correlation between distributional similarity and semantic similarity (compare also Haiman's claim [1983: 783]). I have implemented the idea of correlating distributional and semantic similarity to a larger extent than what could be considered standard until recently (cf. Gries [this volume] for a comparable approach and an overview of previous standards). The principal method of investigation applied in this third section of the case study aims at extracting clues from all elements present in the sentences in which these five

Intentional verbs are used so as to infer different meaning facets of the verbs.

3.1. Data, parameters and method

The source of data is the sixteen-million-word section of the Amsterdam corpus (Barentsen 1999) made up of literary works, originally written in Russian during the 20th century by 100 different authors. Using literary data does not compromise the validity of the results: according to Apresjan (p.c.) research into near-synonyms should preferably be based on sources providing well-monitored language that shuns repetition and favors variation. The exact numbers of examples used are given in Table (1)[8], *predpolagat'* 'intend, propose' and *planirovat'* 'plan' are too infrequent to be considered. Note that, because the absolute frequencies of examples for the near-synonyms differ, the precise data for each verb are converted to relative frequencies, expressed as percentages[9], throughout the remainder of the case study.

Table 1. Corpus examples per verb

Xotet'	Dumat'	Sobirat'sja	Nameravat'sja	Predpolagat'	Planirovat'
278	206	209	100	49	34

Although the numbers may seem rather small for a detailed lexical semantic analysis, for three out of four verbs I analyze more than double the amount of the 100 examples per verb used in the most extensive study available (Apresjan et al. 1999²: 303–308); moreover, 200 to 300 examples per verb is a number for which extensive manual tagging is practically feasible. Coding started from observable formal characteristics of the finite verbs and was extended to include information on other elements of the sentence. Each variable provides an "ID tag" or an "objective indication of semantic identity" (Atkins 1987: 23). Taken together, these ID tags form a "behavioral profile" for each verb (Hanks 1996: 79).

In a first coding round, I zoom in on the formal make-up of the slots in the [V_{FIN} V_{INF}] pattern. Finite verbs do not exist without a specific aspect, mode and tense. Since these characteristics invariably occur together and the verbs of this study owe their Intentional character to the combination with an infinitive, I have correlated the aspect, mode and tense of the finite verb with the aspect of the infinitive in the tags. Besides, I have added those elements that are strictly necessary to form a full-fledged simplex sentence, i.e. information on the type of clause the [V_{FIN} V_{INF}] sequence is used in and, linked to the main- or subordinate status, the case marked on the subject slot. Thirdly, I have encoded whether the sentence qualifies as declarative, interrogative, imperative or exclamative. Taken together these structural data form the skeleton of the sentence. From here, one can fill up constructional slots with lexical elements.

In the second coding round, the tagging is inspired by the meticulous "portrayal" methodology, developed within the Moscow School of Semantics (Apresjan 1995 et al.). In this round, the emphasis lies on a thorough analysis of the variation in combinatorial preferences of the verbs. On the one hand, collocates such as negation particles, types of adverbs and connectors have been tagged for. Yet, these data did not provide any significant results and will therefore be disregarded in this analysis. On the other hand, semantic paraphrases for the subject and infinitive have been used. The subject paradigms are classified along a combination of lines presented in traditional grammars of Russian and corpus-based analyses; "animate" is subdivided into addressable human beings and non-addressable animals, and "non-animate" is classified as concrete items that can be man-made or non-man-made, such as phenomena of nature and body parts, abstract concepts as well as groups and organizations. For the infinitives, I have adopted a labeling system that coincides with the eight "semantic primitives of human behavior" set forth in Apresjan's (1995a) linguistic naïve world view, i.e. *do, say, know, want, perceive, sense,* and *feel*. For physical reactions there does not seem to be a primitive, at least not in Russian. Obvious formal properties underlie these primitives (Apresjan 1967; Fisher et al. 1991: 379). Because verbs that relate to the primitive *do* are extremely frequent, they have been subdivided into six categories on the basis of their argument structure. There are "physical activities" that need only a subject like *sleep, drink*. "Physical other" verbs involve an affected object as in *kill someone*; "physical exchange or transfer" verbs like *sell something* feature unaffected objects that easily introduce a third participant in the form of e.g. a dative *to someone*. "Physical exchange or transfer" verbs resemble activities that involve motion: motion of the subject itself ("physical motion") and motion of an object ("physical motion other"), parallel to the affected self and the affected other in physical activities that do not refer to motion. The three basic groups, "physical", "physical exchange" and "physical motion" have metaphorical counterparts, e.g. *catch a smell, draw someone into an argument.* Of all other primitives, only the perceptuals are further divided into active, conscious, directed perception as in *look* and passive, accidental perception like *see* (cf. Apresjan 1995a: 357). The latter feature of directed versus accidental is closely related to an additional important parameter, i.e. the degree of (objective) controllability of the actions. The tests used in tagging for this variable are inspired by the Vendlerian (1967) stativity tests (see Divjak 2004: 239). There are "controllable actions", such as *copy*, "weakly controllable" activities like *find* and "non-controllable" verbs like *forget*.

All 793 sentences are tagged for the total of 47 parameters. That is to say, the analysis that follows is based on a set of 37 271 manually coded data points. The large volume of data, and the assumption that all elements in the sentence may have a valuable contribution to make in providing clues for the subcategorization and related lexical-semantic description of the four Intentional verbs, make a compelling case for a quantitative approach. It is unlikely indeed that a human analyst could keep track of all the variables when computing the similarities and differences that indicate basic tendencies. Cluster analysis[10] is a technique that is often applied in analyzing large data sets. Although there are different types of clustering techniques (Everitt 1993), in dealing with semantically related verbs Hierarchical Agglomerative Clustering (HAC)[11] seems the most appropriate.

In Section 3.2. I will use behavioral profiles to extract more refined information about the concept INTEND as it is encoded in language. Absence of certain parameters indicates incompatibility of these parameters with the concept in general; parameters that are present can be used to differentiate the four verbs. In order to do so, I will compare the verbs in the structures suggested by the HAC analysis applied to the total behavioral profiles for each of the four verbs (visualized in Dendrogram [3]) as well as to selected combinations of ID tags (see Dendrograms [1] and [2]) and I will propose parameters that contribute to subcategorizing and interpreting the Intentional verbs.

3.2. A tentative radial network[12]

Distributional data forming the behavioral profile for each of the intentional verbs reveal what language can tell us about a concept that is rather abstract and closed to observation like INTEND TO CARRY OUT AN ACTION. Typically, the intention is displayed by human beings and concerns physical, mental and communicative activities. Physiological reactions, physiological conditions and wishes or desires are not represented in the tags; intentions do not seem to apply to these situations. The results of elicitation tests with native speakers confirm this finding (cf. Divjak 2004: 238–239). Although the intention itself can be negated, negation of the activity expressed by the infinitive is rare. As opposed to plans, intentions typically do not occur in the infinitive, imperative or – to a lesser extent – as a participle; naively put, intentions cannot be modified or imposed and can hardly be thought of as a (temporary) property of someone. The absence of perfective counterparts for verbs that express intention as well as the fact that these verbs are not found in the infinitive makes future tense extremely atypical for intentions; intentions seem hard to predict. Adverbial specifications of time, place, manner and reason are rare, but specifications of purpose are found; the latter however, refer to the complex situation of intention and intended activity.

Apart from these characteristics, which all intentional verbs share, the four verbs differ in several respects. First of all, the so-called "semantic dominant" (Raxilina 2000: 283) of the polysemous network each verb belongs to provides important information for contrasting the four verbs and understanding the difference in perspective on a situation they convey. Except for *namerevat'sja* 'intend, mean', the total number of examples for each of the intentional verbs reveals that constructions without infinitive are overwhelmingly more frequent than combinations of these verbs with infinitive. *Dumat'* 'intend, think (of)' is related to thinking, *xotet'* 'want, intend' to wanting and *sobirat'sja* 'intend, be about' to gathering or getting together. *Xotet'* 'want, intend' is the only verb that stems from the volitional domain. This might be the reason why Levontina (in Apresjan et al. 1999: 385), who defines INTEND as "want to do something and be prepared to put in effort to so that", excludes *xotet'* 'want, intend'; maybe, a volition-based intention is not typically thought of as guaranteeing willingness to put in effort. *Namerevat'sja* 'intend, mean' is restricted to combinations with an infinitive; not surprisingly, *namerenie* is the only noun Russian has to express pure 'intention'. Possibly because of its neutral position in this respect *namerevat'sja* 'intend, mean' is listed as heading the intentional series in Evgen'eva (2001, 1: 590).

Supplementary distinctive specifications can be inferred from close inspection of the ID tags and make it possible to discover the differences in the prototype center of each verb (cf. Hirst 1995). HAC analysis is useful here in at least two respects. First, it organizes an enormous amount of data in the most optimal substructures thus greatly reducing the number of variables needed to distinguish the elements. Secondly, it provides an objective basis for drawing a network representation. The relationships between the near-synonyms can best be represented by a radial network (Lakoff 1987: 91–114) as the "elaborative distance" between two nodes (Langacker 1987: 379) can be used to visualize the relation between them: the greater the elaborative distance, the less synonymous the verbs are. In what follows, I will focus on a few salient differences between the verbs and use these to indicate in passing how even in contexts where two verbs may appear to be freely interchangeable the speaker can convey subtle differences in perspective on the situation he is describing. Finally, I will combine the findings and propose a structure for all the verbs in the Intentional category.

HAC analyses carried out on selected tags visualize the respects in which these verbs are most similar and in which other respects they are most dissimilar. Dendrogram (1) shows the cluster solution proposed on the basis of skeletal info, i.e. the exact formal makeup of the constructional slots and the frequency with which they are encountered, excluding collocates and paraphrased semantic information. The idea of empty constructional slots might be of importance for the analysis of near-synonymous verbs. Due to the high similarity and low contrastiveness that characterizes near-synonyms, they are usually defined as "highly intersubstitutable". The more slots in a shared construction the more frequently display identical formal features, the higher the chances are of being able to "automatically" substitute one near-synonym for another. It is surprising that this factor has

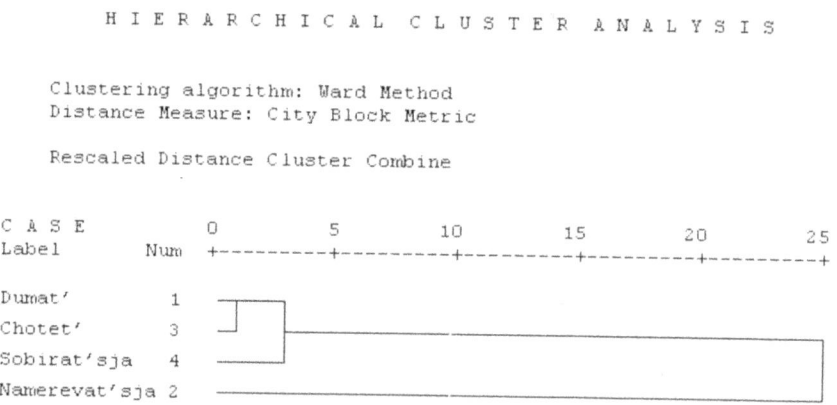

Dendrogram 1. Skeletal data

been largely neglected in previous studies on near-synonymy. In studies on polysemy, on the contrary, the exact form of a verb, its collocates and the frequency with which they occur have been used (cf. Gries [this volume] and references therein) to automatically identify senses, distinguish them or to link them up.

The results of the HAC analysis on skeletal data show that *dumat'* 'intend, think (of)' and *xotet'* 'want, intend' are most closely related. Intra-cluster differences are less important than intercluster differences, however, and there is very little in the range of differences between these two verbs. Basically, *xotet'* 'want, intend' differs most from *dumat'* 'intend, think (of)' in that *dumat'* 'intend, think (of)' occurs more frequently in interrogative clauses. This feature possibly relates to the think-component present in the *dumat'*-type of intention. The questions do not necessarily focus on the presence or absence of the intention, instead, they ask the subject to give his opinion on a particular aspect of the infinitive event, as illustrated in (11).

(11) ***Во сколько,** приблизительно, **месяцев вы думаете покрыть расстояние** между землей и Марсом? – спросил Скайльс* [...].
[A.N. Tolstoj. Aèlita.]
'**In how many**, approximately, **months do you think/intend to cover the distance** between the earth and Mars? – asked Skajl's [...].'

In example (12) the volitional roots of *xotet'* 'want, intend' are revealed by the conditional mode that is not found with *dumat'* 'intend, think (of)' or any of the other verbs.

(12) *Из этого списка **я хотел бы выделить** тех, кто много труда положил в помощь мне, чтобы эта вещь была снабжена* [...]
[A. Solženicyn. Archipelag GULag.]
'And from that list **I would want/intend to single ou**t those who put in a lot of effort helping me [...]'

Let us stay with *dumat'* 'intend, think (of)' and *xotet'* 'want, intend' and look at the collocational respects in which they differ. Dendrogram (2) visualizes the clustering obtained on the basis of paraphrased semantic information relating to the subject and the infinitive alone. In these respects, *dumat'* 'intend, think (of)' and *xotet'* 'want, intend' are rather dissimilar.

```
           HIERARCHICAL CLUSTER ANALYSIS

    Clustering algorithm: Ward Method
    Distance Measure: City Block Metric

    Rescaled Distance Cluster Combine


    C A S E        0        5       10       15       20       25
    Label    Num  +--------+--------+--------+--------+--------+

    Dumat'         1   ─┐
    Namerevat'sja  2   ─┘
    Sobirat'sja    4   ─────────────────────────────────────────
    Chotet'        3   ─────────────────────────────────────────
```

Dendrogram 2. Subject and infinitive related information

Although *xotet'* 'want, intend' has the largest combinability of all intentional verbs, it is most suited to combine with actions that express intellectual activity and communication, including those that escape the subject's sphere of control. This is no surprise, given that volition is less constrained by feasibility than reason.

(13) *Павел смотрел на него с какой-то затаенной злостью, с болью даже, как если бы* **хотел что-то понять** *и никак понять не мог.* [V. Šukšin. Osen'ju.]
'Pavel looked at him with some kind of suppressed anger, with pain even, as if **he wanted/intended to understand something** and by no means could.'

Dumat' 'intend, think (of)', on the other hand, strongly prefers controllable actions and is rarely found in combination with mental activities. Although *dumat'* 'intend, think (of)' is related to reason instead of volition, it likewise signals that the subject is far from sure that the controllable infinitive action will be successfully carried out. Yet, this preliminary assessment does not exclude a positive outcome.

(14) *Я переносила этот разврат, как больной переносит лекарство: он думает этим спасти свою жизнь,* ***я думала спасти свою любовь****.* [M. Ageev. Kokain.]

'I endured this debauchery like a patient endures medicine: he thinks/intends to save his life with it, and **I thought/intended to save my love**.'

In other words, both *xotet'* 'want, intend' and *dumat'* 'intend, think (of)' express a hesitant intention that was inspired by volition or reason respectively. Also, although the subject is emotionally (15) or mentally (16) involved in the choices s/he makes, s/he hasn't really made up his/her mind, and several options are left open:

(15) *Волька повернулся с боку на бок, **хотел что-то ответить Жене, но не ответил**, а быстро вскочил на ноги и бросился в глубь [...]* [L. Lagin. Starik Xottabyč.]
'Vol'ka tossed and turned, **he wanted to answer Ženja something, yet he didn't**, but jumped fast to his feet and threw himself into the abyss [...]'

(16) *Сначала **я думал стать психиатром**, как многие неудачники; но я был неудачником особенным; [...] и **я перешел** на изучение английской литературы [...]*. [V. Nabokov. Lolita.]
'**At first I intended/thought to become a psychiatrist** like many failures; **but** I was an unusual failure [...] and **I switched** to studying English literature [...].'

A third verb, *sobirat'sja* 'intend, be about' occupies the middle position in both dendrograms. Dendrograms (1) and (2) reveal that *sobirat'sja* 'intend, be about' is more similar to the hesitant intentions, *dumat'* 'intend, think of)' and *xotet'* 'want, intend', with respect to the formal make-up of the slots than with respect to the semantic paraphrases for subject and infinitive. In the case of *sobirat'sja* 'intend, be about', nothing is known about the source of the intention. The subject has an intention and is "getting ready" to carry it out, as the active, processual nature of its semantic dominant indicates. *Sobirat'sja* 'to intend' can handle about any infinitive, although it is most often found with infinitives that express physical activities, in particular motion (see [17]).

(17) *Серпилин уже несколько дней **собирался походить** ночью по окопам переднего края, посмотреть, как идет служба.*
[A. Simonov. Živye I Mërtvye.]

'Already a couple of days Serpilin **intended to walk** along the entrenchments of the forward positions at night to see how the active service was going.'

Emotion and perception verbs seem to fit the shade of processuality typical of the intention expressed by *sobirat'sja* 'intend, be about' less well than they fit the type of intention expressed by *xotet'* 'want, intend' and *dumat'* 'intend, think (of)'. At the same time, the activity and processuality of *sobirat'sja* 'intend, be about' make it possible to background the meaning of actually intending to carry out an action, thus foregrounding the visible about-to-happen component. The subject is doing something that may well cause the infinitive event to take place.

(18) *Было бы совершенной неправдой сказать, что за эти несколько минут […] меня нисколько небеспокоило, что я болен, и что* **собираюсь Зиночку заразить**. [M. Ageev. Kokain.]
'It would have been completely untrue to say that in those couple of minutes […] it did not worry me the least that I am ill, and that **I am about/intend to infect Zinočka**.'

Whereas *dumat'* 'intend, think (of)' and *xotet'* 'want, intend' preferably occur in main clauses, *sobirat'sja* 'intend, be about' is found in a variety of subordinate clauses. Roughly, this difference indicates that a "visible" intention such as the one present in *sobirat'sja* 'intend, be about' enters more easily into the type of relation, e.g. time, manner, purpose, condition among others, that can hold between a main clause event and a subordinate clause event than hesitant intentions that are closed to observation. The preference of *sobirat'sja* 'intend, be about' for occurring in subordinate clauses makes the verb resemble *namerevat'sja* 'intend, mean'. The latter verb occurs more specifically in gerundive constructions (19) that relate the intention to carry out a controllable action to the situation expressed in the main clause with respect to time, cause, condition, reason etc. In addition, the subject of main and subordinate clause needs to be co-referential.

(19) *Но это должно быть в большинстве -- испорченные женщины? Ты сама испорченная! -- вскричал* **Николай** *и быстро* **встал, намереваясь уйти**. [A. Gajdar. V dni poraženij i pobed.]
'"But that must be mostly depraved women?" "You are depraved yourself!", **Nikolaj** cried out, and **got up** fast, **intending to leave**.'

The last verb, *namerevat'sja* 'intend, mean' is the only verb that does not relate to a semantic dominant outside the domain of intentions. It expresses a pure intention. The type of intention rendered by *namerevat'sja* 'intend, mean' is nearly exclusively encountered in positive declarative clauses.

(20) Да еще слухи о **земельной реформе**, которую **намеревался произвести** пан гетман, [...] [M. Bulgakov. Belaja Gvardija.]
 'And also the rumors about **the land reform** that the hetman **intended to carry out** [...]'

Skeletal data and the semantic information – however abstract – they convey are obviously important in defining a verb's meaning and hence for distinguishing between two near-synonyms. Dendrogram (2) visualizes the close relation between *namerevat'sja* 'intend, mean' and the type of intention that stems from reasoning, *dumat'* 'intend, think (of)', with respect to the types of subjects and infinitives the verbs preferably combine with. Typically, *namerevat'sja* 'intend, mean' applies to controllable actions, preferably expressing physical effort and motion.

(21) Сергей собирал, где мог, сведения, **намереваясь** при первом же случае **убежать** к партизанам. [A. Gajdar. V dni poraženij i pobed.]
 'Sergej collected, wherever he could, information, because he **intended to escape** to the partisans on the first occasion.'

On the basis of collocational data for the infinitive alone, one might wrongly propose the highest degree of similarity for *namerevat'sja* 'intend, mean' and *dumat'* 'intend, think (of)', verbs that are intuitively rather dissimilar (compare Apresjan et al. 1999: 385–390; Evgen'eva 2001, 1: 590–591).

The intention rendered by *namerevat'sja* 'intend, mean' deviates from the expected pattern and thus demands a fully conscious choice (22) from the subject; often matters of higher importance are at stake (see also [20]).

(22) Стадвухлетний старец заявил, что остаток жизни **намеревается посвятить добрым делам**, и теперь, наверное долго не протянет. [A. and B. Strugackie. Trudno byt' bogom.]
 'The 102 year old man announced that he intended to **devote the rest of his life to good deeds**, and now, he probably won't last long.'

In other words, the intention in *namerevat'sja* 'intend, mean' seems to be a firm one as *tvërdo* 'firmly' in (23) stresses:

(23) Она-то рассчитывала, что, увидев милиционеров, настырный Герман ретируется по-тихому, но он, [...] **твёрдо намеревался отстаивать свое право** на приватную беседу с ней.
[A. Marinina. Čužaja maska.]
'She was counting on it that once stubborn Herman had spotted the policemen, he would silently withdraw, but he **firmly intended to defend his right** to a private conversation with her.'

In a last step I show how these verbs interact and structure the semantic and related conceptual space INTEND TO CARRY OUT AN ACTION. Taking all values obtained for all four verbs on the basis of all sentences in the data sample through the HAC analysis yields Dendrogram (3). Interestingly, the structure in Dendrogram (3) is nearly identical to the structure in Dendrogram (1), computed on the basis of skeletal data alone.

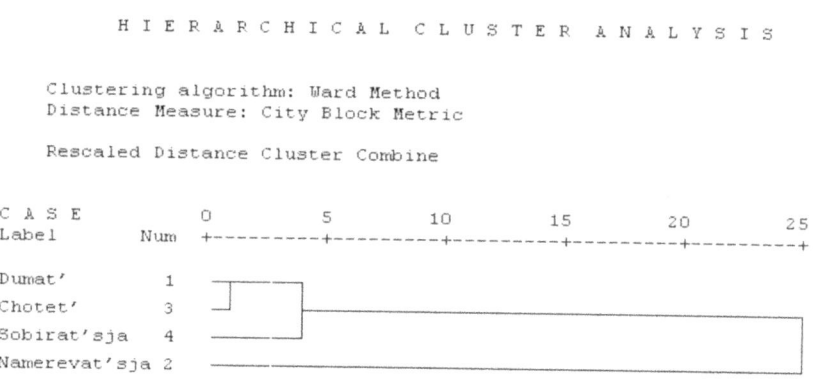

Dendrogram 3. Total behavioral profile

The results from HAC analysis can easily be translated into a radial network representation, giving it an objective and verifiable basis. Given the small number of verbs and the clear structure of the dendrogram I will refrain from inserting a separate network representation. The structure proposed for the group of near-synonyms shows that *dumat'* 'intend, think (of)' and *xotet'* 'want, intend' are very similar, that *namerevat'sja* 'intend, mean' is rather dissimilar, while *sobirat'sja* 'intend, be about' holds the middle ground being on the whole more closely related to *dumat'* 'intend, think (of)' and *xotet'* 'want, intend'. *Sobirat'sja* 'intend, be about' occupies the central position: it relates both to hesitant and firm intentions, yet is not specified in that respect itself. The active, process-like nature of the intention expressed by *sobirat'sja* 'intend, be about' seems an ideal point of reference: interestingly, sentences in the corpus sample that contain two intentional verbs typically contrast *sobirat'sja* 'intend, be about' with any of the other verbs. Compare here examples (24) through (26).

(24) […] *но он своих зрителей **пугать не собирается**, **он хочет показать** им и смешное, и грустное, и печальное,* […]
[V. Koneckij. Nevezučij Al'fons.]
'[…] but **he does not intend to scare** his spectators, **he wants/intends to show** them both what is funny and sad, and grievous […]'

(25) *Лицо ее шло красными пятнами, яркие губы дрожали, словно **она собиралась заплакать**, но она, конечно, **не думала плакать**, она была в бешенстве.* [A. and B. Strugackie. Gadkie lebedi.]
'Her face was covered in red blotches, her bright lips trembled as if **she was about/intended to burst into tears**, but she, of course, **didn't think/intend to cry**, she was enraged.'

(26) *В соответствии с составленным ею же самой планом на день **лениться она собиралась** часов до четырех, после чего **намеревалась приступить к написанию** аналитической справки по убийствам и изнасилованиям в Москве.* [A. Marinina. Posmertnyj obraz.]
'In accordance with the plan for the day she had made herself, she **intended/was about to laze around** until app. 4 pm, and after that **she (firmly) intended to get down to writing** an analytic report about murder and rape in Moscow.'

Going from *xotet'* 'want, intend' and *dumat'* 'to consider, intend, think' over *sobirat'sja* 'intend, be about' to *namerevat'sja* 'to intend, mean', the strength of the intent increases, and with the strength of the intent, the subject's engagement and maybe even his chances of succeeding. Compare here Givón's (1990: 535) scale of intent that likewise suggests an evolution from wishes through intentions to plans. For Russian, the differences in strength of the intent emerging from relatedness to different semantic dominants are clearly less important than the differences between INTEND and

PLAN TO CARRY OUT AN ACTION. The major difference between INTEND and PLAN has been encoded at the level of the constructions each concept takes part in, whereas the minor differences between types of INTEND reside in the way the constructional slots, shared by all INTEND verbs, are formed and filled up. Dendrograms (1) and (3) visualize that the way constructional slots are formed can be decisive in determining the degree of closeness between near-synonyms: the comparison of Dendrograms (2) and (3) reveals that collocational preferences alone yield counter-intuitive results, as I have pointed out for *namerevat'sja* 'intend, mean' and *dumat'* 'intend, think (of)' above. Acquiring abstract concepts requires more experience with language than, for instance, acquiring concrete object nouns for which sensory information is more conclusive (Boroditsky 2001: 20). For this particular abstract concept INTEND, the form-related clues encoded in Russian even outweigh the semantic combinatorial patterns typical of Russian.

4. Summary: A distribution-based view on series of near-synonyms

In conclusion to this paper I would like to stress that the present two-level distribution-based approach to delineating and discovering the structure of near-synonyms seems to offer a valid verifiable and repeatable alternative to meaning-based, introspective methodologies. Data on which slots a verb can open up and how these slots are typically formed and filled up facilitate measuring (dis)similarities in meaning between related lexemes. In addition, comparison with the results of a semantically inspired analysis shows that the differences in combinatorial possibilities and preferences for certain patterns yield intuitively acceptable classifications, reveal important semantic differences and refine introspective analyses by formulating the (dis)similarities in a more precise way.

In the first part of my analysis, I have exploited elicited data on networks of constructions to categorize the four verbs said to express that someone INTENDS TO CARRY OUT AN ACTION in Russian (Levontina in Apresjan et al. [1999: 385–390]). Three alternative construction possibilities reveal argument- and event-structure properties of the four finite verbs that remain implicit in the [V_{FIN} V_{INF}] pattern. Together, these constructions elucidate the direction and degree of integration between the two verbs in the sequence and delineate semantically coherent verb classes. I propose to take the substitutability requirement more seriously with respect to the constructional potential of the verbs. Near-synonyms should be freely interchangeable at the level of the network of constructions they are part of: a network captures the finite verbs' meaning at the coarse grain. According to the syntactic bootstrapping approach to acquisition it is likely that native speakers of Russian have used the formal distinctions to discover the related meaning distinctions. Fisher et al. (1991: 377) hypothesize that "semantic properties that are closed to observation must be marked in the syntax if the language learner is even to discover which words in the languages express them". A syntactic bootstrapping approach to language acquisition implies a strong influence of grammatical structure on cognitive structure; language may partly shape conceptions of events (cf. Slobin 2003 "thinking for speaking"). Yet, in many cases this process is presumably aided by experience: syntactic differences are said to arise over time to signal the difference in meaning; precisely those syntactic differences are chosen that fit the meaning of an item (Croft 1999: 85–87). Language and experience would then mutually support each other. This seems a viable strategy for PLANNING versus INTENDING, which encode activities and states respectively and can be seen as adjacent positions on a scale of degree.

Yet, all the rough, constructional differences taken together provide only part of the meaning of a word; by far not all meaning components are expressed in subcategorization frames. The lexemes *dumat'* 'intend, think (of)', *namerevat'sja* 'intend, mean', *sobirat'sja* 'intend, be about' and *xotet'* 'want, intend' that have very restricted constructional possibilities, i.e. combine exclusively with an infinitive, vary in several respects; these lexical differences are relevant to the language user. In the second part of this paper, I have proposed a verifiable and repeatable solution for the internal structuring of clusters of near-synonyms that also lays the foundation for a fine-grained lexical-semantic description of the verbs in those clusters. Constellations of ID tags and the resulting total behavioral profiles provide a basis for describing the variation between lexical elements. ID tags encode structural and lexical preferences; on the basis of these data they reveal how the near-synonyms have different prototypical distributions and how they each specify a view on a situation.

The present corpus-based analysis can be validated and extended in several (synchronic) respects of which I only mention those for which precise techniques have been developed. First, further quantitative analysis of the behavioral profiles by means of t-values and z-scores sheds light on which of the ID tags exhibit the largest differences between the clusters and the verbs in those clusters (cf. Divjak and Gries to appear). Secondly, larger corpus-samples can be used to extract more precise information on the variables that facilitate distinguishing intentional verbs, e.g. the exact content of the subject or infinitive collocate; these data could then be subjected to strict hypothesis testing. At the same time, the larger samples might shed light on parameters such as the occurrence of specific adverbs that seem of importance, yet do not yield statistically significant differences in the sample used for this paper. Thirdly, the findings could be validated by means of experiments in which native speakers are asked to perform tasks in which the semantic (dis)similarity between the verbs is judged.

Apart from validating the results, it seems beneficial to study the intentional senses of these verbs from the view of the polysemous network they are part of. Knowledge about the semantic dominant that holds a network together would provide insight into the precise nature of the different concepts from which the intentional meanings developed. Obviously, data on the semantic dominant do not reveal what an intention is, yet contribute to understanding the differences between lexemes that express intention.

The linguistic findings presented in this paper can be used as input for cognitive research on the concept INTEND TO CARRY OUT AN ACTION. Through language, human beings have the capacity to construe a "ceived" situation in alternate ways. The preferences and limitations hard-wired into the grammatical and lexical structure of Russian limit the array of coding possibilities for expressing situations that qualify as INTEND; these preferences and limitations provide valuable linguistic data for describing the concept INTEND. On the one hand, insight has been gained into how semantic knowledge about (PLAN and) INTEND is parceled out between grammar and lexicon. In addition, I have elucidated with respect to which properties near-synonymous lexemes are most intersubstitutable. Supplementing these linguistic data with cognitive data will shed light on whether structural or lexical clues are more pervasive when acquiring the meaning of lexemes. This knowledge in turn would contribute to a theory of meaning acquisition and lexical organization. On the other hand, the findings can shed light on how precisely the linguistic structure of a concept relates to the cognitive structure: do elicitation tests with native speakers yield a network similar to the one proposed on the basis of language data (Sandra and Rice 1995)? Clearly, speakers have to respect the grammatical and lexical conventions of their language that can be seen as the result of a process of collectively structuring experiences and expressing these experiences in language (Raxilina 2000: 353). Hence, the categorization of a language may guide the categorization of experiences and the categorization typical of the language one speaks may influence the structure and contents of the concepts one eventually acquires. Mapping the results of extensive linguistic and cognitive research onto each other will reveal whether and to what extent "the limits of one's language mean the limits of one's world".

Notes

* This research was carried out with the financial support of the Science Foundation – Flanders in the form of a research assistantship (K. U. Leuven – Belgium, 2000–2004). Revisions were made during a post doctoral fellowship (UNC at Chapel Hill, 2004–2005) financed by the Francqui Foundation (B.A.E.F.). I would like to thank the ICLC 8 (2003) audience in Spain for interesting questions and remarks, and Bert Cornillie, Laura A. Janda and the editors of this volume for valuable comments on both the contents and presentation of this paper. The usual disclaimers apply.
1. Of course, the absence of a specific pattern in a sufficiently large sample of the language does provide some support for the infelicity of that pattern. Yet, given that a representative (well-balanced and stratified) corpus of Russian is not (yet) available, I will not regard the low-frequency or absence of a pattern as negative evidence. Moreover, the large number of possibly low frequent verbs (of all 300 verbs that combine with an infinitive) makes it virtually impossible to approach this topic from a corpus-based point of view. Research into "alternations" is generally not corpus-based (compare Levin 1993): corpora provide information about which constructions are attested for a particular verb, but native speaker intuitions are used to decide whether a particular construction alternates with another construction.
2. Sometimes, the lexemes that are selected as semantically similar on a distributional basis are antonyms, not synonyms. Given that this phenomenon does not affect the verbs dealt with in this paper, I will not go into this issue but refer to Lin and Zhao (1993) instead.
3. The elicitation experiment with native speakers of Russian was set up as a small number design. Five native speakers between the ages of 25 and 50 were selected to judge the constructional possibilities of 300 verbs on a three-point scale. The experiment was conducted over a period of three months in the form of a weekly interview during which each native speaker was presented with approximately 25 verbs. Several measures were taken to minimize the obvious negative effects of this set-up. Native speakers were asked both to judge ready-made sentences and to form sentences using particular constructional devices; these sentences were on a later occasion presented to the participant who had constructed them as well as to other participants. To guard against lexical effects, the tests were carried using pro-nouns and other pro-forms (cf. Smessaert et al. 2005), which ensures that the mutual effect of lexi-

cal items in a construction is minimized as much as possible; as a result, the acceptability or unacceptability of a particular construction is very unlikely to be influenced by a particular lexical compatibility or incompatibility of words that are not focused on. In the experiment, infinitives were replaced by *(s)delat'* 'do', and the results might therefore be restricted to combinations with infinitives that relate to this action primitive. Moreover, to check for repetition effects in judgments of grammaticality 10 control judgments were collected for every verb in every construction type from an ever varying pool of native speakers. In this case, the trigger questions were mixed with other, non-related questions about aspects of Russian syntax and semantics. Finally, the results obtained have been systematically compared against information contained in dictionaries, and utterances found in the Amsterdam corpus and on the Internet. For a more detailed discussion of the data collection and native speaker survey I refer to Divjak (2004: 19–33).

4. The English translations are word-for-word translations of the Russian original. In Section 2 glosses are provided for the phenomena that are in focus; in Section 3, formal information is irrelevant and is therefore omitted. For the same reason, throughout this article, morphemic alignment of source and goal sentence has not been implemented.

5. Langacker (1990: 269–270) contends that each modal verb "evokes the conception of an associated activity. One does not simply want, know or have a physical capacity in the abstract – rather, one wants, knows, or has the capacity *to do something*. Thus each verb makes schematic reference to another process, which serves as a landmark and as the e-site for a relational complement". The data presented in this paper show that in Russian the infinitive process does not necessarily function like other, typical landmarks and e-sites. Compare also Kemmer and Verhagen (1994: 117–119) who define analytic causatives as conceptually dependent on the effected predicate, since they necessarily evoke the idea of another action or state.

6. Because the constructional possibilities of these verbs are limited to combinations with an infinitive there are no conspicuous formal characteristics that can be used as the basis for further subcategorization. Therefore, the verbs were classified with the help of elicited and non-elicited data on their linear distribution, i.e. their mutual combinatorial possibilities in verb triples. This procedure yielded categories that have received formal underpinning from implication relations and aspectual behavior (Divjak 2004: 143–174). The Intentional category contains five verbs, i.e. *dumat'* 'intend, think (of)', *namerevat'sja* 'intend, mean', *sobirat'sja* 'intend, be about', *predpolagat'* 'intend' and *xotet'* 'want, intend, be about'.

7. Zaliznjak and Šmelev (2000: 21) do not consider the imperfective *sobirat'sja* and the perfective *sobrat'sja* 'intend' as an aspectual pair when the verbs are combined with an infinitive. Instead, they classify the perfective *sobrat'sja* as

"prezens naprasnogo ožidanija" [present of idle expectation], i.e. as a verb with a negated intention.

8. The thousands of examples found for the two most frequent verbs, *xotet'* 'want, intend' and *sobirat'sja* 'intend, be about', constitute a number far too large to be submitted to a thorough manual analysis that aims at tagging all examples for app. 50 parameters. Therefore, prior to closer inspection, the number of examples was reduced to 3 sentences per author, preferably from three different works. For the considerably less frequently used *dumat'* 'intend, think (of)' maximum 5 examples were selected per author, for *namerevat'sja* 'intend, mean' up to 8 sentences were taken and for the rare *predpolagat'* 'intend, propose' all examples were used.

9. Working with relative frequencies causes a problem for *planirovat'* 'plan' and *predpolagat'* 'intend, propose'. Because there are in all 34 and 49 examples containing planirovat' 'plan' and *predpolagat'* 'intend, propose' respectively, the percentages are distorted; given that the verb is becoming obsolete it turned out to be impossible to collect more data from comparable (literary) sources. For this reason, *planirovat'* 'plan' and *predpolagat'* 'intend, propose' will be left out of the cluster analysis.

10. Many thanks to Stefan Th. Gries for advising me to apply clustering techniques to this and similar data sets (see Divjak 2004: 227–293) in order to obtain an objective basis for my decisions, for providing statistical support and for guidance in interpreting the results. I take full responsibility for any descriptive and interpretative shortcomings.

11. The distance between the Intentional verbs is computed using City-block (Manhattan) distance, the average difference across dimensions. The linkage or amalgamation rules are given by Ward's method that uses an analysis of variance approach to evaluate the distances between clusters: it tests for significant differences between means and links the clusters that produce the smallest variance in the merged cluster. In general, Ward's method tends to create clusters of a small size, which is what is needed with an input group of four verbs for which the degree of near-synonymy has to be established. Alternative analyses were carried out using Euclidean distance and the Weighted pair-group average. The Euclidean distance and the Weighted pair-group average seem to be less suited for dealing with data on near-synonyms. Working with Euclidean distance, a minimal distance, does not seem appropriate when the subjects that have to be compared are known to be highly similar. Clustering by means of the Weighted-pair group algorithm is advisable when the cluster sizes are suspected to be greatly uneven: in the computations, the size of the respective clusters (i.e., the number of objects contained in them) is used as a weight. Given that the input group of subjects contains only four elements, there is not much reason to suspect that the clusters will be greatly uneven. In order for a cluster to have autonomy, the distance between the

clusters has to be sufficiently large. The results of analyses with Euclidean distance and the Weighted pair-group average are less clear in this respect and thus harder to interpret: in general, the elements were first clustered at larger distances and the clusters were linked at smaller distances than with City Block distance and Ward's clustering algorithm.

12. Because hierarchical cluster analysis is an exploratory method, results should be treated as tentative until they are confirmed with, e.g. an independent sample. For this reason, from the same Amsterdam corpus a random sample was drawn that, admittedly, partly overlaps with the balanced sample used in this paper. HAC analysis applied on these alternative data sets yielded identical clustering patterns.

References

Apresjan, Jurij Derenikovič
    1967   *Экспериментальное Исследование Семантики Русского Глагола* [An Experimental Investigation of the Semantics of the Russian Verb]. Moskva: Nauka.
    1995a   Образ человека по данным языка: попытка системного описания [The image of man according to language data: an attempt at a systematic description]. *Вопросы Языкознания* [Issues in Linguistics] 1: 37–67.
    1995b   *Избранные труды. Том I. Лексическая Семантика: Синонимические Средства Языка,* 2-е изд. испр и доп [Selected writings. Volume I. Lexical Semantics, 2nd edition, corrected and supplemented]. Moskva: Škola "Jazyki Russkoj Kul'tury" [1974].

Apresjan, Jurij Derenikovič and Erna Pall
    1982   *Русский Глагол – Венгерский Глагол: Управление и Сочетаемость* [The Russian Verb – the Hungarian Verb: Government and Combinability]. Budapest: Tankën'vkiado.

Apresjan, Jurij Derenikovič, Ol'ga Ju. Boguslavskaja, Irina V. Levontina, and Elena V. Uryson
    1995   *Новый Объяснительный Словарь Синонимов: Проспект* [The New Explanatory Dictionary of Synonyms: Prospectus]. Moskva: Russkie Slovari.

Apresjan, Jurij Derenikovič, Ol'ga Ju. Boguslavskaja, Irina V. Levontina, Elena V. Uryson, Marina Ja. Glovinskaja, and Tat'jana V. Krylova
    1999[2]   *Новый Объяснительный Словарь Синонимов Русского Языка. Выпуск I.* [The New Explanatory Dictionary of Synonyms. Volume I]. Moskva: Škola "Jazyki Russkoj Kul'tury".

Apresjan, Jurij Derenikovič, Irina V. Levontina, Ol'ga Ju. Boguslavskaja, Elena V. Uryson, Marina Ja. Glovinskaja, Tat'jana V. Krylova, Svetlana A. Grigor'eva, Valentina Ju. Apresjan, Elizaveta Ė. Babaeva, and A. V. Ptencova
    2000   Новый Объяснительный Словарь Синонимов Русского Языка. Выпуск II. [The New Explanatory Dictionary of Synonyms. Volume II]. Moskva: Škola "Jazyki Russkoj Kul'tury".

Atkins, B. T. Sue and Beth Levin
    1995   Building on a corpus: A linguistic and lexicographical look at some near-synonyms. *International Journal of Lexicography* 8 (2): 85–114.

Barentsen, Adriaan (compiler)
    1999   *The Amsterdam Corpus of Written Russian.*

Boroditsky, Lera
    2001   Does language shape thought? Mandarin and English speakers' conceptions of time. *Cognitive Psychology* 43: 1–22.

Cristofaro, Sonia
    2003   *Subordination.* (Oxford Studies in Typology and Linguistic Theory.) Oxford: Oxford University Press.

Croft, William
    1999   Some contributions of typology to cognitive linguistics, and vice versa. In: Theo Janssen and Gisela Redeker (eds.), *Cognitive Linguistics: Foundations, Scope, and Methodology*, 61–93. (Cognitive Linguistics Research 15.) Berlin/New York: Mouton de Gruyter.
    2001   *Radical Construction Grammar: Syntactic Theory in Typological Perspective.* (Oxford Linguistics.) Oxford: Oxford University Press.

Cruse, D. Alan
    1986   *Lexical Semantics.* Cambridge: Cambridge University Press.
    2000   *Meaning in Language: An Introduction to Semantics and Pragmatics.* Oxford: Oxford University Press.

Divjak, Dagmar
    2004   Degrees of verb integration. Conceptualizing and categorizing events in Russian. Unpublished Ph.D. Dissertation, K. U. Leuven (Belgium), Dept. of Oriental and Slavic Studies.

Divjak, Dagmar and Stefan Th. Gries.
    to appear   Ways of trying in Russian: Clustering behavioral profiles. *Corpus Linguistics and Linguistic Theory* 2 (1).

Edmonds, Philip and Graeme Hirst
    2002   Near-synonymy and lexical choice. *Computational Linguistics*, 28 (2 June), 105–144.

Everitt, Brian S.
    1993[3]   *Cluster Analysis.* London: Arnold.

Evgen'eva, Anastasija P. (ed.)
    2001²   Словарь Синонимов Русского Языка в Двух Томах [Dictionary of Russian Synonyms in Two Volumes]. Moskva: Astrel' AST.
Fisher, Cynthia, Henry Gleitman, and Lila Gleitman
    1991   On the semantic content of subcategorization frames. *Cognitive Psychology* 2: 331–392.
Flank, Susan
    1995   Aspectualizers and scope. Unpublished Ph.D. dissertation, Harvard University (U.S.A.).
Givón, Talmy
    1990   *Syntax: A Functional Typological Introduction*, Volume 2. Amsterdam/Philadelphia: John Benjamins.
Goldberg, Adele
    1995   *Constructions: A Construction Grammar Approach to Argument Structure*. Chicago and London: Chicago University Press.
Gries, Stefan Th.
    (this volume) Corpus-based methods and cognitive semantics: the many senses of "to run". In: Stefan Th. Gries and Anatol Stefanowitsch (eds.), *Corpora in Cognitive Linguistics. Vol. 2: The Syntax-Lexis Interface*. Berlin/New York: Mouton de Gruyter.
Haiman, John
    1983   Iconic and economic motivation. *Language* 59 (3): 781–819.
Hanks, Patrick
    1996   Contextual dependency and lexical sets. *International Journal of Corpus Linguistics* 1 (1): 75–98.
Hirst, Graeme
    1995   Near-synonymy and the structure of lexical knowledge. In: Klavans, J. (chair), *Representation and Acquisition of Lexical Knowledge: Polysemy, Ambiguity, and Generativity. Papers from the AAAI Spring Symposium*, 51–56. Menlo Park: AAAI.
Kemmer, Suzanne and Arie Verhagen
    1994   The grammar of causatives and the conceptual structure of events. *Cognitive Linguistics* 5 (2): 115–156.
Lakoff, George
    1987   *Women, Fire, and Dangerous Things: What Categories Reveal about the Mind*. Chicago: University of Chicago Press.
Langacker, Ronald W.
    1987   *Foundations of Cognitive Grammar: Theoretical Prerequisites*. Stanford: Stanford University Press.
    1991   *Foundations of Cognitive Grammar: Descriptive Application*. Stanford: Stanford University Press.

Lemmens, Maarten
    1998   *Lexical Perspectives on Transitivity and Ergativity: Causative Constructions in English*. (Current Issues in Linguistic Theory 166.) Amsterdam/Philadelphia: John Benjamins.

Levin, Beth
    1993   *English Verb Classes and Alternations: A Preliminary Investigation*. Chicago: University of Chicago Press.

Lin, Dekang and Shaojun Zhao
    2003   Identifying synonyms among distributionally similar words. In: Georg Gottlob and Toby Walsh (eds.), *Proceedings of the Eighteenth International Joint Conference on Artificial Intelligence, IJCAI–03, Acapulco, Mexico, August 9–15, 2003*, 1492–1493. San Francisco, CA: Morgan Kaufmann.

Miller, George A. and Walter G. Charles
    1991   Contextual correlates of semantic similarity. *Language and Cognitive Processes* 6 (1): 1–28.

Mohammad, Saif and Graeme Hirst
    subm.   Distributional Measures as Proxies for Semantic Relatedness.

Plungjan, Vladimir A. and Ekaterina V. Raxilina
    1998   Парадоксы валентностей [Valency's paradoxes]. *Семиотика и Информатика* [Semiotics and Informatics] 36: 108–119.

Pustejovsky, James
    1991   The syntax of event structure. In: Beth Levin and Steven Pinker (eds.), *Lexical and Conceptual Semantics*, 47–81. Cambridge, MA/Oxford, UK: Blackwell Publishers.

Raxilina, Ekaterina V.
    2000   *Когнитивный Анализ Предметных Имен: Семантика и Сочетаемость* [A Cognitive Analysis of Physical Names: Semantics and Combinability]. Moskva: Russkie Slovari.

Rubenstein, Herbert and John B. Goodenough
    1965   Contextual correlates of synonymy. *Computational Linguistics* 8 (10): 627–633.

Sandra, Dominiek and Sally Rice
    1995   Network analysis of prepositional meaning: mirroring whose mind – the linguist's or the language user's? *Cognitive linguistics* 6 (1): 89–130.

Slobin, Dan I.
    2003   Language and thought online: cognitive consequences of linguistic relativity. In: Dedre Gentner and Susan Goldin-Meadow (eds.), *Language in Mind. Advances in the Study of Language and Thought*, 157–192. Cambridge MA: MIT Press.

Smessaert, Hans, Bert Cornillie, Dagmar Divjak, and Karel van den Eynde
    2005   Degrees of clause integration. From endotactic to exotactic subordination in Dutch. *Linguistics. An Interdisciplinary Journal of the Language Sciences* 43: 471–530.

Stefanowitsch, Anatol and Stefan Th. Gries
    2003   Collostructions: investigating the interaction between words and constructions. *International Journal of Corpus Linguistics* 8 (2): 209–243.

Talmy, Leonard
    2000   *Toward a Cognitive Semantics. Vol. 1. Concept Structuring Systems.* (Language, Speech and Communication.) Cambridge MA: MIT Press.

Taylor, John R.
    2003   Near synonyms as co-extensive categories: "high" and "tall" revisited. *Language Sciences* 25: 263–284.

Tsai, Mei-Chih, Chu-Ren Huang, Keh-Jiann Chen, and Kathleen Ahrens
    1998   Towards a representation of verbal semantics – an approach based on near-synonyms. *Computational Linguistics and Chinese Language Processing* 3 (1 February): 61–74.

Vendler, Zeno
    1967   Verbs and times. *Linguistics in Philosophy*, 97–121. New York: Ithaca.

Wierzbicka, Anna
    1985   *Lexicography and Conceptual Analysis.* Ann Arbor: Karoma Publishers.
    1988   *The Semantics of Grammar.* (Studies in Language Companion Series 18.) Amsterdam/Philadelphia: John Benjamins.

Zaliznjak, Anna A. and Aleksej D. Šmelev
    2000   *Введение в Русскую Аспектологию* [Introduction to Russian Aspectology]. Moskva: Škola "Jazyki Russkoj Kul'tury".

Corpus-based methods and cognitive semantics: The many senses of *to run*[*]

Stefan Th. Gries

Abstract

The first major part of this paper is a comprehensive cognitively-oriented analysis of the senses and their interrelations of the verb *to run* along the lines of much recent cognitive work on polysemy. In the second major part, all occurrences of *to run* from the ICE-GB and the Brown Corpus are coded for a variety of linguistic parameters (so-called ID tags), yielding a complete behavioral profile of this verb. On that basis, the paper then discusses several case studies of how such corpus-linguistic quantitative methods can provide objective empirical evidence suggesting answers to some notoriously difficult problems in cognitive linguistics; these include the issue of prototype identification, the (degree of) sense distinctness, the structure of the hypothesized network as well as possibilities of automatic sense identification.

Keywords: polysemy; word sense (disambiguation); behavioral profile; semantic network; cluster analysis.

1. Introduction

The present paper is concerned with word senses from the perspective of cognitive linguistics on the one hand and corpus-linguistics as well as corpus-based lexicography on the other hand. While many recent cognitive-linguistic approaches to polysemy have concerned themselves with polysemous words as network-like categories with many interrelated senses (with varying degrees of commitment to mental representations), corpus-linguistic approaches have remained rather agnostic as to how different word senses are related and have rather focused on distributional characteristics of different word senses. This paper attempts to bridge the gap between these two approaches by demonstrating how cognitive linguistics can benefit from methodologies from corpus linguistics and computational linguistics; it is therefore a plea for more corpus linguistics in cognitive linguistics and structured as follows: Section 2 provides a by necessity very brief overview of cognitive-linguistic approaches towards polysemy and some of their weaknesses (cf. Section 2.1) as well as some corpus-based approaches (cf. Section 2.2). The review can of course not do justice to the large number of studies on polysemy and especially word sense disambiguation; it merely serves to discuss how the problems of identifying the different senses of a polysemous word have been addressed. Section 3 discusses the senses of the highly polysemous English verb *to run* on the basis of British and American corpus data. Section 4 constitutes the central part of this study. It introduces and exemplifies a few methodologies which increase the descriptive adequacy of cognitively-oriented analyses of lexical items as well as resolve some notoriously difficult questions within the cognitive paradigm. Finally, Section 5 concludes with some further extensions.

2. Distinctions between senses and the relations between them: A short review

2.1. Cognitive-linguistic approaches

One of the central areas of research within cognitive linguistics has been the investigation of polysemy of lexemes and constructions. Traditionally, the idea that a word is polysemous entails that the particular lexeme under investigation (i) has more than one distinct sense (otherwise the lexeme would be considered vague) and (ii) that the senses are related (otherwise the lexeme would be considered homonymous).[1]

The former point is usually made on the basis of a variety of well-known ambiguity tests including the logical test, the linguistic (*do so*) test and the definitional test (cf. Geeraerts [1993], Cruse [1986] and Kilgarriff [1997] for detailed discussion). However, these tests often yield mutually contradictory results, which is why cognitive linguists have often posited a continuum of semantic distinctness ranging from clear cases of homonymy on the one hand to clear cases of vagueness on the other hand; cases of polysemy were then located somewhere between these two extremes (cf., e.g., Tuggy [1993] or Croft [1998]). Thus, the distinctness of different senses of a lexeme is considered a matter of degree. Although it is probably fair to say that cognitive linguists have focused on the analysis of how different senses of a word are related to each other, they have of course also been aware that the motivation of sense distinction is a non-trivial issue since the links between senses can only be discussed once the distinctness of senses has been established. Thus, a variety of different approaches have been proposed to deal with this problem; let us briefly consider some examples.

Consider, as a first example, some early studies such as Brugman (1981), Norvig and Lakoff (1987), Lakoff (1987) and Brugman and Lakoff (1988). On the basis of intuition data, nearly every usage event minimally different from another one constitutes a different sense. For instance, Brugman and Lakoff argue that "a polysemous lexical item is a radial category of senses" (1988: 478) and they posit different schemas of the English preposition *over*, which often differ only with respect to properties of the landmark. For instance, in (1a) the landmark (the hill) is vertical whereas, in (1b), it (the yard) is not (Brugman and Lakoff's [1988: 482–483] examples).

(1) a. *The plane flew over the hill* → schema 1 (above and across): vertical extended landmark, no contact
 b. *The bird flew over the yard* → schema 1 (above and across): non-vertical extended landmark, no contact

This so-called full-specification approach (cf. Lakoff 1987) has been criticized for its methodological vagueness (resulting in the high degree of granularity – i.e., minimally different senses – pointed out above), its vagueness of representational convention and its lack of clarity concerning the linguistic and cognitive status of its network architecture (cf. Sandra and Rice [1995] for discussion and exemplification), and other approaches have been adopted to resolve this question on a principled, non-arbitrary basis. For example, Sandra and Rice (1995) as well as Rice (1996) argue in favor of (prepositional) polysemy on the basis of different experimental results. As another alternative, Tyler and Evans (2001) develop a principled-polysemy approach in which a distinct sense of *over* is only posited iff the meaning of *over* in one utterance involves a different spatial configuration from *over* in another utterance and cannot be inferred from encyclopedic knowledge and contextual information.[2]

However, not all these approaches are equally useful. For example, it is unclear whether the results of the sorting tasks of Sandra and Rice (1995) or Rice (1996) can actually be attributed solely to semantic differences of the uses (which also undermines the results' utility in refuting monosemy approaches): unlike recent experimental work by, say, Klein and Murphy (2001, 2002), the experimental sentences were not balanced with respect to all lexical items contributing to subjects' decisions. Moreover, different distance measures and clustering algorithms result in different amalgamation schedules and different degrees of granularity, but Sandra and Rice do not provide such details, which makes the evaluation of their findings difficult.

It is only very recently that cognitive linguists have turned to corpus data as a source of evidence for sense distinctions. For example, Croft (1998: 169) argues in favor of investigating the distinctness and conventionality of senses corpus-linguistically. He points out how semantically different direct objects of *to eat* correlate with uses distinct in terms of the arguments they occur with. In addition, Fillmore and Atkins's (2000) discussion of *to crawl* is cognitive-linguistic in the sense that the relations between different senses of *to crawl* are motivated both experientially and frame-semantically, but also truly corpus-based as it relies on an exhaustive analysis of a complete concordance. Finally, Kishner and Gibbs (1996) (as well as Gibbs and Matlock [2001]) discuss associations (of unmentioned strengths) of different senses of the English adverb *just* and *to make* on the one hand to different R1 collocates (i.e., words at the first slot to the right of the word of interest) and syntactic patterns on the other hand. They demonstrate "that people's choice of a sense of *just* is in part determined by the frequency of co-occurrence of particular senses of *just* with particular classes of words" (1996: 27–28) as well as situational characteristics, which results in some resemblance to a frame-semantic approach. Lastly, they propose that such results generalize to (words of) other syntactic categories, e.g. the verb *to run* and, in Gibbs and Matlock (2001: 234), argue that "if polysemous words are best described in terms of lexical networks, then our findings suggest the need to incorporate information about image schemas and lexico-grammatical constructions in drawing links between different senses of a polysemous word", a proposal to which we will return.

2.2. Corpus-based approaches

Especially the last approach by Kishner and Gibbs bridges the gap between cognitively oriented approaches and the linguistic paradigm in which the question of how to determine whether two uses of a particular word instantiate two different senses or not has probably received most attention, namely (corpus-based) lexicography; we will turn to this approach now.

Organizing and formulating a dictionary entry for a word requires many decisions as to whether two citations of a word instantiate senses differing enough that the word's entry needs to be split or whether the citations instantiate senses similar enough to be lumped together. Although the lexicographer's interest in sense distinctions need not coincide with that of linguists of a more theoretical persuasion, the basic question of course remains the same. Given these questions, recent lexicographic work has arrived at the conclusion that word senses as conceived of traditionally do not exist and has therefore adopted an increasingly corpus-based approach. For example, Kilgarriff (1997: 92) argues in favor of "an alternative conception of the word sense, in which it corresponds to a cluster of citations for a word". In the simplest possible conception, "corpus citations fall into one or more distinct clusters and each of these clusters, if large enough and distinct enough from other clusters, forms a distinct word sense" (Kilgarriff 1997: 108). According to him, much lexicographic work more or less conforms to the following characterization: first, call up a concordance for the word. Then, divide the concordance lines into clusters which maximize intra-cluster similarity and minimize inter-cluster similarity. Third, for each cluster, identify what makes the member of a cluster belong together (and change clusters where necessary), and finally, encode these conclusions in lexicographese (cf. also Biber [1993] and Hanks [1996: 82]). Similarly, Hanks (2000: 208–210) argues for a focus on separate semantic components (jointly constituting a word's meaning potential), which can be weighted in terms of their frequency and predictive power for regular word uses.

However, the above is only a very abstract idealization of the actual cognitive processes underlying sense identification and distinction. This and the fact that many of these processes result in apparently subjective decisions is immediately obvious once a user consults different dictionaries on the same word (cf. Fillmore and Atkins [2000] or Gries [2001, 2003a] for discussion). Therefore, corpus-based lexicographers have begun to formulate strategies to provide a more objective foundation for resolving such issues by, for instance, identifying corpus-based traces of meaning components etc. In order to bring together both cognitive-linguistic and corpus-based lexicographic approaches, it is necessary to briefly review the two lexicographic approaches upon which the present approach relies most.

First, Atkins (1987) discusses what she refers to as "ID tags", i.e. "syntactic or lexical markers in the citations which point to a particular dictionary sense of the word" (Atkins 1987: 24). ID tags are distinguished depending on (i) whether the presence of a particular clue is categorically or probabilistically associated with a particular sense and (ii) whether they testify to a characteristic of the word under investigation directly or indirectly (i.e. via the properties of other words). Atkins then investigates 441 citations of the word *danger* with respect to these ID tags: the word class of *danger* in the citation and more fine-grained distinctions within the word class (e.g. number, countability etc.); the complementation pattern associated with *danger* in the citation (e.g. [$_{NP}$ the danger [$_{PP}$ to [$_{NP}$ health]]], etc.); the function of the phrase in which *danger* occurs (e.g. subject, direct object, complement etc.); and the collocates in a window of ±7 words.[3]

Even without a full statistical analysis, Atkins obtains several useful ID tags. For example, the senses of *danger* that can be paraphrased as 'unsafeness/riskiness' and 'someone/something posing a threat' are associated with, among others, the ID tags in (2) and (3) respectively.

(2) uncountable noun with no support (as in *They are, however, fraught with danger*)

(3) countable noun followed by a PP with *in* without a *that*-clause (as in *There are, he agrees, real dangers in a partisan Civil Service*)

It turns out that the predictive power of some ID tags is fairly high, indicating that the ([semi-]automatic) allocation of citations to senses can be further improved; the approach is thus a forerunner of similar work on the automatic identification of semantic roles by Gildea and Jurafsky (2001).

The second lexicographic approach relevant to the present approach is that of Hanks (1996). He argues that the semantics of a verb are determined by the totality of its complementation patterns (1996: 75, 77) and proposes to analyze the usage of a particular word on the basis of the word's behavioral profile, which basically corresponds to a set of Atkins's (1987) ID tags together with semantic role generalizations. The different senses of words can then be derived from (i) different patterns within a behavioral profile and (ii) the process of triangulation, i.e. the identification of correlations between two or more lexical sets in different slots associated with the verb. Like Atkins, Hanks does not provide data on the predictive power of the behavioral profile of a verb or the different lexical sets, but he does state that many verbs exhibit strong frequency asymmetries of particular patterns and senses that can aid sense identification considerably.

As we have seen, a few cognitive-linguistic studies (most notably Kishner and Gibbs [1996]) have devoted their attention to how word senses correlate with a narrow range of formal characteristics such as complementation patterns, i.e. what corpus linguists have referred to as colligations. Section 3 first provides a cognitively-oriented polysemy analysis of the English verb *to run* to first of all determine its inventory of senses. The set of applications presented in Section 4 extends Kishner and Gibbs's (1996) hypothesis (that colligations similar to the ones discussed for *just* can be found for other word classes) by taking seriously the notions of behavioral profile and triangulation using the set of lexico-grammatical ID tags employed by Atkins (1987). That is, Section 4 outlines several case studies relating *to run*'s cognitively motivated senses to its corpus-based behavioral profile.[4]

3. *To run*: A cognitively-oriented analysis

In this section, I will discuss, and provide the token frequencies of, the different senses of all 815 instances of *to run* from the British component of the International Corpus of English (ICE-GB; n=391) and the Brown Corpus of American English (n=424).[5] The senses were identified manually and mainly on the basis of the match of the citation to senses listed in dictionaries and in WordNet 1.7.1.[6,7] While I will also be concerned with how the different senses of *to run* are related, I will follow Kishner and Gibbs (1996) as well as Fillmore and Atkins (2000) and refrain from elaborating in detail on all cognitive mechanisms relating the different senses, restricting myself to a less rigorous characterization; all examples are taken from the corpus data.

3.1. Intransitive uses of *to run*

The central, or prototypical, sense of *to run* appears to be that of 'fast pedestrian motion' as in (4); cf. Section 4.1 below for a justification of why this sense is considered prototypical.

(4)   *Simons had run down to the villa to get help* [$n_{\text{of this sense in corpus}}$=203]

Other, closely related senses are exemplified by (5) (where motion is still fast but not necessarily pedestrian) and (6) (where the motion even need not be fast anymore) – in this example, however, the sentence also implies that the boat makes this journey regularly, a semantic feature we will find again.

(5) *Yet they keep running from one physician to another* [n=4]

(6) *There are three boats that run from the mainland to the Island* [n=24]

Two senses that are closely related to the sense(s) exemplified in (5) and (6) are 'to move away from something dangerous/unpleasant' and 'to move away to engage in a romantic relationship' in (7a) and (7b); actually, the two senses are similar enough to be considered a single sense provisionally labeled 'to escape'. Similarly closely related to the central sense is the sense of 'to look after' in (7c). These three senses of *to run* need not, but typically do, invoke literal fast pedestrian motion.

(7) a. *When he loses his temper with her she runs off, taking young Jacob with her* [n=28]
 b. *If Adelia had felt about someone as Henrietta felt about Charles, would she have run away with him?* [n=4]
 c. *At an age when they might want to take things easy <,> many women like sixty-three-year-old Eileen Allen are running around after older relatives* [n=1]

A similarly close relationship to the senses in (5) to (7) is exhibited by the senses 'motion without control/restraint' and 'to meet (unexpectedly)' in (8) and (9) respectively.[8]

(8) *Dogs ran about, getting in people's way*

(9) *On my way to the elevator, I ran into Pete*

The sense in (9) can also be extended metaphorically to yield the sense of 'to speak continuously' in (10a) with a metonymic understanding of *the bench* and non-human subjects as in (10b); cf. also (23) and (42) below.

(10) a. *the bench, which numerous times rebuked the Attorney General for letting his witnesses run on* [n=6]
 b. *Then a wild thought ran circles through his clouded brain*

(10) is more remote from the central sense(s) than (8) and (9) – not involving pedestrian motion – but other cases are even more remote: (11a) predicates motion of liquids (i.e. 'to flow') and (11b) refers to the potential result of liquid mixing with color (i.e. 'diffusion of color').

(11) a. *The tears ran down my face* [n=16]
b. *Colors on the towels had run* [n=2]

Then, by some version of the *swarm* alternation (Levin 1993: 53–55) or by what Norvig and Lakoff (1987: 198) have termed profile shift, (12) denotes 'to exist in abundance' (cf. Fillmore and Atkins [2000: 103] on the similar *The kitchen was crawling with cockroaches*).

(12) *Baker, you will have the streets of our American cities running with blood on registration day* [n=1]

Still on the basis of (11) and a profile shift from the liquid to the container out of which it moves, (13) denotes what happens when there is liquid in abundance in a container, namely 'to overflow'.[9]

(13) *So when the Big House filled up and ran over, the sisters-in-law found beds for everyone in their own homes* [n=1]

Finally, (14a) refers to the result of a liquid moving out of a container, namely 'to become used up', which is extended metaphorically to the domain of time in (14b).

(14) a. *It has a shelf life of 100 years and will write for three miles before the ink runs out* [n=14]
b. *Time is running out*

The senses in (14) can also undergo an alternation where the thing becoming used up is demoted from subject status to that of a prepositional complement headed by *out of* and where the former possessor's role is profiled and becomes the subject of *to run out of*, cf. (15a). If the location from which the liquid is moving is conceptualized as causing the liquid's motion, we find the sense 'to emit liquid' as in (15b).

(15) a. *we're running out of tea bags* [n=18]
 b. *She can't tell whether her left nostril is running* [n=1]

Another metaphorical extension of *to run* is used as meaning 'to be in charge of something'. Usually, this sense involves the transitive construction (cf. Section 3.2), but the intransitive use in (16) comes about by a metaphor CHANGE OF STATE IS CHANGE OF LOCATION and the metonymy relating organizations to the people who are part of the organization.

(16) *Thus, if corporations are not to run away with us, they must become quasi-governmental institutions* [n=1]

If the subject is not human but, as in (17), refers to an idea/some information, *to run* can be used to mean that the human referent of the prepositional complement 'fails to control' or 'fails to understand' the subject's referent (via the metaphors IDEAS ARE ENTITIES and UNDERSTANDING/LEARNING IS GAINING PHYSICAL CONTROL OVER AN ENTITY).

(17) *This [finding out the person some description is referring to and what her surname is] is running away with me* [n=23]

In many other instances, the relation to the central sense is similarly less direct. For example, there are different kinds of what Langacker (1987: 168–173) has called abstract motion, i.e. there are instances where the subject of *to run* is still human, but what is denoted is not literal (pedestrian) motion, but 'metaphorical motion' as in (18a) and (18b) (cf. STATES ARE LOCATIONS), there is the sense of 'to be/to become' in (18c), and the sense of 'to deteriorate' in (18d) (cf. GOOD IS UP).

(18) a. *we may conceivably run into trouble here* [n=8]
 b. *He ran into the rapture of the depths* [n=1]
 c. *Chief Bob Moore looked his same hick-self; a man mountain running to lard in his middle-age* [n=4]
 d. *pansy seeds, he told me, soon "run down"* [n=3]

Uses similar to the one exemplified in (18d) are also found in more specific contexts, where *to run down* refers not only to 'to deteriorate', but to the slightly different sense of 'to lose power/efficiency', cf. (19).

(19) *Foster listened with [...] patience until Digby ran down, [...]* [n=1]

Similar cases of abstract motion are 'to check/to rehearse' in (20a) and (20b) and 'to campaign' in (21) (via GOALS ARE DESTINATIONS).[10]

(20) a. *Russ ran through the bills* [n=14]
     b. *Cosmo ran through a few historical dates in his mind*

(21) *[...] when Bush was running for the White House, [...]* [n=28]

Then, by analogy to (10) and (17), in instances such as (22) there is not even a human agent performing the (metaphorical) motion.

(22) *Their policy ran counter to the traditional idea that a good fighter was usually a libertine* [n=21]

To run can also be used like a copular verb to denote 'to have a particular wording' as in (23) (cf. Langacker 1987: 168–169).

(23) *"[...] Say he is a horse thief", runs an old adage* [n=12]

(24) exemplifies an image-schema transformation (and Levin's [1993: Section 4.7.7] *meander* verbs), namely the sense 'to extend spatially'.

(24) *Street car tracks run down the center of Pennsylvania* [n=55]

This sense has been extended (via TIME IS SPACE) to 'to continue (to exist) for a certain time period' (cf. [25a] and [25b]) and to the quantitative senses 'to amount to' and 'to surpass' in (26) and (27) respectively.

(25) a. *It [a play] ran until past one o'clock* [n=22]
     b. *the diplomatic process has run its course*

(26) *[...] the number may run into tens of millions* [n=14]

(27) *Sales of TV sets at retail ran ahead of the like months of 1959* [n=3]

A sense related to (25) is 'to occur regularly/persistently' in (28), differing from (25) since the motion does not occur in the spatial domain.

(28) a. *Naturally curly hair runs in my family* [n=5]
 b. *two streams of development run through the history of twentieth-century American folklore*

While many of these senses are related to the central sense(s) via straightforward metaphorical mappings, other senses of *to run* involve yet other patterns of extension. One frequent sense of *to run* can be paraphrased as 'to function'; the link to the central sense is probably that one can often see that machines are functioning because they and/or their parts move; cf. (29).

(29) *The monitors ran twenty-four hours each day* [n=47]

A more abstract extension denotes 'to be valid' as exemplified in (30).

(30) *But within that period you must have applied for a new one [a vehicle licence], to run from the day after the last one expired* [n=4]

While I did not discuss all details of how different intransitive senses of *to run* are related to each other, they do appear to form some kind of network like those posited for many other words. We now turn to transitive uses.

3.2. Transitive uses of *to run*

The intransitive uses of *to run* discussed above account for about 65% of all uses in my corpus. Most of the transitive uses we discuss now are related to one of the intransitive uses by what Levin (1993: Section 1.1) refers to as "[o]bject of [t]ransitive = [subject] of [i]ntransitive [a]lternations" as in (31).

(31) $NP_i\ V_{intransitive} \rightarrow NP_k\ V_{transitive}\ NP_i$

For a straightforward motion verb such as *to run*, this is exactly what a cognitively-oriented approach predicts, given the prototypical meaning of the transitive construction (cf. Rice 1987) and the fact that omnipresent conceptual metaphors such as STATES ARE LOCATIONS, CHANGE OF STATE IS CHANGE OF LOCATION and CHANGE OF STATE IS CONTROL OVER AN ENTITY RELATIVE TO A LOCATION can be easily exploited; hence, I will proceed in the order of senses in Section 3.1.

The prototypical sense of 'fast pedestrian motion' can also be found in transitive uses where the direct object usually is an event such as a race or a marathon (cf. [32a] and Levin's [1993: 43-4, 266] locative preposition drop alternation) or a concrete object determining the direction/endpoint of movement (cf. [32b], which can then be paraphrased as 'to score points by running to some location'), and (32c). Finally, the direct object can also be a distance/measure phrase (cf. Levin [1993: 266]) as in (32d).

(32) a. *and it's Sibor who leads the way running his own race* [n=12]
 b. *Or even the way you run bases* [n=1]
 c. *Running the rail in the yellow is Honey Church*
 d. *His brother ran a mile to get the father*

The most straightforward and most productive causative extension from one of the central senses follows from the induced action alternation (cf. Levin [1993: 31]) and is correspondingly instantiated by the senses 'to cause motion' in (33) and 'to knock over' in (34), which speaks in favor of 'motion' as the sense from which most others can be most economically derived.

(33) a. *He ran a finger down his cheek, tracing the scratch there* [n=13]
 b. *Suppose he ran up the white flag altogether?*

(34) *The hospitals contain patients [...] run over by sports cars* [n=3]

In the examples in (33), the direct object refers to the thing that is moved, but there are also cases where it is not the direct object that moves; consider (35) for an example of such a profile shift.

(35) *the soldiers were ordered to [...] run through anyone who might step out of line* [n=1]

In the special case where the direct object is an eye (cf. [36]), *to run* means 'to see': directing one's view to the stimulus is conceptualized as moving the sensory organ to the stimulus which, upon contact, is understood as being perceived via the PERCEIVING IS TOUCHING metaphor.

(36) *He ran his eye along the roof copings* [n=1]

The sense of 'to cause motion' in (33) in combination with the conceptual metaphor MORE IS UP results in the sense 'to cause to accumulate' or 'to increase' shown in (37); by extension, if the direct object refers to a part/piece of clothing, *to run up* can also mean 'to sew' as in (38).

(37) *thanks partly to George Herman Ruth's spectacular efforts each season to run his salary higher and higher* [n=1]

(38) *Do you love to run up a hem, sew on buttons, [...]?* [n=1]

Other transitive uses constitute causative extensions from metaphorical intransitive uses. For instance, the metaphorically motivated sense of 'to deteriorate' has a transitive counterpart 'to cause to deteriorate', which is exemplified in (39), and since the mental state of a human being can be worsened by, e.g., criticizing somebody, *to run* has also taken on this sense (cf. [40]).

(39) *Have you had the flu or you've been [...] run down in the last few days* [n=4]

(40) *Casey had made a point of running down all such suggestions* [n=2]

There is also a fairly fixed transitive extension of the intransitive sense of 'diffusion of color' exemplified in (11b) above, namely a sense where *color* becomes the direct object rather than the subject as above (i.e. another alternation of the type schematically represented in [31]).

(41) *the bright V woven into the neckline had melted, running a darker color* [n=1]

A further example of a causative extension of an intransitive sense of *to run* is exemplified in (42), where it means something like 'to cause something to have a particular wording', i.e. 'to formulate'.

(42) *We usually run a social note when somebody moves away* [n=1]

The same mechanism underlies the extension from 'to extend spatially' (cf. [24] above) to that of 'to cause to extend spatially' in (43).

(43) But anybody who promises a substantial volume of business can get a railroad to run a short spur to his plant these days [n=1]

Then, a sense that could be related to both that of 'to function' and 'to amount to' and/or that could be explained with reference to Levin's locative preposition drop alternation is exemplified in (44).

(44) To continue to run a public sector surplus, although [...] [n=3]

The most frequent group of transitive senses of *to run* are causative extensions of 'to function'. One can be paraphrased as 'to execute/operate', the other as 'to manage' (cf. [45] and [46] respectively).

(45) a. Very often the screens are run at too high a brightness level which can quickly tire the eyes and wear out the screen [n=25]
b. Presently they had to give up running the furnace at full capacity

(46) a. she often saw him when she was in Ramsford, [...], where he ran the one-man police station [n=101]
b. The club runs regular trips to the cabins

The difference between the two already emerges from the nearly synonymous paraphrases. On the one hand, the sense of 'to execute/operate' usually involves starting some machine or (software) application which can then operate on its own or on the basis of continuous personal/manual involvement of the operator. On the other hand, the sense 'to manage' usually involves directing some organization or institution on a more abstract level of involvement. Finally, there are some instances where it is not really possible to decide which degree of involvement and, thus, which of these two senses is instantiated; consider (47) as an example (which supports Hanks's [2000: Section 7] discussion of semantic indeterminacy).

(47) When we are able to run a four day first aid course [n=23]

It is unclear whether (47) means 'we taught the course (ourselves)' (as in, e.g., *I've got to run an errand*) or 'we organized the course and let other people teach it'. If we hypothesize that language users have abstracted away from such vagueness, the hypothesized more schematic sense they have stored could be labeled 'to be in charge of something'.

A further extension of the sense of 'to execute/operate' involves a frame addition (cf. Norvig and Lakoff 1987: 197) of what might be called the publication frame, resulting in the sense of 'to broadcast/publish' as in (48).

(48)   *The island's newspaper runs a weekly cartoon showing the adventures of 'Vincey'; in its struggle to survive* [n=5]

Finally, *to run* can be used as a transitive phrasal verb with the particle *off* meaning 'to copy'. While there is some semantic relation of this sense to that of 'to execute/operate', the reason for why the particle *off* is part of this construction remains opaque to me; this is probably motivated by the movements which were once involved in the action of copying.

(49)   *If you give me a tape I've got a tape to tape and I can run it off* [n=1]

3.3. More idiomatic uses of *to run*

This section discusses some senses that, while they can of course also be characterized in terms of transitivity, are semantically much more difficult to integrate into the network, given their lack of compositionality. Since many of these senses are also strongly associated with particular content words as complements,[11] do not appear to be very productive syntactically, and describe recurrent situations of social interest, they qualify as idioms (cf. Nunberg, Sag, and Wasow 1994: 492–493), deserving special mention in their own section. One of these is the sense 'to risk' as in (50).

(50)   *They were reluctant to appoint sheriffs to protect the property, thus running the risk of creating disturbances* [n=12]

Then, there are several idioms which are used to characterize humans' experiences. In (51), *to run the gamut* refers to 'to experience a wide variety of things'; in (52), *to run the gauntlet* means 'to experience being criticized by (many) people', and (53) denotes 'experiencing something very negative'.

(51)   *it [red wine] will have run the gamut of many beguiling and interesting stages* [n=3]

(52) *William and Hamrick did indeed run the ga[u]ntlet* [n=4]

(53) *their cups were already running over without us* [n=1]

A different idiom meaning to 'to ignore' is exemplified in (54).

(54) *Catholics run roughshod over Protestant sensibilities, by failure to consider the reasoning behind the Protestant position* [n=1]

The final idiom depending on particular content words can be paraphrased as 'to be successful' as in (55).

(55) *New Halen running a blinder up in the third* [n=1]

For a representation summarizing the discussion so far, consider Figure 1. Solid lines denote instance and similarity links, dotted lines denote causation alternation links. Note that Figure 1 serves expository reasons only – it is, just like Bartsch's (1984: 48) polysemic complex, merely a notational format and is non-committal with respect to issues of mental representation.

4. Case studies

This section will introduce several very brief case studies discussing the interplay between the behavioral profile of *to run* and the cognitively-motivated senses. As mentioned above, I will not restrict my analysis to R1 collocations as Kishner and Gibbs (1996) but will base it on a much wider variety of ID tags. To that end, the data set, all instances of the lemma *to run* discussed in Section 3 above, were coded for the following direct ID tags; cf. Divjak and Gries, to appear, for a similar way of annotation):

- morphological features of the verb form: tense, aspect, and voice;
- the syntactic properties of the clause the verb form occurs in: intransitive vs. transitive vs. complex transitive use of *to run*, declarative vs. interrogative vs. imperative sentence form, main clause vs. subordinate clause (e.g. regular subordinate clause with or without subordinator, relative clause with or without relative pronoun);

74 Stefan Th. Gries

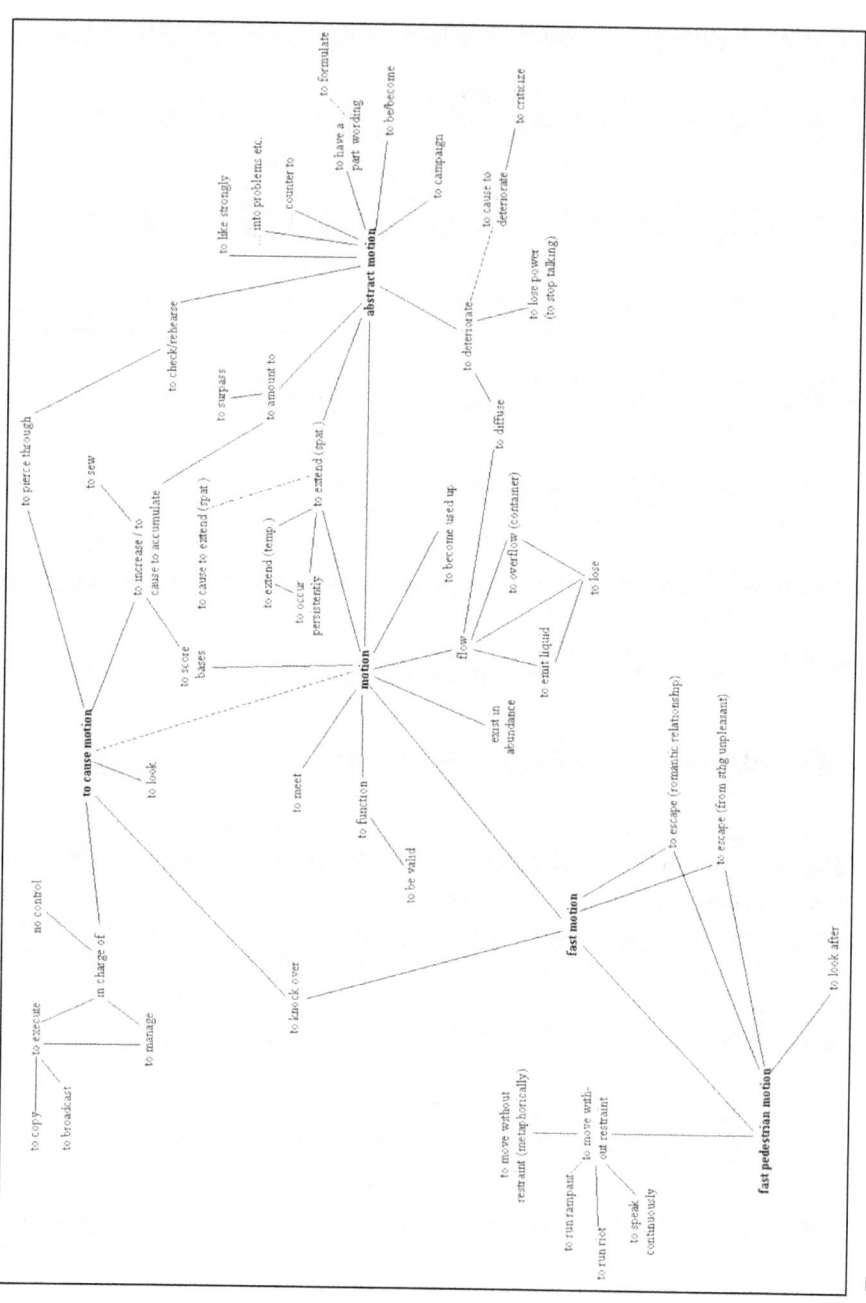

Figure 1. Radial network of *to run*

- semantic characteristics of the referents of the elements co-occurring with *to run*: its subjects/heads, objects and complements (which were coded, e.g., as human, animate, concrete countable objects, concrete mass nouns, machines, abstract entities, organizations/institutions, locations, quantities, events, processes etc.);
- the instance's collocates in the same clause;
- a paraphrase of *to run*'s meaning in the citation.

As a result, I obtained a corpus-based behavioral profile of *to run* based on 815 citations annotated with respect to 252 different ID tags (40% consisting of manually annotated formal and semantic properties mentioned above, 60% consisting of collocates); since the *absolute* sense frequencies varied considerably, I used the *relative* frequencies of each ID tag attribute within each ID tag. The following brief case studies exemplify how these data can be put to use in order to address a variety of questions that virtually all cognitively-oriented analyses of lexical polysemy must address; these questions include the issue of prototype identification, the (degree of) sense distinctness, the structure of the hypothesized network etc.

4.1. Prototypicality of one sense

Let me begin with the question of which sense of *to run* is the prototypical one. This question plays a central role in cognitive-linguistic analyses so various researchers have established a variety of criteria (cf., e.g., Rice [1996: 145–146], Tyler and Evans [2001: Section 3.3]); the following is a non-exhaustive list of such criteria: asymmetrical judgments of goodness or similarity; ease of elicitation; gradation within the category; earliest attested meaning; centrality/predominance in the semantic network; use in composite forms; etc. However, given such an inventory of criteria, conflicts of criteria are the rule rather than the exception (cf. Corston-Oliver [2001] on *by*). The present subsection illustrate how corpus data can be brought to bear on this issue.

Following the argumentation by Norvig and Lakoff (1987: 198) as well as Tyler and Evans (2001, 2003), Figure 1 suggests that 'motion' is the prototypical sense since 'motion' is the sense from which most others can be (most economically) derived. However, both corpus data in general (i.e. data for which no behavioral profile in Hanks's (1996) sense is necessary) and the behavioral profile of *to run* in particular point nearly uniformly into a different direction, namely that, as I claimed above, *to run*'s prototypical sense is instantiated by 'fast pedestrian motion' as in (4). Let us begin with some arguments from general corpus data.

First, the sense 'fast pedestrian motion' is the most frequent sense used in early stages of acquisition, as is shown by an as yet informal analysis of *to run* in the Manchester component of the CHILDES corpus (cf. Theakston et al. [2001] and MacWhinney [2000] respectively), where the only other sense coming close to a similar frequency is that of 'to knock over'.[12]

Second, according to etymological dictionaries, which are based on the analysis of historical texts and, thus, adopt a corpus-based approach, the "exact sem[antic] and [phon]ological originations and interactions are at once complicated and obscure" (Partridge 1961: s.v. *run*), but the diachronically primary senses are 'fast pedestrian motion' and 'to flow'.

Third, a related argument is that, like so many other English verbs, *to run* can be zero-derived to function as a noun, a development which apparently began in the 14th or 15th century. There are 60 such instances in the ICE-GB corpus (*run* and *runs* occur 47 and 13 times respectively),[13] about 75% of which refer to 'fast pedestrian motion' (or the metonymically related sense of 'to score in baseball, cricket etc.'); the few exceptions to this predominance are mainly instances from just one corpus file where *run(s)* refers to experimental trials and a few fixed expressions such as *in the long run*. Also, the 'fast pedestrian motion' sense of the zero-derived noun appears first diachronically (cf. the OED 3.01 on CD-ROM, s.v. *run*).

Nearly all of the general corpus data already point in the same direction, but we can also exploit the behavioral profile for further evidence. For example, the data show that the sense 'fast pedestrian motion' is by far the most frequent one in the corpus (approximately 25% of all instances), which reflects its central status (cf. Durkin and Manning [1989]). Also, it appears to be the formally least constrained sense and can, thus, be considered unmarked and prototypical (cf. especially Lakoff [1987: 60–61] on the relation between prototypicality and markedness).[14] But what does "formally least constrained" mean and how can it be measured? One rather specific example for "formally least constrained" is that the sense 'fast pedestrian motion' is the one with the highest number of differently headed prepositional phrases. A more general, and thus more valuable, finding is that 'fast pedestrian motion' is the sense with the highest number of different 252 ID tag attributes, i.e. it exhibits most variation across all formal and semantic characteristics which were coded, which in turn strongly supports its unmarkedness.

In sum, the above arguments demonstrate the utility of corpus data for prototype identification. While my earlier work on this issue has been concerned with the corpus-based identification of prototypical instances of constructions (verb-particle constructions as well as ditransitives and prepositional datives; cf. Gries [2003b, 2003c]), this work illustrates a similar potential for prototypical intraword senses.

4.2. Distinctiveness of senses

A notoriously problematic issue arising for every polysemy analysis is to decide whether two different citations instantiate distinct senses or just modulations of a more general sense (the lumping vs. splitting issue). Some studies (e.g. Tyler and Evans [2001, 2003]) have addressed this issue by invoking the notion of inferrability by arguing that a particular use of the preposition *over* constitutes a different sense if it profiles a spatial configuration and if the meaning of *over* cannot be inferred from encyclopedic knowledge and contextual information. Let me briefly exemplify this approach on the basis of *to run*. Consider, for example, the meaning of 'to flow'. Given the high degree of granularity of some cognitive-linguistic analyses, one can assume that any cognitively-oriented polysemy analysis of *to run* adopting the full-specification approach would postulate the existence of this sense. However, as the corpus data reveal and as one would expect intuitively, all of the instances of *to run* meaning 'to flow' have as their subject/head a (usually uncountable) noun denoting a liquid. Since the only natural way for liquids to move is by flowing, the sense of 'to flow' is inferable, which in turn would obviate the need to posit a separately stored sense of 'to flow' – rather, positing the sense 'motion' is sufficient since the particular kind of motion is contributed by contextual information tapping into encyclopedic knowledge. A similar line of reasoning applies to the sense of 'to overflow' with the liquid as subject as in *The water ran over*. Once the meaning of 'to flow' is considered compositional, the sense of *The water ran over* can also be inferred from the meaning 'to flow' and the independently established sense of *over* in this expression (cf. Tyler and Evans 2001: 756–757). This argument also 'explains' why no one has, on the basis of examples such as *Back with Gary Pallister who just let the ball run across the touch-line*, ever postulated that *to run* has a sense 'to roll' – the manner of motion is again contingent on (the nature of) the subject.[15]

In spite of the intuitive appeal of this approach, it is worth pointing out that this approach appears to run into problems once it is combined with Tyler and Evans's approach to prototypicality: on the one hand, they should consider the sense 'to flow' prototypical (since it is among the earliest attested senses), but on the other hand it should not be considered an individual sense in the first place (since it is inferable); the latter position, however, I would contend, does probably not really match native speakers' intuitions.

From the corpus-based perspective, however, such a conflict does not even arise in the first place. In a paper on linguists' contribution to questions of how polysemous words are mentally represented, Croft (1998: 169) refers to the senses of *to eat* labeled 'to consume' and 'to dine', arguing that the comitative argument (referring to a fellow eater) occurs only with the latter use in the corpus. That is, one finds sentences of the type *Jack ate lunch with Jill* but not *Jack ate a pizza with Jill*, although the latter would be judged grammatical on introspection. The disjoint syntactic-semantic distribution suggests that 'consume' and 'dine' are grammatically distinct uses of *eat*. (Note how this argument obviously presupposes some version of a behavioral profile of *to eat*.)

If we apply this argument to the example of 'to flow', the citations involving the sense 'to flow' all have subjects being a liquid so that, in accordance with intuitions, this distributional characteristic provides corpus-linguistic evidence for considering 'to flow' a distinct sense. In spite of some lexicographical implications,[16] this example is relatively trivial: even if the subject of *to run* meaning 'to flow' always has a liquid in the behavioral profile, one does not need the behavioral profile to find that out. However, there are less trivial examples to drive home the point that corpus data help to distinguish senses in terms of formal patterns so let us now look at two such examples, one in favor of lumping, one in favor of splitting.

First, this approach would argue in favor of lumping two kinds of usage of 'fast pedestrian motion.' For example, we find cases where *to run* in its sense of 'fast pedestrian motion' is combined either only with a SOURCE argument (cf. [56] and n. 13) and or only with a GOAL argument (cf. [57]).

(56) *and we ran back to my car*

(57) *Durkin and Calhoun came running from the post.*

But, on the basis of the above arguments, we must not infer that the two constitute two different senses of *to run* since there are many examples such as those in (58), where both SOURCE and GOAL are present (in both orders), and, in fact, such cases outnumber those with only a SOURCE.[17]

(58) a. *He was almost breathless from having run towards her uphill from, it could only be, the lake*
  b. *I once ran from the Archive studio to the Start The Week studio*

Second, this approach would argue in favor of splitting the two senses of *to run* that can be paraphrased as 'to move away from something dangerous/unpleasant' and 'to move away to engage in a romantic relationship'. The data show that the former sense is instantiated by the verbs *to run off* and *to run away* (often with a prepositional phrase referring to the negatively evaluated stimulus). The latter sense also occurs as *to run off* and *to run away*, but mostly with a comitative argument. The parallel to Croft's example is that, while a sentence with both a negative stimulus and a comitative argument (e.g. *She ran away with him from all the problems*) appears acceptable, not a single such sentence was attested in my data, which, following Croft's logic, points to the distinctness of the two senses. Again, objective corpus-based evidence could be used to answer an otherwise difficult question or, more modestly, could provide objective *prima facie* evidence in one direction.

4.3. Where to connect a sense in the network

Another interesting possibility of analysis arising from the behavioral profile is concerned with determining the structure of the network representing the senses of *to run* and their relations. Consider again the senses 'to move away from something dangerous/unpleasant' and 'to move away to engage in a romantic relationship'. Devising a lexical network structure of *to run* requires a decision how to connect these two senses to the others. The initial decision would probably be to connect them to the node of the prototypical sense 'fast pedestrian motion' since this is the central sense and 'fast pedestrian motion' is the typical/most basic way to perform these actions. On the other hand, it is equally obvious that fast pedestrian motion is not the only way to move away from something dangerous/unpleasant or to move away to engage in a romantic relationship, which is why the senses 'fast motion' (or just 'motion') appear reasonable points of connection, too.

It is therefore difficult to decide in favor of one of the two alternatives on a principled basis, i.e., to decide how to integrate them into the network such that they connect to the sense they are most similar to. However, one can approximate the semantic similarity of these five senses in terms of their distributional similarity (as is customary in corpus-linguistic or computational-linguistic studies; cf. Biber [1993] for an example and McDonald [1997] for validation).

Previous studies aiming at quantifying the similarity of senses have used hierarchical cluster analyses on semantic similarity judgments or sentence sorting tasks. For the moment, however, the simpler technique of correlation analysis also serves our purpose. I computed all 3,080 pairwise correlations of the 56 senses' ID tag vectors to determine whether this approach is feasible at all. The results support this (in other areas already well-established) approach in many respects: First, the correlation coefficients obtained range from .38 to .93, differentiating across a whole spectrum of degrees of distributional similarity. Second, a brief look at the extreme values shows that the senses least similar to each other are those in (59a) and (59b), an intuitively reasonable result.

(59) a. *their cups were already running over without us*
     b. *He ran his eye along the roof copings*

Third, the result concerning the senses considered most similar to each other by this correlational analysis appears to be even more reasonable, and it also bears directly on our question: the maximum r value (i.e. the highest degree of similarity) is obtained for 'fast pedestrian motion' and 'to escape'. Finally, the five senses we are interested in are on average much more similar to each other than the average pairwise similarity of senses after Fisher Z transformation (mean $r_{\text{all senses}}$ =.545; mean $r_{\text{five senses}}$=.848), as would again be expected intuitively. These results lend credence to the assumption underlying much recent corpus-linguistic work that distributional similarity correlates with semantic similarity.

However, the results are rendered less precise than possible for our actual question since many ID tags occur so infrequently that their percentages are by definition either very small or very large, thereby distorting the results. Thus, I left out the ID tags coding just the presence/absence of a particular adverb or preposition, which left 55 reasonably frequent ID tags for comparison. Then, I computed the correlations between the three motion senses and the two 'to escape' senses (across all 55 relative frequencies).

The results are unequivocal: across all 55 ID tags, the sense 'to move away from something dangerous/unpleasant' is highly significantly more similar to 'fast pedestrian motion' than to the senses 'fast motion' ($z=5.38$; $p<.001$) and 'motion' ($z=5.06$; $p<.001$) while the latter two do not differ significantly from each other ($z=.45$; $p=.665$). The same holds for the sense 'to move away to engage in a romantic relationship', which is very significantly and marginally significantly more similar to 'fast pedestrian motion' than to the senses 'fast motion' ($z=3.17$; $p=.002$) and 'motion' ($z=1.88$; $p<.061$) respectively while, again, the latter two do not differ significantly ($z=1.42$; $p=.156$). That is to say, in absence of further theoretical motivation or evidence to the contrary, one should connect both 'to escape' senses to the prototypical sense rather than to 'motion' or 'fast motion', a decision we could again motivate on the basis of objective evidence.[18]

4.4. Agglomerative clustering of senses

Cluster analyses have been used to determine the similarity of intraword senses or the degree of granularity exhibited by polysemous word senses (cf. Miller 1971; Sandra and Rice 1995; Rice 1996). While clustering is often applied to collocate frequencies (cf. Manning and Schütze 2000: ch. 14), we can apply it to the much more detailed complete behavioral profile of *to run*; cf. Schulte im Walde (2003) for a similar approach. Accordingly, the table of relative frequencies was submitted to a hierarchical agglomerative cluster analysis, resulting in the dendrogram in Figure 2.[19]

Given the limited corpus size, the results can only be preliminary, but in spite of the diversity of authentic corpus data, several noteworthy observations can be made. First, on the right we find a branching which corresponds extremely closely to that of intransitive and transitive (i.e. causative) uses.[20] Then, at the top of Figure 2, the analysis has grouped together most cases of literal motion and a range of cases of abstract motion that have in Section 3 been related straightforwardly via metaphorical mappings and/or image-schema transformations.

Within this larger cluster, several small ones are homogeneous enough to be mentioned: 'fast pedestrian motion' and 'to escape', 'to extend spatially' and 'motion', and 'motion without control/restraint' and 'metaphorical motion without control/restraint'. There is also a cluster subsuming several semantically very similar senses under some general 'to be in charge of' sense. Finally, there is one cluster subsuming four senses which

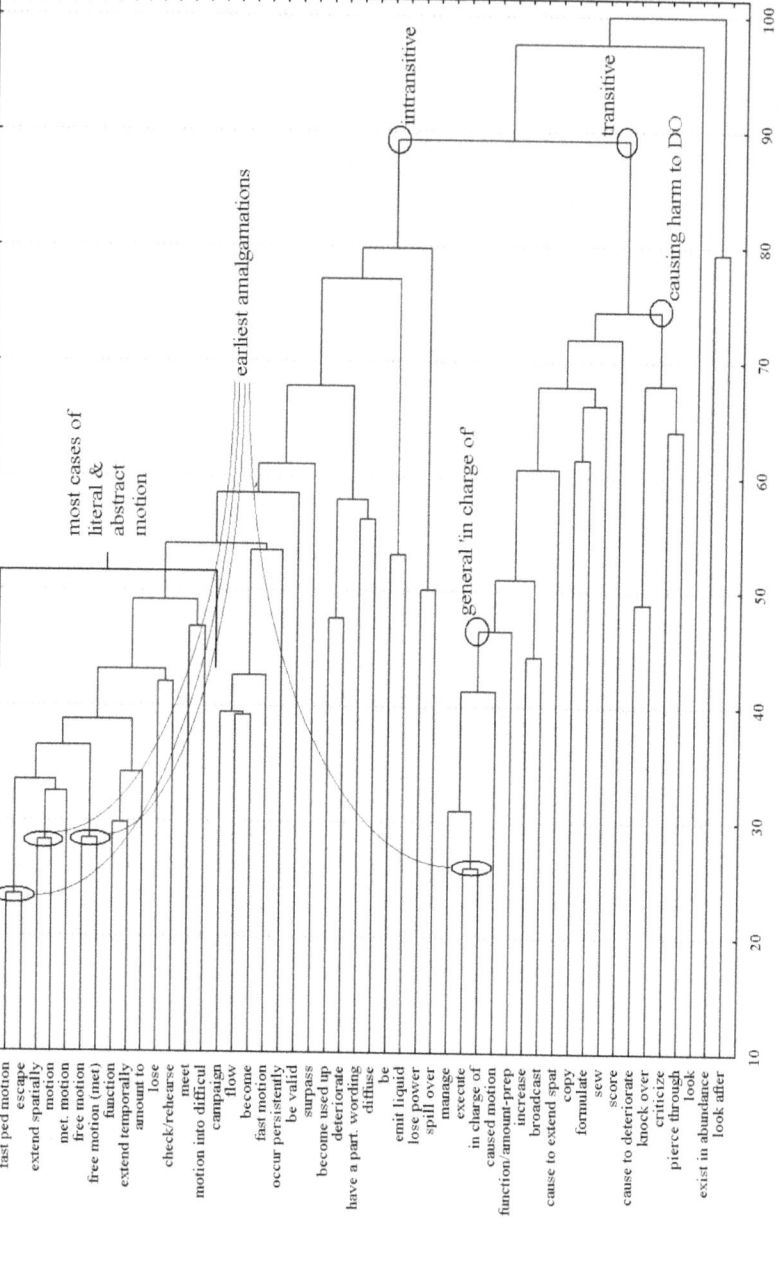

Figure 2. Dendrogram resulting from a hierarchical cluster analysis

all denote that some harm is done to the referent of the direct object; this is of course still a heterogeneous class, but the commonality is striking. In other words, we do find several clusters at about the same level of generality as Sandra and Rice (1995) do in their work on prepositions.

Other findings from Figure 2 are also worth mentioning. For example, the senses amalgamated earliest on distributional grounds are exactly those that are most strongly branching in the network-like representation of Figure 1. Note that this cannot be explained in terms of the senses' frequencies and that particularly the sense of 'fast pedestrian motion' argued to be prototypical is the very first sense to be amalgamated. If this finding could be replicated, it would open up completely new perspectives since corpus-based clustering of objective ID tags can then be considered indicative of, or again more modestly at least correlating with, aspects of category structure.

I hope the brief comments above have outlined the potential of the method. However, given the limited size of the present corpus, the larger data set necessary for a more comprehensive analysis may well result in some changes. For example, there are several high intercorrelations (of the type discussed in Section 4.3) and some clusters which are difficult to explain (e.g., the cluster linking "to increase" and "to broadcast", which are, however, not amalgamated early). Part of such variance is of course due to the fact that cluster analyses are influenced by the amount of noise attributable to corpus data. But since research on clustering of humanly-sorted word senses has also sometimes resulted in low agreement ratios (cf. Jorgensen 1990), the corpus-based method is not by definition an inferior method; currently ongoing work tests corpus-based clusterings of the above sort against experimentally obtained sorting preferences. Be that as it may, depending on the size of the data set and further ID tags one might wish to include (e.g. metaphorical mappings or other mechanisms underlying sense extensions), future analyses can shed much more light on categorical and distributional properties of particular senses.

4.5. Automatic sense identification

I repeatedly referred to the fact that Kishner and Gibbs have argued in favor of adding lexico-grammatical information to the description of (the interrelations of) polysemous words' senses. While such a compilation of a behavioral profile would obviously not only enhance the descriptive adequacy of the analysis as such, the previous sections have, I hope, also demonstrated that the behavioral profile offers a variety of possibilities to arrive at objective answers to notoriously difficult questions. However, such an approach has more to offer once we begin to leave the domain of cognitive linguistics proper. In other words, while we have so far considered the senses as given and have then determined ID tags differentiating between senses, we can also adopt the reverse perspective: how well can we predict the sense of *to run* in a particular citation when we extract this citation's ID tags? More technically, so far we looked at the conditional probability p (ID tag | word sense), but we can equally well determine p (word sense | ID tag[s]), a question central to the issue of word sense disambiguation (WSD) within computational linguistics. If the joint predictive power of several ID tags made it possible to predict a word sense, this would provide further support for the notion of ID tags and analyses relying on them. This is how a very elementary approach would look like; cf. Manning and Schütze (2000: Chapter 7) for much discussion of WSD.

The regular way to determine intercorrelations between a particular meaning of *to run* on the one hand and formal/semantic patterns of the sentences instantiating this meaning on the other hand would be to cross-tabulate all meanings with all ID tags. However, given the large number of potentially relevant features, the number of possible configurations (of different factorial degrees) of ID tags increases so quickly that the observed frequencies for each configuration turn out to be too low to lend themselves to usual statistical approaches (e.g. the χ^2-test), a frequent problem in such applications. In order to overcome a similar problem, Gildea and Jurafsky (2001: Section 4.2) suggested to combine probabilities of a selected variety of meaning-pattern configurations, a technique we can adopt easily.

Assume that a sense recognition system is provided with (i) a general baseline frequency of each sense and (ii) a mechanism to identify ID tags of each sense on the basis of the context of the word. When the system is fed with a sentence to recognize its sense, two things can happen. The usual case would be that the ID tag is not particularly distinctive for, i.e. independent of, the sense, and thus just adds noise to the classificatory problem since combining independent probabilities requires their multiplication. The interesting cases are those where the ID tags recognized by the system are not independent of the sense and, in spite of the statistical tendency of the probabilities to decrease, actually *increase* the system's predictive power.

Let me explain this briefly on the basis of the two most frequent senses of *to run*. The most frequent sense in the present corpus (25% of all tokens) is that of 'fast pedestrian motion'. An automatic sense classification system could already achieve an accuracy of about 25% by simply assigning this sense to every incoming sentence with *to run*. But 'fast pedestrian motion' has some strong probabilistic ID tags: If the system recognizes that the verb is in the past tense (i.e. *ran*), then, since 42.3% of all occurrences of *ran* are instances of 'fast pedestrian motion', the prediction accuracy rises to 42.3%, an improvement of approximately 70%. If the system also recognizes that *ran* is used intransitively, the prediction accuracy is further increased to 49.3%, and if intransitive *ran* is followed by a prepositional phrase headed by *to*, the prediction accuracy is increased to 73.7%. Finally, if the structure [s [NPsubj] [VP *ran* [PP *to* [NP]]]] has a human subject noun phrase, the only attested sense for this configuration of ID tags is in fact 'fast pedestrian motion', i.e. the prediction accuracy amounts to 100%. A similar case can be made for the second most frequent meaning of *to run*, 'to manage'. Its overall relative frequency is 12.4%, but, as is shown in Figure 3, there are several formal, easy-to-recognize ID tags strongly associated with the meaning of 'to manage'.

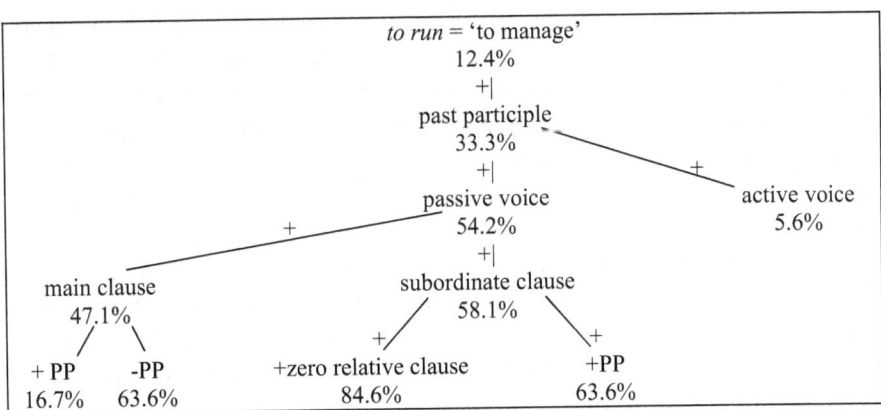

Figure 3. Successive change of prediction accuracy for 'to manage'

Space does not permit detailed discussion of more examples; suffice it to say that similar accuracy improvements are obtained for other sufficiently frequent senses (such as for 'to extend spatially'). In addition, while the above observations have exclusively relied on positive ID tags, i.e. ID tags whose *presence* is probabilistically indicative for a particular sense, senses can of course be equally well predicted given the *absence* of some ID tag; for reasons of space, I will not discuss this phenomenon in detail, but cf. Table 1 for results on the two most frequent senses.

Table 1. The complementary distribution of selected ID tags for the two most frequent senses of *to run*

		'fast pedestrian motion'	'to manage'
verb form	+	*ran*	*run* (past part.)
	−	*runs*	*ran*
transitivity	+	intransitive	transitive
	−	transitive	intransitive
clause type	+	main clause, imperative clause	zero relative clause, zero subordinate clause
	−	(zero) relative clause interrogative clause	main clause
subject	+	human, animate	organization/institution
	−	concrete objects, organization/institution	−
preposition of following PP	+	towards, for, down, after, up	0
	−	−	−

These examples show that the senses of *to run* do have strong probabilistic associations with formal and/or semantic patterns (in our parlance, ID tags) that, according to Kishner and Gibbs, merit inclusion in polysemy networks (if only for the sake of completeness and the utility they may have for explaining psycholinguistic findings and their predictive power for NLP); cf. also Theakston et al. (2002) for similar correlations concerning the acquisition of the verb *to go* as well as Newman and Rice (this volume) for such findings concerning the verbs *to eat* and *to drink*. The most interesting thing about Table 1, however, is that the ID tags also differ across senses unexpectedly: there is no *a priori* expectation that 'fast pedestrian motion' should correlate with past tense whereas 'to manage' and 'to extend spatially' correlate with past participle and third person singular present tense/the present participle respectively. True, it is easy to motivate that 'to manage' is the only sense associated with past participle in passives: it is the only transitive, and thus passivizable, sense of the two singled out for analysis, which is in turn responsible for the expected transitivity preferences. But note that (i) there would nevertheless not have been a reason to posit that 'to manage' is associated with past participle to begin with – could it not equally well prefer the present participle? – and (ii) it does not explain other senses' ID tags or their complementary distributions. In sum, the mere fact that ID tags are powerful enough for the actual prediction of senses already underscores their importance for the analysis of word senses.

5. Conclusion

Before I summarize the most important points of this paper and briefly talk about possible extensions, one caveat is necessary. I have tried to emphasize the benefits of additional corpus-based evidence, but I should like to point out, however, that I do not advocate using corpus evidence alone. Corpus evidence can complement different research methodologies such as (psycho-)linguistic experiments, but it should not replace them. Thus, not all results from above will remain constant across different data, and the above findings will have to be checked against different evidence.

There is yet another aspect of the corpus-based approach that deserves mention. Given the multifactorial approach advocated above, I am the first to admit that the present corpus is not large enough, which is also reflected by the fact that not all senses of *to run* listed in reference works were attested. But in spite of this, it was large enough for us to find (i) which senses are most frequent and whose characterization and cognitive motivation is therefore most relevant and (ii) that some uses of *to run* attested in the corpus data were not listed in (corpus-based) dictionaries such as Cobuild on CD-ROM (1995) or Collins Cobuild E-Dict (1998) and/or turned out to be unfamiliar to some native speakers (e.g. the 'to stop talking' sense and the 'to fail to understand' sense). This is all the more astonishing since these senses or (some aspects of) their distributional behavior are not fully predictable from other senses and should thus be listed in reference works. I interpret this as evidence that it is highly unlikely that intuitions of linguists concerning (i) what are possible uses of a lexeme and (ii) how frequent (or, more cognitively speaking, how entrenched) the uses are will turn out to provide a data base reliable enough for analyzing a word's senses.

I hope the brief case studies discussed in the previous sections have borne out my claim that cognitively-oriented analyses of polysemy benefit from a corpus-based perspective. The hypothesis by Kishner and Gibbs (1996) that comprehenders' choices of a sense of a polysemous item can be influenced by senses' colligations has received support. Also, we have seen that there are many recurrent problems of polysemy analyses (which sense is prototypical?, where do we connect sense X to the network? etc.) to which corpus-based methods can contribute their share of an answer. What is more, I hope to have shown (i) that Kishner and Gibbs's proposal to provide the lexical network description of words' senses with ID tags and frequency information is in fact reasonable and (ii) how this proposal could be implemented since it could be demonstrated that senses often have so strong associations to ID tags that (combinations of) ID tags alone suffice for automatic word sense identification.

Finally, the above observations underscore individual word senses' strong affinity to constructions. The present approach, therefore, bears quite some resemblance to the analyses of collostruction strength (cf. Stefanowitsch and Gries [2003] and Gries and Stefanowitsch [2004a, 2004b]). In these studies, the focus was on measuring the degree of attraction and repulsion of words and constructions by determining the words most characteristic for particular constructions. However, they also point out that the reverse perspective – starting out from a word's behavioral profile – is equally possible. The present study follows up on that proposal: It starts from a single word, and it measures the degree of attraction/repulsion of this word's senses and ID tags, thereby taking into consideration, and simultaneously supporting, recent findings indicating that some distributional patterns are often not *verb*-specific but rather *verb-sense* specific (cf. Roland and Jurafsky [1998, 2002] and Hare, McRae and Elman [2003]). Since these studies are, however, mostly concerned with words having few senses which are much less similar to each other than those of *to run*, the present work with its much more comprehensive and cognitively-oriented behavioral profile also contributes its share to the large area of disambiguation preferences in language comprehension as discussed by Roland and Jurafsky (2002) and Hare, McRae and Elman (2003: 282–284, 295–298). Some possible extensions of this approach will be proposed below.

Let me begin with a major methodological suggestion for improvement. The main multifactorial technique employed above has been the hierarchical agglomerative clustering technique; its main emphasis has been on determining degrees of similarity between (groups of) senses. In passing, we have also briefly looked at to what degree senses can be predicted on the basis of ID tags. Since the number of variables strongly correlating with meanings of *to run* has been very high, it was – as in Gildea and Jurafsky's work – not possible to include all possible combinations of features in the analysis for the latter objective. Therefore, I isolated some ID tags with a strong predictive power on the basis of a manual inspection of hundreds of two- and three-dimensional frequency tables. Given the large number of tables of different factorial degrees requiring manual inspection, this technique must be refined for objective analysis. On the basis of a much larger data set, comprehensive statistical techniques widely used in other disciplines could used, which I would like to briefly outline in the following.

A first such technique is known as hierarchical configural frequency analysis (H-CFA). The basic idea of a regular configural frequency analysis (CFA) is similar to that of a χ^2-test (cf. von Eye [1990] or Krauth [1993] for details). For the present purposes, it determines which of the observed configurations of ID tags of the n-dimensional table are significantly more/less frequently than expected using multiple post hoc tests. For our purpose, however, an extension of this technique, the H-CFA, is more promising: it tests all configurations of ID tags of all factorial degrees. In our case, the analysis would test (i) which of the thousands of configurations of ID tags and senses are frequent enough to be statistically significant and (ii) which of the ID tags are necessary to constitute a particular significant configuration and which can be omitted because they do not discriminate well enough between senses. For example, instances of *to run* meaning 'fast pedestrian motion' are often used intransitively with a human agent – but a temporal prepositional phrase will probably not be distinctive for this meaning. Put differently, human agents and intransitive usage rule out many meanings of *to run* other than 'fast pedestrian motion', but a temporal prepositional phrase denoting the time when the action takes place can be predicated of most meanings of *to run* and is, thus, not useful for the identification of 'fast pedestrian motion'.

Another possible technique which would not require such large sample sizes would not use significance testing but would otherwise generate similar results, namely the technique of association rules frequently used in data mining. Its measures (coverage, support, strength, lift, and leverage) could also identify recurring configurations at different factorial levels.

A much less technical way of extension can be introduced on the basis of two issues already previously mentioned. First, we have seen that recent research on word senses summarized above suggests that it is probably more rewarding to abandon traditional word senses on behalf of meaning components. Second, a more explicit cognitive analysis of *to run* could provide more evidence of the frequencies of mechanisms which figure in extensions of words (i.e. metaphorical, metonymical or image-schematic mappings, profile shifts, frame additions etc.) than the relatively coarse-grained analysis in Section 3. These cognitive mechanisms can be interpreted as constituting, or at least contributing to, the meaning components determining a word's sense, and it would be natural in many cases to expect that the derivation of a new sense via some of these mechanisms would manifest itself not just in the abstract analysis of the linguist, but also in one contextual property, which we have labeled ID tags: obviously, many of the abstract motion senses discussed above differ from the literal motion cases such that their subject is not human or animate, to give just one example. On that basis, the kinds of metaphorical mappings figuring in the senses of *to run* would strongly increase (i) the predictive power of sense recognition and (ii) the descriptive power of the clustering algorithm since, then, senses which are metaphorically closely related but otherwise distributionally dissimilar but would receive higher similarity ratings (e.g. 'to function' and 'to be valid'). Probably more interestingly, it would even be conceivable that further studies could investigate which metaphorical mappings are most entrenched and/or exploited most frequently for extending senses and why.

In that connection, these issues may also be interesting from the perspective of language acquisition. For example, setting up a dynamic behavioral profile of a verb while it is acquired may provide interesting evidence concerning both the salience of the different senses as well as the salience of the cognitively-motivated mechanisms underlying sense extensions during acquisition. For example, such a dynamic behavioral profile would provide information as to which senses are acquired first, which metaphors, metonymies etc. are responsible for the first extensions, what the sequence of acquisition of verb senses tells us about the way children extend senses, and how different formal aspects of the words under investigation (e.g. TAM marking, the distribution of senses within different kinds of clauses etc.) figure in their acquisition; the above-mentioned study of Theakston et al. (2002) is a study in this spirit. The same may hold (though perhaps less directly so) for a diachronic approach towards how the different senses of words develop. Finally, while the present approach has focused on behavioral profiles of different senses of the same word, it can also be applied to the corpus-based cognitive-linguistic investigation of near synonymous words (cf. Divjak [2004, this volume] as well as Divjak and Gries [to appear]).

In sum, for many of these issues which are relevant to cognitive-linguistic approaches, a behavioral profile is, I believe, the most rewarding starting point that will hopefully be utilized more fully in future work.

Notes

*   I thank (in alphabetical order) particularly Ewa Dabrowska and Stefanie Wulff, but also the reviewers, for their detailed feedback and comments; the usual disclaimers apply.
1. In this paper, I will only focus on the synchronic relatedness of senses.
2. The first criterion of this methodology leaves open the question of how word classes other than (usually spatial) prepositions should be investigated.
3. This window is much larger than that for most collocation-based studies, but can be justified given the importance of topical context for word sense disambiguation (cf., e.g., Chodorow, Leacock and Miller 2000).
4. The ideas of ID tags making up a behavioral profile is also compatible with many studies on word sense disambiguation (cf. Ide and Véronis 1998). Given the overlap of issues that both cognitive linguists and WSD studies have been addressing for quite some time (e.g. distinctness of senses, granularity of sense distinctions etc.), it is even a little surprising to note how little cognitive linguists appear to have looked at the accomplishments of these disciplines. Parts of the present paper will therefore also attempt to bridge this gap.
5. This list of frequencies of intraword senses is more than just an end in itself. For example, Williams (1992: 208) discusses "an asymmetry in the amount of priming between central and non-central meanings", proposing that "[o]ne explanation of this asymmetry would be in terms of the relative frequencies of the two meanings". However, he is forced to acknowledge that "[i]n the absence of any data on actual frequencies of use of the meanings of these words, this hypothesis cannot be evaluated". Thus, the knowledge of sense frequencies resulting from the behavioral profile, although of limited use for a traditional cognitive-linguistic analysis of word meaning, are in fact very useful to explain such psycholinguistic findings.
6. The dictionaries used were Cobuild on CD-ROM (1995), Collins Cobuild E-Dict (1998) and Merriam Webster's online dictionary at http://www.m-w.com.
7. I have included all citations of *to run* into the analysis even if this included very creative uses or complex-transitive uses in verb-particle constructions etc. To my mind, this does not constitute a weakness of the present approach: on the one hand, the importance attached to such less central cases can be weighted by their frequency; on the other hand, a truly cognitively-inspired analysis should be able to provide some motivation for extraordinarily creative or more idiomatic extensions anyway. For an earlier analysis of *to run*'s senses, which invokes prototypes, metaphor, and metonymy from a formal semantics perspective, but addresses only a limited number of senses, cf. Bartsch (1984).

8. If the intention to meet the referent of the prepositional phrase headed by *into* is absent, this sense is probably not only related to the sense of 'motion', but probably also to that of 'motion without control/restraint'.
9. The sense 'to overflow' with a liquid as subject (rather than the container) was not attested in the corpus data.
10. Contrary to Lehrer (1990: 226), this sense is neither restricted to, nor significantly preferred in, the corpus of American English.
11. Interestingly, most senses of *to run* that are idiomatic and/or that are tied to particular open-class lexical items involve alliteration: *to run rampant, to run riot, to run roughshod over* NP/S, *to run the risk, to run into rapture*.
12. The analysis counted only complete and completely intelligible utterances by children which were not labeled as imitations or routines; cases where an unambiguous identification was not possible were discarded.
13. The figures result from discounting run/runs as part of proper names – if these were included, the figures would not change markedly, especially since some cases of *run* as part of a proper name refer to racing horses whose main purpose is of course running in the sense of 'fast pedestrian motion', thereby supporting my above claim.
14. Note also that (4) is not only prototypical for *to run* because it exemplifies the sense 'fast pedestrian motion' – it is also a prototypical instance of the sense of 'fast pedestrian motion' because it contains a locative prepositional phrase denoting the goal of the motion like most corpus examples of this sense; corpus examples containing no such prepositional phrase or containing a prepositional phrase denoting the source, direction or origin or goal of the agent's movement are markedly less frequent.
15. Of course, even though the sense of, say, 'to flow' is inferable and need not be stored, it may still be stored just because it is frequent enough to acquire unit status at some point of time.
16. Especially dictionaries often "violate" the criterion of inferrability to provide maximally explicit assistance. I cannot discuss here individual dictionaries' shortcomings or investigate if dictionaries should prefer listing cognitive mechanisms relating different senses over many minimally different senses, but let me provide just a few examples of debatable decisions in favor of splitting from the Cobuild on CD-ROM (1995). Once the 'motion' and 'to cause motion' senses of *to run* have been established, do we really need to distinguish the definitions of (a) and (b) from each other, and the senses in (a) and (b) from the one in (c) in spite of their compositionality?

    (a) 'motion': "If an object such as a ball runs somewhere, it moves smoothly and quickly over the ground. EXAMPLE: *The ball ran to the boundary*" (sense 22) vs. "If you run somewhere in a car, you make a short trip in it. EXAMPLE: *Why don't we run down to Worcester for the afternoon?*" (sense 18) vs., as just discussed above in the main text, "If a

liquid runs somewhere, it flows in a particular place or direction. EXAMPLE: *Tears were running down the side of his face ... The water ran into a bucket.*" (sense 23)
  (b) 'to cause motion': "If you run an object or your hand over something, you make the object or your hand touch it and move over it. EXAMPLE: *He ran his hand over her hair ... She ran her finger down a list of names*" (sense 10) vs. "If you run someone somewhere in a car, you drive them there. EXAMPLE: Would you mind running me to the station?" (sense 19)
  (c) 'motion' or 'to cause motion' (ergative verb): "If you run a vehicle somewhere or it runs there, it moves to a particular place or in a particular direction. EXAMPLE: *Run the car into the garage before you go ... The cart ran down the road out of control.*" (sense 20)
17. In fact, a similar logic can be applied to the potential distinction of *to run* with a DIRECTION argument, which can occur alone (e.g. *He'd heard the shouts and shrieks, had heard Cassie running up the stairs*), but also with a GOAL (e.g. *Russ ran up the steps quickly to the plank porch*).
18. There is nothing in the method implying that there is just one correct way of analysis or connection: of course, multiple connections between different senses are possible – even then, the proposed way of analysis makes it possible to rank the potential connection sites in terms of similarity.
19. Hierarchical agglomerative cluster analysis is a family of methods that aims at identifying and representing (dis)similarity relations between different items (a general comprehensive discussion of clustering can be found in Kaufman and Rousseeuw [1990]). Usually, clustering is performed on the basis of variables that characterize the items or on the basis of a similarity matrix of the items as, for example, obtained from the variables in example above or from similarity judgments or sorting tasks. In our case, the items correspond to the senses of *to run* while the variables are the ID tags.

    A cluster analysis of the kind used here begins by considering each of the n senses as one-sense clusters and proceeds to amalgamate those clusters which exhibit the highest intra-cluster similarity and the lowest inter-cluster similarity successively until all clusters have been amalgamated into a single cluster containing all items. The structure yielded by this amalgamation process is typically represented by means of a so-called dendrogram, i.e. a tree diagram representing the similarities among clusters. In addition, a variety of statistical measures can be outputted that help (i) to determine the number of clusters one should assume as well as (ii) to identify which of the variables are most responsible for the clustering solution obtained.

    Since the choice of the distance measure and the clustering algorithm can bias the results, 48 different cluster analyses were conducted to systematically compare different combinations of distance measures, clustering algorithms and senses and ID tags to include. However, it turned out that in this case the differences were of relatively minor importance. The solution presented above is based on Euclidean distances, the weighted pair-group average, all senses minus the idiomatic ones, and all features.

20. Interestingly, the fact that the coarsest distinction in the corpus data is the syntactic one of transitivity ties in perfectly with a result from a sorting experiment in Miller (1971: 577), where "adult judges seem to work by sorting the items on syntactic grounds before sorting them on semantic grounds."

References

Atkins, Beryl T. Sue
    1987   Semantic ID tags: corpus evidence for dictionary senses. *Proceedings of the Third Annual Conference of the UW Centre for the New Oxford English Dictionary*, 17–36.

Bartsch, Renate
    1988   The structure of word meanings: Polysemy, metaphor, metonymy. In: Fred Landman and Frank Veltman (eds.), *Varieties of Formal Semantics*, 27–54. Dordrecht: Foris.

Biber, Douglas
    1993   Co-occurrence patterns among collocations: A tool for corpus-based lexical knowledge acquisition. *Computational Linguistics* 19 (3): 531–538.

Brugman, Claudia
    1984   The *very* idea: a case study in polysemy and cross-lexical generalizations. *Papers from the Parasession on Lexical Semantics*, 21–38. Chicago, IL: CLS.

Brugman, Claudia and George Lakoff
    1988   Cognitive topology and lexical networks. In: Steven L. Small, Garrison W. Cottrell, and Michael K. Tanenhaus (eds.), *Lexical Ambiguity Resolution*, 477–508. San Mateo, CA: Morgan Kaufman.

Chodorow, Martin, Claudia Leacock, and George A. Miller
    2000   A topical/local classifier for word sense identification. *Computers and the Humanities* 34 (1/2): 115–120.

Cobuild on CD-ROM 1.2.
    1995   Glasgow: Harper Collins.

Collins Cobuild E-Dict.
    1998   Glasgow: Harper Collins.

Corston-Oliver, Monica
   2001   Central meanings of polysemous prepositions: Challenging the assumptions. Poster presented at the ICLC 2001, University of California, Santa Barbara.

Croft, William
   1998   Linguistic evidence and mental representations. *Cognitive Linguistics* 9 (2): 151–173.

Cruse, D. Alan
   1986   *Lexical Semantics*. Cambridge: Cambridge University Press.

Divjak, Dagmar
   2004   Degrees of verb integration. Conceptualizing and categorizing events in Russian. Doctoral dissertation, Katholieke Universiteit Leuven.
   this vol. Ways of intending: Delineating and structuring near-synonyms.

Divjak, Dagmar and Stefan Th. Gries
   to appear Ways of trying in Russian: clustering and comparing behavioral profiles. *Corpus Linguistics and Linguistic Theory* 2 (1).

Durkin, Kevin and Jocelyn Manning
   1989   Polysemy and the subjective lexicon: Semantic relatedness and the salience of intraword senses. *Journal of Psycholinguistic Research* 18 (6): 577–612.

Eye, Alexander von
   1990   *Introduction to Configural Frequency Analysis: The Search for Types and Antitypes in Cross-classifications*. Cambridge: Cambridge University Press.

Fillmore, Charles J. and Beryl T. Sue Atkins
   2000   Describing polysemy: the case of 'crawl'. In: Yael Ravin and Claudia Leacock (eds.), *Polysemy: Theoretical and Computational Approaches*, 91–110. Oxford: Oxford University Press.

Geeraerts, Dirk
   1993   Vagueness's puzzles, polysemy's vagaries. *Cognitive Linguistics* 4 (3): 223–272.

Gibbs, Raymond W. Jr. and Teenie Matlock
   2001   Psycholinguistic perspectives on polysemy. In: Hubert Cuyckens and Britta Zawada (eds.), *Polysemy in Cognitive Linguistics*, 213–239. Amsterdam/Philadelphia: John Benjamins.

Gildea, Daniel and Daniel Jurafsky
   2001   Automatic labeling of semantic roles. *Computational Linguistics* 28 (3): 245–288.

Gries, Stefan Th.
   2001   A corpus-linguistic analysis of *-ic* and *-ical* adjectives. *ICAME Journal* 25: 65–108.

2003a   Testing the sub-test: A collocational-overlap analysis of English *-ic* and *-ical* adjectives. *International Journal of Corpus Linguistics* 8 (1): 31–61.
2003b   *Multifactorial Analysis in Corpus Linguistics: The Case of Particle Placement*. London/New York: Continuum.
2003c   Towards a corpus-based identification of prototypical instances of constructions. *Annual Review of Cognitive Linguistics* 1: 1–27.

Gries, Stefan Th. and Anatol Stefanowitsch
2004a   Extending collostructional analysis: A corpus-based perspective on 'alternations'. *International Journal of Corpus Linguistics* 9 (1): 97–129.
2004b   Co-varying collexemes in the *into*-causative. In: Michel Achard and Suzanne Kemmer (eds.), *Language, Culture, and Mind*, 225–236. Stanford, CA: CSLI.

Hanks, Patrick
1996   Contextual dependency and lexical sets. *International Journal of Corpus Linguistics* 1 (1): 75–98.
2000   Do word meanings exist? *Computers and the Humanities* 34 (1/2): 205–215.

Hare, Mary L., Ken McRae, and Jeffrey L. Elman
2003   Sense and structure: Meaning as a determinant of verb subcategorization preferences. *Journal of Memory and Language* 48 (2): 281–303.

Ide, Nancy and Jean Véronis
1998   Introduction to the special issue on word sense disambiguation: the state of the art. *Computational Linguistics* 24 (1): 1–40.

Jorgensen, Julia
1990   The psychological reality of word senses. *Journal of Psycholinguistic Research* 19 (3): 167–190.

Kaufman, Leonard and Peter J. Rousseeuw
1990   *Finding Groups in Data*. New York: Wiley.

Kilgarriff, Adam
1993   Dictionary word sense distinctions: an enquiry into their nature. *Computers and the Humanities* 26 (1–2): 365–387.
1997   I don't believe in word senses. *Computers and the Humanities* 31 (2): 91–113.

Kishner, Jeffrey M. and Raymond W. Jr. Gibbs
1996   How *just* gets its meanings: Polysemy and context in psychological semantics. *Language and Speech* 39 (1): 19–36.

Klein, Deborah E. and Gregory L. Murphy
2001   The representation of polysemous words. *Journal of Memory and Language* 45 (2): 259–282.

2002 Paper has been my ruin: Conceptual relations of polysemous senses. *Journal of Memory and Language* 47 (4): 548–570.

Krauth, Joachim
1993 *Einführung in die Konfigurationsfrequenzanalyse: [...]*. Weinheim: Beltz, Psychologie-Verlags-Union.

Lakoff, George
1987 *Women, Fire, and Dangerous Things*. Chicago: The University of Chicago Press.

Langenscheidts Grosswörterbuch der Englischen und Deutschen Sprache: "Der kleine Muret-Sanders". 1991 5th ed. Berlin/München: Langenscheidt.

Lehrer, Adrienne
1990 Polysemy, conventionality, and the structure of the subjective lexicon. *Cognitive Linguistics* 1 (2): 207–246.

Manning, Christopher D. and Hinrich Schütze
2000 *Foundations of Statistical Natural Language Processing*. 4th printing with corr. Cambridge, MA: The MIT Press.

MacWhinney, Brian
2000 *The CHILDES Project: Tools for Analyzing Talk*. 3rd ed. Mahwah, NJ: Lawrence Erlbaum Associates.

McDonald, Scott
1997 Exploring the validity of corpus-derived measures of semantic similarity. Paper presented at the 9th Annual CCS/HCRC postgraduate conference, University of Edinburgh.

Miller, George A.
1971 Empirical methods in the study of semantics. In: Danny Steinberg and Leon A. Jakobovits (eds.), *Semantics: An Interdisciplinary Reader*, 569–585. London/New York: Cambridge University Press.

Nordquist, Dawn
2004 Comparing elicited data and corpora: What the (mis)match reveals about the lexicon. In: Michael Achard and Suzanne Kemmer (eds.), *Language, culture, and mind*. Stanford, CA: CSLI.

Norvig, Peter and George Lakoff
1987 Taking: A study in lexical network theory. In: Jon Aske, Natasha. Beery, Laura Michaelis, and Hana Filip (eds.), *Proceedings of the Thirteenth Annual Meeting of the Berkeley Linguistics Society*, 195–206. Berkeley, CA: BLS.

Nunberg, Geoffrey, Ivan A. Sag, and Thomas Wasow
1994 Idioms. *Language* 70 (3): 491–538.

Oxford English Dictionary 2 on CD-ROM V. 1.15. Oxford: Oxford University Press.

Partridge, Eric
   1961   *Origins: A Short Etymological Dictionary of Modern English*. London: Routledge and Kegan Paul.

Rice, Sally
   1987   Towards a transitive prototype: Evidence from some atypical English passives. In: Jon Aske, Natasha Beery, Laura Michaelis, and Hana Filip (eds.), *Proceedings of the Thirteenth Annual Meeting of the Berkeley Linguistics Society*, 422–434. Berkeley, CA: BLS.
   1996   Prepositional prototypes. In: Martin Pütz and Rene Dirven (eds.), *The Construal of Space in Language and Thought*, 135–165. Berlin/New York: Mouton de Gruyter.

Roland, Douglas and Daniel Jurafsky
   1998   How verb subcategorization frequencies are affected by corpus choice. *ACL/COLING Proceedings*, 1122–1228.
   2002   Verb sense and subcategorization probabilities. In: Paola Merlo and Suzanne Stevenson (eds.), *The Lexical Basis of Sentence Processing: Formal, Computational and Experimental Issues*, 303–324. Amsterdam/Philadelphia: John Benjamins.

Sandra, Dominiek
   1998   What linguists can and can't tell you about the human mind: A reply to Croft. *Cognitive Linguistics* 9 (4): 361–378.

Sandra, Dominiek and Sally Rice
   1995   Network analyses of prepositional meaning: mirroring whose mind – the linguist's or the language user's? *Cognitive Linguistics* 6 (1): 89–130.

Schulte im Walte, Sabine
   2003   Experiments on the automatic induction of German semantic verb classes. Doctoral dissertation, University of Stuttgart.

Stefanowitsch, Anatol and Stefan Th. Gries
   2003   Collostructions: Investigating the interactions of words and constructions. *International Journal of Corpus Linguistics* 8 (2): 209–243.

Theakston, Anna L., Elena V. M. Lieven, Julian M. Pine, and C. F. Rowland
   2001   The role of performance limitations in the acquisition of verb-argument structure: An alternative account. *Journal of Child Language* 28 (1) 127–152.
   2002   Going, going, gone: The acquisition of the verb 'go'. *Journal of Child Language* 29 (4):783–811.

Tuggy, David
   1993   Ambiguity, polysemy, and vagueness. *Cognitive Linguistics* 4 (3): 273–290.

Tyler, Andrea and Vyvyan Evans
    2001   Reconsidering prepositional polysemy networks: The case of *over*. *Language* 77 (4): 724–765.

Williams, John N.
    1992   Processing polysemous words in context: Evidence for interrelated meanings. *Journal of Psycholinguistic Research* 21 (3): 193–218.

Go-V vs. *go-and*-V in English:
A case of constructional synonymy?

Stefanie Wulff

Abstract

The present paper deals with the double verb patterns *go-and*-V and *go*-V. While generative approaches have argued that the latter are truncated surface forms derived from the former, the present paper adds to the empirical evidence obtained so far, arguing in favor of the view that the two patterns be adequately conceived of as separate constructions (the notion of construction being defined in terms of construction grammar). On the basis of a large-scale corpus sample, statistical significance tests such as collostructional analysis and distinctive collexeme analysis confirm that *go*-V and *go-and*-V differ substantially in terms of the (aktionsart of the) verbs they attract; moreover, calculating the collexemic overlap between the two constructions, we find that the overlap of verbs shared between the two constructions is significantly smaller than would be expected according to a derivational view.

Keywords: fake coordination; synonymy; collocational overlap estimation; collostructional analysis; distinctive collexemes.

1. Introduction

The present paper deals with two superficially very similar double verb patterns in English, *go-and*-V and *go*-V, as exemplified in (1) and (2).

(1)   *Now, just keep polishing those glasses while I go and check the drinks.*

(2)   *Go find the books and show me.*

In generative approaches, double verb constructions of the kind shown in (2) have been argued to be mere short versions derived from constructions like that in (1), while more functionally oriented researchers have argued that the two patterns behave differently with respect to their semantics, which rules out the possibility of the shorter pattern merely being a surface structure variant of the longer version. In particular, according to one of the central tenets of construction grammar, which is the theoretical framework adopted here, constructional synonymy is ruled out by the *Principle of No Synonymy* (cf. Goldberg 1995: 67, cf. Section 3).

The present paper approaches the question whether *go-and*-V and *go*-V are synonymous patterns from a corpus-linguistic perspective, arguing in favor of the hypothesis that *go*-V and *go-and*-V are not synonymous but rather constitute separate constructions (the notion of construction being defined in terms of construction grammar, cf. Section 3). In what follows, I will first provide a brief overview of previous approaches to *go-(and)*-V in Section 2. The hypotheses that can be derived from a derivational view will be tested on the basis of more than 5,000 instances of *go-(and)*-V obtained from the British National Corpus, the sampling and classification of which I will outline in Section 4. In Section 5, I will present the results produced by several statistical methods such as collocational overlap estimation, collostructional analysis, and distinctive collexeme analysis. The empirical evidence thereby obtained demonstrates that – contrary to the generative account – *go*-V and *go-and*-V do in fact instantiate separate constructions.

2. Previous approaches to *go-and*-V vs. *go*-V

To begin with descriptive grammar books, while it is widely acknowledged that coordinated double verb patterns (mostly referred to as fake coordinations) display a variety of syntactic and semantic idiosyncrasies such as restrictions on the verb forms licensed to be inserted into the V_2-slot, their association with informal style[1] and their often negative or derogatory connotation (cf. Quirk et al. 1985: 978–979; Huddleston and Pullum 2002: 1304), the relationship between *go-and*-V and *go*-V is rarely addressed directly. Eastwood (1994: 147) notes that *go*-V is the American English variant for British English *go-and*-V; however, this claim is proven wrong in view of the 454 examples found in the British National Corpus constituting a part of the data sample to be investigated here.

Carden and Pesetzky (1979: 89) argue that V_1-V_2 constructions like *go-V* are derivates of the corresponding V_1-*and*-V_2 constructions, "presumably by a syntactic rule of Fake-*and* Deletion". They present three arguments to support their claim; however, they themselves have to concede that none of these arguments applies to *go-(and)-V* without confinements. Firstly, they claim that generally, both a V_1-*and*-V_2 pattern as well as its corresponding V_1-V_2 pattern share syntactic constraints such as the *bare stem condition*, which restricts the set of verb forms to be inserted into the patterns' verbal slots to non-inflected forms. However, Carden and Pesetzky (1979: 89) note that while this constraint holds for *go-V*, it does not hold for *go-and-V*; consider their examples in (3) and (4) respectively.

(3) a. *John went visit Harry yesterday.*
     b. *He went and hit me.*

Similarly, with respect to their second argument, saying that the semantics of V_1-V_2 patterns and V_1-*and*-V_2 patterns are identical, Carden and Pesetzky have to point out that while *go-and-V* has a possible "unexpected event reading" (consider [4a] and [4b], taken from Carden and Pesetzky [1979: 89]), *go-V* cannot encode such a meaning.

(4) a. *??As we had arranged, the President went and addressed the graduating class.*
     b. *To our amazement, instead of addressing the graduating class, the President went and harangued the janitors.*

Finally, Carden and Pesetzky point out that the set of verbs licensed in the V_1 position of V_1-V_2 patterns constitute a subset of those of the V_1-*and*-V_2 patterns. Unfortunately, they do not provide any empirical evidence supporting this claim. To conclude, the failure of generative approaches to account for *go-(and)-V* may be due to "a reluctance to think of a sequence that transgresses the boundary of two coordinated clauses as constituting a single grammatical construction" (cf. Hopper 2002: 146), since one of the fundamental commitments in generative grammar is a sharp dividing line between syntax and semantics.

Shopen (1971: 260) adopts a more functionally-oriented approach to V_1-V_2 constructions and argues against the view that V_1-V_2 constructions[2] (to which he refers as *quasi-modals*) are to be considered merely "truncated surface variants of some other expression type". He points towards two semantic differences between V_1-*and*-V_2 constructions and their corresponding V_1-V_2 constructions to support his claim. First, the linkage between the two inserted verbs is much tighter in V_1-V_2 constructions than in V_1-*and*-V_2 constructions. Providing the examples in (5a) and (5b), Shopen (1971: 260) argues that (5a) is unacceptable because the semantics of the two verbs *go* and *leave* are incompatible, while (5b) is acceptable due to the weaker linkage between the two verbs.

(5) a. *They deliberately go leave their wives behind.
    b. They deliberately go and leave their wives behind.

Another difference between V_1-V_2 patterns and V_1-*and*-V_2 patterns Shopen identifies is that while *go* ordinarily allows both agential as well as non-agential interpretations (as in *go-and*-V), in the *go*-V pattern, the interpretation must be agential, which also speaks against the view that *go*-V is only a short form of *go-and*-V. He illustrates his claim with the following examples.

(6) a. The trucks come and pick up the garbage every Monday.
    b. The trucks come pick up the garbage every Monday.

(7) a. Pieces of drift wood come and wash up the shore.
    b. *Pieces of drift wood come wash up the shore.

(8) a. The smoke fumes go and inebriate the people upstairs.
    b. *The smokes go inebriate the people upstairs.

While (6b) is acceptable because the trucks can be associated with an agent, (7b)/(8b) are unacceptable because the subjects *pieces of drift wood* and *the smoke fumes* do not license such an agential interpretation.

3. Construction-based approaches to *go-and*-V

In more recent theoretical frameworks, the strict dividing line between syntax and semantics is no longer upheld; instead, it is assumed that syntax and semantics are systematically intertwined to a considerable degree. One of these theoretical frameworks which appears to be especially well-suited for the explanation of structures like *go-*(*and*)-V and which is also adopted here is construction grammar. In construction grammar as developed by, among others, Goldberg (1995, 1996) and Lakoff (1987), double verb patterns are assigned the status of a construction, the notion of construction being defined as follows:

> A construction is ... a pairing of form with meaning/use such that some aspect of the form or some aspect of the meaning is not strictly predictable from the component parts or from other constructions already established to exist in the language. (Goldberg 1996: 68)

Several analyses have demonstrated that construction grammar can account for coordinate double verb constructions as in (1) in an elegant and straightforward way (cf. Lakoff 1986; Hopper 2002; Stefanowitsch 2000). Since neither of these analyses discusses the question of the relationship between *go-and-*V and *go-*V but exclusively focus on *go-and-*V and its status as a construction, I will not provide a detailed account of these analyses here; instead, the essentials of these analyses will be discussed in Section 5 to the extent deemed necessary in order to compare the semantics of *go-and-*V and *go-*V.

In spite of the fact that the relationship between *go-and-*V and *go-*V has not yet been addressed explicitly from a construction-based perspective, it is possible to derive the hypothesis that *go-*V must be considered a separate construction from established theoretical commitments. According to one of the central tenets of Goldbergian construction grammar, the *Principle of No Synonymy*, "if two constructions are syntactically distinct, they must be semantically or pragmatically distinct" (Goldberg 1995: 67). So far, evidence for this principle comes from classic cases of "alternation" phenomena, such as dative movement, the load/spray alternation, the active/passive alternation, particle movement, and others. Each of these cases has been shown to consist of two distinct constructions, each with its own semantics and/or pragmatics (Goldberg 1995, 2002; Gries and Stefanowitsch 2004a). In all of these cases there is a difference in word order, often with additional lexical differences; however, there is little evidence so far concerning cases which, although one form has been argued to be derived from the other, have not been considered alternants on an equal footing, but where one structure is a shortened surface form of the other.

The present paper takes steps towards closing this gap. The following hypothesis follows from a derivational view: generally speaking, the two constructions should be semantically synonymous (in the absence of systematic semantic differences between the two patterns, the "unexpected event"-reading of *go-and*-V could be ignored as a solitary exception). Strictly speaking, it follows that the verbs inserted into the open slot of the *go*-V pattern should be identical to (or constitute a subset of) those of the *go-and*-V pattern. From a constructionist perspective, we would neither want to rule out that there is some degree of semantic overlap, since it is likely to assume that *go*-V was actually once derived from *go-and*-V (this question being, however, beyond the scope of the present paper), so we can expect to find some semantic commonalities (particularly since a major part of the semantics of both constructions is contributed by the lexical semantics of *go*). However, according to the *Principle of No Synonymy*, we also expect that (i) there is a significant number of verbs in the *go*-V construction which do not occur in the *go-and*-V construction and vice versa, and that (ii) these two groups of verbs can be differentiated systematically with respect to their semantics, thereby legitimating the view that *go-and*-V and *go*-V actually are individual constructions.

4. Data and classification

All instances of *go*-V and *go-and*-V were searched for in the British National Corpus. The initial sample comprising approximately 10,000 items was manually inspected in order to filter out about 5,000 instances of true coordination (and other patterns fitting the structural description). In accordance with the defining criteria for fake coordinations, the final sample did not include

- instances of *go*-PRT-*and*-V: these constitute constructions in their own right (cf. Stefanowitsch 2000);
- items in which a comma, full stop or any other punctuation mark intervened between *go* and the conjunction *and*, or *go* and V_2 (in the case of *go*-V) respectively: these are not instances of *go-(and)*-V, since the punctuation mark signals the beginning of a new clause;
- items in which the conjunction *and* was not directly followed by V_2, but by *then, afterwards*, or any other time adverbial: the presence of such an adverbial strongly indicates that the action denoted by *go* and the action denoted by V_2 are interpreted sequentially, which renders these items cases of true coordination.

The final sample size amounted to 5,320 instances of the *go-and-*V construction (comprised of 492 different V_2 types) and 454 instances of the *go-*V construction (comprised of 115 different V_2 types).

If the constructions actually carry different meanings, this should primarily become evident in the choice of the only variable element in the constructional frame, V_2. Accordingly, all V_2s were classified according to two different semantic classifications schemes. In a first step, the data were coded according to Vendler's (1967) situation types (aktionsarten); consider Table 1, which provides an overview.

Table 1. Situation types (adapted from Vendler 1967)

	punctual	durative
terminal	accomplishment	achievement
non-terminal	activity	state

These aspectual profiles constitute, of course, clausal properties when used in a specific context (cf. also Moens and Steedman [1988: 17]). Indeed, more often than not, only the context helped to unambiguously assign the tokens membership in one of the four classes. Therefore, the context is also provided in the following examples. As can be seen in Table 1, Vendler distinguishes four different situation types which are distinguishable along two dimensions, namely temporal extension (punctual vs. durative) and telicity (telic vs. atelic or, in Vendler's terminology, terminal vs. non-terminal). In other words, any action described by a verb can be distinguished according to (i) whether it extends in time or not and (ii) whether it has a culmination associated with it at which a change of state takes place or not. (9) to (12) provide examples from the present data sample.

(9) a. *He can go and love some other girl and wed her if he can* (state)
    b. *Why doesn't she go live round there or something* (state)
(10) a. *You've gone and achieved something* (achievement)
     b. *Go find the books and show me* (achievement)
(11) a. *Shall I go and knock on her door and ask?* (accomplishment)
     b. *Or you could do an Arnold Schwarzenegger, just go break the lock!* (accomplishment)
(12) a. *let's go and walk by the water's edge!* (activity)
     b. *it would be nonsensical to get Paul Weller to go play live on a kids* (activity)

The second, more fine-grained semantic classification scheme employed here are Levin's (1993) verb classes. Her classification scheme is based on a systematic investigation of the different degree to which verbs do or do not undergo a variety of syntactic diathesis alternations. The primary hypothesis underlying this procedure is that these syntactic properties are semantically determined. As Levin notes,

> [t]he assumption that the syntactic behavior of verbs is semantically determined gives rise to a powerful technique for investigating verb meaning that can be exploited in the development of a theory of lexical knowledge. If the distinctive behavior of verb classes with respect to diathesis alternations arises from their meaning, any class of verbs whose meanings pattern together with respect to diathesis alternations should be a semantically coherent class: its members should share at least some aspect of meaning. (Levin 1993: 14)

Levin's resulting classification scheme comprises 49 different classes covering a wide range of semantic classes such as verbs of putting, image creation verbs, verbs relating to the body, etc. These verb classes are further divided into sub-classes which have been ignored for the purpose of the present study. For reasons of space, not all of Levin's main verb classes can be enumerated here with examples; cf. section 4, where examples are given for those classes actually attested in the present data sample. The classification was based on Levin's own class assignment for each verb. 162 tokens [53 types] from the present data sample are not included in Levin's verb index. In order not to distort the picture unnecessarily, they were excluded from the data sample for this part of the analysis. If class membership was ambiguous (for instance with polysemous verbs like *see*), I determined the appropriate sense by considering the context of the item.

5. Results

5.1. The verbs of *go*-V do not constitute a subset of the verbs of *go-and*-V

In order to test to what extent the two constructions are actually synonymous, the first analysis to be presented here is an ESCO (Estimation of Significant Collocate Overlap) analysis as proposed by Gries (2001). While Gries (2001) originally developed this technique in order to determine the semantic overlap of *-ic* and *-ical* adjectives, the method can be extended beyond the word level without difficulty given a construction grammar approach as adopted here, which postulates no fundamental difference in the constructional status of words and patterns of higher lexico-syntactic complexity. That is, Gries's (2001: 83) assumptions that "(i) word meanings can be differentiated on the basis of significant collocates and [...] (ii) we, thus, interpret a significant collocate of a word as one of its features" hold for more complex constructions as well. Accordingly, adapting Gries's method for *go-and*-V and *go*-V, the following three values enter into the computation of ESCO:

- the number of significant collexemes[3] (i.e., features) that both *go-and*-V and *go*-V exhibit,
- the number of significant collexemes exhibited by *go-and*-V, but not *go*-V, and
- the number of significant collexemes exhibited by *go*-V, but not *go-and*-V.

Figure 1 is a graphic representation of the proportions of these numbers.

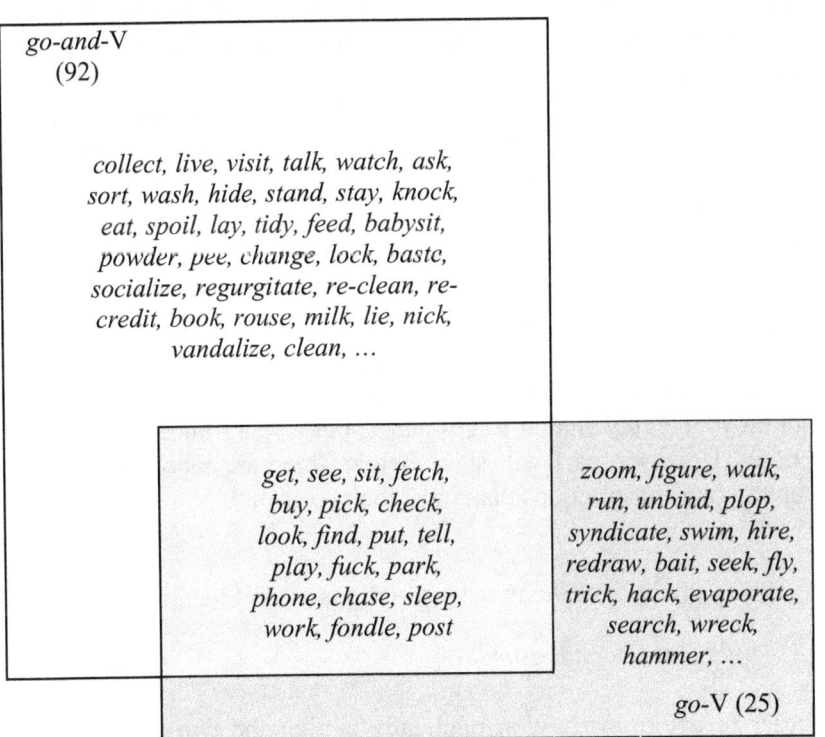

Figure 1. Significantly attracted collexeme set for *go-(and)*-V

As is obvious from Figure 1, the overlap as determined by applying Gries's ESCO analysis is considerable. However, from the overlap percentages (17.9% for *go-and*-V and 44.4% for *go*-V) it is completely unclear whether the overlap is significantly larger than would be expected on the basis of chance alone. To determine whether the overlap is in fact significant, two Monte Carlo simulations were carried out along the lines of Gries, Hampe, and Schönefeld (to appear). First, a list of all verb forms and their probabilities of occurrence in the BNC was obtained.[4] Then 50,000 different samples of 45 verb forms (the number of significant collexemes of *go*-V) were drawn from that list where each verb form's chance of being sampled corresponded to its relative frequency in the BNC. Then for each of the 50,000 samples it was counted how many of the 45 verb forms instantiated one of the 112 significant collexeme lemmas of *go-and*-V to determine how often this happened more than 20 times per sample. The same was done in the other constructional direction with 50,000 samples of 112 verb forms (the number of significant collexemes of *go-and*-V). As it turned out, an overlap of 20 was obtained only once in the (pooled) 100,000 random samples, which is why the overlap represented in Figure 2 must be considered highly significant: p=0.00001.[5]

Note finally that even the direction of derivation that has been assumed by previous analyses is supported. Gries (2001: 105, n. 18) argued that, of the two items investigated, the one exhibiting higher overlap has "less an identity on its own", which is why one can plausibly assume the more strongly overlapping construction to be a derivative of the other. According to Figure 2, *go-and*-V has much more of an identity on its own, sharing only approximately 18% of its collexemes, which is why considering *go*-V a derivative receives some empirical support. On the basis of these findings, it comes as no surprise that much theoretical work has considered *go*-V not only as highly similar to *go-and*-V, but also a truncated derivative of the other. However, as I will show below, there are more differences between the two constructions than meet the eye at first.

5.2. The semantics of the two constructions are not identical

5.2.1. Differences in aktionsart

In order to determine how semantically similar the two patterns actually are, I carried out a so-called collostructional analysis along the lines of Stefanowitsch and Gries (2003); the computations (for all collostructional analyses discussed in this paper) were performed with Coll.analysis 3.2, an R script by, and freely available from, Stefan Th. Gries. By means of this method, it is possible to determine those lexemes in the slots of a construction which are strongly associated with the construction; these lexemes are also referred to as collexemes. In its paying tribute to the fact that the syntax of language is hierarchically structured, collostructional analysis goes beyond simply looking at the words directly preceding or following a word (i.e., the word's collocates), thereby enabling a more accurate description of the interdependency between particular lexemes and the syntactic structures they occur in. In order to test whether a lexeme L is significantly attracted or repelled by the construction C, four frequency values are entered into a 2-by-2 matrix:

- the frequency of L in C,
- the frequency of L in constructions that are not C,
- the frequency of C where the free slot is filled with lexemes that are not L, and
- the frequency of all constructions other than C that are filled with lexemes that are not L.

The significance of the association between L and C is measured in terms of a Fisher-Yates exact test. Moreover, it is possible to identify which of these collexemes are either positively or negatively associated with the construction: if the co-occurrence frequency of L and C is higher than would be expected (given the general frequency of L and C), L is attracted to C; if, on the contrary, L fills the potential slot of C less frequently than would be expected, one can say that L is repelled by C.

As already noted above, the only potential slot to be occupied in the *go-(and)-V* constructions is the V_2 slot, so semantic differences between the two constructions should be detectable by looking at the verbal collexemes.

Let us now turn to the results obtained by the collostructional analysis. First, we will have a look at the 25 most significantly attracted and repelled collexemes.[6] Since it is comparatively difficult to find consistent semantic patterns by looking at the individual verbs alone, we will also consider the data when classified in terms of situation types and Levin's (1993) semantic verb classes.

To begin with *go-and*-V, Table 2 provides the 25 most significantly attracted/repelled collexemes of *go-and*-V. Table 3 displays the distribution of all significant collexemes (i.e., both the attracted as well as the repelled ones) with respect to situation types.

112 Stefanie Wulff

Let us first consider the significantly attracted collexemes of *go-and*-V. As Table 2 in combination with Table 3 shows, verbs denoting accomplishments and achievements are predominant, e.g. *get*, *fetch*, *check*, and *find*, accounting for 2,274 (1,328+946) out of 4,491 items containing a significant collexeme. Pure motion verbs, on the contrary, are rare: of the 2,053 items classified as activities, only 124 items are characterized as "physical" according to Levin's classification scheme. This predominance of telic verbs can be accounted for straightforwardly in terms of construction grammar: assuming that the aspect of "motion"/"dynamics" is an inherent part of the constructional meaning itself (primarily contributed by *go*), the V_2 slot can be employed for encoding (compatible) additional information.

Table 2. Collexemes most significantly attracted to/repelled by *go-and*-V

Attracted collexemes	Collostruction strength	Repelled collexemes	Collostruction strength
get	Inf(inity)	*be*	Inf
see	Inf	*have*	55.879
sit	102.057	*go*	50.157
fetch	100.229	*say*	33.271
buy	68.134	*think*	33.245
pick	30.146	*come*	25.023
check	27.838	*use*	18.055
look	25.325	*become*	11.390
find	23.889	*follow*	9.087
collect	22.886	*believe*	6.579
live	21.892	*allow*	6.381
visit	21.810	*happen*	6.035
talk	20.639	*carry*	5.859
put	18.457	*continue*	5.690
watch	18.176	*involve*	5.328
ask	17.678	*suggest*	5.305
tell	15.269	*run*	5.256
sort	14.618	*offer*	5.099
wash	12.950	*keep*	5.026
play	12.567	*set*	4.517
hide	9.838	*give*	4.438
fuck	8.886	*decide*	4.397
stand	8.239	*reach*	4.105
stay	7.607	*write*	3.613
knock	7.542	*pass*	3.612

Generally speaking, the fact that culmination verbs are so frequent among the significantly attracted collexemes of *go-and*-V does not come as a surprise if one assumes that the two verbs in the construction serve to encode a single event (cf. Lakoff 1986; Stefanowitsch 2000: 260): in an iconic linear ordering sequence, *go* describes the initiation of the event, and the V_2 inserted describes the (way of) fulfillment of this action/event.[7]

Table 3. Distribution of situation types in all tokens of significant collexemes for *go-and*-V

Situation type	Token frequency
Activity	2,049 (45.6%)
Accomplishment	1,328 (29.6%)
Achievement	946 (21.1%)
State	168 (3.7%)
Column totals	4,491 (100%)

Considering the most strongly repelled collexemes in Table 2, we find that the two verbs most strongly repelled by *go-and*-V are *be* and *have*, both of which denote states (other stative verbs among the repelled collexemes are, e.g., *think, believe* and *keep*, amounting to 168 out of 4,491 items including a significant collexeme). So although stative verbs do occur in the construction, which contradicts previous analyses claiming that this is impossible (cf. Hopper 2002), stative verbs occur much less frequently in the construction than their general corpus frequency would lead us to expect. As a matter of fact, this ties in well with Stefanowitsch's (2000: 261) observation that the essential semantic contribution made by *go* in the *go-and*-V construction is "motion along a path", i.e. a dynamic feature. This leads us to expect that V_2 will also be inherently dynamic or at least lend itself to such an interpretation if it is inserted into the construction. Stative verbs, on the contrary, should be disfavored by the construction because they are incompatible with the constructional semantics, and this is exactly what the collostructional analysis tells us (cf. Goldberg 1995: 50–51).

So what about the cases where the verb actually is stative? A construction-based approach can also account for these seemingly contradicting cases. As Stefanowitsch (2000: 261) notes, the semantics of the construction and the lexical semantics of the verb blend into each other such that not only the lexical semantics of the verb adds new information to the construction as a whole, but also vice versa such that the way in which the verb's meaning will be interpreted is strongly influenced by the constructional frame in which it occurs (cf. Stefanowitsch 2000: 261). Consequently, even verbs that are interpreted as stative in the default case can be inserted into the construction given that a more dynamic reading is possible, even if it is one very remote from the verb's core meaning. How the choice of one sense of a polysemous verb is motivated by the constructional semantics is nicely illustrated by the most strongly attracted collexeme *see*: as opposed to its prototypical perceptive meaning (which is relatively stative in nature), in the *go-and*-V construction, it takes on the more dynamic meaning 'watch'/'visit'; consider (13) and (14).

(13)   *I might go and see Aunt Violet*

(14)   *But, we pleaded, can we go and see a proper team like Sunderland next time*

Similarly, the third most strongly attracted collexeme, *sit*, the core meaning of which is also non-dynamic, yields an event-like interpretation in the *go-and*-V construction, as illustrated in (15) and (16).

(15)   *... middle-aged people that could go and sit in there for a drink*

(16)   *Or shall we go and sit at the café?*

So far, the results of the collostructional analysis largely confirm already established claims about the semantics of the *go-and*-V construction. However, the analysis also reveals some aspects about the usage of this construction that have hitherto not been noticed. One interesting aspect – which, admittedly, can only be detected if one considers all 112 significantly attracted collexemes of the construction – is that it is very frequently employed with verbs denoting cleaning and/or bodily hygiene such as *clean, scrub, shower, powder*, and *wipe*; these usages completely lack the derogatory or foolish connotation that typically characterizes a large part of the examples. Consider two typical examples in (17) and (18).

(17)   *go and tidy your rubbish up darling*

(18)   *I think I'll go and wash my hair*

This result is particularly interesting when being combined with the ESCO results (cf. Figure 1), which show that the verbs relating to (bodily) hygiene are all among the group of verbs which exclusively occur with *go-and*-V; this points towards the fact that *go-and*-V in fact has a specified semantic profile that is different from the one of *go*-V.

Let us now turn to the significant collexemes of *go*-V in Table 4 and their distribution with respect to situation types as shown in Table 5.[8]

Table 4. Collexemes most significantly attracted to/repelled by *go*-V

Attracted collexemes	Collostruction strength	Repelled collexemes	Collostruction strength
get	48.177	have	18.330
fuck	19.399	say	3.687
see	14.769	do	1.949
fetch	11.522		
work	6.950		
zoom	6.949		
tell	6.924		
buy	6.626		
look	6.480		
sleep	4.834		
figure	4.736		
walk	4.649		
park	4.140		
phone	3.674		
run	3.448		
check	3.240		
unbind	3.016		
play	2.972		
find	2.749		
plop	2.724		
post	2.719		
syndicate	2.658		
chase	2.636		
swim	2.445		
fondle	2.420		

Table 5. Distribution of situation types in all tokens of significant collexemes for *go*-V

Situation type	Token frequency
Activity	180 (54.4%)
Accomplishment	44 (13.3%)
Achievement	95 (28.7%)
State	12 (3.6%)
Column totals	331 (100%)

Interpreting Table 5, we find that a substantial number of *go*-V's attracted collexemes (44+95/331) belongs to the class of accomplishment and achievement verbs such as *check, fetch, find,* and *get*. However, the share of process verbs which are atelic is also considerably high. As for *go-and*-V, the collexemes most strongly repelled belong to the situation type class of states (cf. Table 3). Once we focus exclusively on the opposition pair of accomplishments/achievements and atelic activities/states, an interesting picture emerges; consider Table 6, which provides the observed frequencies (as well as the expected frequencies in parentheses) for these verb classes.

Table 6. Number of telic vs. atelic verbs for *go-and*-V

	Telic verbs	Atelic verbs	Row totals
go-and-V	2,274 (2,247)	2,217 (2,244)	4,491
go-V	139 (166)	192 (165)	331
Column totals	2,413	2,409	4,822

A Fisher-Yates exact test shows that *go*-V takes verbs denoting accomplishments/achievements less often than would be expected; this tendency is highly significant ($p_{\text{Fisher exact}} < .01$).

To conclude, the results of the collostructional analysis and the interpretation of the results in terms of situation types has shown that the two constructions are not semantically identical because the proportions of verb types they take differ notably. Moreover, these differences are not random, but can be described in a systematic pattern: while *go-and*-V prefers telic verbs, *go*-V preferably takes atelic process verbs. However, the two constructions also share features, e.g., both repel stative verbs.

5.2.2. Differences in terms of Levin's (1993) verb classes

In order to pinpoint the semantic differences between the two constructions, the classification of the verbs according to situation types obviously is too coarse-grained and does not lead us any further. Consider Table 7, which provides an overview of which of Levin's (1993) verb classes were instantiated by how many significant collexemes (of both constructions). For each verb class, at least one example of a significant collexeme is given. The first of the two frequency values given in each cell is the observed number of items among the significant collexemes of the respective construction for each semantic class; the second value in brackets is the expected frequency.[9]

A chi-square test shows that the overall distribution is significant ($\chi^2=301.46$; df=32; p<.001***[10]). Those cells which are responsible for this general significance, i.e., so-called contributions to chi-square, are printed in bold face. Finally, the plus or minus signs at the right top corners indicate whether the observed frequency is significantly higher or lower than expected.

The most interesting fact to be derived from Table 7 is that *go*-V significantly more often attracts verbs classified as relating to the body, motion and perception (I leave aside the statistical significance for the class of destroy verbs because only a single verb yields a significant value). That is to say, *go*-V favors verbs which, in their most typical sense, relate to physical behaviour and activity. In other words, whereas in the *go-and*-V construction, the dynamic aspect is part of the constructional semantics and motivates the choice of a correspondingly dynamic sense of a polysemous verb – even if this sense is a remote one – it appears that *go*-V rather prefers verbs which already carry this semantic property in their more prototypical, default senses.

Table 7. Distribution of Levin's (1993) verb classes

Verb class	Example	*go-and*-V	*go*-V
do	*do*	247 (244)	14 (17)
verbs of (dis)appearance / occurrence	*come, die*	20 (19)	– (1)
aspectual verbs	*start, continue*	12 (11)	– (1)
bear	*bear*	4 (4)	– (–)
body verbs	*sleep, smack*	17 (21)	6$^{\oplus}$ (2)
calve verbs	*foal*	1 (1)	– (–)
verbs of change of possession	*fetch, buy*	1,648 (1,649)	116 (115)
verbs of change of state	*freshen, boil*	9 (10)	2 (1)
verbs of combining/attaching	*baste, lock*	12 (11)	– (1)
communication verbs	*ask, tell*	359 (358)	24 (25)
concealment verbs	*hide*	20 (19)	– (1)
verbs of contact by impact	*knock, smash*	18 (17)	– (1)
verbs of creation/transformation	*change, prepare*	261 (261)	18 (18)
verbs of cutting	*nick*	3 (3)	– (–)
verbs of desire	*wish*	1 (1)	– (–)
destroy verbs	*wreck*	– (1)	1$^{\oplus}$ (–)
verbs of emission	*gurgle*	1 (1)	– (–)
verbs of existence	*live, stay*	103 (96)	–$^{\ominus}$ (7)
verbs of grooming/bodily care	*powder, wash*	38 (38)	– (2)
image creation verbs	*draw, write*	12 (11)	– (1)
verbs of ingesting	*eat, feed*	33 (31)	– (2)
measure verbs	*fit*	1 (1)	– (–)
motion verbs	*jump, run*	54 (74)	25$^{\oplus}$ (5)
perception verbs	*hear, see*	188 (229)	57$^{\oplus}$ (16)
verbs of assuming a position	*kneel, sit*	237 (227)	6 (16)
predicative complement verbs	*discover, prove*	678 (637)	3$^{\ominus}$ (44)
psych-verbs	*encourage, scare*	5 (6)	1 (–)
verbs of putting	*lay, stick*	133 (136)	12 (9)
verbs of removing	*clean, wipe*	24 (22)	– (2)
verbs of searching	*check, inspect*	99 (102)	10 (7)
verbs of sending/carrying	*post, send*	8 (9)	2 (1)
verbs of separating/disassembling	*unhook, unlace*	2 (2)	– (–)
verbs of social interaction	*hobnob, visit*	109 (108)	7
Column totals		4,357	304

5.2.3. Distinctive collexeme analysis

The third corpus-linguistic method applied to the data is a so-called distinctive collexeme analysis, which measures the dissimilarity of semantically similar constructions on the basis of their significant collexemes (cf. Gries and Stefanowitsch's [2004a, 2004b] extension of Church et al.'s [1991] technique to investigate distinctive collocates). Accordingly, the distinctive collexemes of two constructions are those words which distinguish best between the two constructions. Four frequency values enter into the computation of a collexeme's distinctiveness:

- the collexeme's lemma frequency in construction A,
- the collexeme's lemma frequency in construction B,
- the (added) frequencies of all other collexemes in construction A, and
- the (added) frequencies of all other collexemes in construction B.

These numbers are entered into a 2-by-2 matrix and are subjected to a Fisher-Yates exact test. A corresponding *p*-value tells us how distinctive a collexeme is for a particular construction; the smaller the value, the higher the collexeme's distinctiveness.

Let us have a look at the results obtained by the distinctive collexeme analysis and see in how far they support the assumptions made about the difference between the two constructions made so far. Table 8 displays all significant distinctive collexemes for *go-and*-V vs. *go*-V; for both constructions, we find the distinctive collexemes (in decreasing order of their distinctiveness) in the left-hand column, together with the ratio of their frequency in the constructions. For instance, the ratio of 357:8 of the collexeme *have* means that *have* occurs 357 times in the *go-and*-V construction, but only 8 times in the *go*-V construction, which renders *have* highly distinctive for *go-and*-V. In the right-hand column, the corresponding *p*-values for each collexeme are given.

As Table 8 shows, the distinctive collexeme analysis unanimously supports the results gained from the collostructional analysis: with the exception of *talk*, the overwhelming majority of the distinctive collexemes for *go-and*-V are verbs which may either have a stative or, as has been argued above, a dynamic reading which is selected if the verb is inserted into the construction (*have, sit, see, stand*). The distinctive collexemes for *go*-V, on the other hand, are mostly motion verbs (*run, fuck, walk, fly, swim*) or verbs which imply (ongoing physical) activity (*work, seek*). To conclude, the distinctive collexeme analysis supports the hypothesis about the semantic inequality of *go-and*-V and *go*-V.

Table 8. Distinctive collexemes for *go-and*-V and *go*-V

| *go-and*-V | | *go*-V | |
Collexeme	Distinctiveness	Collexeme	Distinctiveness
have (357:8)	5.769	*run* (4:8)	6.294
sit (162:5)	2.134	*fuck* (10:10)	6.138
see (675:40)	2.090	*work* (48:16)	4.640
stand (46:0)	1.640	*walk* (8:7)	4.188
talk (67:1)	1.593	*seek* (1:4)	3.754
collect (37:0)	1.318	*figure* (0:3)	3.318
		zoom (0:3)	3.318
		fly (1:3)	2.742
		give (38:10)	2.458
		sleep (10:5)	2.345
		swim (0:2)	2.211
		tell (101:17)	2.211
		pass (1:2)	1.993
		park (8:3)	1.757
		phone (8:3)	1.307

Moreover, bringing together the results obtained from the collostructional analyses and the ESCO analysis, we find that the group of collexemes which *go*-V does not share with *go-and*-V are exactly the ones which the collostruction and distinctive collexeme analyses identified as the ones best representing its constructional semantics, namely process verbs.

These findings, although they do not strictly preclude the possibility that *go*-V and *go-and*-V are related constructions or even that the shorter one was once derived from the longer one, nevertheless cast serious doubt on the hypothesis that *go*-V simply is a truncated form of *go-and*-V. If this were the case, one would expect that the core constructional semantics of *go-and*-V, namely its dynamism and event-like reading, are inherited by the more specific construction, *go*-V. However, in *go*-V constructions, the constructional semantics are reduced to "initiation of action/event", with a strong focus on the procedural aspects of this action or event, without it necessarily being brought to an (foreseen) end. This also ties in well with Shopen's (1971) above-mentioned observation that the linkage between V_1 and V_2 is stronger in the constructions lacking a conjunction in comparison to those including *and*. Moreover, the auxiliary-like function of *go* as noted by Stefanowitsch (2000) appears to be even stronger for *go*-V than for *go-and*-V, which is also reflected in its closer position to V$_2$.

6. Conclusion

This paper demonstrates that – contrary to the generative account – *go*-V and *go-and*-V do in fact instantiate separate constructions. That is, *go*-V is not a truncated surface variant which means the same as its mother structure, as generative approaches like the *Fake* and *Deletion* rule would imply, but the shortening process has also led to a change, or, more precisely, a reduction and re-focusing, in meaning. That is, while whatever action is denoted by *go-and*-V gains an event-like interpretation and is meant to embrace the whole sequence cascade of a typical event with a beginning and an end, the meaning of *go*-V only denotes the initiation of an action and is inherently atelic, which invites process verbs to occupy the V$_2$ slot. While the *Principle of No Synonymy* has formerly been tested only on the basis of classic 'alternation' phenomena, the results of the present analysis show that it holds also for constructions where one structure is considered a shortened surface form of the other, thereby taking a first step towards closing an empirical gap.

Moreover, this paper has made two strong methodological points. Firstly, it has emphasized the need for large-scale and representative data samples as well as an exhaustive examination of these data in order to yield a comprehensive picture of the actual range of usage of a pattern. The fact that former analyses (irrespective of their theoretical orientation) concluded that *go-and*-V and *go*-V must be synonymous comes as no surprise once we have a look at the collexemic overlap estimation of the two constructions, which nicely illustrated how misleading it may be to consider only the most frequently occurring attestations of a particular pattern. Secondly, the paper has shown how semantic differences between near-synonymous constructions like *go*-V and *go-and*-V can only be identified in combining several corpus-linguistic methods: while the ESCO analysis revealed that indeed a range of verbs occur in both constructions, the collostructional analyses revealed how those verbs which are not shared between the two constructions form fairly homogenous semantic groups in terms of aktionsart and Levin's (1993) semantic classes. Taken together, we find that these semantic differences are neither diffuse nor quantitatively marginal, but highly systematic and quantitatively significant.

Last but not least, in applying the corpus-linguistic techniques developed by Gries and Stefanowitsch to a research question other than the one(s) they were originally designed for, namely the field of constructional synonymy, the present paper may serve as a model how future research in related fields such as polysemy, word sense disambiguation, etc. can benefit from applying these methods, too.

Notes

1. With respect to the claim that *go-and*-V is strongly associated with informal style, I would like to point out that in the present data sample, 54% (2,876 items) of the *go-and*-V data as well as 56% (253 items) of the *go*-V data were obtained from the spoken subcorpus of the BNC, so it does not appear that the constructions are actually only associated with informal and colloquial register, but they are also frequently employed in written language.
2. It has to be noted here that with the exception of the work of Stefanowitsch (2000), all other approaches to V_1-(*and*)-V_2 constructions discussed here do not employ the term construction in the sense of construction grammar, but rather in a traditional sense.
3. A collexeme is any verb inserted into the V_2-slot of *go*-V/*go-and*-V which is significantly associated with the respective construction; cf. Section 5.2, where the method(s) employed for obtaining each construction's significant collexemes is explained in more detail.
4. I included only those forms which were unambiguously tagged as verbs or had a portmanteau tag with the verb tag first.
5. One final comment is in order here. One might object to the above kind of simulation since Figure 2 was concerned with significant collexemes while the Monte Carlo simulation was not – it counted collexemes irrespective of whether they had a significant association to any construction. However, performing the test as reported here should be an even more stringent test of the overlap hypothesis because the percentage of overlapping significant collexemes is much smaller than those of all collexemes (17.4% for *go-and*-V and 74.7% for *go*-V), so if the simulated overlap figures do not even reach the lower percentages of the significant collexemes, they cannot possibly reach those of all collexemes.
6. For reasons of space, I decided to present only the first 25 most significantly attracted/repelled collexemes for each construction. The overall number of significant collexemes amounts to 112 attracted/76 repelled collexemes for *go-and*-V and 45 attracted/3 repelled for *go*-V.

7. In the publications introducing collostructional analysis, the strength of association and repulsion is measured by the *p*-value of a Fisher-Yates exact test. In the present work, I use the negative logarithm to the base 10 of this *p*-value because the resulting numbers are easier to interpret. Accordingly, to reach a 5% level of significance, the value must be higher than 1.3, and a difference of one between two verbs' collostructional strength corresponds to a difference of one order of magnitude. For cases like *get* and *see* in Table 2 where the *p*-values are so small that the default settings of Coll.analysis 3 report them as infinite, I determined the actual ranking of the verbs by setting the program to use log-likelihood values (1,884.34 and 1,494.72 respectively) for ranking instead.
8. The fact that *go*-V has fewer significant collexemes than *go-and*-V can be seen as a mirror image of the general frequency of these constructions, *go*-V being much less frequent than *go-and*-V (454 vs. 5,320 tokens in the present data sample), as well as the correspondingly smaller number of different V_2 types occurring in the respective constructions (115 vs. 491 types).
9. *Do* and *bear* are not assigned membership in any particular class but are treated separately in Levin's (1993) analysis, which is why they are itemized here.
10. Strictly speaking, one cannot use the chi-square test for this table since more than 20% of the expected frequencies are smaller than five. The exact alternative which is not sensitive to such distributions, the Freeman-Halton test, proved to be computationally too expensive for such a large sample. Therefore, I conducted two Monte-Carlo-like simulations of multinomial tests to assess the degree of deviation between observed and expected cell frequencies (using mult.nom.test 1.0, an R script by, and available from, Stefan Th Gries). In the first simulation, I tested whether the observed distribution of verb classes for *go-and*-V could be obtained when the expected distribution is that following from the *go*-V verb classes. Thus, I drew 100,000 random samples of 4,491 constructions with the input probabilities of the *go*-V distribution and counted how often I obtained a distribution that deviated from the observed one as extremely or even more extremely. The second simulation was performed in the reverse direction, asking how often the distribution of verb classes for *go*-V was obtained when the expected frequencies followed from the *go-and*-V distribution. In both cases, i.e. all 200,000 simulations, not a single such distribution was obtained, which reflects that the distributions of verb classes in both constructions differ very strongly.

References

Carden, Guy and David Pesetzky
    1979   Double-verb constructions, markedness, and a fake co-ordination. *CLS* 13: 82–92.

Church, Kenneth W., William Gale, Patrick Hanks, and Donald Hindle
    1991   Using statistics in lexical analysis. In: Uri Zernik (ed.), *Lexical acquisition: Exploiting on-line resources to build up a lexicon*, 115–164. Hillsdale, NJ: Lawrence Erlbaum.

Eastwood, John
    1994   *Oxford Guide to English Grammar*. Oxford: Oxford University Press.

Goldberg, Adele E.
    1995   *Constructions: A construction grammar approach to argument structure*. Chicago/London: University of Chicago Press.
    1996   Construction grammar. In: Keith Brown and Jim Miller (eds.), *Concise Encyclopedia of Syntactic Theories*, 68–71. Oxford: Pergamon.
    2002   Surface generalizations: An alternative to alternations. *Cognitive Linguistics* 13 (3): 327–356.

Gries, Stefan Th.
    2001   A corpus-linguistic analysis of *-ic* and *-ical* adjectives. *ICAME Journal* 25: 65–108.
    to appear   New perspectives on old alternations. *CLS* 39.

Gries, Stefan Th., Beate Hampe, and Doris Schönefeld
    in press   Converging evidence II: More on the association of verbs and constructions. In: John Newman and Sally Rice (eds.), *Empirical and Experimental Methods in Cognitive/Functional Research*. Stanford, CA: CSLI Publications.

Gries, Stefan Th. and Anatol Stefanowitsch
    2004a   Extending collostructional analysis: A corpus-based perspective on "alternations". *International Journal of Corpus Linguistics* 9 (1): 97–129.
    2004b   Covarying collexemes in the into-causative. In: Michel Achard and Suzanne Kemmer (eds.), *Language, Culture, and Mind*, 225–236. Stanford, CA: CSLI Publications.

Hopper, Paul
    2002   Hendiadys and auxiliation in English. In: Joan L. Bybee and Michael Noonan (eds.), *Complex sentences in grammar and discourse: Essays in honor of Sandra A. Thompson*, 145–173. Amsterdam/Philadelphia: John Benjamins.

Huddleston, Rodney and Geoffrey K. Pullum
 2002 *The Cambridge Grammar of the English Language.* Cambridge: Cambridge University Press.
Jaeggli, Osvaldo A. and Nina M. Hyams
 1993 On the independence and interdependence of syntactic and morphological properties: English aspectual *come* and *go*. *Natural Language and Linguistic Theory* 11: 313–346.
Lakoff, George
 1987 *Women, Fire, and Dangerous Things. What Categories Reveal about the Mind.* Chicago/London: University of Chicago Press.
Levin, Beth
 1993 *English Verb Classes and Alternations. A Preliminary Investigation.* Chicago/London: Chicago University Press.
Moens, Marc and Mark Steedman
 1988 Temporal ontology and temporal reference. *Computational Linguistics* 14 (2): 15–28.
Quirk, Randolph, Sidney Greenbaum, Geoffrey Leech, and Jan Svartvik (eds.)
 1985 *A Comprehensive Grammar of the English Language.* London: Longman.
Shopen, Timothy
 1971 Caught in the act. *CLS* 7: 254–263.
Stefanowitsch, Anatol
 2000 The English *GO*-(PRT)-*AND*-VERB construction. *BLS* 26: 259–270.
Stefanowitsch, Anatol and Stefan Th. Gries
 2003 Collostructions: On the interaction between verbs and constructions. *International Journal of Corpus Linguistics* 8 (2): 209–243.
Vendler, Zeno
 1967 *Linguistics in Philosophy.* Ithaca, NY: Cornell University Press.

Syntactic leaps or lexical variation? – More on "Creative Syntax"

Beate Hampe and Doris Schönefeld[*]

Abstract

Based on a search in the British National Corpus for all occurrences of the verbs *encourage, fear, support,* and *bore* in complex-transitive argument-structures, which are more typically associated with other (causative) verbs, we continue to study the kind of creativity at work in "syntactic blends". The corpus data call for an extension of Goldberg's (1995) "fusion model" and suggest (i) that inputs of differing levels of schematicity may be involved: from fixed collocations, via (lexical) variations thereof to verb-class-specific and (finally) even fully schematic argument-structure constructions; and (ii) that lower-level schemas in the form of partially filled constructions with one or more variable slots (underlying strong lexical constraints) play a more important role than previously assumed. From this, we hypothesize that processes of schematisation over usage patterns plausibly also extract *item-based, mid-level schemas*, which must be assumed to be central to the creation of the expressions at issue.

Keywords: syntactic creativity; argument-structure construction; lower-level schema; quantitative corpus linguistics.

1. Introduction

1.1. Summary of preceding work

In "Creative Syntax" (Hampe and Schönefeld 2003), we started to explore the kind of syntactic creativity that can be observed whenever a verb is used with an argument structure much more typically associated with that of other verbs (/verb classes), as in the following examples randomly collected from journalistic and literary prose (1) and (2):[1]

(1) a. *He* supported *them through the entrance door.* (vs. push *through the door*)
　　b. *She* bore *them stupid.* (vs. make *stupid*)
　　c. *An Oxford student is* feared *drowned.* (vs. consider *drowned*)

(2) a. *She* paid *herself in at the hotel. (vs.* check *in)*
　　b. *The boiler* shuddered *to a halt. (vs.* come *to a halt)*

Each of these examples exhibits an extended verbal meaning and unusual syntactic structure, which could be said to be borrowed, derived, or "inherited" from these other verbs (/verb classes):

> ... a word can have distributional and semantic properties that *overlap with the properties of certain other words (or word-classes)*. We might say it "inherits" some of its grammatical properties, *in this use*, from the associated word. (Fillmore and Atkins 1992: 96, emphasis ours)

We argued that these creative verb uses presented instances of "syntactic blending" – quite analogously to such cases of morphological blending, as presented in (3).

(3)　*alcoholic, brunch, smog, infotainment*

While these are obviously created from two lexical items, whose formal integration (cf. Gries 2004a, 2004b) iconically signals simultaneous integration at the conceptual level (cf. Ungerer 1999), we also hypothesized the examples in (1) and (2) to be created through the formal integration of two verbal expressions such that one verb appears in the expression, but with the argument structure of the other.[2] Working within a semiotic framework, we speculated that, in each such example (at least as long as it is not yet available to speakers as an entrenched unit), the unusual, quasi-borrowed argument structure serves as a (diagrammatic) *iconic* clue to the intended interpretation in that it triggers the retrieval of at least one other verbal concept, more typically associated with the respective argument structure and fitting the contextual requirements. The intended meaning was hypothetically proposed to be arrived at through the conceptual integration/blending of the two verbal concepts thus activated.[3]

In (1c) *student feared drowned*, for instance, the hypothesis was that the verbal expression iconically triggered by the unusual argument structure in which the verb *fear* here occurs was one that more typically realises this argument-structure construction.[4] We intuitively regarded as potential candidates such verbs as the light verb *find* in its cognition sense, or perhaps the semantically less ambiguous mental verb *consider*, both exemplified in the following examples from the BNC (see Section 2.1 for corpus data concerning this issue).[5]

(4) a. *What if I* find *certain issues or situations difficult.*
    b. *Many people who use drugs regularly,* find *it difficult to exist in a drug-free world.*
    c. *And I shall* find *you empty of that fault.*

(5) a. *However, the reputation of the cataloguer may be in some instances* considered *decisive.*
    b. *Irish catholics were represented in the dominant culture as an inferior race, ridiculed and* considered *incompetent and beastly.*

1.2. Open issues: Construction-based "fusion" vs. verb(class)-based "blending"

> We have much more of an idea of the nature of the stuff that comes out of the mixer than we do about what goes into it. Blending by its nature obscures the input to the blend. (Barlow 2000: 324)

As an explicitly item-(/verb class) based explanation of syntactic creativity, our (2003) approach contrasted to some extent with the model currently dominant in construction grammar, Goldberg's "fusion model" (Goldberg 1995: 50–66; Goldberg and Jackendoff 2004: 534). Construction grammar (Goldberg 1995: 72–81) traditionally represents motivational links between constructions as "inheritance links", which capture the commonalities between constructions, while preserving the differences. In the normal mode of inheritance, also called "inheritance with overrides" (Lakoff 1987; Goldberg 1995: 73–74)

> ... information is inherited from dominant nodes transitively as long as that information does not conflict with information specified by nodes lower in the inheritance hierarchy. (Goldberg 1995: 73)

The fusion model is a special case of "inheritance with overrides" in which a verb "inherits" a syntactic slot from an argument-structure construction (ASC) it is not usually associated with. More specifically, the (fully schematic) ASC provides both a very generic meaning and a syntactic template (see the box in Figure 1), which gets fused with the semantic and syntactic frame of the verb at issue (see the dashed arrows in Figure 1). The ASC thus licenses both the semantic change incurred and the appearance of additional syntactic slots (see the bold arrow in Figure 1):

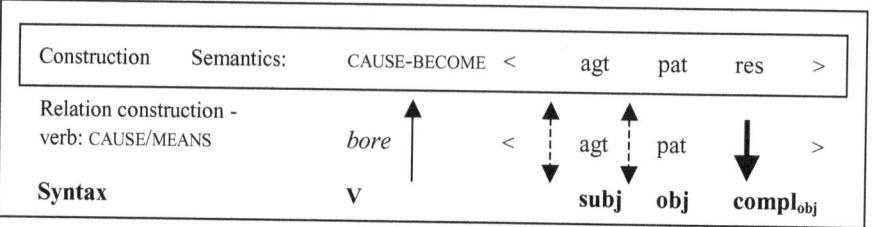

Figure 1. Role fusion for *bore somebody stupid* ("resultative" construction +*bore*) (cf. Hampe and Schönefeld 2003; adapted from Goldberg 1995: 54)

> An important innovation in the constructional view is that ... the VP's complement structure is not determined by the verb alone ... argument structure is determined by the *composite effects of the verb and the construction* ... the *verb does not change its meaning* so as to license these extra arguments. (Goldberg and Jackendoff 2004: 534, emphases ours)

On the one hand, our suggestions were in accordance with Goldberg's in that we did *not* assume creative verb uses to originate in extended verb meanings either. More specifically, we also avoided positing any immediate changes of the verbal semantics directly in the lexical entry – e.g., via "lexical rules" acting "directly on the verb's semantic representation transforming it into a new one", as suggested by Pinker (1989: 63, cf. also 1984), in whose model any changes in syntactic structure automatically arise from preceding changes in the semantic representation of the verb entry. A reverse process, however, in which frequent experiences of a verb in an unusual ASC may eventually result in the acquisition/entrenchment of new, extended verb senses, seemed highly plausible to us (see also the discussion of the corpus data in Section 2.2).

On the other hand, our suggestions diverged from Goldberg's in that we envisaged the ASC to play a *different* role than in her fusion model: we hypothesized the ASC to act as a trigger to the activation of another verb (/class) as input to a blending process.

Within the theory of conceptual integration as developed by Fauconnier and Turner (1995, 1998, 2002), Goldberg's "fusion" is treated as a form of grammatical blending. Fauconnier and Turner (1996), however, are not fully explicit about the exact nature of the inputs to this blending process in that they leave open whether these are the typical verbs (/verb classes) or the argument-structure constructions as fully schematic syntactic templates.

In fact, this difference is a very subtle one, and certainly very difficult, if not impossible, to determine solely on the basis of corpus data. While these are necessary to uncover plausible potential input candidates on the basis of associations in the lexicon, which cannot be identified through introspection, experimental evidence is needed to ascertain which of these are actually used/activated in on-line processing (see also Section 4; for a relevant methodological discussion, see Gries, Hampe and Schönefeld, in press a, in press b).

1.3. Methodological considerations

As our first attempt was not founded on corpus-linguistic methods, we were not able to determine what it meant for a verb to appear in an "unusual", "borrowed" or "inherited" syntactic structure, apart from intuitions mainly based on semantic considerations. This is an aspect of the problem at issue, however, which *can* be dealt with on the basis of corpus data alone.

We surmise that it makes sense to start out from a determination of the *typical*, rather than the unusual case. Depending on the perspective chosen, a typical verb use could be either of two things:

(a) A particular verb instantiates a given construction significantly more frequently (compared to other verbs) than expected on the basis of pure chance.

(b) A particular construction is significantly more frequent in the entire usage of a given verb (compared to other constructions) than expected on the basis of pure chance.

In the truly novel, creative case, in contrast, neither (a) nor (b) would be expected to hold, so that such verbal uses must be extremely rare in any corpus.

We will start out in Section 2.1 from an exemplary analysis of ASCs with adjectival object complements in the ICE-GB, a syntactically parsed one-million word corpus of contemporary written and spoken British English. As a means to check up on the intuitions presented above, we use a so-called "collexeme analysis" (Stefanowitsch and Gries 2003; Gries, Hampe and Schönefeld, in press a, in press b) for the determination of the verbs most typically realising this ASC, thus following perspective (a). This method from the family of "collostruction analyses" provides a measurement of the attraction between a construction and the lexical items realising it in a corpus by taking into account all of the frequencies given in Table 1 and calculating the significance of the differences between what has been observed and what would be expected to hold on the basis of chance alone by means of a Fisher-Yates exact test (cf. Stefanowitsch and Gries 2003; Gries, Hampe and Schönefeld, in press a, in press b):

Table 1. Input data for a collexeme analysis of a given construction

	Construction Y	¬ Construction Y
Verb X	A: *X in Y*	B: *X in other constructions*
		(= lemma frequency of X–A)
¬ Verb X	C: *Y with other verbs* (= construction frequency – A)	D: *Other verbs in other constructions* (= no of ASC – (A+B+C))

We retrieved all complex-transitive argument-structure constructions with adjectival object complements, by using the ICE-CUP software package to create queries for all verb phrases parsed as "complex-transitive" with an adjectival phrase non-immediately following or preceding a (notional) direct object (6a, b). The output was manually coded for true hits and provided us with 766 verb tokens of the ASC containing 45 different verb types.

(6)   a.   (,(, VP(cxtr) OD ,, AjP))
      b.   (,(, VP(cxtr) NOOD ,, AjP))

In Section 2.2, we follow perspective (b) – asking in what particular (grammatical) constructions a given verb tends (not) to appear – because this view enables lexically defined corpus searches. Since a corpus of one million words cannot provide a sufficient number of rare/unusual syntactic realisations, we used the entire British National Corpus (BNC 2, world edition: 100 million words), rather than the ICE-GB, to check all occurrences of four from our previous random collection of (supposedly) creative verbs – *encourage, support, bore, fear* – searching for any unusual syntactic realisations. In order to assess these frequency data with regard to what they reveal about lexical associations, we calculated the "collocation strength" (i.e., significance of co-occurrence) between the verbs and the lexical heads of the complement phrases (adjectival phrase/prepositional phrase) on the basis of the observed frequencies of co-occurrence in the corpus and the values expected from the corpus frequencies of the separate items (see Table 2). A parts-of-speech query provided by "Sara", the standard software accompanying the BNC2-world edition, was used to retrieve these frequencies: we only searched for items unambiguously tagged for the respective word class. Following Stefanowitsch and Gries (2003: note 6), the calculation of the significance of the relevant co-occurrence frequencies was again done by means of the Fisher-Yates exact test.

Table 2. Input data for a collexeme analysis of a given construction

	Lexical item Y	**¬ Lexical item Y**
Verb X	A: *X with Y*	B: *X with other lexical items* (= lemma frequency of X–A)
¬ Verb X	C: *Y with other lexical items* (= lemma frequency of Y–A)	D: *Other lexical items* (= corpus size – (A+B+C))

All of our results, both the collostruction-strength value and the collocation-strength values, are given in the form of the logarithm of the p-value: [*-log (Fisher-Yates exact, 10)*], from which the strength of attraction (positive value) or repulsion (negative value) can be directly read off:

- A collocation-strength value > 3 equals p<0.001.
- A collocation-strength value > 2 equals p<0.01.
- A collocation-strength value > 1.30103 equals p<0.05.

All calculations were done with an interactive program in R ("coll.analysis 2.1") written by Stefan Th. Gries and available from ⟨http://people.freenet/Stefan_Th_Gries⟩.

2. Presentation and discussion of the corpus results

2.1. (Classes of) verbs typically "attracted" by ASC

Of the 45 different verb types represented in the corrected corpus output for the argument-structure construction with adjectival object complements, traditionally called "resultative construction" in construction grammar, *make* turned out to be the most closely associated item, with *find* and *keep* next in the collexeme ranking (see Table 3). *Consider*, in contrast, did not turn out to be as strongly associated with the construction as assumed (with a p-value only marginally significant). The light verb *make* can be seen to represent an entire class of causative verbs, including also *render, get, set,* etc., all of which denote causation of change and are thus truly "resultative". Semantically closely related (in force-dynamic terms) is the light verb *keep* and the class it stands for (*leave, hold, have,* etc.), which denote the maintenance of a given state, and thus the *prevention*, rather than the causation, of change.

Table 3. Most strongly attracted collexemes of the "resultative" construction (Object complements = AjP) in the ICE-GB

collexeme	*obs. freq.*	*lemma freq. in the ICE-GB*	*exp. freq.*	*faith*	*collostruction strength* -log (Fisher exact, 10) attraction: (> 1.30103 => p<0.05)
1. *make*	359	1951	10.87	0.1840	INFINITE
2. *find*	109	941	5.20	0.1158	**106.1538549**
3. *keep*	79	412	2.28	0.1917	94.7225748
4. *leave*	36	583	3.22	0.0617	25.3462236
5. *render*	10	19	0.10	0.5263	17.6566792
6. *get*	53	3275	18.09	0.0162	11.1025367
7. *set*	8	323	1.78	0.0248	3.3076526
[...]					
16. *consider*	4	265	1.46	0.0151	1.2182389
total no of verb types: 45			**total number of verb tokens: 766**		

In contrast, the light verb *find*, which is also very closely associated with the ASC and appears in second position in the collostruction-strength ranking, represents a completely different class of verbs, to which *consider* belongs too, namely cognition verbs denoting the ascription of a property to the referent of the object noun phrase.[6] We call this second major verb class in the complex-transitive construction with adjectival object complements "attributive", rather than "resultative", to mark out the semantic difference.[7]

It has been argued (cf. Croft 2003) that such verb classes should be acknowledged as constructions in their own right (i.e., "verb-class specific constructions"), rather than be treated as the subsenses of one superordinate construction. The results of our collexeme analysis support this, which, for the present purposes, eliminates the question whether such a superordinate construction, i.e., the (fully schematic) ASC, is either polysemous, or semantically even more generic than the two verb-class specific meanings are.[8]

While this, as a theoretical issue, may be beyond our immediate concerns anyway, it is of much concern that the light verb *find* in the complex-transitive argument-structure construction with adjectival object complements – or rather: the entire "attributive" verb class it represents – provides a formally integrated clausal representation of a type of scenario/situation in which the subject-referent assigns a property to the object-referent. This is exactly what we expected an expression like (1c) *student feared drowned* to draw on. Note that the ASC with adjectival object complements, whose generic meaning is specified in Goldberg's (1995) constructional account as "resultative" (X CAUSE Y BECOME Z), does not provide the relevant semantics (X THINK Y BE Z) to be "inherited" by the verb use at issue here (see also Section 4).

We consider the use of *fear* in that construction (and "attributive" sense) as creative, because *fear* is an emotion verb not normally belonging to the verb class specified and not normally denoting this type of scenario. Secondly, our collexeme analysis also confirms that, at least in the ICE-GB, emotion verbs are generally not associated with this ASC – not a single instance of this class is to be found among the 15 significantly attracted verb types (nor among the 42 types not significantly repelled). The use of *fear* is still not unmotivated here, however, because the aspect of fear is so salient in a situation where one must consider someone dead or at least in great danger that it is chosen to encode the whole situation, and the "coercion" power (Taylor 1998: 194–195) of the "attributive" verb class in that ASC is seemingly strong enough to ascertain the right (i.e., "attributive") interpretation.

2.2. The converse perspective: (A-)typical syntactic uses of verbs

For all four verbs, whose complete usage data were retrieved from the BNC: *encourage, support, bore, fear,* it turns out that their instantiations in complex-transitive patterns with prepositional phrases and adjectival phrases, traditionally called "caused-motion" and "resultative" constructions, respectively, are both rare and felt to be unusual/creative to various degrees.[9]

(7) a. caused motion (literal): *He* supported *them* through *the entrance door.* / *We should be* encouraging *more shoppers* into *the town ...*
b. caused motion (metaphorical): *She ... refused all his efforts to* encourage *her* into *a more luxurious life.* / *Both families are staying close,* supporting *each other* through *their ordeal.*

(8) a. resultative: *She* bore *them* stupid.
b. attributive: *They* feared *him* drowned.

Table 4. Verb occurrences in complex-transitive constructions with object complements (PP/AjP) in the BNC

Verbs	Verb lemma frequency (BNC world-edition)	Frequency in caused-motion/ Resultative constructions (per cent)
encourage	10,650	81 (0.76 %)
support	15,317	38 (0.25 %)
bore	1,279	91 (7.11 %)
fear	4,045	38 (0.94 %)

To comment briefly on our terminology, we generally use the term "caused-motion construction" for complex-transitive patterns with object-related directional adverbials (prepositional phrase/adverbial phrase) – no matter whether literal or metaphorical – and employ the terms "resultative" and "attributive" to refer to the two formally similar, but semantically different ("verb-class specific") constructions with AjP/NP.

For reasons of feasibility, we restrict ourselves in this paper to a closer analysis of constructions with object-related complements in the form of either a prepositional phrase or an adjectival phrase as exemplified in (7) and (8).

2.2.1. The creative use of encourage

The frequency-based CCELD (1987: 464) records that encourage exhibits a mono-transitive argument structure (9a),[10] and that it also regularly occurs in a complex-transitive pattern with object-related *to*-infinitive denoting an event (cf. [9b]):

(9) a. V + O$_D$: *A natural substance that encourages cell growth.* (CCELD)
    b. V + O$_D$ + [$_{NFC}$ *to*-inf.]: *We want to encourage people to go fishing.* (CCELD)

In the more untypical cases given in (10a–d) below, which make up less than one per cent of all occurrences of the verb lemma *encourage* in the BNC (see Table 4), there are object-related adverbials instead, realised by prepositional phrases. This creative extension does not really present a syntactic leap to an entirely new argument-structure, but is a mere change from one complex-transitive pattern to another, less entrenched one. What gives the expressions their special – creative and expressive – feel, is that the originally spatial motivation of the *to*-infinitive re-appears in the caused-motion pattern, more specifically the directional adverbial.[11]

(10) a. *... this is as important as a varied diet to* encourage *birds* to *the garden / ... creating a pleasant 'shopping experience', possibly even* encouraging *tourists* into *the area.*
    b. *... if we are to support children in their reading we need to* encourage *them* into *libraries / ... more teachers should be* encouraged into *primary schools (especially men).*
    c. *The Open College of the Arts* encouraged *me* to *a course in music. / She hoped the award would* encourage *more women* into *industry. / ... schemes to* encourage *women* into *physics, chemistry or engineering are missing.*
    d. *Positive achievements act as good models and* encourage *other members* into *action. / ... an instrument to* encourage *the working classes* into *frugality.*

The examples in (10a–d) illustrate that there are fully literal as well as metonymic and metaphorical realisations of the caused-motion pattern. They show that processes of metonymy and metaphor either apply to varying extents to the landmarks only – realised by the respective noun phrases or by gerunds functioning as complements of the prepositions – or apply to the event as a whole. *Encourage* in the caused-motion syntax can thus refer to:

(a) the causation of literal movement as listed in (10a),
(b) motion to a goal which can be construed both spatially and metonymically, as in (10b),
(c) the metaphorical construal of a goal which can be traced back to the kind of metonymy presented in (b), as in (10c), and
(d) metaphorical conceptualizations of causation in terms of motion as licensed by the event-structure metaphor, as in (10d).

These usage data reveal collocational (i.e., lexical) restrictions in the realisation of the caused-motion pattern (see Table 5). More specifically, prepositions denoting goal-directed motion (*to, towards, into*) occur in the great majority of cases, while prepositions denoting the reversed direction are markedly absent: the one example with *away from* in the entire corpus (cf. [11]) is coordinated with a PP containing *towards*, thus additionally specifying the source of the movement – but not solely movement away from the goal:

(11) *She believed this was a prime factor* encouraging *Laura's shirt [an enterprise]* away from *garments* towards *home furnishing.*

The collocation-strength ranking reveals that *towards* and *into* are the only items significantly associated with the verb *encourage* ($p<0.001$) in the caused-motion use.

As regards the form of the complements of the prepositions, these are much more frequently realised as noun phrases than as gerunds. In fact, only 10 out of all the caused-motion uses of the verb *encourage* in the BNC exhibit the latter format, seven with *into*, exemplified in (12a), and three with *towards*, exemplified in (12b).[12]

Table 5. Caused-motion uses of *encourage*

Encourage: Constructions with object-related adverbial [PP]: 81				
word 1: *encourage*			freq 1: 10650	
word 2	freq 2	co-occ. freq	coll. strength	association
toward(s)	27272	14 (exp. 2.90)	**5.6301212**	attraction
into	157631	39 (exp. 16.79)	**5.6050512**	attraction
onto/on to	939878	5 (exp. 100.1)	35.7144275	repulsion
to	912606	20 (exp. 97.19)	20.8691484	repulsion
through	62347	1 (exp. 6.64)	2.0013825	repulsion
across	20708	2 (exp. 2.21)	0.2067287	repulsion
away from*	11417	1 (exp. 1.22)	0.1825167	repulsion
			* in coordination with *towards*	

(12) a. ... *the Kayan and the Penan peoples are being* encouraged – *some would say* coerced – *into leaving their scattered forest homes.* / ... *and friends often* encourage *each other* into *taking the drugs.* / ... *the success of Hammer* encouraged *other companies* into *working the same scene.*

 b. ... *it also* encouraged *me* towards *directing my own training school* / *This is the approach which* ... *seeks to* ... encourage *them [pupils]* towards *accepting* ... *that viewpoint.* / *The concept* encourages *South East arts* towards *passing over responsibility.*

In all constructions with gerund, the directional adverbials serve as metaphorical goals. The nominalized entities complementing the spatial prepositions are construed as profiled "abstract regions" (or unbounded things), i.e. as reified instances of a process type which are left "ungrounded" (cf. Langacker 1991: 33–34). In this respect, these expressions parallel example (10d) above: *encourage someone into action*, in which an event is likewise conceptualized as an abstract region, and metaphorically represented as a spatial goal of movement. Of all three potential constructions expressing caused, goal-oriented motion/action: (i) the *to*-infinitive, (ii) directional preposition plus noun phrase, and (iii) directional preposition plus gerund, the third possibility is the most marked one. It is more marked than (ii), as it competes with the *to*-infinitive itself – in that both the infinitive and the gerund directly evoke an instance of an entire event type expressed by a verb and its complementation. Thereby the *to*-infinitive is still closer to a verbal construal, allowing for aspect incorporation (Langacker 1991: 420–421). In contrast, in the more common construction with *to*-infinitive (i), the metaphorical conceptualization of causation as caused motion has entirely bleached out (see also note 11).

2.2.2. The creative use of *support*

There is a real syntactic leap to another argument structure in the case of *support*, which the CCELD (1987: 1469–1470) lists as exhibiting a monotransitive argument structure, referring to both spatial (ex 13a) and various metaphorical scenarios (13b–d).

(13) a. V + O_D: *He had to sit down because his knees wouldn't support him anymore.* (CCELD)
   b. V + O_D: *I've always supported her and I still do.* (CCELD)
   c. V + O_D: *They supported the war effort.* (CCELD)
   d. V + O_D: *She supports a family of three./ The valley had a vast population to support.* (CCELD)

The usage data from the BNC (see Table 4) show that, in a tiny fraction of all its occurrences, the verb also occurs in the caused-motion pattern, though there are less than 50 instances of it in a total of almost 16,000 occurrences of the lemma *support*, i.e. 3 per mille.

Again, there are in the corpus literal as well as metaphorical instantiations thereof, whereby the latter predominate with 33 out of 38 examples. The five literal instantiations of the caused-motion pattern, which are listed in (14) involve the causation of real movement, whereby often the complete path is specified by a whole sequence of prepositional phrases:

(14) *... and* supported *her up the stairs, past the paintings and the roses, and into her bedroom. / ... and he* supported *him out through the theatre door towards the car. / ... were* supported *into the inn / ...* supported *the old man over to his bed... / ... he ...* supported *him through to the bedroom.*

In the overwhelming majority of cases, the directional adverbial is metaphorically construed (15a–d):

(15) a. ... supported *Gwen, his third wife,* through *her battle against breast cancer over the last years* / ... *whose faith* ... supported *them* through *the hardships and challenges of recent years.* / ... *tutors will* support *learners* through *the process of problem-solving.* / ... *the ceramic society* supported *Mike* through *this transition.* / ... supporting *the counsellee* through *the process of change* ... / ... *we have lost many rituals that in the past have* supported *us* through *the various stages of grief.*
b. ... supporting *them* into *old age.* / ... *bizarre that he'd have to* support *me* into *my 30s.*
c. ... *they'd recommend the bank's board to* support *him* through *thick and thin.* / ... *she* ... supports *her husband* through *thick and thin.* / ... *the trade unions* supported *the party* through *thick and thin.* / ... *fans* ... supporting *the team* through *thick and thin.* / ... *the banks* ... supported *them* through *thin times and thick.* / ... *from the responsibility of* supporting *their corporate clients* through *thin times.*

The realisation of the newly acquired argument slots in the creative uses of *support* also underlie collocational constraints, with *through* being by far the most frequent preposition – as well as the only highly significantly associated one (see Table 6 below). Most restricted are metaphorical expressions, which almost exclusively exhibit prepositional phrases containing *through* (31 of 33 instances), with the exception of the two expressions with *into* given in (15b). The few literal uses in (14) seem slightly more flexible in that other prepositions do occur, but often in sequences of several prepositional phrases specifying together entire paths of movement, always containing as one of their elements again either *through*, or *into*.

In all 33 metaphorical uses, the landmark noun phrases complementing the prepositions exclusively denote some sort of crisis, hardship or undesirable change (ex [15a, 15b]). A special case of this is presented by the repeated occurrence, often in playful variation, of the fixed idiomatic expression *through thick and thin* (full list presented in [15c]).[13] The verb *support*, though certainly not negative by itself, thus carries a clear negative semantic "prosody" in the caused-motion construction,[14] reflecting that – in British culture – people are not generally conceptualized as being in need of support when experiencing good times.

Table 6. Caused-motion uses of *support*

Support: Constructions with object-related Adverbial [PP]: 38				
word 1: *support*			freq 1: 15317	
word 2	freq 2	obs. co-occ. freq	coll. strength	association
through	62347	32 (exp. 9.55)	**8.0701957**	**Attraction**
*up**	3424	1 (exp. 0.52)	0.3891795	Attraction
*past**	6269	1 (exp. 0.96)	0.2095515	Attraction
to	912606	2 (exp. 139.78)	56.9866492	Repulsion
into	157631	4 (exp. 24.14)	6.2662512	Repulsion
*toward(s)***	27272	1 (exp. 4.18)	1.1002954	Repulsion

* in conjunction with a sequence of PPs containing *into*
** only in conjunction with another PP containing *through*

2.2.3. The creative use of bore

Though the CCELD (1987: 154) documents that *bore* most typically/frequently exhibits a mono-transitive argument structure (16a), it also lists both the caused-motion construction (16b) and the resultative construction (16c) as possible uses of *bore*:

(16) a. V + O$_D$: *I won't bore you with the details.* (CCELD)
 b. V + O$_D$ + Adv$_O$ [PP]: *I like acting, but the film world bores me to tears.* (CCELD)
 c. V + O$_D$ + Compl$_O$ [AjP]: *The subject bores them stiff.* (CCELD)

In our data, *bore* instantiates these patterns in more than 7 per cent of all occurrences of the verb lemma (cf. Table 4). In contrast to the two verbs previously discussed, these uses of *bore* are clearly more entrenched as they are not only more frequent, but also show considerably higher "collocation-strength" values. They are recognized by lexicographers as "fixed informal expressions". The CCELD, for instance, lists the following realisations of the object-related adverbial (17a) and complement (17b), respectively:

(17) a. X *bore* Y [$_{PP}$ *to tears/death*]
 b. X *bore* Y [$_{AjP}$ *stiff*]

The corpus results (see Table 7) indicate that this inventory of idiomatic expressions can be extended for British English, including at least also *X bore Y [AjP stupid]* – with *stupid* representing a further closely associated adjective class, and *X bore Y [PP out of Y's mind]* (see [19a] below).

The results further demonstrate that the lexically determined PPs/AjPs do allow for limited (though sometimes semantically rather rash) variations of these phrases. More specifically, other lexical elements from the same semantic fields as *tears/death,* and *stiff/stupid* appear (ex [18a,b]), which relate to either highly undesirable states-of-mind, or – more extremely – to death. All variations in the attributive syntax (18b) are closely associated with the verb in this pattern ($p<0.001$), i.e., are relatively entrenched.

(18) a. variations of the landmark of the PP of (16a):[15]
  – to *distraction* (3x, see idiomatic phrase *drive to distraction*), to *malevolence*
  – to *pieces*
 b. variations of the object complement of (16b):[16]
  – *witless*
  – *rigid* (9x)

The instances in the data set, where the preposition itself is varied to *out of* (19a), or *into* (19b), go beyond such closely analoguous cases, with the former preposition also being strongly associated with the verb ($p<0.001$) and the latter being the only one repelled by it (see Table 6).

(19) a. variations of the form *bore X [out of NP]*:[17]
  – out of *one's mind* (9x), out of *one's brain*, out of *one's ear*, out of *one's skull*
 b. variations of the form *bore X [into NP]*:[18]
  – into *stone*

Mostly, the items used in the variations of the constructions with a prepositional phrase (ex [18a, 19a, 19b]) are highly expressive, and are related to the model items *[to death], [to tears]* and *[out of one's mind]* via metonymy, usually involving hyperbole.

There are basically two different construals to be found within the caused-motion uses of *bore*. In the majority of cases, the person is construed as the trajector of the preposition (= the direct-object noun phrase), as in *bore sb. to distraction*. The examples in (20a, 20b) with the preposition *off*, however, reveal that the person can also be construed as the landmark of the preposition, and that this preposition is also very strongly associated with the verb (p<0.001). In these expressions with the preposition *off*, a taboo body part (20a) and, euphemistically, pieces of clothes (20b), respectively, serve as the trajector of the preposition. Since this second construal is marked by a change in word order (i.e., person as prepositional instead of direct object), this variation is no longer purely lexical, though it appears lexicalized as one major caused-motion use of *bore* in contemporary British English:

(20) a. bore *the ass* off *sb.* (2x.)[19]
     b. bore *the pants* off *sb.* (3x)[20]

In sum, though the use of the verb *bore* in the caused-motion and resultative patterns has to be regarded as firmly entrenched, there is also some lexico-syntactic variation to be found in the usage data, including some bolder variations in construal – all of which appear to be significantly associated with the verb, i.e. relatively entrenched.

Table 7. Survey of caused-motion and resultative uses of *bore*

Bore: Constructions with object-related adverbial [PP]/ object complement [AjP]: 91				
	word 1: *bore*		freq 1: 1279	
word 2	**freq 2**	**obs. co-occ. freq**	**coll. strength**	**association**
construal (1): person as direct object (trajector of PP)				
to tears	208	15 (exp. 0.02)	**51.00379**	attraction
to death	1739	19 (exp. 0.01)	**48.59901**	attraction
out of x's mind	379	9 (exp. 0.04)	**26.44583**	attraction
stiff	966	19 (exp. 0.01)	**53.480631**	attraction
rigid	1407	9 (exp. 0.02)	**21.293606**	attraction
stupid	3089	4 (exp. 0.04)	**7.009998**	attraction
witless	38	2 (exp. 0.00)	**6.939776**	attraction
out of	46889	12 (exp. 0.60)	**11.6058833**	attraction
to	912606	39 (exp. 11.67)	**9.7377729**	attraction
into	157631	1 (exp. 2.02)	0.3963701	repulsion
construal (2): person as prepositional object (landmark of PP)				
off	8060	5 (exp. 0.10)	**7.0541873**	attraction

2.2.4. The creative use of *fear*

Fear most typically exhibits a mono-transitive argument structure (CCELD 1987: 522), whereby the objects can be instantiated by noun phrases or non-finite clauses (21a/b):

(21) a. V + O$_D$: *A woman whom he disliked and* feared. / *He* feared *nothing.* (CCELD)
   b. V + O$_D$: *Some pilgrims ventured no further than this,* fearing *to disturb the priest.* (CCELD)

In our data, it also marginally, i.e., in less than one per cent of all occurrences of *fear* (cf. Table 4 above), appears in what we have called the "attributive" pattern (see Section 1.1). More specifically, of a total of about 4,000 occurrences of the verb lemma, there are 38 examples exhibiting an object-related adjectival complement, as in (22):

(22) *Hundreds of people are* feared dead *after a mining disaster.*

Table 8. Resultative uses of *fear*

Fear: Total number of constructions with object complement [AjP]: 38

word 2	word 1: *fear* freq. 2	obs. co-occ. freq.	freq. 1: 4045 coll. strength	association
dead	10873	19 (exp. 0.44)	24.068433	attraction
drowned	230	4 (exp. 0.01)	9.520830	attraction
killed	216	3 (exp. 0.01)	6.963216	attraction
trapped	151	2 (exp. 0.01)	4.733976	attraction
buried	153	2 (exp. 0.01)	4.722532	attraction
damaged	1	1 (exp. 0.00)	4.393081	attraction
kidnapped	1	1 (exp. 0.00)	4.393081	attraction
murdered	230	2 (exp. 0.01)	4.368405	attraction
missing	1430	2 (exp. 0.06)	2.793608	attraction
lost	2255	2 (exp. 0.09)	2.407473	attraction

There are again restrictions on this particular usage, both of a lexical and syntactic type. Regarding the latter, it is noteworthy that all of our examples are in the passive voice, and all, except one, have human object-referents (here occurring in the subject position of the passive clauses). As for the former, half of our examples employ the adjective *dead* as an object-related complement, which is also the by far most closely associated collocate (see Table 8), while all other adjectives come from the same semantic field and are either hyponyms to the model-adjective *dead* or are otherwise closely related to it in the relevant semantic frames.[21] The only exception to this in the data is presented in (23). This example has an inanimate subject-referent (*supplies*) and, accordingly, an adjectival complement reflecting this.

(23) *Tests are carried out on* supplies feared damaged *in a major chemical fire*.

The collocation-strength values given in Table 8 show all of the lexical variations found to be significantly associated with the verb *fear*: the verb use, in terms of entrenchment, is thus not too different from what has been presented in the previous section for *bore*, even though (1) the percentage of complex-transitive uses is much smaller in the case of *fear* (see Table 4), and (2) even though the attributive use of *fear* is not recorded in dictionaries (yet) – and the OED (Online) does not record its use in that structure to date.

3. Speculating about the origin of syntactic creativity

On the basis of data on lexical associations in the BNC, we will now speculatively discuss what potential motivations for the attributive use of, e.g., *fear* might have looked like – i.e., from which other constructions *fear* might have "inherited" aspects of its resultative usage. The "attributive", verb-class specific ASC with adjectival object complements, represented by the light-verb construction with *find*, provides a relevant generic meaning, but would – even in combination with the lexical verb to *fear* – still not be sufficient to motivate the collocational restrictions uncovered for the "attributive" use of *fear* – there are other things to be feared, after all, besides death. If this is not just an accident, it might stem from the nature of the input material(s) to the blending/fusion process.

In the previous section, we identified the collocation of *fear* with *dead* as a kind of "master collocation", because of its exceptionally high collocation strength (see Table 8), and regarded as mere variations on this model all other expressions, the adjectival slots of which are either filled by hyponyms of *dead* or frame-semantically closely related adjectives. As all expressions instantiating it occur only in the passive voice, we suggest the relevant lower-level schematization to be more specifically (24). Its only variable constituent is the direct object of the verb surfacing in the corpus occurrences as the passive subject and being almost exclusively realised by a noun phrase referring to a human being:[22]

(24) *X (be) feared dead*

The identification of this lexically determined pattern for an explanation of the creative uses of *fear* is begging the question, however, since the pattern itself must at some stage have emerged as an extended, unusual use of the verb *fear*. Collocational data from the BNC regarding the complex-transitive uses of *find* in its various literal and non-literal uses, might at least provide further hints at the kinds of material that might have motivated the original, "creative" production of (24) in the first place:

Find as a light verb in the "attributive construction" does *not* collocate with *dead* in the BNC. Instead it co-occurs with – predominantly negatively connoted – adjectives such as *hard, difficult, boring, tiring, depressing, impossible, frustrating*, making up about two thirds of all cases. Occasionally, it also co-occurs with positively connoted adjectives, such as *useful, easy, fascinating, interesting, appealing, exciting, helpful*:

(25) *I* found *it very traumatic and distressing. / I'm* finding *that totally impossible. / I* find *it fascinating. / I've never* found *writing easy.*

Find, as a main verb, however, *does* collocate with the adjective *dead*, almost exclusively in fully literal, passivized expressions (*find dead*: obs. 305, exp. 9.82; colloc. strength (-log(fisher exact, 10)): INFINITE ATTRACTION, $p < 0.001$). These expressions refer to another, highly specific and more concrete scenario, in which the object referent is literally found in the state denoted by the adjective *dead* (example 26), thus also denoting an attributive relation between the two:

(26) *A man has been* found *dead in a police cell at Greenock, Strathclyde / ... the bookseller was* found *dead in his office in circumstances suggesting foul play.* (BNC)

From this, we hypothesize that the use of *fear* in the syntax of the attributive construction is probably motivated by multiple inputs of varying levels of abstraction, or schematicity:

- Potential model verbs, from the class of cognition verbs strongly associated with the syntactic construction and represented by the light-verb *find*, provide integrated scenarios of mental events, in which an experiencer attributes a feature/quality to the direct-object referent.
- Further model verbs may even provide lexically filled model collocations, such as *X (be) found dead*, from which a specific "creative" collocation like *X (be) feared dead* may be formed by lexically manipulating the model pattern in only one slot, creating an otherwise highly analoguous expression. Such a single creative collocation may in turn give rise to lexical variations of its own slots, as observed in the previous section.

A similar speculation could be applied to the caused-motion uses of *encourage* and *support*, which also show clear master collocations, namely: *encourage X towards/into Y* and *support X through Y*. It is not implausible to assume that these, too, are likely to be modelled after the more entrenched uses of other verbs in that pattern with exactly these prepositions. Sometimes a particular expression, such as the first example of the *into*-causative in (12a): *... the ... peoples are being encouraged – some would say coerced – into leaving their scattered forest homes*, gives away a candidate for a more entrenched model collocation: *coerce X into Y* (obs: 63, exp: 0,21, collocation strength: 136.98735 ATTRACTION, $p < 0.001$). For the caused-motion uses of *encourage* in general, it could also be such caused-motion verbs *drive X into Y* (obs: 119, exp: 19.45; collocation strength: 51.911644 ATTRACTION, $p < 0.001$), or *steer X towards Y* (obs: 5, exp: 0.27; collocation strength: 5.011313 ATTRACTION, $p < 0.001$). For the caused-motion uses of *support*, for instance, these might be such caused-motion verbs as *guide X through Y* (obs: 14, exp: 0.11; collocation strength: 24.633 ATTRACTION, $p < 0.001$)., *escort X through Y* (obs: 5, exp: 0.04; collocation strength: 9.009 ATTRACTION, $p < 0.001$).

In sum, the birth place of syntactic creativity might be presented by fully lexical, and highly local processes of analogical variation, with the mechanism being strongly reminiscent of the local, lexicon-driven processes found in children's first acquisition of ASCs (see: the "verb-island" hypothesis, Tomasello 2000b). Rather than being merely motivated by ASCs, "creative syntax" – with the term misleadingly implying a dominant role of high-level schematizations – may turn out to be a matter of "inheritance"/ "fusion" between constructions at various levels of schematicity, particularly (partially) lexically filled ones.

4. Summary and conclusions: Beyond the fusion model

We showed three of the verbs discussed, *encourage*, *support*, and *fear*, to be used "creatively" in a tiny fraction of all of their occurrences (less than one per cent), in which they exhibit an extended semantics, i.e. a "causative" or "attributive" sense, as well as an argument slot not present in their most typical uses. This contrasted to some extent with the usage of the verb *bore*, in which caused-motion and resultative uses, though still not central, are relatively more frequent (about seven per cent), and must be regarded as firmly entrenched – in particular as they are lexicalized as caused-motion/resultative idioms. The collocation-strength values of many of the collocations found with the other verbs, and especially those found with *fear*, however, show this difference to be one of *degree*, not kind. More exactly, they can be related to the extent to which a given construction, however "creative" when first used with an atypical lexical item, may get gradually more entrenched among language users. Vice versa, the collocation-strength values also mark out some variations of entrenched patterns as novel/unusual.

As our speculation about such novel uses already suggests, we take the corpus results presented in Sections 2.1 and 2.2 to indicate that the creativity at issue is not necessarily *merely* syntactic in nature – i.e., not *exclusively* based on the respective ASC (fully schematic syntactic templates) as second input to processes of fusion/blending.

From the collexeme analysis in 2.1 we concluded that the complex-transitive construction with object-related adjectival complements, as a fully schematic syntactic template, is in principle unspecified for either a strictly "resultative" (X CAUSE Y BECOME Z) or an "attributive" (X THINK Y BE Z) interpretation, and thus cannot bring any of these meanings to a process of "fusion" or "blending" with verbs that do not already exhibit these as part of their established semantics. Therefore, we suggested that it may instead be the most strongly attracted light verbs *make* and *find* (together with the entire verb-classes they represent in that construction). In Section 2.2, we demonstrated that the newly acquired argument-slots (i.e., the object complements) of all creatively used verbs underlie strong *collocational restrictions*. This is our most important finding, which a model of fusion with the ASC alone would neither predict nor explain. Neither would they be expected from an extended model of fusion based on verb-class specific meanings, or the corresponding light-verb constructions. We speculated in the previous section that these collocational constraints may indicate that what is treated as a merely syntactic (i.e., ASC-driven) type of creativity in Goldberg's "fusion model" may be governed, to variable extents, by lexical processes. These may occur at even lower levels of schematicity than that presented by the verb-class specific/light-verb constructions, such that the "syntactic leap" from one ASC to another may have its origin in the lexical manipulation of "master collocations" serving as models for closely analoguous uses.

We take our corpus data to indicate two points: Firstly, argument-structure constructions are not as central to the process as some lower-level (i.e., partially lexically filled) constructions, including the verb-classes represented by the most closely attracted light verbs (vis-à-vis fully schematic argument-structure constructions), and might play a more important role than hitherto assumed in construction-based accounts. Secondly, multiple related inputs of varying degrees of schematicity may be involved, with completely lexically filled schemas (fixed expressions) at the one end of the continuum – and syntactic templates, i.e., argument-structure constructions at the other end of it. We would like to stress, though, that any such conclusions cannot be drawn on the basis of corpus data alone, but would have to be corroborated by experimental evidence.

Still, on a more general plane, the tendency towards a heightened role of lower-level schemas in the process of extending a language's resources is also in line with the assumption of collocations, or rather lexically filled chunks, as elements of a usage-based model of syntax and as plausible elements of a speaker's linguistic repertoire (Schönefeld 2001: 244f). It has been stressed before in the literature (e.g., Barlow 2000: 324) that such chunks can be modified in various ways as well as combined – in the sense of truly blended – as required by the ideas to be verbalized.

> ... lower-level schemas, expressing regularities of only limited scope, may on balance be more essential to language structure than high-level schemas representing the broadest generalizations. (Langacker 2000: 3)

Notes

* The order of the authors merely follows the alphabet. This paper originated in a talk given at the *4th Symposium on Iconicity in Language and Literature* (Louvain-la-Neuve, March 2003). We wish to thank the editors as well as anonymous reviewers for their insightful comments on earlier versions of this paper; we would also like to acknowledge valuable feedback on various occasions by Sylvia Adamson, Holger Diessel, Olga Fischer, Ad Foolen, Adele Goldberg, Willem Hollmann, and Michael Tomasello, which helped us a lot to clarify our ideas. All remaining insufficiencies are entirely our own.
1. The exact sources from which these isolated authentic examples were collected are given in Hampe and Schönefeld (2003).
2. An interesting question to pose in this context concerns the role of intention in the creation of "syntactic blends", as the processes involved in speech errors of the syntactic contamination type, which result in similarly mixed expressions, may be the same.
3. In detail, we hypothesized several formal cues of the "deviant" form to be iconic reflections of the blending processes going on at the conceptual level, which might instruct the listener how to unpack the meanings of verbs that occur with verbal complementations usually not "their own": (i) retrieve the concept referred to by the verb occurring in the expression, (ii) retrieve a second verbal concept, normally and more typically occurring in the syntactic frame of the expression at hand, (iii) meaningfully blend the two concepts to produce a third, contextually appropriate event conceptualization. The cues involved in part (ii) of this "instruction" were specified as being diagrammatic icons of the second degree, whereas (iii) exposes a process-related type of iconicity.
4. The construction in question is the complex-transitive argument-structure construction with adjectival object complements, usually called "resultative construction" (cf. e.g. Goldberg 1995).
5. If not indicated otherwise, all examples in the text are quoted from the BNC 2 (world edition).
6. For an in-depth analysis of a closely related construction, the *as*-predicative, in terms of collostruction strength rankings vs. frequency rankings, see Gries, Hampe and Schönefeld (2005).
7. There is even a third verb-class specific meaning detectable in the data, which we call the "denominative" meaning of the ASC with adjectival object complements. It is represented in the list of collexemes by *declare* (14th position [coll. strength = 1,4425, p<0.05]) and *call* (not significantly attracted, coll strength = 0.8136). The latter light verb is the one item most strongly attracted to the ASC with nominal object complements (see note 8).
8. Parallel ICE-GB investigations for the constructions with object-complements

as noun phrases (and object-related adverbials as prepositional phrases yielded the following results [Hampe 2005]: in the former, the light verbs *call* [coll strength: 150.406, other significantly attracted verbs in the order of decreasing coll. strength: *proclaim, declare, dub*] and *make* [coll strength: 73.388, other items: *render*] turned out to be most strongly attracted to the ASC, representing what we call the "denominative" and the "resultative" class, respectively. The "attributive" verb class, again represented by *find* [coll. strength: 1.463; other verbs: *feel, see, think*] is less central: In the caused-motion pattern with the prepositional phrase, the light verbs most strongly attracted were *put* [attraction: inf] and *keep* [attraction: 67.544] representing the "causation of motion" sense/verb class [other significantly attracted verbs in the order of decreasing coll. strength: *bring, get, place, take*] and a related "maintenance of location" sense/verb class [other verbs: *have, leave*], respectively. The "resultative" sense of the caused-motion pattern with the prepositional phrase is a third, less central, class, with *turn* being most strongly associated [pos. 9 in the ranking, coll. strength: 16.602, other verbs: *convert, reconvert, remodel, transform, shape*]).

9. The resultative construction was originally assumed to be metaphorically related to the caused-motion construction at the level of the ASC (Goldberg 1995: 81–89): In the complex-transitive pattern SUBJ V OBJ COMPL [PP], the prepositional phrase often denotes a location only metaphorically, and refers to a goal-state resulting from a given action (*X drive Y to despair*), rather than to a location reached as the result of some motion (*X drive Y to the station*). This is very close to the pattern with object-related complement: SUBJ V OBJ COMPL [AjP], in which the adjectival phrase refers to the resulting state of an action (*X drive Y mad*). Quirk et al. (1985: 732–733) noted that the more traditional distinction between complements and adverbials breaks down here, as such metaphorical prepositional phrases behave like complements rather than adverbials. The distinction between "caused-motion" and "resultative" construction has not been maintained by some authors in more recent work (Bencini and Goldberg 2000: 646; Boas 2003: 88–117; Broccias 2003: 2; Goldberg and Jackendoff 2004).

10. CCELD stands for *Collins Cobuild English Language Dictionary*. London, etc.: Collins 1987.

11. This may be seen as a return to a motivation previously lost in the process of grammaticalization (cf. Fischer 1999: 357), as the metaphors, which originally motivated the complex-transitive pattern with *to*-clause, were spatial ones involving directions and goals of movement. Under the EVENT-STRUCTURE METAPHOR complex, *to*-clauses construe an entire event as a bounded region, the goal, with *to* serving as a marker of directionality. The non-finite clause can thus appear in the same position as the adverbial in the SVOA pattern of caused motion: *They encouraged her to finish her thesis./*They encouraged*

her finish her thesis./*They encouraged her finishing her thesis. With such verbs as *encourage*, the pattern has thus come to denote "abstract" causation (cf. Fischer 1999: 357).

12. The gerunds with *into* are instances of the so-called *into*-causative (Gries and Stefanowitsch 2004): it is noteworthy that the semantics of *encourage* is notably different (in that it is strongly positively connoted) from that of the lexical items most closely associated in the corpus used for their study: *trick, fool, coerce, force, mislead, bully, deceive, con, pressurize, provoke*.

13. The verbs habitually co-occurring with [PP *through thick and thin*] in the BNC are either stative verbs (*stand/stick by sb.; back sb*)., movement verbs (*come, follow sb.*), or action verbs (*carry sb.*). All of these have the prepositional phrase *through thick and thin* as an adjunct, rather than a complement (as in the caused-motion pattern). One example in the Collins Online, however, unambiguously requires a caused-motion interpretation: "... Shelter ... will *see us through thick and thin*." (CO, *ephem*) We would like to argue that the caused-motion syntax forces onto all examples in (14b) the argument reading of the prepositional phrase.

14. The term "semantic prosody" is used to refer to a collocational phenomenon: The analysis of patterns to be found around words – in our case the verb *support* – reveals associations with particular types of events – here unpleasant ones – though the words (verbs) by themselves are unmarked (or "innocent") for the respective association. Sinclair (1987: 155–156) uses the term "prosody" in the same sense as Firth, thus indicating that the phenomenon named by it extends over more than one unit (cf. Louw 1993: 158).

15. Additional variations to be found in the British part of the "Collins Online": *bore sb. to hell/defeat/shit*.

16. Additional variations to be found in the British part of the "Collins Online": *bore sb. senseless/silly/sick/shitless/frustrated*.

17. Additional variation to be found in the British part of the "Collins Online": *bore sb. out of their wits*

18. Additional variations to be found in the British part of the "Collins Online": *bore sb. into surrender/coma/hypnosis/trouble/mistake*.

19. Additional variation to be found in the British part of the "Collins Online": *bore the hell out of sb*.

20. Additional variation to be found in the British part of the "Collins Online": *bore the anoraks of sb*.

21. Additional variation to be found in the British part of the "Collins Online": *feared abducted/incapable*.

22. Our usage of the term "schema" corresponds to Langacker's (1991: 1–10) understanding, who defines (constructional) schemas as both schematic and symbolically complex units – at different levels of specificity – reflecting the commonality observable across a set of complex expressions.

References

Barlow, Michael
    1996   Corpora for theory and practice. *International Journal of Corpus Linguistics* 1: 1–37.
    2000   Usage, blends and grammar. In: Michael Barlow and Suzanne Kemmer (eds.), *Usage-based Models of Language*, 315–346. Stanford, CA: CSLI Publications.

Barlow, Michael and Suzanne Kemmer
    1994   A schema-based approach to grammatical description. In: S. Lima, R. Corrigan, and G. Iverson (eds.), *The Reality of Linguistic Rules*, 19–42. Amsterdam/Philadelphia: John Benjamins.

Bencini, Giulia M. L. and Adele E. Goldberg
    2000   The contribution of argument-structure constructions to sentence meaning. *Journal of Memory and Language* 43: 640–651.

Biber, Douglas, Susan Conrad, and Randi Reppen
    1998   *Corpus Linguistics. Investigating Language Structure and Use*. Cambridge: Cambridge University Press.

Boas, Hans C.
    2003   *A Constructional Approach to Resultatives*. Stanford, CA: CSLI Publications.

Broccias, Cristiano
    2003   *The English Change Network. Forcing Changes into Schemas*. Berlin/New York: Mouton de Gruyter.

Croft, William
    2003   Lexical rules vs. constructions. A false dichotomy. In: Cuyckens, Hubert, René Dirven, and Klaus-Uwe Panther (eds.), *Motivation in Language*, 49–68. Amsterdam/Philadelphia: John Benjamins

Fauconnier, Gilles and Mark Turner
    1996   Blending as a central process of grammar. In: Adele E. Goldberg (ed.), *Conceptual Structure, Discourse and Language*, 113–130. Stanford, CA.: CSLI Publications.
    2002   *The Way We Think. Conceptual Blending and the Mind's Hidden Complexities*. New York: Basic Books.

Fillmore, Charles J. and Beryl T. Atkins
    1992   Towards a frame-based lexicon: the semantics of RISK and its neighbors. In: Adrienne Lehrer and Eva Feder-Kittay (eds.), *Frames, Fields and Contrasts*, 75–102. Hillsdale, NJ: Lawrence Erlbaum.

Fischer, Olga
    1999   On the role played by iconicity in grammaticalization processes. In: Max Nänny and Olga Fischer (eds.), *Form Miming Meaning. Iconicity in Language and Literature*, 345–374. Amsterdam/Philadelphia: John Benjamins.

Goldberg, Adele E.
    1995   *Constructions. A Construction-Grammar Approach to Argument Structure*. Chicago, IL: The University of Chicago Press.
    1997   The relationship between verbs and constructions. In: Marjolijn Verspoor, Kee-Dong Lee, and Eve Sweetser (eds.), *Lexical and Syntactical Constructions and the Construction of Meaning*, 383–398. Amsterdam/Philadelphia: John Benjamins.
    1998a   Patterns of experience in patterns of language. In: Michael Tomasello (ed.), *The New Psychology of Language*, 203–219. Hillsdale, NJ.: Lawrence Erlbaum.
    1998b   Semantic principles of predication. In: Jean-Pierre Koenig (ed.), *Discourse and Cognition: Bridging the Gap*, 41–54. Stanford, CA: CSLI Publications.
    1999   The emergence of argument structure semantics. In: Brian MacWhinney (ed.), *The Emergence of Language*, 197–212. Hillsdale, NJ: Lawrence Erlbaum.

Goldberg, Adele E., Devin M. Casenhiser, and Nitya Sethuraman
    2004   Learning argument-structure generalizations. *Cognitive Linguistics* 15: 289–316

Goldberg, Adele E. and Ray Jackendoff
    2004   The English resultative. A family of constructions. *Language* 80: 532–568

Gries, Stefan Th.
    2004a   Shouldn't it be *breakfunch*? A quantitative analysis of the structure of blends. *Linguistics* 42: 639–667.
    2004b   Isn't that fantabulous? How similarity motivates intentional morphological blends in English. In: Achard, Michel and Suzanne Kemmer (eds.), *Language, Culture, and Mind*, 415–428. Stanford, CA: CSLI Publications.

Gries, Stefan Th. and Anatol Stefanowitsch
    2004   Covarying collexemes in the *into*-causative. In: Michel Achard and Suzanne Kemmer (eds.), *Language, Culture and Mind*, 225–236. Stanford: CSLI Publications.

Gries, Stefan Th., Beate Hampe, and Doris Schönefeld
    2005   Converging evidence: Bringing together experimental and corpus data on the association of verbs and constructions. *Cognitive Linguistics* 16: 635–676.

in press   Converging evidence II: More on the association of verbs and constructions. In: Sally Rice and John Newman (eds), *Empirical Evidence in Linguistics. Proceedings of the 7th Conference on Conceptual Structure, Discourse and Language.* Standford: CSLI (UCP).

Hampe, Beate
  2005   To keep (or not to keep) the caused-motion and resultative constructions apart. A collostruction approach. Paper accepted for presentation at "New Directions in Cognitive Linguistics", Brighton, Oct. 2005.

Hampe, Beate and Doris Schönefeld
  2003   Creative syntax. Iconic principles within the symbolic. In: W. G. Müller and O. Fischer (eds.), *From Sign to Signing. Proceedings of the 3rd Symposium on Iconicity in Language and Literature,* 245–263. Amsterdam/Philadelphia: John Benjamins.

Harris, Catherine L.
  1998   Psycholinguistic studies of entrenchment. In: J. P. Koenig (ed.), *Discourse and Cognition: Bridging the Gap,* 55–70. Stanford, CA: CSLI Publications.

Lakoff, George
  1987   There constructions. In: *Women, Fire and Dangerous Things. What Categories reveal about the Mind,* 462–585. Chicago/London: The University of Chicago Press.
  1993   The contemporary theory of metaphor. In: A. Ortony (ed.), *Metaphor in Language and Thought,* 2nd edition, 202–251. Oxford: Oxford University Press.

Lakoff, George and Mark Johnson
  1999   *Philosophy in the Flesh: The Embodied Mind and its Challenge to Western Thought.* New York: Basic Books.

Langacker, Ronald W.
  1991   *Foundations of Cognitive Grammar,* Volume 2. Stanford: Stanford University Press.
  2000   A dynamic usage-based model. In: Michael Barlow and Suzanne Kemmer (eds.), *Usage-based Models of Language,* 1–64. Stanford, CA: CSLI Publications.

Louw, Bill
  1993   Irony in the text or insincerity in the writer? The diagnostic potential of semantic prosodies. In: M. Baker, G. Francis, and E. Tognini-Bonelli (eds.), *Text and Technology,* 156–176. Amsterdam/Philadelphia: John Benjamins.

Pawley, Andrew and Francis H. Syder
    1983   Two puzzles for linguistic theory: Native-like selection and native-like fluency. In: Jack Richards and Richard W. Schmidt (eds.), *Language and Communication*, 191–226. London: Longman.

Pinker, Steven
    1993   *Learnability and Cognition. The Acquisition of Argument-Structure.* Cambridge, MA: The MIT Press.

Schönefeld, Doris
    2001   *Where Lexicon and Syntax Meet.* Berlin/New York: Mouton de Gruyter.

Sinclair, John McH. (ed.)
    1987   *Looking up. An Account of the COBUILD Project in Lexical Computing.* London etc.: Collins.

Stefanowitsch, Anatol and Stefan Th Gries
    2003   Collostructions: Investigating the interaction between words and constructions. *International Journal of Corpus Linguistics* 8: 209–243.
    2005   Covarying collexemes. *Corpus Linguistics and Linguistic Theory* 1 (1): 1–43.

Taylor, John R.
    1998   Syntactic constructions as prototype categories. In: Michael Tomasello (ed.), *The New Psychology of Language*, 177–202. Hillsdale, NJ: Lawrence Erlbaum.

Tomasello, Michael
    2000a   First steps towards a usage-based theory of language acquisition. *Cognitive Linguistics* 11: 61–82.
    2000b   The item-based nature of children's early syntactic development. *Trends in Cognitive Sciences* 4: 156–163.

Ungerer, Friedrich
    1999   Diagrammatic iconicity in word formation. In: Max Nänny and Olga Fischer (eds.), *Form Miming Meaning. Iconicity in Language and Literature.* 307–324. Amsterdam/Philadelphia: John Benjamins.

The place of prototypicality in corpus linguistics: Causation in the hot seat[1]

Gaëtanelle Gilquin

Abstract

This paper seeks to define prototypical causation as applied to English periphrastic causative constructions. More precisely, it compares three models of prototypical causation described in the literature with the most frequent types of constructions found in corpus data. It is shown that, on the whole, and despite some reconciling factors, linguistic frequency does not coincide with (what is presented in the literature as) cognitive salience. A number of hypotheses are put forward to explain this discrepancy, all of which underline the need to investigate the notion of prototypicality more thoroughly.

Keywords: prototypicality; causation; cognition; salience; corpus; frequency.

1. Introduction

The notion of prototypicality lies at the heart of cognitive linguistics. As Geeraerts (1988: 207) nicely puts it, "[p]rototype theory is as it were part of the prototypical core of the cognitive paradigm in semantics, particularly in lexical semantics". So much so, in fact, that prototypicality has come to be used in different senses and has become some sort of "catch-all notion" (Wierzbicka 1985: 343), a label under which diverse phenomena have been lumped together (Geeraerts 1989: 606). In particular, cognitivists tend to consider the prototype as the cognitively most salient exemplar, while corpus linguists often equate it with the most frequently corpus-attested item (cf. Stubb's [2004] equation of "prototypical" and "high frequency" exemplars). Most of the time, the (often implicit) assumption is that the two coincide with one another. Yet, some voices have been raised to claim that corpus linguists and cognitivists examine different things when they study frequency and salience, respectively (e.g. Shortall, in preparation; see later). Taking causation as a starting point, I will compare the models of cognitive salience found in the literature with the most frequent patterns as attested in corpus data. More precisely, I will investigate how English periphrastic causative constructions (i.e. constructions such as *He makes me laugh* or *I had my watch repaired*) behave according to these two definitions of prototypicality.[2]

After giving an overview of the way prototypicality was born and later extended to the field of linguistics, I will present three models of prototypical causation, one concerning the ordering of the participants, and two describing their nature. I will also show how corpus data reflect the notion of prototypicality, and how they have indeed been used as a tool to pinpoint prototypes. Using data from the British National Corpus (BNC), I will then investigate the link between prototypical causation and frequency in authentic language. This analysis will lead me to some concluding remarks on prototypical causation and on the nature of prototypicality itself.

2. The notion of prototypicality

The notion of prototypicality originated from the field of psychology, mainly in the work of Eleanor (Heider) Rosch. Through various experimental tests, she established the existence, within a category, of more representative and less representative members. Thus, a robin is considered a better example of the bird-category than a penguin, and a chair a better example of the furniture-category than a telephone (see Rosch 1975). The most representative member of a category is called the prototype,[3] i.e. "the best, clearest and most salient exemplar among the members of a category and [serving] as a kind of cognitive reference point with respect to which the surrounding, 'poorer' instances of the category are defined" (Radden 1992: 519–520). As demonstrated by Rosch, prototypes have particular features. They are acquired earlier by children, tend to be produced more rapidly in naming tasks, are perceptually more salient (see Rosch's experiments on focal vs. non-focal colours; Heider 1971, 1972) and are more easily memorised (cf. her experiments on square-like shapes among the Dani, a non-Westernised culture in Papua New Guinea; Rosch 1973).

The emergence of prototypicality has revolutionised the conception of categorisation.[4] While the classical, so-called Platonic view preaches the discreteness of categories and the existence of a limited set of necessary and sufficient properties defining them (see Givón 1986), cognitivists claim that natural categories contain good and less good examples, which possess a larger or smaller number of characteristic properties. To illustrate this with a classic example (Fillmore 1977: 68–69), a "bachelor" is defined, in the classical perspective (or "checklist theories of meaning", see Fillmore 1975), by the properties [+ male] and [+ single], which are both necessary (a person must have these two properties to be called a bachelor) and sufficient conditions (a person need only have these two properties to be called a bachelor). In the cognitive perspective, on the other hand, the bachelor-category is organised around a prototype, namely a 30-year-old single man who has not yet married, but it includes other, more marginal members (e.g. a baby boy, a pope or a divorced man).

While the notion of prototype was first used with reference to concrete objects (furniture, vehicles, colour chips, etc.), and then with respect to the meaning of words (cf. "bachelor"), it was later "extended to additional levels of linguistic representation" (Tsohatzidis 1990: 2). One of the first attempts to describe a linguistic category in terms of prototypicality is Hopper and Thompson's (1980) study of transitivity. Whereas transitivity is traditionally characterised by the presence of a direct object, Hopper and Thompson regard it as a continuum and claim that clauses can be ranked according to their degree of transitivity. Their hypothesis is that transitivity is the result of the combination of a number of parameters (number of participants, affirmation, mode, individuation of the object, etc.). The more features a clause has, the more transitive it is, and the closer it is to what Hopper and Thompson call "cardinal Transitivity".

Similarly, Taylor (1989) demonstrates the pervasiveness of prototypicality in linguistic categorisation. The past tense, for example, is primarily used "to locate an event or state at some point or period in time prior to the moment of speaking (or writing)" (Taylor 1989: 149) – as its name indicates. Nevertheless, it has at least two other meanings in English, viz. counterfactuality, as in *if*-conditionals or suppositions, and "pragmatic softening", e.g. *Excuse me, I wanted to ask you something* (Taylor 1989: 149–151). The reference to past time is the prototypical use of the past tense, while the other two meanings are more peripheral.

Syntactic constructions too exhibit prototype effects (Taylor 1989: 197–221; see also Taylor [1998] and Winters [1990]). To give but one example, the central use of the possessive genitive "identifies one entity, the 'possessed', with reference to its possession by another, the 'possessor' " (Taylor 1989: 202), e.g. *John's house*. The other uses somehow diverge from this central sense. In *the dog's bone*, the possessor is non-human and therefore non-prototypical. In *the secretary's typewriter* (meaning 'the typewriter assigned to the secretary for regular use'), the rights of the secretary to use the typewriter are only limited, thus differing from a prototypical construction such as *John's car*, where John has unlimited rights over the car.

Besides this extension to more abstract categories, studies have also revealed the prototypical organisation of apparently discrete categories such as odd numbers or squares, for which informants acknowledge the existence of good and less good examples (Armstrong et al. 1983; Fehr and Russell 1984).

3. Prototypical causation

Causation, like a number of other abstract concepts, has been described in the cognitive literature in terms of prototypicality. Here, we will see how these descriptions can be applied to periphrastic causative constructions. A distinction will be made between two aspects of prototypical causative constructions, viz. the ordering of the different elements that make up the construction and the nature of these elements. Note that, while these two aspects examine fundamentally different things, it will be shown that there is actually considerable overlap and that the presence of prototypical participants[5] almost always implies prototypical ordering.

3.1. Ordering of the participants

The definition of the prototypical ordering of the participants in a causative construction is based on the principle of iconic sequencing (see e.g. Haiman 1985: 91), which establishes a relationship between the ordering of the linguistic elements and the sequence of events as we mentally conceive them. This principle, for example, accounts for the oddity of a sentence such as *He poured himself a glass of wine and opened the bottle*, taken from Ungerer and Schmid (1996: 251), where the ordering of the linguistic elements does not reflect the sequential order of events in reality or, for that matter, events as we mentally conceive them.

A periphrastic causative construction can be described as an action chain (Langacker 1991: 283), as shown in Figure 1, where a "head", the CAUSER, transmits its energy to a second entity, the CAUSEE, which can consume the energy or transmit it further to a third entity, the PATIENT, which absorbs the energy and thus represents the "tail" of the action chain (as indicated by the jagged arrow in Figure 1). The two cases can be illustrated, respectively, by:

(1) That's my fear coming, that's what **makes** me run away from her. <BNC:S:KBX 625>

(2) Or **get** your father to run us out and taxi back. <BNC:S:KE6 9074>

The transmission of energy can also be of a more symbolic nature, as in:

(3) It has become common form to invoke the magic names of the French theorists, as if the names alone would **cause** a torpid academic establishment to collapse. <BNC:W:A1A 172>

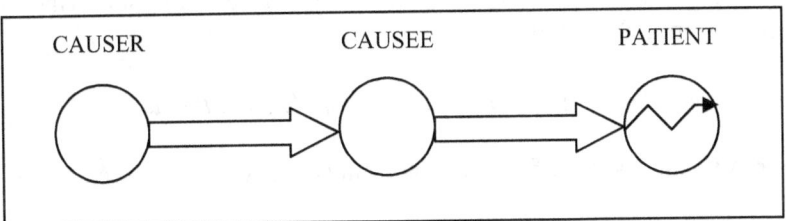

Figure 1. Action chain of a periphrastic causative construction with a PATIENT

Following the principle of iconic sequencing, the most likely ordering of the linguistic elements in a periphrastic causative construction is CAUSER, CAUSEE and PATIENT, if any, since it reflects the ordering of the participants along the action chain. A sentence such as *I got him to close the door* is therefore more prototypical than one such as *He was made to close the door*, which begins with the CAUSEE, or *I had the door closed (by him)*, where the CAUSER is followed by the PATIENT.[6]

3.2. Nature of the participants

The second aspect of prototypicality concerns the nature of the different elements making up the causative construction. The cognitive literature contains two major definitions of prototypical causation, viz. "billiard-ball causation" and "direct manipulation".

The billiard-ball model is to be linked to the notion of action chain, as it represents the flow of energy from one object to another. More precisely, Langacker (1991: 13) explains this model as follows:

> We think of our world as being populated by discrete physical objects. These objects are capable of moving about through space and making contact with one another. Motion is driven by energy, which some objects draw from internal resources and others receive from the exterior. When motion results in forceful physical contact, energy is transmitted from the mover to the impacted object, which may thereby be set in motion to participate in further interactions.

Brugman (1996: 33) refers to billiard-ball causation as the "typical" model of causation. Along the same lines, Itkonen (1983: 18) defines the "paradigmatic type of causation" as "an object A colliding with an object B and making it move in a way it would not otherwise have moved". Talmy's (2000: 418) definition of prototypical causation, which he calls "onset causation of motion" and which is illustrated by (4), seems to subscribe to the billiard-ball model as well.

(4)   *The ball's hitting it **made** the lamp topple from the table.*

Put simply, the model of billiard-ball causation can be expressed as follows:[7]

BILLIARD-BALL CAUSATION

> A single, specific, physical CAUSER transmits energy to a single, specific, physical CAUSEE, which can absorb the energy or transmit it further to a single, specific, physical PATIENT.
> e.g. *The rolling circle causes the central circle to rotate.*
> *The tree falling on it made the lorry lose its loading.*

The second type of prototypical causation is that of direct manipulation, described by Lakoff and Johnson (1980: 69–76) and Lakoff (1987: 54–55) as a cluster of the following interactional properties:

1)   There is an agent that does something.
2)   There is a patient that undergoes a change to a new state.

3) Properties 1 and 2 constitute a single event; they overlap in time and space; the agent comes in contact with the patient.
4) Part of what the agent does (either the motion or the exercise of will) precedes the change in the patient.
5) The agent is the energy source; the patient is the energy goal; there is a transfer of energy from agent to patient.
6) There is a single definite agent and a single definite patient.
7) The agent is human.
8)
   a) The agent wills his action.
   b) The agent is in control of his action.
   c) The agent bears primary responsibility for both his action and the change.
9) The agent uses his hands, body, or some instrument.
10) The agent is looking at the patient, the change in the patient is perceptible, and the agent perceives the change.

(Lakoff 1987: 54–55)

The examples that exhibit all ten properties are the most prototypical ones (cf. Lakoff's examples: *Max broke the window, Brutus killed Caesar*). Those that lack a number of characteristics are less prototypical. This is the case of, say, non-human agency or involuntary causation, but also of periphrastic causative constructions, which fail at least property 3.[8] In order to apply to periphrastic causative constructions, however, Lakoff's list of ten properties has to be slightly adapted. The main change has to do with the nature of the second participant (what has here been called the CAUSEE), which is both agent and patient. In *The teacher made Susan read the book*, Susan is affected by the teacher's action (an affected state which is indicated by the grammatical case of the pronoun, if any, cf. *The teacher made her read the book*), but she also performs an action herself by reading the book. As can be expected from this agentive nature, and as confirmed by other scholars (e.g. Kemmer and Verhagen 1994: 129), the prototypical CAUSEE should be human, resulting in "person-to-person" causation (Goldsmith 1984: 126). As for the PATIENT, it is optional in periphrastic causative constructions (compare *The teacher made Susan read the book* and *The teacher made Susan laugh*).[9] Finally, although it is implicit in Lakoff's definition of prototypical causation (cf. "There is a single definite agent *and* a single definite patient"), it should be emphasised that the participants should be distinct from one another. (5) is more prototypical than (6), where the CAUSEE takes the form of a reflexive pronoun (*myself*), or (7), where the CAUSEE, albeit not mentioned, is co-referential with the CAUSER ("I'll get myself to do my geography project").

(5) *So he **got** you to move it in the end?* <BNC:S:KCY 363>

(6) *I wanted to get ready to come away but I **made** myself sit and really give him time.* <BNC:S:KBF 952>

(7) *Then I'll **get** my geography project done, I can't do anything until I've got this bloody project out the way, can I?* <BNC:S:KCE 6364>

The model of direct manipulation can therefore be expressed succinctly in the following way:

DIRECT MANIPULATION

> A single, definite, human CAUSER manipulates a single, definite, human CAUSEE, distinct from the CAUSER, into producing a volitional and material EFFECT, which can affect, or not, a single, definite and distinct PATIENT.
> e.g. *I'll **make** her go up there.*
> *I **got** John to repaint the wall.*

3.3. Foundations of prototypical causation

Up to now, the three prototypical models presented above have been taken for granted and their origins have not been questioned. Yet, a close look at the literature reveals that the exact nature of these models is far from clear. True, they seem to rely on some deeply-rooted (and elsewhere demonstrated) cognitive principles, such as the primacy of the concrete over the abstract in neural representations (see MacLennan 1998). But on the whole, the sources of prototypical causation as it is described in the literature remain rather obscure. Lakoff (1987: 55) vaguely refers to "representative examples of *humanly relevant* causation" [emphasis mine] and Lakoff and Johnson (1980: 75) maintain that their model of direct manipulation "emerges directly from our experience", but there does not seem to be any experimental basis for their claims.[10] The same holds true for the billiard-ball model, which Langacker (1991: 13) simply introduces with the words "we think of our world as...".

When we move from a purely cognitive approach to a more corpus-based cognitive approach, the establishment of the prototype apparently has stronger empirical foundations, relying as it does on the frequency of linguistic items in naturally-occurring language. Kemmer (2001) and Stefanowitsch (2001), for instance, both seem to equate the notion of prototypicality with what is most frequent in their corpus data.[11] Contrary to Langacker or Lakoff, they do not seek to define prototypical causation as a whole, but the prototypical *have*-causative, the prototypical CAUSEE in *make*-constructions, etc. However, it may reasonably be assumed that what is true of (the elements making up) the causative constructions equally applies to causation itself. In other words, we may hypothesise that what is presented as prototypical causation in the literature corresponds to causation as it is most frequently expressed in authentic language. This is what will be explored in the next sections.

4. Prototypicality and corpus linguistics

4.1. Fuzziness of corpus data

"[I]f there is one lesson to be learnt from studying and analysing corpus examples", Mair (1994: 128) points out, "it is the 'basic non-discreteness of categories' " (see also Teubert 1996: v). Before use was made of authentic data in the form of large machine-readable collections of texts, linguistic categories were largely presented as clear-cut and well-defined. Corpus linguistics, however, by confronting linguists with large quantities of real data, revealed the fuzziness of category membership in language, as well as the prevalence of continua, as opposed to dichotomies. The difference between animacy and inanimacy (Yamamoto 1999), for instance, or between nouns and pronouns (Sugamoto 1989) turned out to be best described as a cline, and even the (apparently) fundamental distinction between lexis and grammar was shown to be invalid (cf. the concept of "lexico-grammar" found in e.g. Sinclair 1991). This radical shift, made possible by the advent of corpus linguistics, can be summarised by quoting Čermák (2002: 273; emphasis original), who notes that

> the historical scarcity of data ... evoked the impression that language data is comfortably discrete and of an entity-like quality. What huge corpora show

is rather different: most of the information is scalar, obtainable in stepwise batches with hazy edges only, where the best help available is often statistics and fuzzy approaches and no longer black-and-white truths and clear-cut classification boxes. To put it differently, instead of insisting on getting straightforward answers of the *yes-no* type we have to elicit answers of the type *rather this than that*, or *more of this and less of that*.

So it seems as if, almost by definition, corpus data reflect the cognitive notion of prototypicality, with some elements more representative of a linguistic category and others, more marginal.

4.2. Link between prototypicality and frequency

Some linguists have elevated the link between corpus data and prototypicality to the status of principle. Thus, Schmid (2000: 39) proposes the "From-Corpus-to-Cognition Principle", according to which "frequency in text instantiates entrenchment in the cognitive system". Put differently, what is most frequent in language is claimed to be most salient and so, most prototypical (remember Radden's [1992] definition of the prototype as the "most *salient* exemplar"). Consequently, establishing a prototype would simply mean determining the most frequent exemplar of a category. Given the vagueness surrounding the term "prototype", as well as the complexity involved in testing linguistic prototypicality experimentally (how does one get people to judge the "goodness-of-example" of, say, a particular transitive clause?), it comes as no surprise that frequency in linguistic usage has regularly been used as a methodological shortcut to establish the prototype. In his study of two Dutch verbs, for example, Geeraerts (1988) examines the actual facts of language in an attempt to uncover the quantitatively most prominent, and so, arguably, most salient, kinds of usage.

The role of frequency in prototypicality cannot be denied. Aitchison (1998: 229), referring to Rosch's (1975) experiments, which were carried out in California, notes that, since nectarines and boysenberries are more common in California than mangoes or kumquats, it is not surprising that the former were regarded by informants as more representative of the fruit-category than the latter. No doubt the results would have been different if the experiments had taken place, say, on the African or Asian continent. Geeraerts (1988: 221–222), giving a similar example, goes even further and establishes a link between *linguistic* frequency (not just *referential* frequency) and prototypicality. Nectarines being more common than mangoes in California, people are more likely to talk about the former – hence a higher linguistic frequency. Frequency of linguistic occurrence, therefore, can be seen as a "heuristic tool in the pinpointing of prototypes" (Geeraerts 1988: 222) – which, incidentally, seems to be confirmed by Geeraerts's results.

However, not everybody agrees that cognitive salience is reflected in linguistic usage. Shortall (in preparation) points out that, while all language users have prototypes about aspects of language use, these may conflict with the evidence of what is most frequent. He illustrates this with the example of *there*-constructions. Whereas in elicitation tasks people tend to produce sentences with a concrete noun, e.g. *There is* a book *on the table* (about 60% of the cases), in the British spoken section of the Bank of English, abstract nouns are predominant (59%). Similarly, Sinclair (1991: 36) notes about common words that, as a rule, "the most frequent meaning is not the one that first comes to mind". This hypothesis is confirmed by other studies which compare the results of elicitation tests, aimed at bringing to light the most salient elements (i.e. those that first come to mind), and the results of corpus analyses, revealing the most frequent kinds of usage, and which come to the conclusion that the two do not necessarily coincide with one another (see e.g. Roland and Jurafsky 2002; Nordquist 2004). And Aitchison (1998: 229) herself, although she notes the link between frequency and prototypicality (see above), suggests that frequency does not explain everything, as appears for instance from the fact that rare items such as "love seat" or "davenport" rate higher on Rosch's (1975) furniture list than a more common item like "refrigerator". The next section seeks to provide an answer (if only partial) to the question of the relation between frequency and prototypicality with respect to the phenomenon of causation in English.

5. Prototypical causation in corpus data

5.1. Material used

The corpus data against which the cognitive models of prototypical causation will be compared consist in a 10-million-word subcorpus from the British National Corpus (5 million words of spoken English and 5 million words of written English). All the constructions with the main periphrastic causative verbs (*cause*, *get*, *have* and *make*) were extracted, which represents a total of 3,574 constructions (see Table 1). Each of these constructions was analysed according to the parameters defining prototypical causation, and summarised in Table 2.[12]

Table 1. Absolute frequency (n) and relative frequency (per 100,000 words) of the causatives

	N	Relative Frequency
CAUSE	200	2.04
HAVE	813	8.29
MAKE	1,251	12.76
GET	1,310	13.36
TOTAL	3,574	36.46

The analysis presented in the next section relies on a strict definition of prototypicality, according to which prototypical members should manifest *all* the prototypical features (see Cruse 1990: 391). If the data pass this extreme test, we can be sure that the models have empirical validity. If they fail, it might be that a looser definition would produce better results, a possibility that will be briefly discussed in Section 5.3.

5.2. Results

Table 3 gives the results for the three models of prototypical causation presented in Sections 3.1 and 3.2. Before going on to the discussion of these results, let us underline a point that does not appear from this table, viz. the large degree of overlap between iconic sequencing on the one hand and the models of billiard-ball causation and direct manipulation on the other hand. A causative construction displaying one of the two last mentioned models almost always displays iconic sequencing too. There are just two exceptions in the data, namely (8) and (9), which use the model of direct manipulation, but whose participants are not ordered iconically.

Table 2. Parameters of the models of prototypical causation

		Iconic Sequencing	Billiard-Ball Model	Direct Manipulation
CAUSER		1st participant	– single – specific – physical	– single – definite – human
CAUSEE		2nd participant	– single – specific – physical	– single – definite – human – distinct from CAUSER
(PATIENT)		(3rd participant)	(– single – specific – physical)	(– single – definite – distinct from CAUSER and CAUSEE)
EFFECT			– material	– material – volitional
CLAUSE			– affirmative	– affirmative

(8) *Our period opens with the imperial coronation of 962; shortly after its close, in 1165, Frederick Barbarossa **had** Charlemagne canonized by his anti-pope Paschal III.* <BNC:W:BMV 1285>

(9) *I **had** it [hoe] <pause> sharpened by Hector* <BNC:S:KC0 6551>

Taking this overlap into account, we can say that the models of prototypical causation presented in the literature only account for some 45% of all the causative constructions (1,632 out of 3,574), which leaves about 55% of the data unaccounted for (i.e. exhibiting neither prototypical ordering, nor prototypical participants) – e.g. constructions such as (10), where the participants (CAUSER and CAUSEE) are neither human beings nor physical objects, or (11), which starts with the CAUSEE and whose EFFECT is neither material nor volitional.

(10) *The regulation of population density can only be a consequence of migration, not the reason why natural selection **causes** the habit to evolve.* <BNC:W:GU8 672>

(11) *At the same time, the reader can be **made** to feel that, on closer inspection, the country's politics might prove to be antics too.*
<BNC:W:A05 70>

So clearly, these models do not seem to be fundamental organising principles in naturally-occurring language. This is particularly true of the billiard-ball model which, with a percentage of 0.06%, is insignificant in the data, and the model of direct manipulation, which represents a proportion of some 5% only.

Table 3. Models of prototypical causation in corpus data

	Iconic Sequencing		Billiard-Ball Model		Direct Manipulation	
	N	%	N	%	N	%
CAUSE	150	75.0	0	0.00	0	0.0
HAVE	133	16.4	0	0.00	17	2.1
MAKE	947	75.7	1	0.08	51	4.1
GET	400	30.5	1	0.08	121	9.2
TOTAL	1,630	45.6	2	0.06	189	5.3

A closer look at Table 3 also reveals a great deal of variation among the different verbs. Using the chi-square test, one can test the distribution for significance so as to determine which model of causation is correlated with which verb. With the exception of the billiard-ball model, which exhibits very low values and so cannot be tested for significance, the distribution of the other two models is highly significant (χ^2 = 504.03 for iconic sequencing and 68.38 for direct manipulation[13]). While iconic sequencing significantly prefers *cause* and *make* and significantly disprefers *have* and *get*, direct manipulation significantly prefers *get* but disprefers the other verbs.

Let us now briefly comment on some of the most striking correlations between the verbs and the models of causation, starting with iconic sequencing and its significant dispreference for *have* and *get*.[14] It is interesting to note that the non-canonical ordering with these two verbs is almost always coupled with the ellipsis of the CAUSEE. Sentences such as (12) and (13), where the CAUSEE is mentioned and follows the PATIENT, are very rare indeed (3 instances with *get* and 10 with *have*).

(12) *Marriages of persons over that age, but under 18, are completely valid; and the only check on such marriages without the consent of parents or guardians is the difficulty of **getting** them celebrated by the clergyman or proper officer without making a false declaration, which involves penal consequences.* <BNC:W:ABP 384>

(13) *This stands for Cooperative Awards in Science and Engineering and erm under this scheme, a company erm can **have** a problem tackled by a research student working in a university and erm a supervisor, and indeed in this case, the input, the financial input, by the company may be quite small, may only amount to a few hundred pounds.* <BNC:S:KRH 874>

This can be explained, especially in the case of *have*, by the common reference to established scenarios, e.g. the "hairdressing" scenario in (14), where the mention of the CAUSEE (here, a hairdresser) would be redundant.[15] In the case of *get*, the ellipsis of the CAUSEE is mainly a consequence of its co-referentiality with the CAUSER, as in (15). Making the two participants explicit, here, would result in unnecessary repetition.

(14) *I just told them you'd **had** your hair cut really short*
 <BNC:S:KC2 3072>

(15) *Sorry, I've nearly finished this. <pause> I'd like to **get** it done before I ...* <BNC:S:KB0 3215–3216>

Turning to the billiard-ball model of causation, it should be emphasised that this model is associated with the natural sciences (Lakoff 1987: 55) and is typically used to describe scientific experiments. We would therefore expect it to be most frequent with the verb *cause*, which is predominantly used in scientific and technical genres (over 50% of its occurrences, see Gilquin 2004). Yet, it appears from Table 3 that *cause* never expresses billiard-ball causation in the corpus data. While it shares a number of characteristics with this model, the main problem has to do with the semantic category of the participants, and more particularly that of the CAUSER. Most of the CAUSERS involved in a causative construction with *cause* refer to abstract entities (almost 80%), as in (16), whereas it will be remembered that according to the billiard-ball model, they should be concrete and physical objects, cf. (17).

(16) The importance and complexity of financial matters *have **caused** special procedures to be evolved to deal with them.* <BNC:W:C8R 703>

(17) *Some children get worried or feel uncomfortable because they fail to chew and then try to swallow* large lumps of food which ***cause*** *them to gag and vomit.* <BNC:W:CGT 1363>

Get, have and *make,* by contrast, are hardly ever used in a scientific context (5% with *make* and less than 1% with *get* and *have*). Accordingly, *have* never expresses billiard-ball causation and *get* and *make* are only used once each with this model, see (18) and (19).

(18) *It's got a tube that would **make** the <pause> the other one go.* <BNC:S:KC1 1042>

(19) *Yes, that should physically click on the pin to **get** the wire to connect.* <BNC:S:KD5 9113>

It is therefore obvious that, albeit regularly mentioned in the literature as a model of prototypical causation, the billiard-ball model may be said to have no impact on language usage – at least in the form of a periphrastic causative construction.

The situation is slightly different for the model of direct manipulation, although, here too, the percentages of constructions corresponding to the model are surprisingly low, as illustrated in Table 3. They range from 2.1% with *have,* to 4.1% with *make* and 9.2% with *get. Cause* is never found with this model in the corpus data. The latter result mainly follows from the inanimacy of the participants in causative constructions with *cause,* as noted by e.g. Chuquet and Paillard (1989: 170). On the basis of the statements found in the literature with respect to the nature of the participants with the other three causatives, however, one would have expected these verbs to rate much higher. It is often claimed that *get* and *have* are used with animate participants only (see e.g. Belvin [1993: 64] for the CAUSER of *have*). And while a corpus analysis reveals some cases where the CAUSER or the CAUSEE is inanimate with *get* and *have* (see Gilquin 2004), these are indeed extremely infrequent. As for *make,* it is very often presented in the literature as implying coercion, on a par with *force* (e.g. Faure and Casanova 1968: 192; Werner et al. 1990: 392), which makes it an ideal candidate for expressing direct manipulation. So how can we explain the low results exhibited by the corpus data for these three verbs? For *get* and *have*, the results should be seen in parallel with the remarks concerning iconic sequencing. As noted earlier, the two verbs tend to prefer a non-prototypical ordering of the elements, together with an ellipsis of the CAUSEE. Now, the model of direct manipulation requires that the CAUSEE should be single, definite, human and distinct from the CAUSER, but also, of course, that there should be a CAUSEE in the first place. Moreover, as already mentioned, *get* has this particular characteristic that the CAUSER is clearly co-referential with the (often implicit) CAUSEE, and hence non-prototypical, in 40% of the cases (as compared to 10% with *have*, 3% with *make* and 0% with *cause*), e.g.

(20) *Anyway, I'm going to get ready or we'll never **get** the shopping done before you go to work.* <BNC:S:KB8 4041>

With *make*, the explanation for the low percentage of the model of direct manipulation essentially lies in the distorted picture that is given of this verb in the literature. Contrary to what is often suggested, the combination of an animate CAUSER, animate CAUSEE and volitional EFFECT, which underlies the meaning of coercion and the model of direct manipulation (see [21]), represents a proportion of 18% only. The most frequent combination, actually, is that of an inanimate CAUSER, animate CAUSEE and non-volitional EFFECT, as in (22).

(21) *At least by the eleventh century every king expected to recruit a part of his army by paying mercenaries, or from knights who received a fee not in land, but in cash; though he did his best to **make** his great nobles provide contingents for which he did not have to pay, or (at least in the twelfth century) pay him in cash if they did not serve him in person.* <BNC:W:BMV 184>

(22) *Er I, I was going in the evening you know, doing the tailoring class but of course my <pause> illnesses have stopped me doing all of that and **made** me realize I can't do it all.* <BNC:S:KBF 5023>

All in all, what this analysis shows is that the models of prototypical causation described in the cognitive literature account for an astonishingly small proportion of the corpus data. This conclusion, however, should be qualified in a number of ways, as will be shown presently.

5.3. Bridging the gap between prototypicality and corpus data

The first qualification has already been alluded to before and concerns the structure of the construction considered. An infinitive structure such as *He got me to open the door* is more likely to reflect one of the models of prototypicality than a past participle structure like *He had the door opened*. This is true, obviously, for the model of iconic sequencing, but also, to a certain extent, for the other two models, since in the second sentence, one of the participants, the CAUSEE, is left unmentioned and so cannot participate in the elaboration of the model. This explains why, for example, the proportion for the model of direct manipulation with *get* rises from 9.2% to 26.6% if we only take infinitive constructions into account.[16]

Second, it should be reminded that the analysis of Section 5.2 relies on a strict definition of prototypicality, requiring the presence of *all* the prototypical features. If we accept a looser definition of prototypicality, where the prototype possesses the greatest number of features (but not necessarily all of them, see e.g. Givón 1986: 79), the picture changes somewhat, for it appears that, although the particular combination of elements making up the model may be infrequent, some of the individual properties can be quite common. As an illustration, let us examine how *make* fares with respect to the different parameters defining direct manipulation, disregarding the PATIENT (see Figure 2). We can see that, while some parameters represent a small proportion (cf. volitionality of the EFFECT), others, such as the distinction between the CAUSER and the CAUSEE or the definiteness of the CAUSER or CAUSEE, respect the model much better.

The next step would be to determine whether all the parameters equally contribute to the model or whether some of them are more important than others, in which case a particular "weight" would have to be assigned to each parameter defining the prototype. This is what Gries (2003) undertakes in his analysis of the dative alternation. On the basis of corpus data and using the notion of "cue validity",[17] he mathematically identifies the attributes that most strongly support the choice of the ditransitive construction and those that most strongly support the choice of the prepositional construction. He also shows that the high cue validity of these attributes is confirmed by the results of an experiment where subjects were asked to rate the naturalness of several instances of both constructions. Since we are not starting from the corpus data here, but instead are comparing the theoretical models against authentic language, and since the models as described in the literature do not assign any particular weight to the different parameters,[18] this question will not be elaborated on.

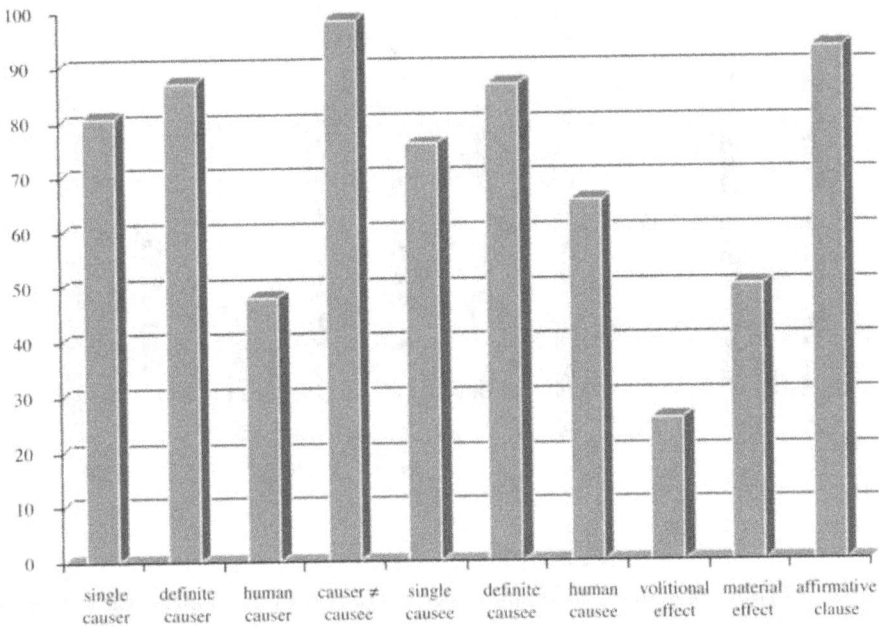

Figure 2. Make and the model of direct manipulation

Finally, medium also seems to play a role in the establishment of prototypical causation, at least as far as the nature of the participants is concerned (iconic sequencing shows no such variation). A comparison of spoken and written corpus data reveals a number of significant differences, as illustrated in Figure 3 for the model of direct manipulation with *make*, with a tendency for speech to come closer to prototypicality than writing. Thus, human CAUSERS and human CAUSEES are significantly more frequent in speech than in writing (χ^2 = 11.96 and 30.97 respectively, p<0.005)[19] and the "single CAUSEE" and "definite CAUSEE" parameters display a marginally significant difference (χ^2 = 6.78 and 7.66 respectively, p<0.01). No parameters rate significantly higher in writing than in speech.

While these elements bridge the gap between prototypicality and frequency to some extent, it is nonetheless true that what is presented in the literature as prototypical causation does not account for a large proportion of the use of periphrastic causative constructions in authentic language. This discrepancy calls for an explanation, which I will try to offer in the next section.

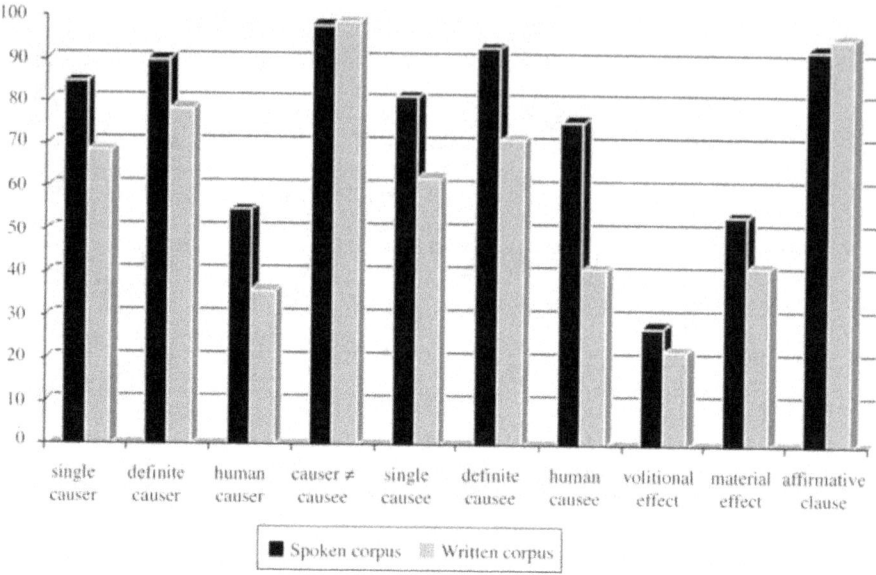

Figure 3. *Make* and the model of direct manipulation in spoken and written corpus data

5.4. Interpretation

A number of hypotheses can be put forward to explain the lack of correspondence between the literature and the corpus data. The first one is that cognitive salience (i.e. "prototypicality") is simply different from frequency in language. What comes first to people's minds may rely on principles, such as the primacy of the concrete over the abstract, which are not at work (or, at least, not to the same extent) in language usage. Several studies have already been alluded to which seem to point in that direction, and preliminary investigations carried out on causative constructions actually confirm this (Gilquin 2004). But the same investigations also show that informants' elicited production of a causative construction does not reflect the models found in the literature either, which suggests a problem with the models themselves.

Another hypothesis, therefore, is that the models proposed in the literature are not valid descriptions of prototypical causation. It will be reminded that these models do not seem to have any experimental foundation and, given the haziness surrounding their origins, we may assume that they (partly) rely on their authors' intuition. Now, one thing that corpus linguistics has clearly brought to light since its advent is the limitations of intuition – whether it comes from linguistically naïve people or from the most competent linguists.[20] So perhaps the models of iconic sequencing, billiard-ball causation and direct manipulation are just theoretical constructs that do not correspond to anything concrete in the English language.

Alternatively, these models may not be appropriate for the description of periphrastic causative constructions. The phenomenon of causation can be expressed through a wide variety of linguistic devices and these may not all exhibit the same prototypical properties. The model of direct manipulation, for example, had to be adapted in order to apply to periphrastic causative constructions and Lakoff (1987: 54–55) himself, although he mentions the periphrasis *cause to die*, quotes as typical examples of direct manipulation the sentences *Max broke the window* and *Brutus killed Caesar*, both of which contain a lexical causative. On the basis of these two examples, and taking the reasoning one step further, maybe Lakoff's model can be said to describe prototypical transitivity, rather than prototypical causation.[21] Causation has often been compared, sometimes confused, with transitivity (e.g. Croft 1994). Kemmer and Verhagen (1994) establish a correspondence between transitive clauses and what they call "intransitive causative constructions" (i.e. periphrastic causative constructions with an intransitive EFFECT, e.g. *I made Mary cry*) and the description they give of the prototypical transitive event is indeed very similar to the models of prototypical causation that have been used here, the main difference being the presence or not of an intermediate participant:[22]

> [The prototypical transitive (or two-participant) event] has an agentive participant, that is, a highly individuated entity capable of volition, and volitionally exerting physical energy on a second participant, which is also a highly individuated participant. This participant absorbs the energy, whereby it undergoes a change of state that would not have taken place without the exertion of energy. The effect on the second participant is direct, that is, there are no observed intermediaries such as a third participant; the effect is complete; there is physical contact between the two participants; and this contact is seen as giving rise to the change of state. (Kemmer and Verhagen 1994: 126)

If the models of prototypical causation found in the literature do not characterise causation *per se*, we can expect problems to arise if we try to apply them to causative constructions.

Finally, a more radical explanation consists in claiming that there is no such thing as prototypical causation. Hampton (1981) has shown that the prototype structure of abstract concepts cannot always be demonstrated, and perhaps causation is one of these. In this case, the literature would seek to describe, and we would try to track down in a corpus, something that simply does not exist – and so cannot be found.

These are only hypotheses, and pinpointing one of these as the actual reason for the discrepancy between prototypicality and frequency would require further research, including psycholinguistic experiments on periphrastic causative constructions. There is certainly a lot to be done in this area for, while many such studies have been devoted to causal relations expressed by means of connectives (e.g. Noordman and de Blijzer 2000; Roebben 2004), periphrastic causative constructions, on the other hand, have been sorely neglected. But the hypotheses proposed here, shaky though they may be, make it possible to gain some insight into the very nature of prototypicality, as will be briefly set out in the next section.

6. The nature of prototypicality

The one thing that should be obvious by now is that the notion of prototypicality is far from straightforward. In fact, Geeraerts (1989) has demonstrated that prototypicality is itself a prototypical notion, with fuzzy boundaries and central and more peripheral instances. And the incursion of prototypicality into linguistics seems to have added to this fuzziness. As rightly pointed out by Tsohatzidis (1990: 8), the "undeniable heuristic value of the notion of prototypicality should not obscure the fact that its exact theoretical shape is less clear than one might have wished, *especially when it is transferred from purely psychological to specifically linguistic domains of investigation*" [emphasis added].

In view of the results of this and other studies, it looks as if prototypicality is perhaps best described as a multi-faceted concept, bringing together (1) theoretical constructs found in the cognitive literature and relying on deeply-rooted neurological principles such as the primacy of the concrete over the abstract, (2) frequently occurring patterns of (authentic) linguistic usage, as evidenced in corpus data, (3) first-come-to-mind manifestations of abstract thought, as revealed through elicitation tests and (4) possibly other aspects that contribute to the cognitive salience of a prototype.[23] The various facets of prototypicality can converge, when they all point in the same direction, but they can also be (wholly or partly) divergent and reflect different realities. In the former case, the prototype may be said to be more prototypical than in the latter case.

At the same time, this analysis has underlined the necessity to investigate the phenomenon of prototypicality more thoroughly. Having a clear idea of what is meant by "prototypicality" is a *sine qua non* if one wants to extend the scope of this notion, not only within the fields of psychology and linguistics, where its existence is already quite well established, but also beyond these fields, in domains as diverse as pedagogy (Niemeier 2003), marketing (Veryzer and Hutchinson 1998) or graphology (Caffray, Schneider, and Devaux 1998), where it is gradually setting up, and perhaps other, less expected domains which will perceive the relevance of the concept to their discipline.

7. Conclusion

In an attempt to come to a better understanding of the concept of prototypicality, and in particular prototypical causation, this article has compared two competing tools for pinpointing prototypes, viz. the theoretical constructs found in the literature and claiming to describe cognitively salient models, and frequency of linguistic usage as evidenced in corpus data. This analysis has revealed a discrepancy between the results obtained through the two methods. While some factors can be introduced which reduce the distance between cognitive salience and frequency (e.g. medium), this lack of overlap nonetheless questions our deepest intuitions and calls for an explanation.

This article is also a plea for a more thorough investigation of prototypicality, which, though one of the most popular concepts in cognitive linguistics, is still extremely obscure. What is most definitely needed at present is a refined and more detailed description of this concept, which might involve multi-faceted characterisation and/or additional adjustments, such as assigning a particular weight to each parameter defining the prototype. Hopefully, thanks to this clarification, the "uses" of prototypicality (see Wierzbicka 1990) will progress, while its "abuses" will melt away.

Notes

1. This work was carried out with the gratefully acknowledged support of the Belgian National Fund for Scientific Research (FNRS). Special thanks are due to the editors of this book, Stefan Th. Gries and Anatol Stefanowitsch, for their insightful comments.

2. I will use the following terms when referring to the different elements making up the periphrastic causative construction: *He* <CAUSER> **got** *the boy* <CAUSEE> *to open* <EFFECT> *the door* <PATIENT>. The CAUSER is an entity, force or event that changes or influences the CAUSEE, and thereby produces an EFFECT. The PATIENT, when present, represents the entity that is acted on by the CAUSEE.
3. A term which, as noted by Ungerer and Schmid (1996: 10), Rosch borrowed from earlier research on pattern recognition (e.g. Reed 1972).
4. Posner (1986: 54) talks of the "Roschian revolution", describing it as a genuine revolution "because it was a part of a general new conceptualization of human thought in terms of bounded rationality that has important implications for psychology and the social sciences".
5. I use the term "participant" in a broad sense, here, to cover all the elements making up the causative construction, including the verbal element (the EFFECT).
6. See also Van Valin (2001), who argues that *Jean* in (i) is "in the **canonical** position for interpretation as direct object (undergoer) of *laisser* and as subject (actor) of *manger*" [emphasis mine], unlike *Jean* in (ii), which is coded as an indirect object, a function which, in simple clauses, is not interpreted as being an actor-like argument.
    (i)   *Je laisserai **Jean** manger les gâteaux.*
          'I will let John eat the cakes'
    (ii) *Je ferai manger les gâteaux à **Jean**.*
          'I will make eat the cakes to John'
   Van Valin also notes that sentences such as (i) appear before structures such as (ii) in child language – a property which, it will be reminded, is considered as characteristic of prototypes.
7. Langacker's (1991: 13) idea of discreteness of the objects interacting energetically with one another has here been equated with the linguistic notion of specificity (as opposed to generic entities).
8. As noted by Fodor (1970) and others, the main difference between morphological causative verbs such as *kill* and periphrastic causative constructions such as *cause to die* is that the former, unlike the latter, imply an overlap in time and space between the causing event and the caused event. Compare: **John killed Bill on Sunday by stabbing him on Saturday* and *John caused Bill to die on Sunday by stabbing him on Saturday* (Fodor 1970: 433). See, however, Lemmens (1998: 23–24) for an (authentic) example where *kill* involves a temporal separation between the *cause*-component and the *die*-component, and for an explanation for this apparent counter-example.
9. As far as I know, nothing in the literature allows us to decide whether a PATIENT should be present or not in a prototypical periphrastic causative construction. In Degand's (2001) corpus of Dutch, causative constructions with an (explicit) PATIENT are more frequent, but this does not imply that they are

prototypical (see later). Both types of structures will therefore be taken into account here.
10. In fact, Lakoff (1982: 164) himself admits that "the question of how accurate [the] conditions [making up the model of direct manipulation] are, and what other properties there might be" "is a matter for further empirical study".
11. See e.g. Stefanowitsch's (2001: 133) remark that the service frame with the *have*-causative "accounts for 72.0% of all examples in the corpus, *and can thus clearly be seen as the prototype*" [emphasis mine].
12. The classification of the data according to the different parameters was in fact more complex than it may sound, for some category boundaries are themselves fuzzy and difficult to draw at times. As a rule, only unquestionable cases were included. Thus, human-like participants were not taken into account in the model of direct manipulation (i), nor were constructions where the relation between the CAUSER and the CAUSEE (co-referential or not) is ambiguous (ii).
    (i) *Even the famine area was **made** to pay one-half of the supplemental tax levied for famine relief.* <BNC:W:A64 1127>
    (ii) *I'll have to <pause> see if I can **get** some banana skins put on the stairs [to bump him off].* <BNC:S:KB7 15681>
    Intermediate cases for the other parameters were handled in the same way.
13. Strictly speaking, a chi-square test is not possible for the model of direct manipulation either, given that one of the cells equals zero. However, a test based on random sampling of 1,000,000 tables with the same marginal totals yielded the same result. I thank Stefan Th. Gries for help with the statistics.
14. It might be argued that such preferences or dispreferences in sequencing are not effects of prototypicality, but of complementation possibilities. However, it should be noted that, although past participle constructions represent the most frequent complementation pattern with *have* and *get* (82% and 61% respectively), which might explain the dispreference of these two verbs for iconic sequencing, speakers still have the possibility of organising the participants iconically if they want to, by choosing an infinitive or a present participle construction – even if, of course, there are many other elements that contribute to the choice between a past participle, present participle or infinitive. In the same vein, while past participle constructions are impossible with *cause* and highly restricted with *make* (Van Ek and Robat [1984: 327] limit the *make* + past participle construction to instances where the EFFECT denotes "the exercise and recognition of influence in the widest sense"), there are other ways in which the prototypical ordering of the sentence with these two verbs can be disrupted, namely by passivising the main clause (*He was caused/made to...*) or, in the case of *cause*, using a passive infinitive (*He caused it to be removed*) – two possibilities which do not exist (or only very marginally) with *get* and *have*.

15. Albeit possible, such constructions with *get* are less common and when they do occur, the focus is more on the idea of difficulty, typical of *get* (see Gilquin 2004), than on the scenario, as clearly appears from a comparison of the following two sentences, taken from the British component of the International Corpus of English (ICE-GB):
    (i) *Ironic, since fashion has gone full-circle and kids actually ask to **have** their hair cut short now.* <ICE-GB:W2F-004#23:1>
    (ii) *Alternatively, they might rebel and become violently opposed to short hair, refusing to allow their children to **get** their hair cut.* <ICE-GB:W2B-017#77:1>
16. The rise, admittedly, is less sharp for *make* and *have* (from 4.1% to 4.4% for the former and from 2.1% to 9.1% for the latter).
17. As Rosch and Mervis (1975) point out, "the validity of a cue is defined in terms of its total frequency within a category and its proportional frequency in that category relative to contrasting categories".
18. Lakoff (1982: 164) notes that the ten properties making up the model of direct manipulation "are obviously not all equally important", but he leaves it for further research to investigate their relative importance.
19. Because a chi-square test has to be carried out for each of the ten parameters of the model, the so-called Bonferroni correction has to be applied and the p-value normally used to determine significance has to be divided by the number of tests. Consequently, each of the ten results has to be significant at the level of 0.005 in order to be regarded as statistically significant and at the level of 0.01 for marginal significance.
20. See, for instance, Sampson's (1980: 152) observation that "[s]peakers are often straightforwardly, and startlingly, wrong in their sincere convictions about even the most elementary facts of their own languages" or Fillmore's (1992: 35) remark that every corpus that he has examined, however small, has taught him facts that he could not have found out about in any other way.
21. I thank Maarten Lemmens for this observation. In 1977, Lakoff actually described this model (with minor differences) as that of "prototypical agent-patient sentences" (Lakoff 1977: 244).
22. Notice, also, the reference to counterfactuality ("a change of state that would not have taken place without the exertion of energy"), reminiscent of the definitions of causative relations found in the literature, e.g. Shibatani (1976: 1–2), who notes that the dependency between the causing event and the caused event in a causative construction "must be to the extent that it allows the speaker to entertain a counterfactual inference that the caused event would not have taken place at that particular time if the causing event had not taken place, provided that all else had remained the same".
23. Winters (1990) makes a similar point when she lists the different features of a syntactic prototype, including among others frequency, salience and naturalness.

References

Aitchison, Jean
    1998   Bad birds and better birds: prototype theories. In: Virginia P. Clark, Paul A. Eschholz, and Alfred F. Rosa (eds.), *Language. Readings in Language and Culture,* 6th edition, 225–239. Boston: Bedford/St. Martin's.

Armstrong, Sharon Lee, Lila R. Gleitman, and Henry Gleitman
    1983   What some concepts might not be. *Cognition* 13 (3): 263–308.

Belvin, Robert S.
    1993   The two causative *haves* and the two possessive *haves*. In: Katharine Beals, Gina Cooke, David Kathman, Sotaro Kita, Karl-Erik McCullough, and David Testen (eds.), *Papers from the 29th Regional Meeting of the Chicago Linguistic Society. Vol. 1: The Main Session,* 61–75. Chicago, IL: Chicago Linguistic Society.

Brugman, Claudia
    1996.   Mental spaces, constructional meaning, and pragmatic ambiguity. In: Gilles Fauconnier and Eve Sweetser (eds.), *Spaces, Worlds, and Grammar,* 29–56. Chicago, IL: University of Chicago Press.

Caffray, Christine M., Sandra L. Schneider, and Michele R. Devaux
    1998   Guessing who you are by your handwriting: Prototypicality helps accuracy but not confidence. Poster presented at the *1998 Annual Meeting of the Society for Judgment and Decision Making,* abstract available at <http://www.sjdm.org/programs/98posters.html> (last accessed on 23 January 2004).

Čermák, František
    2002   Today's corpus linguistics. Some open questions. *International Journal of Corpus Linguistics* 7 (2): 265–282.

Chuquet, Hélène and Michel Paillard
    1989   *Approche linguistique des problèmes de traduction anglais ↔ français. Edition révisée.* Gap: Ophrys.

Croft, William
    1994   Voice: Beyond control and affectedness. In: Barbara A. Fox and Paul J. Hopper (eds.), *Voice: Form and Function,* 89–117. Amsterdam/Philadelphia: John Benjamins.

Cruse, D. Alan
    1990   Prototype theory and lexical semantics. In: Savas L. Tsohatzidis (ed.), *Meanings and Prototypes. Studies in Linguistic Categorization,* 382–402. London/New York: Routledge.

Degand, Liesbeth
    2001   *Form and Function of Causation. A Theoretical and Empirical Investigation of Causal Constructions in Dutch.* Leuven: Peeters.

Faure, G. and J. Casanova
  1968   *Nouvelle grammaire anglaise*. Paris: Hatier Université.
Fehr, Beverley and James A. Russell
  1984   Concept of emotion viewed from a prototype perspective. *Journal of Experimental Psychology: General* 113 (3): 464–486.
Fillmore, Charles J.
  1975   An alternative to checklist theories of meaning. In: Cathy Cogen, Henry Thompson, Graham Thurgood, Kenneth Whistler, and James Wright (eds.), *Proceedings of the First Annual Meeting of the Berkeley Linguistics Society*, 123–131. Berkeley: Berkeley Linguistics Society.
  1977   Scenes-and-frames semantics. In: Antonio Zampolli (ed.), *Linguistic Structures Processing*, 55–81. Amsterdam: North-Holland Publishing Company.
  1992   "Corpus linguistics" or "Computer-aided armchair linguistics". In: Jan Svartvik (ed.), *Directions in Corpus Linguistics. Proceedings of Nobel Symposium 82. Stockholm, 4–8 August 1991*, 35–60. Berlin/New York: Mouton de Gruyter.
Fodor, Jerry A.
  1970   Three reasons for not deriving "kill" from "cause to die". *Linguistic Inquiry* 1 (4): 429–438.
Geeraerts, Dirk
  1988   Where does prototypicality come from? In: Brygida Rudzka-Ostyn (ed.), *Topics in Cognitive Linguistics*, 207–229. Amsterdam/Philadelphia: John Benjamins.
  1989   Introduction: Prospects and problems of prototype theory. *Linguistics* 27: 587–612.
Gilquin, Gaëtanelle
  2004   Corpus-based cognitive study of the main English causative verbs. A syntactic, semantic, lexical and stylistic approach. Ph.D. dissertation, Centre for English Corpus Linguistics, Université catholique de Louvain.
Givón, Talmy
  1986   Prototypes: Between Plato and Wittgenstein. In: Colette Craig (ed.), *Noun Classes and Categorization*, 77–102. Amsterdam/Philadelphia: John Benjamins.
Goldsmith, John
  1984   Causative verbs in English. In: Veena Mishra Testen and Joseph Drogo (eds.), *Papers from the Parasession on Lexical Semantics*, David 117–130. Chicago Linguistic Society.

Gries, Stefan Th.
    2003   Towards a corpus-based identification of prototypical instances of constructions. *Annual Review of Cognitive Linguistics* 1: 1–28.

Haiman, John
    1985   Symmetry. In: John Haiman (ed.), *Iconicity in Syntax. Proceedings of a Symposium on Iconicity in Syntax. Stanford, June 24–6, 1983*, 73–95. Amsterdam/Philadelphia: John Benjamins.

Hampton, James A.
    1981   An investigation of the nature of abstract concepts. *Memory and Cognition* 9 (2): 149–156.

Heider, Eleanor R.
    1971   "Focal" color areas and the development of color names. *Developmental Psychology* 4: 447–455.
    1972   Universals in color naming and memory. *Journal of Experimental Psychology* 93: 10–20.

Hopper, Paul J. and Sandra A. Thompson
    1980   Transitivity in grammar and discourse. *Language* 56 (1): 251–299.

Itkonen, Esa
    1983   *Causality in Linguistic Theory. A Critical Investigation into the Philosophical and Methodological Foundations of 'Non-Autonomous' Linguistics.* London/Canberra: Croom Helm.

Kemmer, Suzanne
    2001   Causative constructions and cognitive models: The English *make* causative. In: *The First Seoul International Conference on Discourse and Cognitive Linguistics: Perspectives for the 21st Century*, 803–846. Seoul: Discourse and Cognitive Linguistics Society of Korea.

Kemmer, Suzanne and Arie Verhagen
    1994   The grammar of causatives and the conceptual structure of events. *Cognitive Linguistics* 5 (2): 115–156.

Lakoff, George
    1977   Linguistic gestalts. In: Samuel E. Fox, Woodford A. Beach, and Shulamith Philosoph (eds.), *Papers from the Thirteenth Regional Meeting of the Chicago Linguistic Society*, 236–287. Chicago, IL: Chicago Linguistic Society.
    1982   Categories: An essay in cognitive linguistics. In: The Linguistic Society of Korea (ed.), *Linguistics in the Morning Calm. Selected Papers from SICOL-1981*, 139–193. Seoul, Korea: Hanshin.
    1987   *Women, Fire, and Dangerous Things. What Categories Reveal about the Mind.* Chicago/London: The University of Chicago Press.

Lakoff, George and Mark Johnson
    1980   *Metaphors We Live By.* Chicago/London: The University of Chicago Press.

Langacker, Ronald W.
    1991   *Foundations of Cognitive Grammar. Vol. II. Descriptive Application.* Stanford, CA: Stanford University Press.

Lemmens, Maarten
    1998   *Lexical Perspectives on Transitivity and Ergativity. Causative Constructions in English.* Amsterdam/Philadelphia: John Benjamins.

MacLennan, Bruce J.
    1998   Finding order in our world: The primacy of the concrete in neural representations and the role of invariance in substance reidentification. *Behavioral and Brain Sciences* 21 (1): 78–79.

Mair, Christian
    1994   Is *see* becoming a conjunction? The study of grammaticalisation as a meeting ground for corpus linguistics and grammatical theory. In: Udo Fries, Gunnel Tottie, and Peter Schneider (eds.), *Creating and Using English Language Corpora. Papers from the Fourteenth International Conference on English Language Research on Computerized Corpora, Zürich 1993*, 127–137. Amsterdam/Atlanta, GA: Rodopi.

Niemeier, Susanne
    2003   Applied Cognitive Linguistics: The notion of boundedness/unboundedness in the foreign language classroom. In: International Cognitive Linguistics Association (ed.), *8th International Cognitive Linguistics Conference. Cognitive Linguistics, Functionalism, Discourse Studies: Common Ground and New Directions. Logroño, July 20–25, 2003*, 109. Logroño, Spain: University of La Rioja.

Noordman, Leo G. M. and Femke de Blijzer
    2000   On the processing of causal relations. In: Elizabeth Couper-Kuhlen and Bernd Kortmann (eds.), *Cause – Condition – Concession – Contrast. Cognitive and Discourse Perspectives*, 35–56. Berlin/New York: Mouton de Gruyter.

Nordquist, Dawn
    2004   Comparing elicited data and corpora. In: Michel Achard and Suzanne Kemmer (eds.), *Language, Culture, and Mind*, 211–224. Stanford, CA: CSLI Publications.

Posner, Michael I.
    1986   Empirical studies of prototypes. In: Colette Craig (ed.), *Noun Classes and Categorization*, 53–61. Amsterdam/Philadelphia: John Benjamins.

Radden, Günter
    1992   The cognitive approach to natural language. In: Martin Pütz (ed.), *Thirty Years of Linguistic Evolution. Studies in Honour of René*

Dirven on the Occasion of his Sixtieth Birthday, 513–541. Amsterdam/Philadelphia: John Benjamins.

Reed, Stephen K.
    1972   Pattern recognition and categorization. *Cognitive Psychology* 3: 382–407.

Roebben, Nicolas
    2004   Etude de l'impact des connecteurs de cause sur la compréhension des textes expositifs. Ph.D. dissertation, Université catholique de Louvain.

Roland, Douglas and Daniel Jurafsky
    2002   Verb sense and verb subcategorization probabilities. In: Paola Merlo and Suzanne Stevenson (eds.), *The Lexical Basis of Sentence Processing: Formal, Computational, and Experimental Issues*, 325–346. Amsterdam/Philadelphia: John Benjamins.

Rosch, Eleanor
    1973   On the internal structure of perceptual and semantic categories. In: Timothy E. Moore (ed.), *Cognitive Development and the Acquisition of Language*, 111–144. New York/San Francisco/London: Academic Press.
    1975   Cognitive representations of semantic categories. *Journal of Experimental Psychology, General* 104 (3): 192–233.

Rosch, Eleanor and Carolyn B. Mervis
    1975   Family resemblances: Studies in the internal structure of categories. *Cognitive Psychology* 7: 573–605.

Sampson, Geoffrey
    1980   *Schools of Linguistics*. Stanford, CA: Stanford University Press.

Schmid, Hans-Jörg
    2000   *English Abstract Nouns as Conceptual Shells: From Corpus to Cognition*. Berlin/New York: Mouton de Gruyter.

Shibatani, Masayoshi
    1976   The grammar of causative constructions: a conspectus. In: Masayoshi Shibatani (ed.), *The Grammar of Causative Constructions*, 1–40. New York/San Francisco/London: Academic Press.

Shortall, Terry
    in prep.   Corpus, Cognition, and Curriculum. Ph.D. dissertation, The University of Birmingham.

Sinclair, John
    1991   *Corpus, Concordance, Collocation*. Oxford: Oxford University Press.

Stefanowitsch, Anatol
    2001   Constructing causation: A construction grammar approach to analytic causatives. Ph.D. dissertation, Rice University.

Stubbs, Michael
   2004   On very frequent phrases in English: Distributions, functions and structures. Plenary lecture given at ICAME 25, the 25th anniversary meeting of the International Computer Archive for Modern and Medieval English, Verona, Italy, 19–23 May 2004. (Slightly revised version available at <http://www.uni-trier.de/uni/fb2/anglistik/Projekte/stubbs/icame-2004.htm>, last accessed on 12 April 2005.)

Sugamoto, Nobuko
   1989   Pronominality. A noun-pronoun continuum. In: Roberta L. Corrigan, Fred R. Eckman, and Michael Noonan (eds.), *Linguistic Categorization*, 267–291. Amsterdam/Philadelphia: John Benjamins.

Talmy, Leonard
   2000   *Toward a Cognitive Semantics. Vol. I. Concept Structuring Systems.* Cambridge, MA/London, England: The MIT Press.

Taylor, John R.
   1989   *Linguistic Categorization. Prototypes in Linguistic Theory.* Oxford: Clarendon Press.
   1998   Syntactic constructions as prototype categories. In: Michael Tomasello (ed.), *The New Psychology of Language. Cognitive and Functional Approaches to Language Structure*, 177–202. Mahwah, NJ/London: Lawrence Erlbaum.

Teubert, Wolfgang
   1996   Editorial. *International Journal of Corpus Linguistics* 1 (1): iii–x.

Tsohatzidis, Savas L.
   1990   Introduction. In: Savas L. Tsohatzidis (ed.), *Meanings and Prototypes. Studies in Linguistic Categorization*, 1–13. London/New York: Routledge.

Ungerer, Friedrich and Hans-Jörg Schmid
   1996   *An Introduction to Cognitive Linguistics.* London/New York: Longman.

Van Ek, Jan A. and Nico J. Robat
   1984   *The Student's Grammar of English.* Glasgow: Bell & Bain.

Van Valin, Robert D. Jr.
   2001   The acquisition of complex sentences: A case study in the role of theory in the study of language development. *Chicago Linguistic Society. Parasession Papers* 36: 511–531. Available at <http://linguistics.buffalo.edu/research/rrg/vanvalin_papers/Acq_of_complex_sent.pdf> (last accessed on 5 February 2004).

Veryzer, Robert W. and J. Wesley Hutchinson
   1998   The influence of unity and prototypicality on aesthetic responses to new product designs. *Journal of Consumer Research* 24 (4): 374–394.

Werner, Patricia K., John P. Nelson, and Lida R. Baker
   1990   *Mosaic II. A Content-based Grammar. Second Edition.* New York: McGraw-Hill.

Wierzbicka, Anna
   1985   *Lexicography and Conceptual Analysis.* Ann Arbor, MI: Karoma.
   1990   "Prototypes save": On the uses and abuses of the notion of "prototype" in linguistics and related fields. In: Savas L. Tsohatzidis (ed.), *Meanings and Prototypes. Studies in Linguistic Categorization*, 347–367. London/New York: Routledge.

Winters, Margaret E.
   1990   Toward a theory of syntactic prototypes. In: Savas L. Tsohatzidis (ed.), *Meanings and Prototypes. Studies in Linguistic Categorization*, 285–306. London/New York: Routledge.

Yamamoto, Mutsumi
   1999   *Animacy and Reference. A Cognitive Approach to Corpus Linguistics.* Amsterdam/Philadelphia: John Benjamins.

Passivisability of English periphrastic causatives

Willem Hollmann

Abstract

Causatives in English and other languages display differences in passivisability. In line with e.g. Rice (1987) it is argued that this variation is due to different degrees of semantic transitivity. Transitivity is defined in terms of Hopper and Thompson's (1980) parameters, modified in the light of typological research on causatives. The British National Corpus was used to obtain examples of both active and passive periphrastic causative *make*, semantically the most general causative. A comparison between these two data sets yields quantitative evidence for a number of correlations between transitivity properties and passivisability. Because of the generality of *make* the results may be extended to other causatives. And due to the grounding in typological work the correlations can be stated as implicational universals. These universals explain many of the facts of differential passivisability but some additional hypotheses are made to account for more. A few questions remain, but these may evaporate if we allow for the possibility that some semantic factors are more important than others.

Keywords: causatives; passive; transitivity; typology.

1. Introduction

This paper sets out to account for the differences in passivisability of English periphrastic causatives – i.e. causative constructions with infinitival complements – such as *cause, force, get, have, make, persuade*.[1] Compare for instance *make*, which passivises readily, to *have*, which does not:

(1) *Recruits [...] were made to hop on the spot.* (BNC CJR 460)

(2) **Recruits were had to hop on the spot.*

The inherently causative predicates *force* also passivises easily, which, interestingly, is also true in languages where more general causatives are more resistant to passivisation:

German (cf. Nedjalkov 1971: 27):[2]

(3)　*Der Student wurde gezwungen abzureisen.*
　　　'The student was forced to leave.'

(4)　**Der Student wurde abzureisen gelassen.*
　　　the student was leave let

Dutch:

(5)　*De student werd gedwongen (om) te vertrekken.*
　　　the student became forced (for) to leave
　　　'The student was forced to leave.'

(6)　**De student werd laten/doen vertrekken.*[3]
　　　the student became let/do to leave

Spanish:[4]

(7)　*El estudiante fue obligado a salir.*
　　　'The student was forced to leave.'

(8)　**El estudiante fue hecho (/dejado) a salir.*
　　　the student was made (/let) to go

Get is somewhere in between, accepting passive only marginally (informal inquiries among American English speakers suggest increased acceptability if *got* is replaced with *gotten*):

(9)　??*Recruits were got to hop on the spot.*

(10)　*The agreeableness of a thing depends [...] on the number of people who can be got to like it.* (*OED*, likeableness)

English *persuade* patterns with *make* and *force*, accepting passivisation easily: *cause* also accepts passivisation, though not as readily as *force*, *make* and *persuade*.[5]

(11) *Essentially, people in their work roles are caused to respond from their unconscious world of internal objects.* (BNC CBH 599)

(12) *It was not until early in 1984 that Branson was finally persuaded to stop living on the houseboat, by his doctor, after he had contracted a severe case of pneumonia.* (BNC FNX 1408)

The evidence for these differences in passivisability comes not only from casual observation and informal native speaker judgments, but also from corpora.[6] Gilquin (2004) used the British National Corpus[7] to shed light on the frequency of passivisation of *cause, get, have* and *make*. Basing herself on a 9.8 million words subcorpus of spoken and written texts (cf. Gilquin 2004: 186–191) she finds that *make* passivises in more than 8 per cent of cases (Gilquin 2004: 256), while for *cause* the ratio is significantly lower, at .5 per cent (Gilquin 2004: 257). Due to the design of Gilquin's search algorithm she does not report on the frequency of passive *get* and *have* in her subcorpus (2004: 257), but having also carried out a less automated search of the whole BNC for these verbs she does not provide any unambiguous examples of passive *have* and *get* either. (She seems to analyse *The argument is not that the check is fallible, for if it were we might still hope that enough memories could be **got to** prop each other up, as Ayer suggests (Ayer, 1954).* [BNC F9K 1333] as an unambiguous example [Gilquin 2004: 257] but the problem here is that memories are not normally thought of as being consciously manipulable in this fashion, and so an interpretation on which *got* means something like 'obtain' and the *to*-infinitive clause is an adjunct would be more plausible.) An analysis of the FLOB corpus[8] (one million words, British English) yields similar results. There are 8 tokens of passive *make* out of a total of 156, i.e. 5.1 per cent. There are no passive tokens of the less passivisable constructions *cause* and *get* – not very surprising given that the total numbers are only 22 and 20, respectively – and, as expected, none of *have* either. The FLOB data also confirm the ease of passivisation of *force* and *persuade* (not included in Gilquin's study): 30 out of 68 *force* tokens (44.1 per cent) can be classified as passive; for *persuade* the frequency is 11 out of 44 (25.0 per cent). Whilst these percentages are so high that one may be tempted to argue for a higher degree of passivisability than in the case of *make*, the problem is that for these two constructions the passive constructions shades into the copula construction. Consider, for instance, that in an example like *Few of them [...] will ever be persuaded to accept at face value Mr. Saddam's periodic offers of am-*

nesty to Kurdish refugees (FLOB A04 178) we could insert an intensifier such as *fully, entirely* or *completely* as a modifier of *persuaded*, suggesting that the participle may function here as an adjective. Note also that by replacing *be* with *feel* the meaning of the sentence changes only very little. A similar argument can be made in relation to some cases involving *force*: e.g. *But Dickon was no match for the team of four galloping greys and disconsolately, she was forced to give up the chase* (FLOB P28 67) could be rephrased as *But Dickon [...] found herself forced [...]* The prudent solution to this classification problem taken here is to equate *force, make* and *persuade* in terms of passivisability.

Despite the considerable amount of attention causatives have received in the literature crossconstructional variation in passivisability has not been extensively studied at all. The only previous in-depth study I am aware of apart from Gilquin (2004) is Stefanowitsch (2001: 196–209). Focusing on *force, get, have* and *make* he argues that passivisability depends on the compatibility between the semantics-pragmatics of the passive construction, and of the relevant causative construction. The function of the passive is to increase the salience of the O argument (the causee) at the expense of A (the causer).[9] The details of Stefanowitsch's semantic analysis would take us too far afield but briefly, *make* and *force* are analysed as construing the causative event such that the causee not the causer is in focus. This meaning dovetails nicely with that of the passive (Stefanowitsch 2001: 202–204). *Have*, by contrast, features a relatively salient causer and so is naturally less congruous for passivisation (Stefanowitsch 2001: 204–205).

Using careful corpus-based semantic analysis, Stefanowitsch provides an attractive account of the passivisation facts of *make, force* and *have*. However, he abstracts away from the marginal passivisability of *get* (2001: 205; cf. examples [9–10], above). Analysing its meaning as parallel to that of *have* he sees the causer as more in focus than the causee. Admittedly, Stefanowitsch seems to suggest that in *get* the causee may be more salient than in *have*: he argues that in the former it "is affected in a sense: it is convinced or tricked into doing something it would not have done otherwise, i.e. there is a change of opinion with respect to the willingness to perform the result" (2001: 205). If the causee is therefore less backgrounded in *get* than in *have*, the facts of (marginal) passivisation are less surprising. However, Stefanowitsch also implies that the causer is more salient in *get* than in *have*, since in the former but not the latter he sees it as "very agentive, having to act on the causee for a prolonged period of time" (2001: 205). Stefanowitsch's prediction regarding the effect of the non-punctuality of the causing event on passivisability is contradicted by Hopper and Thompson (1980), as I explain below. For now, the problem is that if *both* causer and causee should be more salient in *get* than in *have* it does not follow that the overall balance of focus in *get* is less skewed towards the causer. In other words, Stefanowitsch's account does not easily accommodate passive *get*.

Stefanowitsch would also have to account for the ease of passivisation of *cause*. One of his arguments for excluding *cause* is that compared to *force, get, have* and *make* it is "much more abstract" (2001: 161).[10] To the extent that this is true – with Dixon (1991, 2000), I argue in §2, below, that it is not –, Stefanowitsch (2001) does not explicitly describe how the (relative) ease of passivisation of *cause* falls out of its semantics: how does abstractness relate to relative salience of causer and causee? Stefanowitsch (personal communication) suggests that the passivisability of *cause* can actually be explained by recognising some aspects of the semantics of the construction, notably the lack of benefit on the part of the causer and the negative semantic prosody with intransitive lower clauses (cf. Stubbs 1995: 43 for a similar suggestion concerning non-infinitival complements of *cause*), implying a highly affected causee. It follows that the causer is relatively non-salient, and the causee, salient.

Persuade is also ignored in Stefanowitsch's discussion on passivisation. Elsewhere in his study he notes that it is more specific in meaning than e.g. *make*, in that it "typically, but not necessarily, suggest[s] some type of verbal interaction between the causer and the causee" (2001: 40). Drawing on Rice (1987) I argue below that this specificity contributes significantly to its ease of passivisation. Note, though, that this semantic dimension cannot be captured in terms of relative salience of causer/causee in any obvious way.

The account presented below is similar in spirit to Stefanowitsch's study in that it, too, traces the differential passivisability of the various causatives to differences in meaning. In view of the connection between passivisability and (semantic/conceptual) transitivity (see e.g. Bolinger 1978; Hopper and Thompson 1980; Keenan 1985; Rice 1987)[11] the starting point of the present account is Hopper and Thompson's (1980) empirically well-supported parameters of transitivity. This allows the conclusions about the relation between functional properties of the constructions and passivisability to be stated as implicational universals. Herein lies the main contrast with Stefanowitsch's study: given the explicit grounding in typological research the conclusions can be more straightforwardly extended to other languages.

2. Methodology

At first blush the most obvious approach to studying the correlation between the semantics (transitivity) and passivisability of periphrastic causatives might seem to be simply to analyse their meaning and see which properties appear to be responsible for the differences in passivisability. An important problem emerges, however: for some causatives it is hard to pin down their semantics to anything very specific; *make* is the clearest example. Inoue suggests that its semantics only consist of the component [+cause], i.e. it merely represents the fact of causation (1992: 132). Similarly, Dixon, recognising that scholars commonly assume that *cause* is the most neutral causative, argues that because of the association of *cause* with indirect causation (for the notion of directness cf. §2.2.3., below) *make* is actually the least specific (Dixon 1991: 194, 294, 2000: 36–37; using data from the FLOB corpus Hollmann [2003] has found some evidence to support the notion that *make* is compatible with most types of causation, see e.g. p.156).

I set out to turn this generality of *make* into a virtue. By carefully analysing and comparing instances of active versus passive *make* in terms of a substantially revised version of Hopper and Thompson's transitivity parameters I will demonstrate what semantic properties go hand in hand especially naturally with passive coding. The basic procedure here is to score every active and passive example for each of the transitivity parameters; more about this in §2.3. Properties of transitivity that feature significantly more frequently in passive than active *make* should correspond to properties that are typically present in other causatives that passivise readily as well, both in English and – because of the crosslinguistic validity of the parameters involved – in other languages. Conversely, parameter values that are not significantly more frequent in passive *make* than in the active are not expected to be relevant to a given construction's degree of passivisability. The underlying suggestion here is that passive being associated with increased semantic transitivity, passive *make* will tend to be used for situations which are conceptually highly transitive. These situations will have certain characteristics. And depending on their semantics, I contend, other causatives will be more or less compatible with those characteristics.

Thus, based on the parameters that are found to yield statistically significant differences in active vs. passive *make* I will come up with some hierarchies – and corresponding universals – of transitivity/passivisability of causatives. The possibility of using (testing) these universals in (against) other languages is of course subject to the language in question having a reasonably clear active/passive distinction.

Testing the hypotheses against crosslinguistic data would be highly desirable. Careful intralinguistic analysis is a useful basis for discovering crosslinguistic universals (Croft 2001: 107) but one expects that in the light of crosslinguistic data a certain amount of fine-tuning may be required: if one focuses on a single language one may easily miss distinctions, i.e. if the different values are coded in the same way in the language under investigation.

It is worth underlining that the universals will be of the implicational type. That is, I will *not* argue that certain types of causative verbs will *always* allow passivisation and others *never*. Instead, the generalisations will be of the form: if causative construction X passivises, then any other construction that is higher on the scales of transitivity will also passivise, but not necessarily ones that are lower on the hierarchies.

In addition, the scope of passive varies for each language, and so the cut-off points (or regions, consider English *get*) between causatives that do and those that do not passivise will not be constant crosslinguistically: languages that allow passivisation of relatively intransitive predicates in general will also be expected to allow passivisation of causatives that are low on transitivity; conversely, languages that allow passivisation of only highly transitive predicates will only have a passive for accordingly highly transitive causatives.

The remainder of this section, §§2.1.–2.3., describes three methodological issues in some detail. First, I show how I went about finding a corpus large enough to get a solid number of examples of causative *make*. The second aspect of my methodology concerns Hopper and Thompson's (1980) transitivity parameters: since their account is designed to accommodate clauses in general it must be rendered more suitable for causatives. The third methodological dimension described below is the scoring system.

2.1. The corpus

In my quest for a sufficiently large corpus to get several hundreds of examples of active and passive causative *make*, the British National Corpus (BNC) was a natural choice. I searched it by means of the University of Zürich interface.[12] For reasons to do with size and clarity (see Hollmann 2003: 180–181), I used the 90 million word written part.

Passive periphrastic causative *make* is not very common so I collected examples from the entire written part. My search string was *BE made to*[13] (where the capitals indicate that I looked for all forms of *be*). For the active, I searched for *make* in all its morphological guises. Since the verb *make* is very frequent indeed, this time I restricted my search to one of the subcorpus options, i.e. "beginning sample".[14] The subcorpus in question runs to some 21 million words, which allowed me to find sufficiently high numbers of examples.

I restricted myself to the simple present and the simple past, taking 100 examples of each of these tense-aspect constructions for the active and for the passive, yielding a data base of 400 examples in total. The reason why I chose the simple present and past is that these are the only TA constructions that occur 100 times (in fact, more often than that; the first 100 unambiguously causative[15] examples were selected). I excluded examples where *make* was preceded by a modal verb:

(13)   *For that violation they can and should be made to pay.*
       (BNC ACS 1047)

The reason for excluding these was the resulting changes in transitivity caused by the modals.[16] The decreased transitivity of example (13) is purely due to the modal auxiliary; it is not related to the semantics of the periphrastic causative construction itself – which is what the present study sets out to explore.

2.2. The semantic parameters: Modifying Hopper and Thompson (1980)

Hopper and Thompson's (1980) parameters form the starting point of this investigation, but I modify them substantially. This is necessary because Hopper and Thompson's account was designed for clauses in general. As a result, first, not all their parameters are relevant to causatives. Second, some parameters must be more precisely/clearly defined to make them more suitable for causatives. Third, Hopper and Thompson's account misses out on a few semantic distinctions that contribute to differences in transitivity in causatives.

Table 1 below presents Hopper and Thompson's parameters with their high and low transitivity values:

Table 1. Hopper and Thompson's parameters of transitivity (1980: 252)

Parameter	High transitivity	Low transitivity
participants	2 or more participants	1 participant
kinesis	action	non-action
aspect	telic	atelic
punctuality	punctual	non-punctual
volitionality	volitional	non-volitional
affirmation	affirmative	negative
mode	realis	irrealis
agency	A high in potency	A low in potency
affectedness of O	O totally affected	O not affected
individuation of O	O highly individuated	O non-individuated

There are certain interrelations between properties. These interconnections determine the structure of the discussion in the rest of §2 and §3. The parameter groupings are as follows:

1. causality (volitionality, agency, affectedness and participants)
2. aspect (kinesis, aspect and punctuality)
3. modality (affirmation and mode)
4. individuation of O (consists of various subparameters, cf. Hopper and Thompson 1980: 253).

I discuss causality in §2.2.1., below. To see that kinesis, aspect and punctuality hang together one should for instance consider that a non-action such as liking beer is always atelic and nonpunctual, and that a punctual event (achievement) such as knocking someone down is inherently telic. Affirmation and mode are connected in that negative sentences are always irrealis. Modality plays no further role in my account. This is because it is not a property of the causative construction itself but a function of higher level constructions in which the causative may be embedded, such as the Negative construction. In other words, to the best of my knowledge there is no language where affirmative vs. negative and realis vs. irrealis corresponds to coding distinctions in causatives. The same applies to individuation of O, which is therefore also omitted from the rest of the discussion.

§§2.2.1.–2.2.2. below describe causality and aspect in more detail; §2.2.3.–2.2.5. discuss three further dimensions of transitivity in causatives: directness, sphere of control and specificity. As regards the actual scoring of the corpus examples, only causality, aspect and directness are used. The values for sphere of control and specificity are constant across the data, i.e. *make* is invariably neutral with respect to the sphere of control frame and always relatively unspecific. As a result, while these parameters are felt to be significant, the implicational universals hypothesised below capturing the relation between sphere of control/specificity on the one hand, and passivisability, on the other, are not supported by corpus data.

2.2.1. Causality

One of the properties of causality is affectedness of O. Hopper and Thompson are less than fully transparent about this parameter. They describe it as "how completely that patient is affected" (1980: 253) and illustrate this by pointing out that the patient is affected "more effectively in, say, *I drank up the milk* than in *I drank some of the milk*" (Hopper and Thompson 1980: 253). Example (14), below, also features "complete" affectedness (confusingly also called "total"), while (15) does not:

(14) *Jerry knocked Sam down.* (Hopper and Thompson 1980: 253)

(15) *Jerry likes beer.* (Hopper and Thompson 1980: 253)

In the typological literature affectedness is sometimes analysed as a complex property, consisting of 2 dimensions. The first has to do with the object itself and concerns the distinction between the causee being affected in his/her/its entirety by the caused event or only in part. Referring to Aikhenvald (2000: 158) Dixon states that Tariana makes a morphological distinction between full and partial affectedness: the objects in sentences corresponding to English *You made my house fall down completely* and *They made some woodchips fall* (2000: 67) are marked differently. The idea here is that the woodchips are conceptualised against the larger domain of the entire house. Dixon's first example also illustrates the highly transitive value on the second subparameter, which involves not so much the participant acted on but the change-of-state event it is subjected to, specifically, whether that event is completed. The house falling down completely is conceptualised as the natural endpoint of the process in question. By contrast, scratching the surface of the house counts as incomplete affectedness, as one can always do some more scratching. The same goes for making a few woodchips fall.

Causative situations such as the event described by *mow the lawn* show that the twin dimensions of affectedness are very often two sides of the same coin. Indeed, Dowty has proposed an insightful unidimensional account of affectedness, in terms of the so-called "incremental theme" (1991: 567–571 and *passim*; see also Hay, Kennedy, and Levin 1999; Croft in prep.), which I will follow. The central idea is that the extent to which the lawn has been affected by the mowing (i.e. the area that has been mowed) parallels the extent to which the activity of mowing the lawn is complete. Put differently, the affecting event and the affected object are "homomorphic" (Dowty 1991: 567). The incremental theme, labelled "verbal scale" by Croft (in prep.), represents the extent to which the O argument, or more accurately some property of O, has been affected in the event. The property in question depends on the lexical semantics of the predicate. Thus, in the case mowing the lawn it is the degree to which the lawn is mowed; in the case of making someone/something engage in/undergo some event, the extent to which one succeeds in this.

The causatives presently studied are incompatible with zero success; for these situations so-called non-implicative causatives, such as *ask*, *order* or *tell* may be used:

(16) *The sergeant made the recruits hop on the spot, but they didn't do it.*

(17) *The sergeant ordered the recruits to hop on the spot, but they didn't do it.*

Alternatively, of course, the implicative causative may complement a verb such as *try* or *want* (*The sergeant tried/wanted to make the recruits hop on the spot, but they didn't do it*) but then it is the matrix verb not the causative that codes the lack of success.[17]

Thus, the possibilities for the incremental theme/verbal scale in terms of transitivity are twofold. Full affectedness is maximally transitive:

(18) *Having Goldberg in the room with it, as he has been in my life since that first day at college, made me grasp clearly, for the first time, just what it is I have been after, he wrote.* (BNC A08 2766)

Cases where the degree of success is somehow not full are minimally transitive:

(19) *He is the only pianist I have ever heard who does not make Balakirev's Islamey sound clumsy in places.* (BNC BMC 2438)

(20) *During interrogation some detainees were made to kneel for long periods, in some cases on bottle tops and pebbles.* (BNC CFH 95)

In (19) the event of making the piece sound clumsy in places is viewed against the background of making it sound clumsy in its entirety. In interpreting (20) some detainees are seen to be affected, while others are not. Labelling a lack of full affectedness "partial" affectedness, we get the hierarchy below, where the left-hand side is associated with maximal transitivity, the right hand side, with minimal transitivity:

full < partial

Moving on to the properties volitionality and agency, let me first note that they are interrelated in that volitionality implies high potency. Hopper and Thompson define agency and volitionality only relative to A, but in causatives O also potentially displays these characteristics, i.e. if human or at least animate. More generally, Os – especially if human/animate – have the potential to put up *resistance* (cf. Talmy 2000: 416, 458; see Hollmann [2003: Ch.2] for some discussion). Overcoming that amounts to increased transitivity. A related consideration here is the increased salience of mental participants as compared to inanimates (cf. Hopper and Thompson 1980: 253). This implies that causation where the causer and causee are mental entities is more transitive than causation where both are things (all other things being equal).[18] Talmy (1976, 1985, 1988; cf. also Croft 1991) has proposed a four-way classification of causation types based on the animate vs. inanimate distinction in causers and causes:

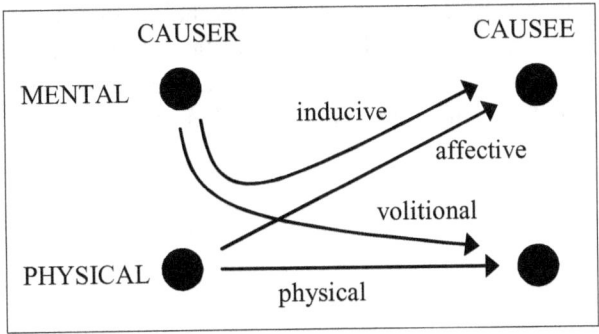

Figure 1. Talmy's typology of causation types (after Croft 1991: 167)

In terms of this classification, a partial ordering presents itself with respect to transitivity. Physical causation is the least transitive, as both A and O are inanimate. The inducive type, conversely, is the most highly transitive, featuring as it does an animate causer and causee. Volitional and affective causation are somewhere in between, both of them having one mental and one inanimate participant. In order to distinguish between these types, I tentatively suggest that due to the inherent salience associated with the matrix clause subject position as compared to the lower clause subject, an animate causer is more salient than an animate causee (again, all other things being equal). This yields the following hierarchy:

inducive < volitional < affective < physical

Hopper and Thompson's participants and affectedness of O parameters, finally, are also connected: consider that a unary participant clause implies that the patient is not affected (since there is none). One might perhaps question the usefulness of the participants parameter in the context of causatives, as the presence of a causer and a causee might seem to imply the presence of two participants. This is not strictly speaking true, however:

(21) *If people try to apply a "turning off the tap" strategy when they are hopping up and down in scalding water they may merely make themselves feel worse.* (BNC CKS 1425)

In (21) the causer and causee are identical. Talmy's concept of the "divided self" is useful here. He uses it to explain the force dynamics of a situation such as the one portrayed by *He thinks he should go* (2000: 451): human beings can apparently conceive of the psyche as internally divided, the different parts being in force-dynamic conflict. Prototypical unary causal chains are a logical impossibility, but (21) demonstrates that cases of the divided self do exist. They are analysed as being lower in transitivity than binary chains:

$$\text{binary} < \text{divided self}^{19}$$

2.2.2. Aspect

Here the scales remain unchanged:

$$\text{action} < \text{non-action}$$
$$\text{telic} < \text{atelic}$$
$$\text{punctual} < \text{non-punctual}$$

2.2.3. Directness

In typological(ly oriented) studies on causatives there has been a lot of debate on "directness" (e.g. Fodor 1970; Fillmore 1972; Jackendoff 1972; Wierzbicka 1975; Givón 2001; Cristofaro 2003). Duffley (1992), Fischer (1995) and Stefanowitsch (2001) have also discussed this, though only with regard to English.

Synthesising the literature, I analyse directness as consisting of three parameters. The first is unity of time. This concerns the temporal relation between the causing and caused events, i.e. whether they occur (or are conceptualised as occurring) hand-in-hand, or with a discontinuity between them (see e.g. Fodor 1970: 432–423; Wierzbicka 1975: 497–499). Presence of unity of time is analysed as more highly transitive than a delayed caused event:

$$\text{presence of unity of time} < \text{absence of unity of time}$$

The overwhelming majority of my examples feature cotemporality of causing and caused events, but some do not. In the literature absence of unity of time is usually exemplified with made-up sentences containing temporal adverbials (cf. Fodor's example *Floyd caused the glass to melt on Sunday by heating it on Saturday*) but many corpus examples are less clear-cut. One is often forced to rely on careful consideration of the context:

(22) *Walker also found that none of the 11 pronouns resolved correctly by the original BFP but not by Hobbs were made to fail when the alteration was made.* (BNC 898 B2X 831)

Here, the alteration that is referred to as the event causing the computer program to fail clearly precedes the failure itself. (BFP is a computer algorithm designed to carry out pronoun resolution; the cognitive scientist Jerry Hobbs has developed a program with the same function.)

The second relevant distinction presence of unity of space vs. a spatial remove between the causing and caused events (see e.g. Fillmore 1972: 4; Wierzbicka 1975: 494–495). Spatial coincidence of causing and caused events is analysed as more highly transitive than a remove:

presence of unity of space < absence of unity of space

Most of my *make* examples feature the more transitive value, i.e. presence of unity of space, but there are some exceptions. While (23), below, shows that sometimes the classification is facilitated by a place adverbial (i.e. *there*), (24) shows that once again, matters are not always that straightforward, and the context must be taken into account:

(23) *One of these areas was Russia, especially because the interest that his work had aroused there made him consider the previously unthinkable possibility of a communist revolution occurring in that country.* (BNC A6S 604)

(24) *CINEMA [sic] workers were made to take lie detector tests after thousands of pounds went missing from a 10-screen UCI complex.* (BNC CBF 12020)

Example (23) describes the effect that the Russians' reaction to Karl Marx's books had on him, at a point when he was clearly not in Russia. In (24) the cinema workers are presumably told at work to go and take the lie detector test at some place like the police station.

While unity of time and unity of space are applicable relatively straightforwardly to my corpus, the third parameter is not. This parameter concerns the absence or presence of another causal participant in between the causer and the causee (see e.g. Jackendoff 1972: 28; Dixon 2000: 70). If such an intermediary party is absent, the causer transfers force to the causee directly and the event is thus more transitive than if there *is* such an intermediary. For a clear illustration of a tripartite causal chain consider:

(25) *I had her lose her temper by sending John over to taunt her.*
(Givón 1975: 65)

The speaker did not *directly* make *her* lose her temper. Instead, this was brought about by the intermediary event of John's taunting her.

The problem in the present study is that in the passive the causer is almost always left out. This renders it hard to determine whether there is a third (implicit) causal participant. To see that this is so, consider the passive version of (25) presented below as (26), which is admittedly strained but serves to illustrate the point (the causative verb in this case has been changed to *make* since passive *have* would have been ungrammatical):

(26) *She was made to lose her temper.*

How now, can one be sure what/who is the causer? And so how does one decide between presence and absence of an intermediary party? The corresponding active sentence might be (25) but for all we know (26) could also be the passive of a direct causal chain:

(27) *I made her lose her temper (by taunting her).*

For this reason the property of absence vs. presence of an intermediary causal party is omitted from the present investigation. One might argue that as a result too much weight is shifted toward unity of time/space, but I suggest in §4 that there is a more serious problem. In practice, the omission of the third subparameter means that in scoring the examples directness can be treated as ternary:

unity of space and time < absence of unity of space/time < absence of unity of space and time

2.2.4. Sphere of control (SC)

Hopper and Thompson do not discuss this dimension, but it has been alluded to by Katz (1977: 216), Givón (1980: 368), Shannon (1987: 8, 11, 173, 182–183), Duffley (1992: 71), Fischer (1996: 256) and Stefanowitsch (2001: 136–137, 152) though never explicitly in relation with transitivity. The basic idea here is that causation is sometimes seen as occurring against a background assumption of inherent control of the causer over the causee. The following examples show that this control frame is part of the semantics of *have*:

(28)   *He had his secretary order some coffee, then closed the door and sat down behind his desk.* (BNC ECK 2589)

(29)   ?*She had her boss order some coffee.*

Force is in this respect the opposite of *have*: it codes a clear absence of a control frame; this is the very reason why the use of force must be resorted to. The use of force renders the causative situation more highly transitive than situations portrayed by *have*, where the successful outcome of the causer/causee manipulation is already implicit in the social/physical power relation between them. As the causatives *cause, get, make* and *persuade* do not seem to portray either a strong presence or absence of a control frame, the hierarchy has three values:

$$-SC < \pm SC < +SC$$

2.2.5. Specificity

Specificity is not mentioned by Hopper and Thompson (1980) but Rice argues that it plays a role in transitivity, such that all other things being equal more specific events are more highly transitive than less specific ones:

(30)   *The narrow footbridge was walked on / tread on / run on / trampled on / stumbled on / wobbled on / slid on / slipped on / *gone on by the kindergartners.* (Rice 1987: 98)

Make is always equally unspecific. However, Hollmann (2003: Chs. 5–6, cf. also 2005) shows, on the basis of (FLOB) corpus data, that variation does obtain *across* causatives. Specifically, in addition to a general lack of specificity, causatives may be restricted to a particular type of causer/causee configuration. *Force*, for instance, which occurred 68 times, never had an inanimate causee. Similar degrees of specificity hold for most of the other causatives under consideration, viz. *cause, get* and *have*. *Persuade* is even more specific: not only does it almost without exception code inducive causation (93 per cent of cases), it typically specifies that the causer interacted with the causee *verbally*. This suggests the following 3 point scale:

> verbal inductive < causation type restricted < causation type underspecified

2.3. The scoring system

Every example is rated against each of the properties making up the 3 parameters causality, aspect and directness. In the scoring process I assigned the score 0 to the minimally transitive value, every more highly transitive value receiving a rating of the next integer, i.e. 1, 2 or 3 (with 4 points the causation type hierarchy has the highest number of values). It is crucial to observe that the parameters are analysed as ordinal, as opposed to interval or ratio variables. That is, while the higher value associated with a higher point on a given hierarchy represents increased transitivity as compared to a lower point, I make no assumptions as to the exact quantitative nature of this increase. For example, with reference to the 4 point causation type scale, inducive causation (e.g. ex. [24]) receives a score of 3 but this type is not seen as 1.5 times as transitive as volitional causation (e.g. ex. [19]) – which is scored 2 – or 3 times as highly transitive as affective causation (e.g. ex. [23]) – which gets a score of 1. Contrast this with a ratio variable, e.g. length: 2 inches is exactly twice as long as 1 inch. Moreover, interpreting the properties as ordinal variables also implies that I do not assume that the difference in degree of transitivity between the affective and the volitional type is necessarily the same as that between the latter and inducive causation. Compare in this connection again a ratio variable such as length (the difference between 1 inch and 2 inches equals that between 2 and 3 inches) or an interval variable such as temperature (although 3 degrees Celsius cannot be meaningfully said to be 1.5 times as warm as 2 degrees and 3 times as warm as 1 degree, the increments between the temperatures of 1, 2 and 3 degrees are exactly the same). The only thing that matters is the *ranks* of the points: thus, in the case of causation type the score of 3 merely codes the fact that the inducive type is more transitive than volitional causation, which, in its turn outranks affective (and physical; e.g. ex. [31], below) causation.

(31)   *The jacket was very fitted and single-breasted, cutting in sharp at the waist – which made the trousers balloon right out.* (BNC A6E 452)

In other words, as long as one makes sure that the scores associated with the different points reflect the ranking, in terms of transitivity, of the causation types, one could equally well choose, say, 5, 6, 14 and 80. Moreover, as what matters are ranks not absolute values, my scores do not imply that the highest value on the 4 point causation type scale (scored 3) is more highly transitive than that on a binary scale such as punctuality (scored 1). In fact, anticipating the discussion of the results in Section 4, let me note that initially equal weighting of the parameters will be assumed, i.e. scoring the maximum value on one parameter is analysed as contributing to overall transitivity just as much as on another property.

The issue of inter-rater reliability deserves to be mentioned here as a methodological limitation in my methodology (as well as in that of corpus linguistic studies rather more generally [Stefanowitsch personal communication]). Very briefly, the problem is that different analysts may arrive at different interpretations of some examples. Thus, for instance, on my interpretation of example (24), above, the explicit mention of the cinema in the word *CINEMA workers* implies spatial (and temporal) distance between the main clause and lower clause events. It is not inconceivable, however, that another analyst would take a more coarse-grained view of the space (and time) frame, and judge this to be a case of spatiotemporal contiguity. Ideally, then, one would have several people analyse the same data then average the results. For reasons of time this has not been attempted here.

3. Results

Below, the results the past and present corpora are considered separately and together. Given the ordinal nature of the variables, in determining the significance (or lack thereof) of the differences between active and passive the Mann Whitney U-test (1-tailed) was used.

3.1. Causality

Affectedness of O and participants do not yield significant results; causation type does:

Table 2. U-scores of the past, present, and combined corpora for causation type

Simple past	Simple present	Past + Present
2403.5	2526	9872.5

The differences are very highly significant (p<.001) across the board here, conforming to the implications of Hopper and Thompson (1980).

3.2. Aspect

Kinesis and aspect are not significant but punctuality is, at least to some extent:

Table 3. U-scores of the past, present, and combined corpora for punctuality

Simple past	Simple present	Past + Present
4950	4700	19500

For the simple past there is no significant difference but there is in the simple present data (p<.05), where the passive causatives are on the whole more transitive than the active ones. For the combined corpus p drops to .13. This is not normally seen as significant but the U-test is a relatively weak test (this is because it makes very few assumptions concerning the interpretation of the differences between values and regarding the distribution, as compared to e.g. the t-test). Thus, the result for the combined corpus warrants the hypothesis that there is a correlation, and that a statistically significant result may be obtained with a larger corpus.

3.3. Directness

Table 4. U-scores of the past, present, and combined corpora for directness

Simple past	Simple present	Past + Present
4740	4901	19685.5

The differences do not pass the test for significance at p<05 but for the past there is an association between passive and increased transitivity at the p=.13 level. This, as argued in §3.2., suggests that a correlation may well exist. For the present and combined corpora p drops to .21 and .28, but one still suspects that a larger sample would yield more conclusive evidence for the hypothesised correlation (see further §4, below).

4. Implicational universals

This section presents the implicational universals that may be proposed to capture the relation between the semantics of causatives and their degree of passivisability. After the statement of each universal I outline its implications concerning the expected degree of passivisability of the causatives considered in addition to *make*. In the process I draw on the corpus-informed semantic analysis of causatives presented most elaborately in Hollmann (2003, cf. also 2005). There is no space here to present the details of this analysis. The first universal, arising from my corpus data on aspect, concerns causation type:

> *Implicational universal 1 (causation type)*
> If a language allows passivisation of causative constructions towards the lower, less transitive end of the causation type scale then constructions toward the higher, more transitive end of the scale will also be passivisable (all other things being equal).

Get, have and *persuade* prototypically portray inducive causation (>90 per cent of cases in my FLOB data) and are thus highly transitive. *Cause* is on the other end of this dimension of transitivity, as it typically occurs with inanimate causers (physical/affective causation, >85 per cent). *Force* is somewhere in the middle: it often features a human causer and causee (inducive causation, 46 per cent) but also freely takes inanimate causers (the affective type 54 per cent). *Make* is similar to *force* in not being clearly associated with either end of the scale, but in addition to the inducive (33 per cent) and affective (42 per cent) types it is not infrequent with the volitional and physical configurations (13 and 12 per cent, respectively).

The second parameter describes the effect of punctuality:

Implicational universal 2 (punctuality)

If a language has passivisable causative constructions that (prototypically) describe non-punctual, then punctual causatives are also passivisable (all other things being equal).

Cause, get, have and *make* prototypically describe punctual causation and therefore outrank *get* and *persuade* on this parameter, as the latter are associated with non-punctual causation (these facts have been established mainly on the basis of collocation with adverbials coding duration of time, such as *gradually* or *finally*, cf. e.g. [12], above).

Directness is the third property. The results did not unambiguously suggest that it played a significant role. However, *make* was an unfortunate choice to test its bearing on passivisability/transitivity, because it almost invariably features direct causation. In a follow-up study one might want to investigate a causative that is more compatible with both values. It is not clear that there is such a construction in English. The ones considered here all usually describe direct causation, except for *cause*, which is strongly associated with indirectness. If a suitable causative could be found, in English or elsewhere, the expected universal would be:

Implicational universal 3 (directness)

If a language allows passivisation of causative constructions prototypically portraying indirect causation then constructions describing direct causation will also be passivisable (all other things being equal).

Thus far I have focussed on the role of the parameters that could be tested on the corpus data. But in §§2.2.4.–2.2.5. I argued that the sphere of control frame and specificity also play a role. And indeed universals 1–3 are clearly not sufficient to account for the English facts. Consider for example that *have* is situated at the maximally transitive ends of the punctuality, causation type and directness scales but does not passivise. Also, *get* and *persuade* are semantically identical with respect to punctuality, causation type and directness, yet the former only passivises marginally. Moreover, it is not obvious from the three universals proposed so far how the relative ease of passivisation, crosslinguistically, of "force" type causatives (see examples [3–8], above) is to be explained.

The universals arising from my discussion of the impact, on transitivity, of the sphere of control frame and specificity go some way towards explaining these facts:

Implicational universal 4 (sphere of control)

If a language allows passivisation of causative constructions which specify that causation occurs against the background of a sphere of control, then causatives that do not feature that background assumption also passivise (all other things being equal).

Implicational universal 5 (specificity)

If a language allows passivisation of causative constructions prototypically associated with the lower end of the specificity scale then constructions that are associated with the higher end of the scale will also be passivisable (all other things being equal).

Given the presence of a control frame (SC) in *have*, and the absence thereof in *force* universal 4 helps explain the lack of passive causative *have*, and the relative ease of passivisation of *force*, in English and in other languages. Universal 5 sheds light on the higher degree of passivisability of *persuade* as compared to *get*, while also reinforcing the high transitivity, across languages, of 'force' type causatives as compared to the more neutral constructions.

Universals 4 and 5 have brought us closer to a comprehensive explanation of the facts passivisation of causatives. However, some problems still remain, as becomes clear from Table 5 below, which presents the scores of the causatives under consideration across the five parameters. The transitivity scores are represented as high-low or high-mid-low, depending on whether the parameter in question has two or three values.

Table 5. Scores for *cause, force, get, have, make* and *persuade* on the transitivity parameters

	Causation type	Punctuality	Directness	SC	Specificity
cause	low	high	low	mid	mid
force	mid	high	high	high	mid
get	high	low	high	mid	mid
have	high	high	high	low	mid
make	mid	high	high	mid	low
persuade	mid	low	high	mid	high

I suggest that the problems may be due to the assumption that all parameters are equally important. First, comparing *cause, get* and *make* on the one hand, to *have*, on the other, the equal weighting assumption would predict that *have* would be easier to passivise than *cause, get* and *make*. *Have* outscores *cause* on directness, *get* on punctuality, *make* on specificity, and both *cause* and *make* on causation type. The absence of a +SC component in the semantics of *cause, get* and *make* is therefore presumably significant enough, relative to directness, punctuality and specificity, to give them the overall edge over *have*. Second, the greater ease of passivisation of *cause* as compared to *get* suggests that punctuality is substantially more important than causation type and directness together, for it is on the former property that *cause* outscores *get*. On the latter two the tables are reversed. Third, to the extent that *cause* is lower in passivisability than *persuade* one may infer that specificity is relatively salient, too, compared to causation type and directness. This is because if punctuality weighs more heavily than causation type and directness, then specificity is the only parameter from which the higher degree of transitivity of *persuade* as compared to *cause* may derive. Note, incidentally, that *cause* is also less passivisable than *force* and *make*, but in contrast to *persuade* these constructions are not outranked by *cause* on punctuality.[20] (Hollmann [2004] argues that differential weighting raises some questions in relation to semantic theory.)

5. Conclusion

In this paper I have tried to account for the facts of passivisation of English periphrastic causatives. This has not often been attempted before, Stefanowitsch (2001) being the only other detailed study. The main advantage of the present discussion is that the conclusions have taken the guise of implicational universals. (Nonetheless, it should not be surprising if the need arises for minor adjustments in the light of crosslinguistic evidence).

Elevating the discussion to a more abstract level, let me briefly reflect on the innovative aspect of the approach taken here to a motivated correspondence between linguistic form (passivisability) and function (transitivity). I have shown how, in cases where one has reason to suspect that several semantic factors are at work, one may go about approaching the issue from a quantitative point of view. Corpus data may be collected and scored for the factors in question. Using statistical tests one may then assess the relevance of the various parameters. The analysis should not be carried out too mechanically or "blindly". The present study was limited by certain aspects of the meaning of *make*, such as its prototypical association with directness. It was seen that by keeping one's eyes open to these limitations, which sometimes creep in almost inevitably, one may still be able to draw conclusions, or at least propose educated hypotheses (such as implicational universal 3, above) regarding issues where the limitations obscure the quantitative evidence.

Notes

1. Bill Croft and David Denison provided invaluable advice on many of the issues dealt with here. My gratitude extends to Sylvia Adamson, Stefan Th. Gries, Dick Hudson and Anatol Stefanowitsch for useful discussion of several points.
2. I am grateful to Gary Toops for drawing my attention to this reference.
3. This example features the so-called *Ersatzinfinitiv* (viz. *laten* 'let', *doen* 'do'), i.e. an infinitive where one would normally expect a participial complement. The use of the infinitive in this example is motivated by a rare example of passive causative *laten* found on the internet:

   (i) *Niemand heeft in maanden aan Banana gedacht, totdat*
       no one has in months on Banana thought, until
       hij leeg werd laten lopen door Ramon.
       he empty became let walk by Ramon
       'For months no one thought of Banana [an inflatable banana shaped toy, WBH], until it was deflated by Ramon.'
       ⟨http://www.geocities.com/bacardifela/banana2.html [3 October 2002]⟩

   This example does not prove that periphrastic causative *laten* is generally passivisable. Talmy (2000: 413, 419) argues that the kind of causative relation portrayed by (i) is notionally very different from the intended meaning in (6), the former but not the latter involving enablement/permission (what Talmy calls "cessation of impingement"). This special category of causatives is beyond the present scope, but see Hollmann (2003: 207–208) for some discussion.

4. I would like to thank María Eugenia Vázquez Laslop for her helpful suggestions concerning the Spanish facts.

5. I focus on *cause, force, get, have, make* and *persuade* partly because scholars (e.g. Baron 1977) often treat *get, have* and *make* as the "central" periphrastic causatives. Sometimes, *cause* and/or *force* are also discussed (see e.g. Dixon 1991). *Persuade* is included mainly because it is semantically similar to *get* yet differs in terms of passivisability. In addition, in my data (the FLOB corpus; see main text and n. 8) it is rather frequent, being the most common periphrastic causative after *make* and *force*.

6. While corpus evidence is important in this connection, in the sense that given a sufficiently large and representative corpus there must be some correlation between the percentage of passive tokens of a construction and its passivisability, I would not necessarily *equate* corpus frequency with degree of passivisability. See in this connection e.g. Schütze (1996: 2) for a vindication of native speaker intuitions (though cf. also Schütze [1996: 4] for the suggestion that this methodology is usually not used with appropriate scientific rigour).

7. The BNC is a 100 million word corpus of spoken and written Present-day English; for more information see e.g. Aston and Burnard (1998).

8. FLOB contains 1 million words of Present-day British English newspaper prose (for more information see e.g. ⟨http://helmer.aksis.uib.no/icame/ manuals.html⟩ [28 May 2004]).

9. The infinitival complement clause may itself contain an A/O distinction, and indeed passivisation may not only occur on the causee but on the O argument of such a transitive lower clause as well: *[...]he used to go on board with his book and get it signed by the mate or the er captain of the ship* (BNC ADM 2056), where the corresponding form with an active complement clause would be *he used to [...] get the mate or the captain of the ship to sign it*. This type of passive will not be considered here, but see Stefanowitsch (2001).

10. The other reason why *cause* is not seen as basic in the same way as *force, get, have* and *make* is token frequency: in Stefanowitsch's data (based on the Switchboard corpus, a 3 million corpus of spoken American English telephone conversations; for more information see e.g. ⟨http://wave.ldc.upenn.edu/Catalog/docs/switchboard/manual.html⟩ [28 May 2004]) *cause* is considerably less frequent than the four causatives he does discuss. However, Hollmann (2003: 156) found that at least in the FLOB corpus it was more frequent than *have* and (marginally) *get*. This suggests that *cause* may be seen as a less peripheral construction if other varieties and/or text types/registers are considered as well.

11. See Siewierska (1984) for a critical appraisal of this position.
12. For more information see ⟨http://www.linguistlist.org/issues/13/13-1709.html⟩ [21 August 2002].
13. It is possible that this search string made me miss out on examples with an adverbial in between *made* and *to*.
14. The other options are "middle sample", "end sample" and "mixed". Beginning sample was the most suitable as it features the highest number of texts. Other ways to restrict the corpus (author gender, author age, dialect, etc.) were also considered but rejected as no such restrictions were imposed on the corpus used for the passive examples. The beginning sample restriction was not imposed there either, but this was less likely to skew the results than sex, age, etc., which sociolinguists have shown often play a role in variation.
15. For an example of ambiguity consider *These safety necessities are cleverly hidden behind panels which were made to look like original military equipment* (BNC CGL 1534), where it is not clear whether *make* is used in its causative or 'create' sense (on the latter interpretation the *to*-infinitive introduces a purpose clause).
16. Another concern here is that while Hopper and Thompson (1980) only distinguish between realis and irrealis it is not clear that a variation on (13) such as *For that violation they* will *be made to pay* is equally transitive as ...*they* might *be made to pay*. Intuitively, the higher likelihood of the caused event in the first example implies higher transitivity. Similar observations may be made for deontic modality; consider e.g. *For that violation you must make them pay* vs. *For that violation you may make them pay*. A more sophisticated scale than Hopper and Thompson's may be desirable, drawing on typological work such as Givón's (1980) binding hierarchy proposal. However, this will not be attempted here.
17. Stefanowitsch (2001) also considers affectedness; it is an important dimension of his notion of causee salience. He does not clearly define it, however. At some points it is associated with resistance on the part of the causee (Stefanowitsch 2001: 208) but elsewhere affectedness and resistance are presented as more independent parameters (Stefanowitsch 2001: 87). Stefanowitsch also analyses causees as being more affected to the extent that they are acted on by the causer for a more extended period of time (2001: 209). He does not motivate this connection, and, if anything, it would seem to go against Hopper and Thompson's account of punctuality: punctual events (including causation) are more transitive than non-punctual events. Finally, it may useful to observe that, differently from the position taken here – i.e. that periphrastic causatives always code some degree of impingement hence affectedness –, Stefanowitsch suggests that "the causee ... may be *affected* or *non-affected* by the entire event" (2001: 87; emphasis original).

18. Following common practice in scholarship on causatives I analyse human institutional entities such as companies, schools and governments as human, hence mental, entities (see e.g. Verhagen and Kemmer 1997: 64).
19. The implication is that in a comprehensive study of transitivity (i.e. not just causatives) along the lines of Hopper and Thompson (1980) I would argue for a three-way hierarchy with divided self outranking unary.
20. Another line of explanation might be to argue that there are more parameters to be considered. However, one would expect that between Hopper and Thompson (1980), Rice (1987) and the (typological) literature on causatives a reasonably complete picture has emerged.

References

Aikhenvald, Alexandra Y.
    2000   Transitivity in Tariana. In: R. M. W. Dixon and A. Y. Aikhenvald (eds.), *Changing Valency. Case Studies in Transitivity*, 145–172. Cambridge, MA: Cambridge University Press.

Aston, Guy and Lou Burnard
    1998   *The BNC Handbook: Exploring the British National Corpus with SARA.* Edinburgh: Edinburgh University Press.

Baron, Naomi S.
    1977   *Language Acquisition and Historical Change.* Amsterdam: North-Holland.

Bolinger, Dwight
    1978   Passive and transitivity again. *Forum Linguisticum* 3: 25–28.

Cristofaro, Sonia
    2003   *Subordination.* Oxford: Oxford University Press.

Croft, William
    1991   *Syntactic Categories and Grammatical Relations: The Cognitive Organization of information.* Chicago: University of Chicago Press.
    2001   *Radical Construction Grammar. Syntactic Theory in Typological Perspective.* Oxford: Oxford University Press.
    in prep.   Verbs. Aspect and argument structure. Oxford: Oxford University Press.

Dixon, R. M. W.
    1991   *A New Approach to English Grammar, on Semantic Principles.* Oxford: Clarendon Press.
    2000   A typology of causatives: Form, syntax and meaning. In: R. M. W. Dixon and Alexandra Y. Aikhenvald (eds.), *Changing Valency: Case Studies in Transitivity*, 30–83. Cambridge: Cambridge University Press.

Dowty, David
    1991   Thematic proto-roles and argument selection. *Language* 67: 547–619.

Duffley, Patrick J.
    1992   *The English Infinitive.* New York: Longman.

Fillmore, Charles J.
    1972   Subjects, speakers, and roles. In: Donald Davidson and Gilbert Harman (eds.), *Semantics of Natural Language,* 1–24. Dordrect: D. Reidel.

Fischer, Olga
    1995   The distinction between bare and *to*-infinitival complements in late Middle English. *Diachronica* 12: 1–30.
    1996   Verbal complementation in early ME: how do the infinitives fit in? In: Derek Britton (ed.), *English Historical Linguistics 1994,* Amsterdam/Philadelphia: John Benjamins.

Fodor, Jerry
    1970   Three reasons for not deriving "kill" from "cause to die". *Linguistic Inquiry* 1: 429–438.

Gilquin, Gaëtanelle
    2004   Corpus-based cognitive study of the main English causative verbs. A syntactic, semantic, lexical and stylistic approach. Ph.D. dissertation, Université Catholique de Louvain.

Givón, Talmy
    1980   The binding hierarchy and the typology of complements. *Studies in Language* 4: 333–377.
    2001   *Syntax. An Introduction.* 2 vols. Amsterdam/Philadelphia: John Benjamins.

Hay, Jennifer, Christopher Kennedy, and Beth Levin
    1999   Scalar structure underlies telicity in "degree achievements". In: Tanya Matthews and Devon Strolovitch (eds.), *Proceedings of SALT 9,* 127–144. Ithaca, NY: CLC Publications.

Hollmann, Willem B.
    2003   Synchrony and diachrony of English periphrastic causatives: a cognitive perspective. Ph.D. dissertation, University of Manchester.
    2004   Semantic maps for complex cognitive domains: The case of transitivity of causatives. Paper presented at the Forum for Kognitiv Vitskap, University of Bergen, Bergen.
    2005   The iconicity of infinitival complementation in present-day English causatives. In: Constantino Maeder, Olga Fischer, and William Herlofsky (eds.). *Iconicity Inside-Out. Iconicity in Language and Literature 4,* Amsterdam/Philadelphia: John Benjamins.

Hopper, Paul and Sandra A. Thompson
   1980   Transitivity in grammar and discourse. *Language* 56: 251–299.
Inoue, Kazuko
   1992   *Cause* and *make* in semantic representation. *English Linguistics* 9: 132–151.
Jackendoff, Ray
   1972   *Semantic Interpretation in Generative Grammar.* Cambridge, MA: MIT Press.
Katz, Jerrold J.
   1977   *Propositional Structure and Illocutionary Force: A Study of the Contribution of Sentence Meaning to Speech Acts.* Hassocks: Harvester Press.
Keenan, Edward L.
   1985   Passive in the world's languages. In: Timothy Shopen (ed.), *Language Typology and Syntactic Description, Vol. 1: Clause Structure,* 243–281. Cambridge: Cambridge University Press.
Nedjalkov, Vladimir P.
   1971   *Kauzativnye Konstrukcii v Nemeckom Jazyke. Analiticheskij Kauzativ.* Leningrad: Nauka.
Rice, Sally A.
   1987   Towards a cognitive model of transitivity. Ph.D. dissertation, University of California.
Schütze, Carson T.
   1996   *The Empirical Base of Linguistics: Grammaticality Judgements and Linguistic Methodology.* Chicago, IL: University of Chicago Press.
Shannon, Thomas
   1987   *Aspects of Complementation and Control in Modern German: The Syntax and Semantics of Permissive Verbs.* Göppingen: Kümmerle.
Siewierska, Anna
   1984   *The Passive. A Comparative Linguistic Analysis.* London: Croom Helm.
Stefanowitsch, Anatol
   2001   Constructing causation: A construction grammar approach to analytic causatives. Ph.D. dissertation, Rice University.
Stubbs, Michael
   1996   *Text and Corpus Analysis. Computer-Assisted Studies of Language and Culture.* Oxford: Blackwell.
Talmy, Leonard
   1976   Semantic causative types. In: Masayoshi Shibatani (ed.), *Syntax and Semantics. Volume 6. The Grammar of Causative Constructions,* 43–116. London: Academic Press.

1985	Lexicalization patterns: Semantic structure in lexical forms. In: Timothy Shopen (ed.), *Language Typology and Syntactic Description. Vol. 3: Grammatical Categories and the Lexicon*, 57–149. Cambridge: Cambridge University Press.
1988	Force dynamics in language and cognition. *Cognitive Science* 12: 49–100.
2000	*Toward a Cognitive Semantics. Volume I: Concept Structuring Systems*. Cambridge, MA/London: MIT Press.

Verhagen, Arie and Suzanne Kemmer
    1997   Interaction and causation: causative constructions in modern standard Dutch. *Journal of Pragmatics* 27: 61–82.

Wierzbicka, Anna
    1975   Why "kill" does not mean "cause to die": The semantics of action sentences. *Foundations of Language* 13: 491–528.

Transitivity schemas of English EAT and DRINK in the BNC

John Newman and Sally Rice

Abstract

This paper adopts a corpus-based methodology, relying upon the British National Corpus (BNC), in order to re-examine properties of intransitive and transitive uses of EAT and DRINK in English. The contrast between spoken and written modalities proves to be highly relevant to a number of properties: there is a greater incidence of transitive usage of these verbs in the spoken sub-corpus, and individuation of objects appears greater in the spoken sub-corpus. The nature of lexical items which occur as part of the subject and object noun phrases is also examined and the results suggest interesting correlations, e.g., more generic nouns like *food* and *meat* appear preferentially as the object in habitual contexts, rather than as the objects of verbs in the simple past tense. This study reaffirms the value of a corpus-based approach to analyzing syntactic patterns such as transitivity. The idea of an *inflectional island* is further proposed, as a way of explicitly acknowledging the uniqueness of a construction or collocational patterning associated with a specific inflected form of the verb.

Keywords: corpus linguistics; British National Corpus; transitivity; collocation; n-gram; inflection.

1. Introduction

In a chapter called "The floating nature of transitiveness" in his multi-volume *Grammar of Late Modern English*, Hendrik Poutsma (1926: 54) wrote:

> Almost all verbs are used both transitively and intransitively.
> a) Sometimes the two applications appear to be equally natural, so that it would be difficult, or indeed impossible, to tell which is the original.
> b) Sometimes one application is clearly felt to be a modification of the other. It is especially this transition which is of particular interest to the student of English.

Transitivity, as a lexico-syntactic phenomenon, has long attracted attention in linguistics as an object of inquiry and as the subject of countless articles, monographs, and dissertations. The present study takes a very particular spin on the topic by examining and qualifying not the essence of transitivity, but merely the use of a verb as transitive or intransitive in particular contexts.[1] Moreover, we scrutinize only two verbs, the relatively basic English verbs EAT and DRINK.[2] However, we observe and quantify the transitivity of these two verbs across thousands of spoken and written examples from the British National Corpus (henceforth sBNC or wBNC to indicate the two sub-corpora, respectively, or BNC for the database as a whole) in the hopes of answering when and why these two highly volatile verbs enter into diathesis alternations – that is, alternations in the syntactic expression of arguments – in the first place.

The value of relying on the BNC as a source of diathesis alternation data can be appreciated in the (a) and (b) sentences in (1) and (2):

(1) a. *Well that put you in your place if you ate too many potatoes.* (sBNC)
 b. *If I don't smoke, I eat.* (sBNC)

(2) a. *You just drank all my milk!* (sBNC)
 b. *If you bet on horses or drink then it cost you money.* (sBNC)

We find that even such simple sentences as these are far more revealing as illustrative examples of the phenomenon under study than the examples found in the typical pedagogical grammar of English or treatise on theoretical syntax. One may note, for example, the presence of *too many* and *all* in the object phrases of the transitive (a) examples (indicative of a larger trend we established in our database); a preference for *I* and *you* as subjects in the spoken corpus; and an habitual use of the simple present in the intransitive (b) examples. Moreover, we feel that sentences like these can offer more insight into the polyvalency of verbs than the highly artificial and contrived examples in much of the literature with their requisite third person subjects, specific direct objects, simple present tense forms, and little in the way of adverbial modification.

The full range of diathesis alternations observed for EAT and DRINK in the BNC reveals that these verbs do indeed behave differently in both their argument structure and in the interpretation of their subject and object depending on genre, register, or modality (by which we mean spoken vs. written corpus). More significantly, we found that the overt valency of these verbs is strongly tied to their particular tense/aspect/mode (TAM) marking; the person, number, and specificity of their subject; as well as semantic properties of their propositional and extra-propositional collocates. In short, there is nothing binary nor straightforward about the so-called transitivity alternation. This paper summarizes the findings of our large-scale corpus inquiry on the grammatical patterning of EAT and DRINK. It also re-introduces a number of concerns about the structure and content of lexical entries (either theoretical or descriptive) as well as the "floating" nature of transitivity itself.

The choice of EAT and DRINK as the focus of our study is not arbitrary. These items constitute a closely related pair of verbs within the same semantic domain,[3] comparable in their degree of (in)formality of usage, with each displaying the syntactic alternation of interest to us. In their uses with objects, they could be regarded as quintessential transitive verbs. In their uses with and without objects, they are the verbs of transitivity diathesis *par excellence*. In so far as they refer to bodily actions and everyday physiological experiences common to all humans, they could be called "basic" verbs. As such, they are natural candidates for sources of figurative and metaphorical extension and idiomatic usage. They are obvious objects of interest and research for linguists with a cognitive linguistic orientation. Comparable research undertaken on other basic verbs from a cognitive linguistic viewpoint includes: sense-perception verbs (Sweetser 1990: 32–48); COME and GO (Radden 1996; Shen 1996; Lichtenberk 1991); STAND and LIE (Serra Borneto 1996); SIT/STAND/LIE (Newman 2002; Newman and Rice 2004); SEE (Alm-Arvius 1993); GIVE and TAKE (Newman 1996, 1998); TAKE (Norvig and Lakoff 1987); HAVE (Wierzbicka 1988); and EAT and DRINK (Wierzbicka 1988; Newman 1997); and miscellaneous verbs referring to bodily acts (Pauwels and Simon-Vandenbergen 1995). For an overview of this and similar research see Newman (2004).

After reviewing some relevant proposals concerning transitivity in Section 2, we explain in Section 3 the corpus-based methodology that we have adopted for the purpose of this study. The distinction between spoken versus written modalities pervades our discussion and we consider some larger findings in terms of modality differences in Section 4. We examine in Sections 5 and 6 object and subject phrases in greater detail and discuss – where appropriate – the relevance of our results to claims about transitivity.

2. Models of transitivity alternations

In the approach adopted here, we understand "transitive" in a conservative manner. "Transitive" designates a construction in which a verb is used with a direct object, whereas "intransitive" refers to a construction in which a verb is used without one. While neither "construction" nor "direct object" is unproblematic as a theoretical term, these labels are nevertheless useful in helping us to delineate the intended sense of transitivity. The linguistics literature offers quite a range of interpretations. Huddleston (1988: 59–60) happens to illustrate the traditional view of transitivity (and omitted object constructions) with an EAT example, repeated here as (3), where S = subject, P = predicate, and O^d = direct object.

(3) a. *She ate.*   Intransitive   S P
     b. *She ate an apple.*   Monotransitive   S P O^d

The sentence in (3a) is deemed intransitive and not further distinguished from what we might recognize as a traditional intransitive like *She died*. Huddleston (1988: 60) describes the propositional relationship in (3a) in the following way: "… the participant role of the subject-referent remains constant and the intransitive clause simply leaves unexpressed the second participant. *She ate* entails that she ate something but doesn't specify what." So-called monotransitives like (3b) receive little in the way of further analysis. Rather, it is the intransitive alternate in (3a) which attracts all the attention. We believe that each of the constructions represented in (3) is worthy of study in its own right and neither is derivative of the other.

Huddleston and Pullum (2002: 303–305) refine Huddleston's notion of intransitivity by offering a sub-categorization of types of "unexpressed objects" of intransitive verbs. EAT and DRINK participate in two such patterns of omissibility: "specific category indefinites" and "normal category indefinites". The former refers to the possibility of understanding the intransitive uses of EAT and DRINK specifically as 'eat a meal' and 'drink alcoholic drink' respectively; the latter refers to the use of intransitive EAT and DRINK when the unexpressed object is interpreted as the "indefinite, typical, unexceptional" exemplar ('food' in the case of EAT, 'water' or 'beverage' presumably, in the case of DRINK).

The traditional view of an intransitive vs. (mono)transitive distinction, as enunciated in Huddleston (1988) and Huddleston and Pullum (2002), is by no means compelling. One could just as well argue that the intransitive use in (3a) really involves one participant (the agent phrase) and describes an activity of that participant, similar to the way in which the intransitive verb *run* in English describes an activity of a runner. Other associated entities can be a necessary part of a larger semantic frame of intransitive verbs (legs in the case of *run*, food in the case of *eat*), but this does not require us to say that they are second participants which are simply unexpressed. In our discussion below, we investigate properties of intransitive and transitive uses of verbs separately, without any assumption that the intransitive use is reducible to the transitive use with the direct object unexpressed. We regard intransitive and transitive uses of EAT and DRINK as separate constructions, or *schemas*, with a host of quite different properties. These schemas are associated with preferred kinds of subjects and objects in terms of both grammatical and lexical content and with preferred co-occurrence patterns of subject, object, and TAM marking.

A more provocative view of transitivity can be found in Van Valin and LaPolla (1997: 115). They speak of the English predicate as having either one or two arguments in its logical structure, similar to Huddleston's distinction between intransitive and monotransitive uses of EAT. Their representation of the logical form of EAT expresses the alternatives through the parenthesized (y) embedded in the argument structure.

(4)   do' (x, [eat' (x, (y))]
      x = CONSUMER, y = CONSUMED

Van Valin and LaPolla distinguish the semantic roles as found in logical structure (agent, patient, etc.) and what they call "macroroles" (actor, undergoer). Applying a notion of transitivity at the level of macroroles ("M-transitivity"), they draw a three-way distinction between *atransitive*, *intransitive*, and *transitive* verb types, as shown in Table 1.

There is a partial overlap with the traditional notion of transitivity in so far as *He ate* is intransitive in both systems and *He ate the plate of spaghetti in ten minutes* is transitive in both systems. A non-referential, "inherent" argument, as found in *He ate spaghetti for ten minutes*, however, does not have an undergoer macrorole assigned to it. Verbs with such inherent arguments are "intransitive" in terms of M-transitivity in Van Valin and LaPolla (1997: 147–154). A search in the sBNC shows, incidentally, that the use of non-referential objects with *ate* is relatively rare: of 155 instances of the verb form *ate* in the BNC, in only three cases do we find non-referential objects: *And it turned out that there was a big goblin that lived on this island and he just ate fairies; Mind you, I ate conga; They ate boiled eggs for breakfast.*

Table 1. An illustration of M-transitivity, based on Van Valin and LaPolla (1997: 99, 147, 150) (eat$_1$ is considered an activity verb, while eat$_2$ is an active accomplishment verb)

Verb	Example sentence	Semantic valence	Macrorole number	M-transitivity
rain	*It rained.*	0	0	Atransitive
eat$_1$	*He ate.*	1 or 2	1	Intransitive
	He ate spaghetti for ten minutes.			
eat$_2$	*He ate a plate of spaghetti in ten minutes.*	2	2	Transitive

In distinguishing referential and non-referential kinds of arguments – a distinction with important morphosyntactic ramifications in some languages – Van Valin and LaPolla achieve a certain refinement of the concept of transitivity, though it is at odds with the traditional account. Not only are the M-transitive and M-intransitive classes not identical with their traditional counterparts, the M-intransitive uses of EAT are not to be understood as simply reduced versions of the M-transitive uses (a view we also endorse). Van Valin and LaPolla (1997: 112) explicitly remark that "... *eat* is not inherently telic, unlike *kill* and *break*; hence it must be analyzed as an activity verb, with an active accomplishment use". For them, the "activity verb" use (*He ate*, *He ate spaghetti for ten minutes*) is the "basic" meaning of EAT. The examples used by Van Valin and LaPolla to illustrate EAT used as an activity verb and as an activity accomplishment verb are, of course, constructed examples. Again, a search of the sBNC can offer insights into the naturalness, or lack thereof, in having a *for*-phrase in their examples containing syntactic objects in Table 1. Again, of the 155 instances of *ate* in the sBNC, there is no example of any usage which conforms to the constructional pattern [Subject-NP *ate* Object-NP *for* Time-Phrase], whereas the construction [Subject-NP *ate* Object-NP *in* Time-Phrase] is attested in a couple of examples, e.g., *Six swallows ate three hundred flies in five hours.*

An influential and far-reaching re-conceptualization of the notion of transitivity is that found in Hopper and Thompson (1980). They identify 10 parameters which distinguish high and low transitivity of clauses, as summarized in Table 2.

Table 2. Scalar transitivity according to Hopper and Thompson (1980: 252)

		HIGH	LOW
A.	PARTICIPANTS	2	1
B.	KINESIS	action	non-action
C.	ASPECT	telic	atelic
D.	PUNCTUALITY	punctual	non-punctual
E.	VOLITIONALITY	volitional	non-volitional
F.	AFFIRMATION	affirmative	negative
G.	MODE	realis	irrealis
H.	AGENCY	A high in potency	A low in potency
I.	AFFECTEDNESS OF O	O highly affected	O not affected
J.	INDIVIDUATION OF O	O highly individuated	O not individuated

The high values for these parameters are claimed to co-vary with one another within a language and cross-linguistically; similarly for the low values. While Hopper and Thompson are not directly concerned with the kind of transitive/intransitive alternation found with EAT and DRINK, their account of transitivity – a clause-level phenomenon for them, rather than simply a verbal one – posits a scale of transitivity allowing for varying degrees to which each of the 10 parameters could be said to be either "high" or "low". Hopper and Thompson's work suggests that there are additional distinctions that might profitably be drawn amongst the syntactically transitive EAT/DRINK uses (in terms of kinesis, aspect, etc.), just as there are additional distinctions that can be made amongst the syntactically intransitive EAT/DRINK uses. Presence or absence of a syntactic object, in other words, is not the only factor of relevance in considering the Transitivity of a clause (written here with a capital T to indicate the Hopper and Thompson sense of transitivity); it is merely one of 10 Transitivity parameters that might be examined.[4]

Recently, Thompson and Hopper (2001) have revisited Transitivity through an exploration of the syntactic patterning found in spontaneous conversation. They arrive at a number of conclusions with relevance to the present study. One result from their corpus-based research is that Transitivity, understood as a kind of additive phenomenon with respect to the number and value of the parameters in Table 2, is very low in spontaneous conversation. This result immediately suggested a line of inquiry with respect to EAT and DRINK and consequently we applied selected Hopper and Thompson (1980) Transitivity parameters to our search returns from the BNC. Thompson and Hopper (2001: 43) acknowledge that, even within a language, there will be variation amongst verbs with respect to their parameters. Thus, the specific behaviour of EAT and DRINK needs to be determined in its own right for each of these verbs, even if we accept their claim that, overall, Transitivity has been found to be low in spontaneous conversation. Thompson and Hopper (2001) is instructive, too, in its usage-based approach to investigating Transitivity. Their focus was spontaneous conversation and their methodology involves a close examination of real examples taken from interactional communication. In other words, they adopt a corpus-linguistic approach and arrive at usage-based results which hold true for a particular genre. In so doing, they distinguish themselves from traditional approaches to grammar which are neither corpus-based nor particularly sensitive to genre or modality differences.[5]

The recent and prestigious *Cambridge Grammar of the English Language* by Huddleston and Pullum (2002) already cited above is typical of this tradition, though perhaps it is more explicit about its assumptions than most other grammars. The authors aim for a grammatical description which is "neutral between spoken and written English" (Huddleston and Pullum: 11). They justify this approach with the claim that "[s]harp divergences between the syntax of speech and the syntax of writing, as opposed to differences that exist between styles within either the spoken or the written language, are rare to the point of non-existence" (Huddleston and Pullum: 13). We believe there is sufficient evidence to justify modality-specific grammatical descriptions and, in the approach adopted here, the contrast in the morphosyntactic behavior of these two key verbs in spoken vs. written modality is a pervasive and crucial feature of our analyses. Our corpus-based approach and the findings which we turn to next ensure a naturalness in our examples, as opposed to the many constructed examples of a grammar such as Huddleston and Pullum (2002).[6]

3. Methodology

The British National Corpus World Edition (BNC) was used as the basis for all searches discussed below. Initially, the entire spoken sub-corpus of the BNC (10 million words) was searched for the word forms *eat, eats, eating, ate, eaten* and *drink, drinks, drinking, drank, drunk*, without recourse to tags. All these results were saved (2,623 hits for EAT, 934 hits for DRINK). The written sub-corpus of the BNC (90 million words) was searched using the same keyword list, but owing to the vast size of the corpus, only a random sampling of 2,000 hits for each of EAT and DRINK was saved. These search returns – the exhaustive sBNC search and what we hope is a representative wBNC search – form the basis of the analysis presented here.

The 7,557 (= 2,623 + 934 + 2,000 + 2,000) examples of EAT and DRINK downloaded from the BNC and used in our analyses were exported to a FileMaker Pro™ database where each return was individually examined and coded as its own record. To begin with, each record was checked for whether or not it represented a form of the relevant verb. Thus, the adjective *drunk* 'intoxicated' was excluded from further analysis, as were the nominal uses of *drink, drinks, eats,* and *EAT* (Employment Appeal Tribunal). We excluded *-ing* forms in compounds such as *eating habits, eating disorders, eating places, drinking fountains,* etc. Each legitimate verb usage was coded for its source corpus (sBNC or wBNC), the part of speech and inflectional class of the key word, and whether the usage had an overt direct object (transitive) or not (intransitive). Moreover, both the subject noun phrase and the direct object, if present, were identified in separate fields. We were thus able to quantify the exact number of usages, for example, of *had eaten* with a first person plural subject and an omitted object or all instances of *drinks* with an unspecified third person subject and overt object.

A small proportion of the examples were deemed uninterpretable (and these were linked exclusively to the sBNC). We downloaded the keyword in our searches, e.g., *eats,* with a limited amount of left and right context (40 characters on each side of the keyword for the sBNC) although in some cases the context may not have been large enough to retrieve the information we wished to identify. However, it is a fact about spontaneous conversation that there will be interruptions, false starts, incomplete utterances, and so forth, and even looking up the full context of usage may not yield information about the subject, object, etc. We adopted a conservative approach to the interpretation of the returns from the sBNC, coding uses as "uninterpretable" unless we were very confident about the meaning. A less conservative approach might have classified a number of these instances as indeed interpretable. It is unlikely that the subsequent subclassification of these unclear instances (e.g., determining the relative proportions of 1SG, 2SG/PL, 3SG subjects) would be seriously affected by a different stance with respect to their inclusion. The examples in (5) illustrate some of our "uninterpretable" instances, these being cases where we were unable to confidently identify a subject of EAT or DRINK.

(5) Examples of an unidentifiable or <u>uninterpretable subject</u> in the coding (key verb underlined)

    a. *Potatoes and er Yeah. Sussed it! bread and <u>eat</u> Yeah. things like that.*
    b. *Yeah, but you can also get it with salt mm Can't <u>eat</u> popcorn then.*
    c. *No I don't think you'll have both Why not? <u>eat</u> it in the evening?*
    d. *Yeah. I thought it'd have something <u>eat</u> it. Your joking! Well erm hello!*
    e. *Baa, baa black. Come on stop it, supposed to be <u>eating</u>. Baa.*
    f. *Well he went to someone's house and all the <u>eats</u> hem so he ate it.*
    g. *Oh dear. And did she take her cup out? Yeah <u>drink</u> about tea.*
    h. *Er this fellow come up fair blue devil go <u>drinking</u>, er he hadn't a, he hadn't.*

While the identification of an object phrase presented few difficulties, identifying and coding the subject phrase posed a number of problems. We distinguished "specified" and "unspecified" subjects, consistent with a contemporary linguistic approach. Even so, it was necessary to make decisions relating to just how narrow or broad our categorizations were going to be. We took "specified subject" to be an overt phrase functioning as the subject of a finite clause containing EAT or DRINK in the main verbal complex or as the phrase functioning as the understood subject of a nearby participial or infinitival phrase. Specified subjects were then sub-categorized for number and person. The examples in (6), taken from our database, illustrate a variety of specified subject phrases of EAT and DRINK.

(6) Examples of a <u>specified subject</u> in the coding (subject phrase underlined)

    a. *She felt <u>she</u> might never eat again.*
    b. *<u>He</u> managed to eat most of the cream.*
    c. *Can I mummy? No <u>You</u>'re not big enough to drink wine ...*
    d. *... when <u>you</u> first start to drink spirits you feel Oh dear, Yeah.*
    e. *<u>They</u> used to cut it up and pretend to eat it.*
    f. *... made <u>him</u> promise never to eat again.*
    g. *... watching <u>other monkeys</u> trying to eat these insects.*
    h. *... but then <u>I</u> hate drinking milk anyway.*
    i. *<u>You</u>'ll soon get fed up eating it.*
    j. *Next to me <u>a girl</u> eating a box of chocolates ...*
    k. *<u>He</u> was sitting there eating...*
    l. *... <u>the poor</u>, who live, cook, eat, and sleep ...*

"Unspecified subject", on the other hand, was taken to refer to an unexpressed, but understood, generic agent associated with an infinitival or *-ing* form. The examples in (7) illustrate such cases with *eat* and *eating*. Sometimes, it is possible in the unspecified subject constructions to relate the eating or drinking to a person referred to elsewhere in the sentence or larger context. For example, in (7b), it is obviously Annie who is the intended eater of the currants. Although it is possible in many such cases to identify a specific agent, we took the construction itself to have an unspecified subject, despite the inferences the larger context allows.

(7) Examples of an <u>unspecified subject</u> in the coding (the relevant verb form is underlined)
  a. *I haven't had a thing to <u>eat</u> for hours.*
  b. *Carolyn gave Annie a saucer of currants to <u>eat</u>.*
  c. *... in case we don't encounter a suitable place to <u>eat</u>.*
  d. *To <u>eat</u> chalk is as foolish as to try to write on a blackboard with cheese!*
  e. *But I would always ask, Is it safe to <u>drink</u> the water out the taps?*
  f. *The best way to protect the pig is to <u>eat</u> it.*
  g. *<u>Eating</u> apples is good.*
  h. *It claimed Elton John was hooked on <u>eating</u> food and spitting it out.*
  i. *But, sad to say, talking and <u>drinking</u> got the better of him.*

4. Spoken vs. written results

As a point of departure, let us look at some of the most striking and macro-level results from our BNC searches. Figure 1 compares the number of EAT and DRINK verbs in our database. In this table, as throughout, the written corpus is the *sampled* wBNC, obtained as described in the preceding section and one should be wary of making direct comparisons between the raw numbers in our spoken and written samples. Figure 1 includes specified and unspecified verb forms, as well as the verb forms which had "uninterpretable" subjects, but excludes non-verb forms of EAT and DRINK.

As can be readily seen in Figure 1, there is a clear preponderance of EAT forms over DRINK in both the spoken and written corpora. The higher frequency of EAT is only one way in which it is more salient than DRINK. EAT also has special status vis-à-vis DRINK in terms of the relative order one tends to use in describing the combination of the two types of consumption: *eating and drinking*, rather than *drinking and eating*. To corroborate this intuition about sequential ordering of EAT and DRINK words, we conducted

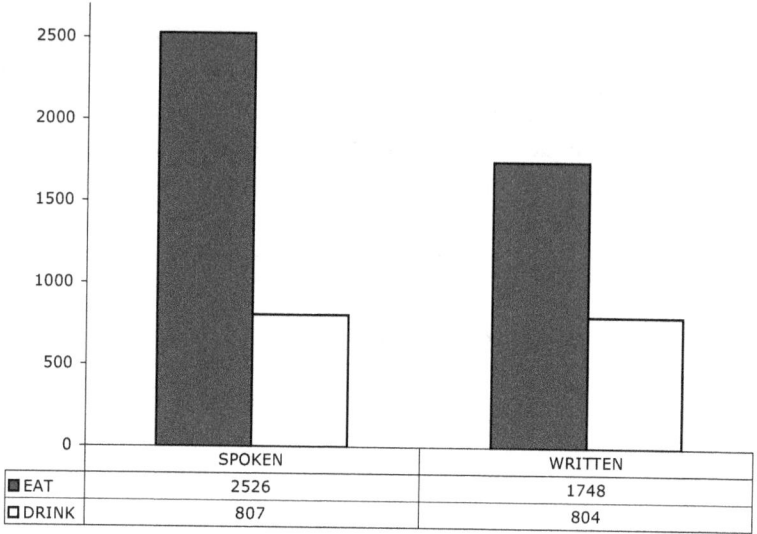

Figure 1. The incidence of EAT and DRINK verbs by sub-corpus of the BNC

a series of searches on the conjunction of the inflected forms of EAT and DRINK in the whole BNC (*eat and drink, drink and eat, eats and drinks*, etc.). The results of these searches, shown in Table 3, confirm this preference in the relative ordering of EAT and DRINK in conjoined phrases. With the exception of the second row, the results are all highly significant as determined by two-tailed binomial tests ($p<0.0001$, $p=0.625$, $p<0.0001$, $p<0.0001$). The results are reminiscent of what we found elsewhere with the verb set SIT, STAND, and LIE, where corpus research shows a relative frequency of SIT > STAND > LIE (cf. Newman and Rice 2001), matching a preference for the same order in phrasal combinations. Higher frequency and priority in sequential ordering are both potential indicators of experiential salience: when we eat and drink, the drinking is an accompaniment to the eating, rather than the other way around. The preferred order of EAT and DRINK words could be seen as an instance of the more general Food and Drink Hierarchy (Fish > Meat > Drink, etc.) proposed by Cooper and Ross (1975), though Cooper and Ross based their hierarchy on nouns rather than verbs.

Table 3. Frequencies of conjoined EAT and DRINK in the whole BNC

eat and drink	66	drink and eat	2
eats and drinks	3	drinks and eats	1
ate and drank	25	drank and ate	2
eating and drinking	70	drinking and eating	8

Though sceptical based on our previous corpus research (cf. Newman and Rice [2001], Rice and Newman [2004], and Newman and Rice [2004]), we were initially mindful of Huddleston and Pullum's pronouncement, quoted above, that the syntax of spoken and written language is virtually the same. We took this as a sort of null hypothesis as we began our investigation of the rather robust diathesis alternations affecting EAT and DRINK across modalities. Admittedly, we were more sympathetic to Thompson and Hopper's claim that Transitivity is very low in spontaneous conversation and expected the incidence of overt vs. omitted objects for these two verbs to vary greatly by corpus. As it happens, our results contravened both accounts.

As shown in Figure 2, not only were these verbs being used transitively, with full-blown objects, most of the time, the incidence of transitive usages was greatest in the spoken corpus for both verbs. In short, pace Huddleston and Pullum, the relative distribution between transitive and intransitive usages – whatever it is – is not consistent across modalities. Figure 2 presents lemmatized totals for these verbs across the two contrasting argument structures. Later, we will give totals for the relative distribution across inflectional forms (by both person and number of subject and TAM marking on the verb), argument structures, and sub-corpus. While one might wish for a relevant measure of statistical significance in evaluating Figure 2, it is not at all clear what the appropriate measure would be. Recall that the "written" counts are based on samples from the wBNC (2,000 hits for each of the lemmas EAT and DRINK), whereas the "spoken" counts are based on total occurrences in the whole of the sBNC (10 million words). Familiar statistical tests such as chi square appear to be inappropriate in this case, given the discrepancy in the nature and size of the written and spoken results on which the comparison is based (cf. Kilgarriff 2001: 124).

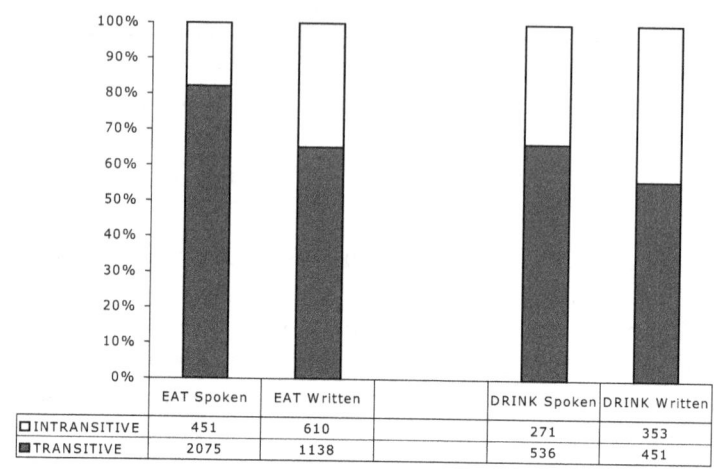

Figure 2. Percentage of transitive and intransitive usages of EAT and DRINK by sub-corpus of the BNC

The findings summarized in Figure 2 also appear to contradict the results of Thompson and Hopper (2001) who claim that low Transitivity is a feature of spontaneous conversation. Some qualifications concerning this comparison are in order, however. Firstly, Transitivity is a composite of 10 parameters, only one of which relates to the presence of an object (parameter A, participants). The transitivity reported on in Figure 2, on the other hand, is the traditional notion and concerns merely the presence or absence of an object. Secondly, one cannot equate Thompson and Hopper's 2-participant clauses with the presence of an object in the BNC cases. A transitive use of EAT or DRINK, for example, may occur without any expressed subject (unspecified subject constructions, imperatives, etc.), in which case the clause would count as a 1-participant clause. Thirdly, it should be remembered that Thompson and Hopper base their conclusions on spontaneous conversation only, whereas the sBNC includes a variety of genres (monologue, dialogue) and domains (educational, business, public, leisure). While these are real considerations, our results on transitivity would still appear to be at odds with Thompson and Hopper (2001).

The difference in the behaviors of EAT and DRINK is also noteworthy. There is proportionately more intransitive usage with DRINK than there is with EAT. The difference is arguably influenced by the existence of specialized meanings associated with the intransitive (the "specific category indefinite" kind of interpretation à la Huddleston and Pullum [2002: 303–

305] or Rice [1988]). In the case of EAT the specific interpretation is "meal", whereas with DRINK it is "alcoholic beverage" (especially when consumed in an habitual and/or excessive manner). This use of intransitive DRINK is a very familiar one in casual conversation (some examples from sBNC are *All they do in that house is drink and smoke*; *Because her daddy drinks in there in the pub[...]*; *He bought a bottle of brandy at the first liquor store he found and he began to drink*), reflecting the prominence of alcohol consumption as a topic of discourse. Comparing EAT and DRINK in this way is instructive for demonstrating the kind of variation that can exist between lexical items, even those which define and exhaust a class (cf. Levin 1993: 213–214). The variation becomes more pronounced in the next set of results.

Figure 2 above only summarizes the relative frequencies of transitive and intransitive usage, ignoring the variation that exists between modalities and between different subject choices. By contrast, Figures 3 and 4 show more detail of this variation in the relative frequencies of transitive and intransitive uses for the lexical forms (not the lemmas) *eat* and *drink*, respectively.[7] These are the forms which occur as finite verbs (*We eat dinner at 6.00pm*), as well as infinitival forms (*We like to eat dinner late, We may eat dinner late, There's too much to eat*, etc.) and imperative forms. While there is, overall, a higher percentage of transitive than intransitive usage for EAT and DRINK, these figures reveal the varying percentages evident in more specific inflections. Indeed, the intransitive usage is the dominant usage in some instances. In the case of *eat*, for example, the intransitive usage is greater with first person plural (1p) subjects in both spoken and written corpora. With *drink*, on the other hand, transitive usage is greater with 1p subjects. In the case of third person plural (3p) subjects, the intransitive use of both *eat* and *drink* is also greater than the transitive use in the spoken corpus. It can be seen in Figures 3 and 4 that there is a preference for intransitive use of *eat* with (1st and 3rd person) plural subjects. Possibly, the experiential realities of eating limit the range of possible objects of *eat* with plural subjects (it is more natural for one person to eat a specific item of food than it is for a group of people to do so). Figures 3 and 4 are meant to give some sense of the variation that exists across different subjects, between the corpora, and between the two lexical items (see Appendices 1 and 2 for the frequencies and percentages underlying this figure). While there is an abundance of similar results that one could generate from our database, we content ourselves here with exemplifying the considerable variation that is lurking within Figure 2.

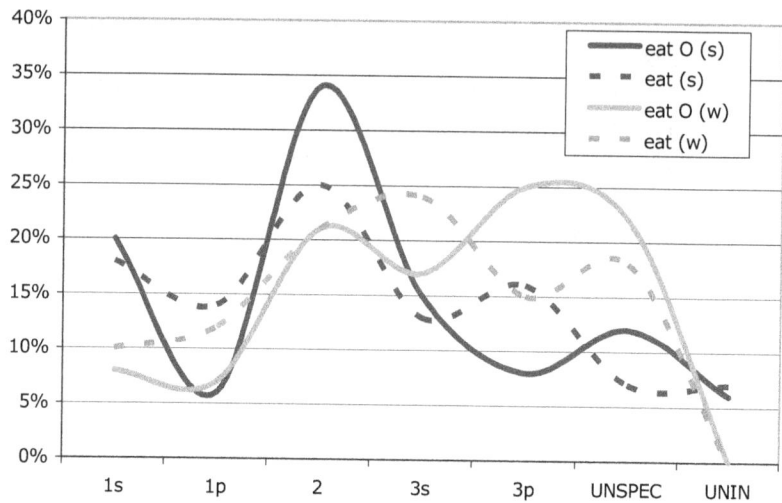

Figure 3. Percentage use of *eat* with (solid lines) and without (broken lines) an object in the sBNC and sampled wBNC

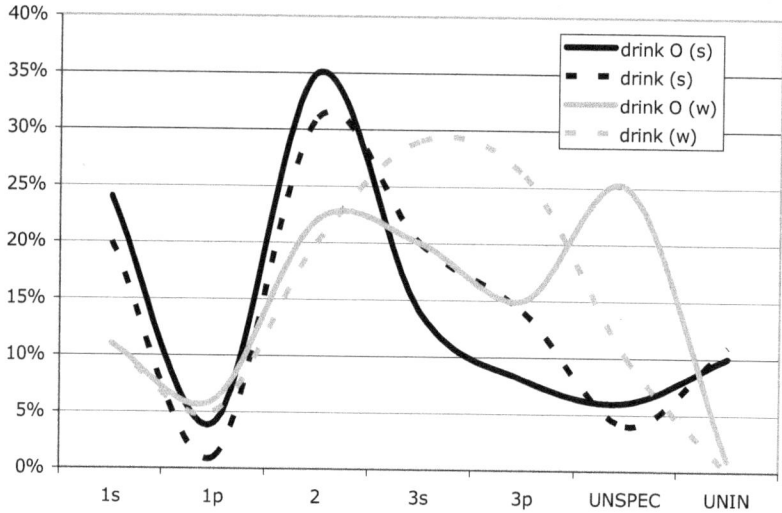

Figure 4. Percentage use of *drink* with (solid lines) and without (broken lines) an object in the sBNC and sampled wBNC

5. Objects

In this section we examine in more detail properties of the objects of EAT and DRINK. We will look at a number of properties which can be successfully researched and described in a quantifiable way, consistent with the orientation of the present study.

5.1. Individuation of O

We explored the degree of individuation of the object (parameter J for Hopper and Thompson [1980]) evident in our data from sBNC and the sampled wBNC. Pronouns are high in individuation and since they are easily identified and searched in a corpus, they are an effective means of measuring individuation. Thompson and Hopper (2001: 36), for example, determine the frequency of pronominal objects in their corpus as a way of quantifying individuation. We followed a similar methodology, though we relied entirely on electronic corpus linguistic tools, as is necessary when working with a database of the size we were dealing with. We used Wordsmith™ to produce frequency lists of the individual words occurring within the object phrases of EAT and DRINK. Our procedure did not differentiate between a single pronoun as object (as in *eat it*) and the relatively infrequent case of a pronoun occurring in a modifying phrase within the object (as in *eat some of it*). This indeterminacy about the syntactic status of the pronouns within the object field in our database is a small cost for the larger benefit of using automated frequency counts with a large database.

We present the results of the object listings in Tables 4 and 5 in terms of frequency-ranking, i.e., the rank occupied by an item in terms of its frequency of occurrence in the domain of the search (in this case, the object field). The highest rank is occupied by the most frequently occurring word (or set of words if the words have identical frequencies). In the case of the lemma EAT, both *it* and *them* appear in the top ten rankings in both the sBNC and the wBNC. However, in both cases, their ranking is higher in the sBNC than in the wBNC. In the case of EAT, which comfortably allows for singular or plural objects, we find higher rankings in the sBNC compared with the wBNC (rank 1 vs. rank 5 for *it*, rank 3 vs. rank 9 for *them*). An even more striking difference is found with the lemma DRINK where only *it*, and not *them*, occurs in the top 10 rankings. There is an experiential rationale for this: we drink liquids which are commonly referred to by mass nouns (hence, treated as singular). Furthermore, we tend to drink one type of beverage at a time. We find that *it* is, in fact, the single most frequently occurring word in the object position with DRINK in the sBNC.

Table 4. The 10 highest frequency-rankings of single words in the object phrases of EAT in the sBNC and wBNC (*it* and *them* in bold)

EAT (sBNC)			EAT (wBNC sample)		
rank	object keywords	N	rank	object keywords	N
1	**it**	**375**	1	the	157
2	the	189	2	of	136
3	**them**	**155**	3	a	133
4	all	148	4	and	86
5	that	133	5	**it**	**82**
6	of	132	6	what	67
7	a	109	7	food	65
8	what	102	8	much	38
9	your	83	8	something	38
10	something	76	9	**them**	**31**
			10	foods	29
			10	more	29

Table 5. The 10 highest frequency-rankings of single words in the object phrases of DRINK in the sBNC and wBNC (*it* in bold)

DRINK (sBNC)			DRINK (wBNC sample)		
rank	object keywords	N	rank	object keywords	N
1	**it**	**104**	1	of	79
2	a	57	2	the	58
3	that	51	3	a	57
4	of	47	4	much	51
5	tea	46	5	coffee	43
6	coffee	41	6	tea	39
7	what	31	7	wine	33
8	the	28	8	water	32
8	your	28	9	too	31
9	much	25	10	**it**	**27**
10	lot	23			
10	milk	23			

These results clearly indicate a higher individuation of objects in the spoken modality compared with the written, as well as a certain difference in this Transitivity parameter between EAT and DRINK. The higher individuation with EAT and DRINK in the spoken corpus would appear to contradict Thompson and Hopper's claims about Transitivity being relatively low in spontaneous conversation. However, even for them, the individuation parameter did not show up as a high value amongst objects in 2-participant clauses. It was one of three parameters which they describe as being divided more or less evenly between high and low values in spontaneous conversation, the other two being volitionality and mode. Our results, however, do not support an even balance of individuation between spoken and written modalities; rather, we find the spoken modality favoring high individuation. The same qualification needs to be made here as above concerning the genres examined by Thompson and Hopper and those in the present study. They base their conclusions on spontaneous conversation only, whereas the sBNC includes a variety of genres (monologue, dialogue) and domains (educational, business, public, leisure).

5.2. Affectedness of O

We also examined the affectedness of O (parameter I for Hopper and Thompson) by considering the type and frequency of "excessive" modifiers or quantifiers that appeared in the object phrase. To help us efficiently identify recurring patterns, we obtained trigrams, or 3-word clusters, from the object phrases. Trigrams typically include combinations of full lexical items and functional words, e.g., *a lot of, a cup of, cup of tea,* etc. As such, they reveal more of the affectedness of the object than do bigrams, which will include combinations of function words only, e.g., *in a, of the*. Trigrams within the objects were calculated separately for EAT and DRINK for each of the spoken and written corpora. Tables 6 and 7 summarize the results of this operation, showing the top 20 trigrams as listed by Wordsmith™. "Top 20" refers to the first 20 trigrams (in order of decreasing frequency) which appear in the list of word clusters compiled by Wordsmith™. There may be additional trigrams (in the 21st, 22nd position, etc.) with identical frequencies as the 20th trigram in some of these lists but, for the sake of ease of comparison of results, these are not included in the tables. As happens with n-gram analyses, some word sequences will appear as separate n-grams when, in fact, they are overlapping sub-parts of a larger construction. So, for example, both *twice as much* and *as much as* will be treated as separate trigrams in the phrase *twice as much as*. Some overlapping of this sort is evident in these tables.

Table 6. Top 20 trigrams from object phrases of EAT in the sBNC and wBNC (trigrams with "excessive" descriptors in bold)

rank	EAT (sBNC) top trigrams	N	EAT (wBNC sample) top trigrams	N
1	***a lot of***	14	*as much as*	7
2	*as much as*	10	*twice as much*	4
3	*a little bit*	5	*a dish of*	3
4	*kind of things*	5	***a lot of***	3
5	*one of these*	5	*a piece of*	3
6	*sort of thing*	4	*bread and cheese*	3
7	***a bit more***	3	*fruit and vegetables*	3
8	*a couple of*	3	***most of the***	3
9	***all of them***	3	*some of the*	3
10	*any more of*	3	*a bar of*	2
11	*as you like*	3	*a healthy diet*	2
12	***little bit more***	3	*a healthy well*	2
13	***more of that***	3	*bar of chocolate*	2
14	***most of the***	3	*bread and jam*	2
15	*of the things*	3	*fish and chips*	2
16	*one of them*	3	*foods rich in*	2
17	*one of those*	3	*good country food*	2
18	***quite a lot***	3	*healthy well-balanced*	2
19	*the pink bits*	3	*kind of food*	2
20	*three hundred flies*	3	***large amounts of***	2

The trigrams in these two tables reveal a propensity towards lexical items relating to an increased or excessive degree of consumption for both EAT and DRINK, as found in each of the corpora though more so in the sBNC. The relevant trigrams are shown in bold in these tables: *a lot of, all of them, most of the, more of the, loads and loads, endless cups of, large amounts of,* etc. We consider these results to be of some interest in that they draw attention to a pattern of usage of transitive EAT and DRINK which is rarely acknowledged, for example, in dictionaries. It is well-known that the intransitive usage of DRINK has associations of an habitual and excessive consumption of alcohol, a meaning regularly recognized in dictionaries. But the idea of excessiveness is also salient in the overt, expressed object phrases of transitive DRINK, as it is for EAT. Likewise, there are more excessive descriptors with DRINK in the sBNC than in the sampled wBNC. This finding should be qualified, however, since quantifier phrases containing "excessive" notions, such as *a lot of* are well represented in spoken corpora generally, especially in comparison to written (cf. Biber et al. 2000: 277–278).

Table 7. Top 20 trigrams from object phrases of DRINK in the sBNC and wBNC (trigrams with "excessive" descriptors in bold)

	DRINK (sBNC)		DRINK (wBNC sample)	
rank	top trigrams	N	top trigrams	N
1	**a lot of**	8	a cup of	5
2	a bottle of	6	**a little too (much)**	5
3	a cup of	5	**little too much**	5
4	cup of tea	5	a bottle of	4
5	your orange juice	4	cup of tea	4
6	a pint of	3	a mug of	3
7	bottle of wine	3	**endless cups of**	3
8	cup of coffee	3	or fruit juice	3
9	**lot of beer**	3	water or fruit	3
10	**lot of it**	3	a litre of	2
11	bottle of gin	2	**a lot of**	2
12	drop of milk	2	a pint of	2
13	**gallons of it**	2	as much as	2
14	little drop of	2	cups of coffee	2
15	**loads and loads**	2	cups of tea	2
16	red hot stuff	2	half a bottle	2
17	**too much coffee**	2	mineral water or	2
18	two or three	2	mug of tea	2
19			one of the	2
20			pints of lager	5

5.3. Preferred objects of consumption

Since one of our goals was to better understand the nature of the overt objects occurring with EAT and DRINK, we identified the most common kinds of nouns referring to foods and meals (with EAT) and beverages (with DRINK). For this, we relied upon wordlists, by descending order of frequency, generated by Wordsmith™. We then extracted from those wordlists the top 20 such nouns occurring in these wordlists. Tables 8 and 9 summarize these results.

Table 8. Top 20 food-type nouns from object phrases of EAT in the sBNC and wBNC (most generic items in bold)

	EAT (sBNC)		EAT (wBNC sample)	
rank	top food types	N	top food types	N
1	***food***	57	***food***	65
2	***dinner***	40	***foods***	29
3	meat	28	fish	27
4	cake	22	bread	24
5	bread	21	meat	23
6	chocolate	21	***meals***	17
7	fish	21	***breakfast***	16
8	cheese	20	cheese	16
9	chicken	18	***lunch***	14
10	chips	18	***meal***	14
11	fruit	18	cake	13
12	flies	16	chocolate	12
13	***breakfast***	15	cream	12
14	***tea*** (meal sense)	14	leaves	10
15	biscuits	11	fibre	9
16	***meal***	11	cakes	8
17	toast	10	rice	8
18	vegetables	10	sandwiches	8
19	cream	9	***supper***	8
20	***lunch***	9	vegetables	8

In the case of the lemma EAT, one can observe something of the varied (and not entirely unhealthy) eating habits of the British, bearing in mind that the occurrence of so many *flies* in Table 8 is due to one particular repetitious classroom lesson. An interesting difference between spoken and written modalities is the occurrence of both *fish* and *chips* in the top 10 of the spoken corpus, whereas only *fish* occurs in the top 20 of the written. This could be a reflection of rather different preferences associated with informal and formal social settings. It can be seen that the most frequent object word in both the spoken and written corpora is *food*. In addition to the generic *food*, the top 20 lists for both corpora include names for meals, e.g., *breakfast, lunch, tea, supper, dinner*, as well as the words *meal* and *meals* themselves. It is commonplace in dictionaries to recognize a "food" and "meal" kind of understood object of intransitive EAT, corresponding to Huddleston and Pullum's (2002) categories of "normal category indefinites" and "specific category indefinites". Our results show that these two categories are a feature of the *transitive* use of EAT as well. Intuition tells us that EAT can occur with such object nouns, but only a corpus linguistic study as we have done tells us something about the robustness of this pattern. Note also the differing relative frequencies with which the main "meal" words are mentioned in spoken and written corpora. In the sBNC, the relative frequency is *dinner* (40) > *breakfast* (15) > *tea* (14) > *lunch* (9), whereas in the sampled wBNC it is *breakfast* (16) > *lunch* (14) > *supper* (8). While we find *breakfast* > *lunch* in both corpora, the high frequency of *dinner* in the sBNC is noteworthy (*dinner* does not even appear in the top 20 food-type nouns of the sampled wBNC). Well over half of the *dinner* object phrases in the sBNC involve a possessive pronoun (*my dinner, your dinner*, etc.), typically used reflexively to refer back to the subject as in *I didn't eat my dinner*. We see here, perhaps, a subtle difference between spoken and written usage.

Table 9. Top 20 beverage-type nouns from object phrases of DRINK in the sBNC and wBNC (alcoholic items in bold)

	DRINK (sBNC)		DRINK (wBNC sample)	
rank	top beverage types	N	top beverage types	N
1	tea	46	coffee	43
2	coffee	41	tea	39
3	milk	23	**wine**	**33**
4	water	22	water	32
5	**wine**	**15**	**beer**	**26**
6	drink	10	**alcohol**	**18**
7	juice	9	milk	14
8	orange	9	juice	9
9	**beer**	**8**	**champagne**	**8**
10	coke	8	**brandy**	**6**
11	**alcohol**	**7**	fruit	6
12	**spirits**	**7**	**sherry**	**6**
13	**gin**	**6**	**whisky**	**6**
14	**sherry**	**6**	blood	5
15	**whisky**	**6**	**lager**	**4**
16	drinks	4	mineral	4
17	**ale**	**3**	**whiskey**	**4**
18	**brandy**	**3**	**ale**	**3**
19	**methylated**	**3**	**booze**	**3**
20	pop	3	fluids	3

With DRINK, we do not find an object noun *drink* or *beverage* occurring with the same kind of frequency as *food* does in the case of EAT. Neither *drink/drinks* nor *beverage* occurs in the top 20 object nouns in the wBNC, for example. Instead, we find words with more specific kinds of meanings. Clearly, alcohol is a common type of object of transitive DRINK and not just a feature of the interpretation of intransitive DRINK. The occurrence of names for alcoholic beverages is striking, accounting for a clear majority of the top 20 beverage-type nouns as objects in both spoken and written corpora. Nevertheless, it is worth noting that *tea* and *coffee* are the most frequent in both corpora. *Tea* is the most common beverage-type noun in the sBNC, while *coffee* is the most common such noun in the wBNC, reflecting (as with *fish* and *chips* above) possible differences in preferences in informal versus formal settings. Ethnographically speaking, we also notice that this famously ale-drinking culture has discovered the grape: there are more instances of *wine* in the object phrase than *beer* in both corpora.

We find these results concerning the top 20 food and drink objects of some interest. Lexicographic practice typically identifies specialized intransitive uses of EAT and DRINK involving the specific interpretations of 'eat a meal' and 'drink alcohol', but omits any mention of these meanings with the transitive usage. This is understandable when a dictionary is intended to be used primarily to help users decode a particular usage of a verb. One might, for example, rely on the dictionary to "fill in" an understood, but unexpressed object. As defensible as it may be for lexicographers to make inferences explicit in one case (the intransitive), but not the other (the transitive), this practice has the drawback of suggesting a difference between transitive and intransitive use when, as in this case, none exists. We stress, again, the virtue of corpus linguistic techniques for the descriptive linguist and lexicographer alike. By sampling thousands of instances of actual uses of an item, the full extent of inferences and collocational properties associated with a verb becomes apparent and the ensuing description becomes more observationally adequate.

Further differentiation of object nouns according to the inflected form of the verb yields additional information. Tables 10 and 11 provide a breakdown of the top 20 food-type nouns by inflected form of EAT. The lists in these tables provide tantalizing glimpses into interactions between TAM marking and lexical properties of the objects. For example, while the superordinate term *food* is the most frequent word in almost all these lists, it is conspicuously absent with the simple past tense *ate* in the sBNC. Note also that *meat* is absent as an object of *ate* and *eaten* in both tables, both telic and highly episodic inflections of the verb EAT. These two object nouns, *food* and *meat*, occur most typically in "habitual" contexts (e.g., *The rich eat too much meat and suffer from chronic constipation*, from the sBNC). The absence of *food* and *meat* in these cases may be motivated by a disharmony between these words (and their habitual associations) and the simple past tense (with more "past" and "completed" associations).

Table 10. Top 20 food-like nouns with inflected forms of EAT in the sBNC

lexeme	head nouns in object phrase (N)
eat	**dinner (33), food (30)**, *meat* (18), *cheese* (14), *chips* (13), *bread* (12), *cake* (12), *fruit* (11), **breakfast (11)**, *fish* (11), *chicken* (10), **tea (10)**, *flies* (9), *biscuits* (8), *chocolate* (8), **meal (8)**, *vegetables* (8), *apples* (6), *sandwiches* (6), *toast* (6)
eats	**food (8)**, *cheese* (4), *meat* (4), *fish* (3), *cake* (2), *flies* (2), *fruit* (2), *salads* (2), *sweets* (2)
eating	**food (14)**, *chocolate* (7), *cake* (6), **dinner (5)**, *fish* (5), *meat* (5), **supper (5), breakfast (4)**, *crisps* (4), **lunch (4)**, *bread* (3), *chicken* (3), *cream* (3), *fruit* (3), **meal (3), tea (3)**, *butter* (2), *chips* (2), *chocolates* (2)
ate	*flies* (4), *bread* (3), *chocolate* (3), *biscuit* (2), *cake* (2), *chips* (2), *cream* (2), *eggs* (2), *margarine* (2), *potatoes* (2), *pudding* (2), *stuffing* (2), *vegetables* (2)
eaten	**food (5)**, *toast* (3), *birds* (2), *bread* (2), *cheese* (2), **dinner (2)**, *fish* (2), *hat* (2), *sausage* (2)

One particular sequence of specific words in our database that deserves comment is *something to eat*. This sequence is, in fact, the most frequent trigram which includes a form of EAT or DRINK in our database. We returned to the BNC, making use of the additional options in the BNCWeb application, to check on the statisitical significance of *something to eat*. We chose *to eat* as the node phrase and sought statistics on the word occurring immediately to the left. In the sBNC we found that *something to eat* occurred 53 times (mutual information score 6.65, Z-score 72.30); in the whole wBNC, *something to eat* occurred 153 times (mutual information score 7.48, Z-score 164.28). These scores indicate significant collocations in both corpora. Again, a corpus-based approach to language analysis can draw our attention to common usage, as opposed to the constructed examples of grammar books. Though *something to eat* is the most common trigram in our database, it is a usage of EAT which is often marginalized in discussions of transitive verbs. Indeed, the infinitival complement of a noun is a frequently omitted construction type or category entry in reference grammars of English.

Table 11. Top 20 food-like nouns with inflected forms of EAT in the sampled wBNC

lexeme	head nouns in object phrase (N)
eat	*food* **(31)**, meat (16), bread (14), *fish* (14), *foods* **(13)**, **meals (8)**, cake (7), *fruit* (7), **breakfast (6)**, **lunch (6)**, **meal (6)**, cheese (5), cream (5), fibre (5), grass (5), salad (5), vegetables (5), cakes (4), chocolate (4), ice (4),
eats	*food* **(4)**, *fish* (2), meat (2)
eating	*food* **(17)**, *foods* **(14)**, cheese (7), **breakfast (5)**, chocolate (5), fish (5), fruit (5), **meals (5)**, sandwiches (5), bread (4), cream (4), fibre (4), animal (3), berries (3), cake (3), cereals (3), fat (3), heart (3), leaves (3), **meal (3)**
ate	*food* **(9)**, **lunch (6)**, *fish* (5), eggs (4), **meals (4)**, apple (3), beans (3), bread (3), **breakfast (3)**, cheese (3), chocolate (3), cream (3), rice (3), biscuits (2), cakes (2), cereal (2), chips (2), crisps (2), **dinner (2)**, ice (2)
eaten	*food* **(4)**, **meal (3)**, bread (2), **breakfast (2)**, cake (2), *foods* **(2)**

6. Subjects

It is natural that there should be more focus on the nature of the object than the subject in discussions of transitivity. However, we are interested in gaining a better understanding of the whole transitive construction in English which includes both a subject and an object. We therefore examined properties of the subject phrases as well as the object phrases. In our database, a non-animate subject was extremely rare, though they did occur. Examples of inanimate subjects with EAT are given in (8). Newman (1997) discusses the metaphorical mappings that underlie these extensions and other ones based on EAT in English.

(8) Inanimate subjects (underlined) occurring with EAT
   a. A tall order, when <u>tennis time</u> eats into valuable study time. (sBNC)
   b. ... because <u>a hangover</u> had already eaten into his small reserves of patience and equanimity. (wBNC)
   c. If your water is soft and acid, <u>it</u> will eat into the shell and dissolve it. (wBNC)
   d. If she will be earning, <u>that</u> will eat into her profit. (wBNC)
   e. <u>Every mile of dual carriageway</u> eats up twenty-six acres of countryside. (sBNC)

We coded subject phrases by number and person for EAT and DRINK in both corpora. Figures 5 and 6 summarize the results based on counts of lemmatized EAT and DRINK. These results show parallel patterns for EAT and DRINK in each corpus (the sBNC and the sampled wBNC), though the difference between the spoken and written modalities is quite striking. In the spoken modality, the contour is defined by peaks at 1st singular, 2nd singular/plural, and 3rd singular, with a certain number of uninterpretable subjects as part of the corpus. In the written modality, on the other hand, 3rd singular, 3rd plural, and unspecified subjects predominate, with no uninterpretable subjects. These different distributions conform to some expected patterns, e.g., the high incidence of reference to speech act participants in the spoken language, at least in conversation. Conversely, there is a predominance of "others", i.e., 3rd person forms, and unspecified subjects in the written corpus. While the overall trends evident in these figures may be well motivated, one cannot predict the specific distributions of individual verbs such as EAT and DRINK without an examination of a corpus. By the same token, one would need to carry out a comparable analysis of other verbs to be confident about the extent to which the profiles in Figures 5 and 6 (or even Figures 3 and 4) are replicated for other verbs.

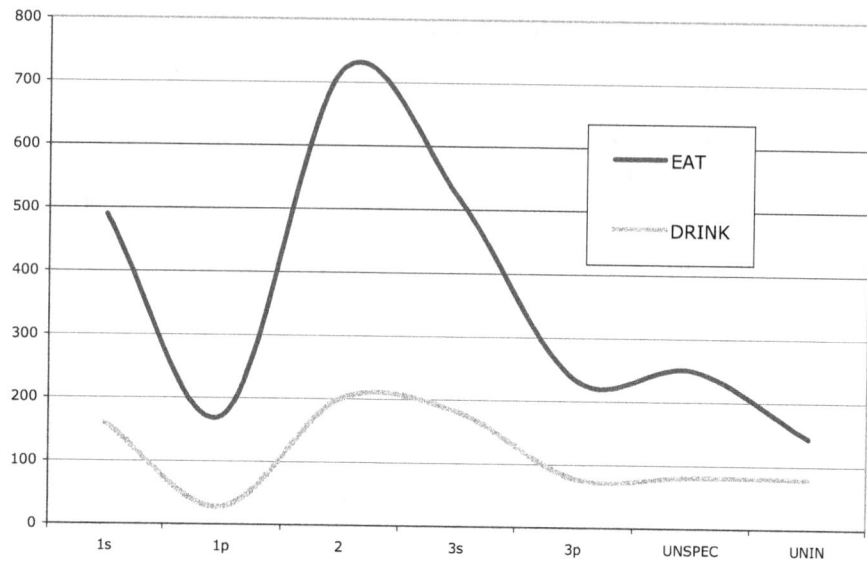

Figure 5. Raw frequencies of the lemmas EAT and DRINK by subject NP in the sBNC

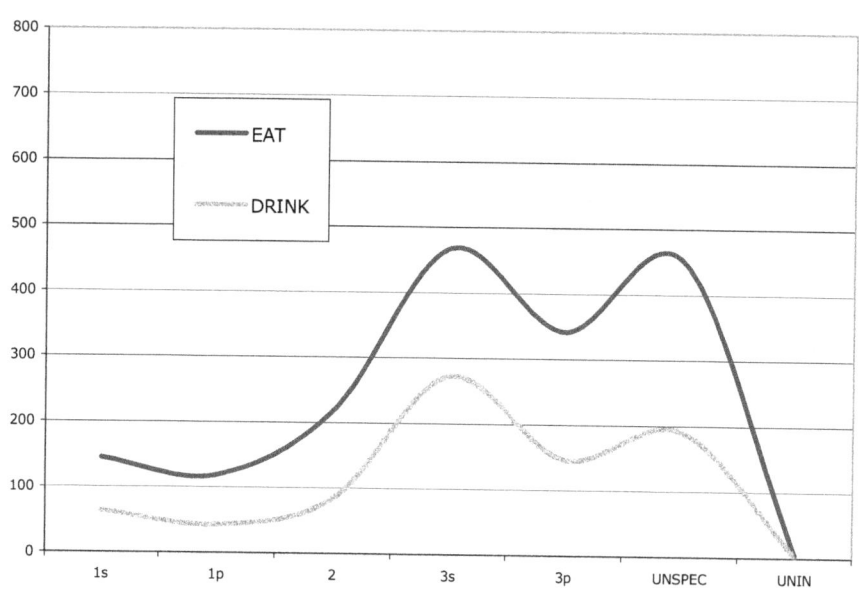

Figure 6. Raw frequencies of the lemmas EAT and DRINK by subject NP in the wBNC sample

7. Beyond (and below) the transitivity of EAT and DRINK

A couple of broad conclusions can be drawn from our corpus study into the transitivity alternations evinced by English EAT and DRINK. First of all, we completely concur with Hopper and Thompson's (1980) view that transitivity is scalar and that a verb's transitivity profile can vary (a variant of which was expressed in Rice [1987]). However, is the phenomenon of transitivity the rightful place to start? We have found ample evidence that the presence or absence of an object phrase can vary by inflection and modality. Furthermore, the semantic properties of a verb and its overt or supressed arguments are construction-specific. Conversely, a verb's argument structure(s) should not be construed as hard-wired in the verbal lexicon, but as emergent from patterns of usage (which, needless to say, are genre- and modality-specific). This conclusion, self-evident to any linguist who works with a corpus, is only recently finding its way into theories of syntax, which have long been dominated by claims that context-free, language-wide, and universally inspired phrase structure patterns are the relevant unit of analysis. Where once truth was sought in the most generalized, category-based phenomena, we prefer to seek truth as it presents itself to us in the specifics of usage.

There is a growing realization amongst cognitively and functionally minded linguists that individual words, together with their co-occurring collocates, are not just a proper "unit" of analysis, but represent a desirable descriptive and analytical starting point. That is to say, it is not just at the categorial level (N, NP, etc.) or the level of the lemma (EAT, DRINK) where we find patterns worthy of study. Words (*eat*, *drink*, etc.), together with their collocational forms, have become a focus of interest in a number of current approaches, notably Langacker's Cognitive Grammar (1987, 1991). It is an idea which also finds expression in Croft's Radical Construction Grammar (Croft 2001). Croft allows for specific constructions such as [*roasted* MEATNOUN] and [*toasted* BREADNOUN], alongside the superordinate construction [TRVERB-PASSPART NOUN]. Here, the specific words *roasted* and *toasted* help define two separate constructions, at one level of analysis. In essence, a verb's selectional restrictions, once exclusively relegated to the lexicon, are allowed to direct the syntax, at least in certain cognitively inspired theories of grammar. Moreover, Renouf and Sinclair (1991) have tracked the incidence of "frames" such as *a(n) X of* (e.g., *a lot of*, *a kind of*, *an example of*); *too X to* (e.g., *too late to*, *too much to*); *many X of* (*many years of*, *many thousands of*) and show how the frame provides a significant context for the keyword X and vice versa (i.e., specific keywords dominate the frame). Similarly, Stefanowitsch and Gries' (2003) idea of a *collostruction*, understood as constructions in which particular lexical items play a key role, e.g., the [INTO-causative] construction or the [NP WAITING-TO-HAPPEN] construction, takes the study of grammar in similar directions.

In the same vein, Thompson and Hopper (2001: 44) recognize a crucial lexico-syntactic level of analysis which is built around a specific verb and its collocational forms. They write:

> ... among the things speakers know about verbs is the range of forms they collocate with according to the different senses they have ... [T]he more different types of language speakers are exposed to and participate in, the wider the range of options for a given verb sense they are likely to have entered and stored ... *[S]ome collocations involving specific verb senses develop lives of their own.* [Italics ours]

We would add that some collocations involving specific verbs *in specific inflections* develop lives of their own. It is not just certain verb lemmas which show an affinity for particular subject and TAM inflection or for realized or implied objects, but also the inflected forms themselves which do.

Some recent case studies of individual verbs in English have detailed such inflectional idiosyncrasy. Tao (2001, 2003) shows that the transitive lemma REMEMBER is overwhelmingly used, in the three spoken corpora he investigated, without an object complement, in the simple present tense, with first person singular (*I remember*) or null subjects (*remember?*), and at utterance boundaries. He concludes that the verb is well on its way to grammaticalizing into a discourse particle which regulates participant interaction in conversation and considers that a preoccupation with REMEMBER's argument structure and lexical meaning is misplaced. Scheibman (2001), in a study of informal conversation, found that 1st singular and 2nd singular subjects occur with particular verbs of cognition with a relative high frequency (*I guess, I don't know, you know, I mean*) reflecting the pragmatic value of such combinations in conversation. Scheibman (2001: 84) emphasizes the need to examine "local" patterns in grammatical research and cautions against relying just on the superordinate grammatical categories (person, verb type, tense etc.). More recently, Newman and Rice (2004) describe the emergence of a *SIT around and...* construction where the meaning relates to futile, lazy, or otherwise unproductive activity rather than the posture of sitting. The presence of the lexical item *around* is a crucial part of this construction. They also report on how the inflectional differences between the *-ing* and past tense forms in the pairs *sitting and…/sat and…, standing and…/stood and, lying and…/lay and…* profoundly influence the range of following verbal collocates. Finally, Rice and Newman (2004), in a study of aspectual uses of English prepositions, note that with the "resumptive" construction *V on with*, just three collocate verbs (*get, carry,* and *go*) account for 90% of the 506 examples in the sBNC. They show, too, that the inflectional categories are distributed in construction-specific ways. Thus, the V in the "continuous activity" *V on* construction occurs preferentially as a bare stem, whereas the V of the "semeliterative" or "corrective" *V over* construction occurs preferentially in the simple past.

The main message we want to impart is that inflected verb forms have their own semantic and constructional properties (hence, the reference to "below transitivity" in the title of this section) and these merit serious descriptive and theoretical consideration. To that end, we propose the notion of an *inflectional island*, taking Tomasello's (1992) notion of a *verb island* a step further. He coined this term to describe the fact that morphosyntactic inflection tends to affect individual verbs in early child language and that syntactic development emerges from one verb to another and not across a lexical class as a whole. We use *inflectional island* in a similar fashion: syntactic/semantic properties tend to inhere in individual inflections of a verb in a register-specific manner. Furthermore, these properties may not extend across all the inflections to characterize the lemma as a whole. For us, the notion of a dictionary entry based on a lemma is still inadequate. Langacker's (1987: 63–76) dictum that grammar is a structured inventory of conventionalized units continues to provide a reliable and insightful way of conceptualizing language. The onus falls on us to identify and describe the level and nature of this conventionalization.

Appendix 1

Raw frequencies and percentages of person/number occurrences with the word form *eat* in our database.

S	*eat* O (s)		*eat* (s)		*eat* O (w)		*eat* (w)	
1s	291	20%	48	18%	49	8%	28	10%
1p	80	6%	38	14%	41	7%	33	12%
2	486	34%	67	25%	129	21%	55	21%
3s	214	15%	34	13%	101	17%	65	24%
3p	121	8%	44	16%	152	25%	40	15%
UNSPEC	176	12%	18	7%	133	22%	47	18%
UNIN	81	6%	20	7%	1	0%	0	0%
TOTALS	1449	100%	269	100%	606	100%	268	100%

Appendix 2

Raw frequencies and percentages of person/number occurrences with the word form *drink* in our database.

S	*drink* O (s)		*drink* (s)		*drink* O (w)		*drink* (w)	
1s	86	24%	25	20%	21	11%	13	11%
1p	14	4%	1	1%	12	6%	6	5%
2	123	35%	39	31%	42	22%	24	20%
3s	49	14%	25	20%	39	20%	35	29%
3p	27	8%	18	14%	29	15%	31	26%
UNSPEC	21	6%	5	4%	48	25%	12	10%
UNIN	35	10%	14	11%	2	1%	0	0%
TOTALS	355	100%	127	100%	193	100%	121	100%

Notes

1. An earlier version of this paper was presented at the theme session on *Language Between Text and Mind: The Use of Corpora in Cognitive Linguistics* at the 8th International Cognitive Linguistics Conference in July, 2003. We would like to thank our research assistants, Hui Yin and Hideyuki Sugiura, who carried out preliminary coding of our corpus search results. Thanks also to the editors and reviewers of this volume who provided helpful feedback.

2. We use small capital letters to denote a lemma which subsumes all the inflected forms, e.g., EAT, and italics to denote a particular word form or lexical item. Thus, EAT subsumes *eat, eats, eating, ate, eaten*.
3. For Levin (1993: 42, 213–214), EAT and DRINK exhaust their particular subclass of what she calls *Verbs of Ingesting*, an exclusivity which makes them all the more intriguing.
4. Note that Van Valin and LaPolla's (1997) distinction between non-referential objects (*He ate spaghetti in ten minutes*) and referential objects (*He ate the plate of spaghetti in ten minutes*) is construable as a special case of parameter J, individuation of the object, in Hopper and Thompson's (1980) model of Transitivity.
5. We reserve the term "modality" for spoken versus written modes of communication, whereas we take "genre" to mean a register difference within a modality, e.g., spontaneous conversation, story-telling, or ceremonial language.
6. Despite our qualms, this grammar is a prodigious achievement nevertheless.
7. We have opted to use lines instead of bars to express quantities in many of the following figures. We felt a need to collapse information between corpus, verb, and transitivity class, as well as across inflectional category. We do not intend for these line-based figures to give the impression of continuous functions across what are obviously discrete categories. However, the lines constitute a distributional "profile" which is easier to assess and compare than what would otherwise be a proliferation of individual bars. We use the following abbreviations in these figures: 1 = 1st person, 2 = 2nd person, 3 = 3rd person, s = singular, p = plural, UNSPEC = unspecified, UNIN = uninterpretable.

References

Alm-Arvius, Christina
    1993   *The English Verb* SEE: *A Study in Multiple Meaning*. Göteburg: Acta Universitatis Gothoburgensis.

Biber, Douglas, Stig Johansson, Geoffrey Leech, Susan Conrad, and Edw. Finegan
    2000   *Longman Grammar of Spoken and Written English*. Harlow: Pearson Education Limited.

Cooper, William E. and John R. Ross
    1975   Word order. In: R. E. Grossman, L. J. San, and T. J. Vance (eds.), *Papers from the Parasession on Functionalism*, 63–111. Chicago, IL: Chicago Linguistic Society.

Croft, William
    2001   *Radical Construction Grammar: Syntactic Theory in Typological Perspective*. Oxford: Oxford University Press.

Hopper, Paul J. and Sandra A. Thompson
　1980　　Transitivity in grammar and discourse. *Language* 56: 251–299.
Huddleston, Rodney
　1988　　*English Grammar: An Outline*. Cambridge: Cambridge University Press.
Huddleston, Rodney and Geoffrey K. Pullum (eds.)
　2002　　*The Cambridge Grammar of the English Language*. Cambridge: Cambridge University Press.
Kilgarriff, Adam
　2001　　Comparing corpora. *International Journal of Corpus Linguistics* 6: 97–133.
Langacker, Ronald W.
　1987　　*Foundations of Cognitive Grammar, Vol. I, Theoretical Prerequisites*. Stanford, CA: Stanford University Press.
　1991　　*Foundations of Cognitive Grammar, Vol. II, Descriptive Application*. Stanford, CA: Stanford University Press.
　2001　　A dynamic usage-based model. In: Michael Barlow and Suzanne Kemmer (eds.), *Usage-based Models of Language*, 1–63. Stanford, CA: CSLI Publications.
Levin, Beth
　1993　　*English Verb Classes and Alternations*. Chicago, IL: University of Chicago Press.
Lichtenberk, Frantisek
　1991　　Semantic changes and heterosemy in grammaticalization. *Language* 67: 475–509.
Newman, John
　1996　　*Give: A Cognitive Linguistic Study*. Berlin/New York: Mouton de Gruyter.
　1997　　Eating and drinking as sources of metaphor in English. *Cuadernos de Filología Inglesa* (Special volume on Cognitive Linguistics) 6: 213–231.
　2004　　Motivating the uses of basic verbs: Linguistic and extra-linguistic considerations. In: Günther Radden and Klaus-Uwe Panther (eds.), *Motivation in Grammar*, 193–218. Berlin/New York: Mouton de Gruyter.
　1998　　(ed.) *The Linguistics of Giving*. Amsterdam/Philadelphia: John Benjamins.
　2002　　(ed.) *The Linguistics of Sitting, Standing, and Lying*. Amsterdam/Philadelphia: John Benjamins.

Newman, John and Sally Rice
2001 English SIT, STAND, and LIE in small and large corpora. *ICAME Journal* 25: 109–133.
2004 Patterns of usage for English SIT, STAND, and LIE: A cognitively-inspired exploration in corpus linguistics. *Cognitive Linguistics* 15: 351–396.

Norvig, Peter and George Lakoff
1987 Taking: A study in Lexical Network Theory. In: *BLS* 13: 195–206.

Pauwels, Paul and Anne-Marie Simon-Vandenbergen
1995 Body parts in linguistic action: Underlying schemata and value judgements. In: Louis Goossens, Paul Pauwels, Brygda Rudzka-Ostyn, Anne-Marie Simon-Vandenbergen, and Johan Vanparys (eds.), *By Word of Mouth: Metaphor, Metonymy and Linguistic Action in a Cognitive Perspective*, 35–69. Amsterdam/Philadelphia: John Benjamins.

Poutsma, Hendrik
1926 *A Grammar of Late Modern English, Part II: The Parts of Speech, Section II: The Verb and the Particles*. Groningen: P. Noordhoff.

Radden, Günther
1996 Motion metaphorized: The case of "coming" and "going". In: Eugene H. Casad (ed.), *Cognitive Linguistics in the Redwoods: The Expansion of a New Paradigm in Linguistics*, 423–458, Berlin/New York: Mouton de Gruyter.

Renouf, Antoinette and John M. Sinclair
1991 Collocational frameworks in English. In: Karin Aijmer and Bengt Altenberg (eds.), *English Corpus Linguistics: Studies in Honour of Jan Svartvik*, 128–143. London/New York: Longman.

Rice, Sally
1987 Towards a cognitive model of transitivity. Ph.D. dissertation, Department of Linguistics, University of California, San Diego.
1988 Unlikely lexical entries. *BLS* 14: 202–212.

Rice, Sally and John Newman
2004 Aspect in the making: A corpus analysis of English aspect-marking prepositions. In: Michel Achard and Suzanne Kemmer (eds.), *Language, Culture, and Mind*, 313–326. Stanford, CA: CSLI Publications.

Scheibman, Joanne
2001 Local patterns of subjectivity in person and verb type in American English conversation. In: Joan Bybee and Paul Hopper (eds.), *Frequency and the Emergence of Linguistic Structure*, 61–89. Amsterdam/Philadelphia: John Benjamins.

Serra Borneto, Carlos
   1996   *Liegen* and *stehen* in German: A study in horizontality and verticality. In: Eugene H. Casad (ed.), *Cognitive Linguistics in the Redwoods: The Expansion of a New Paradigm in Linguistics*, 459–505. Berlin/New York: Mouton de Gruyter.

Shen, Ya-Ming
   1996   The semantics of the Chinese verb "come". In: Eugene H. Casad (ed.), *Cognitive Linguistics in the Redwoods: The Expansion of a New Paradigm in Linguistics*, 507–540. Berlin/New York: Mouton de Gruyter.

Stefanowitsch, Anatol and Stefan Th. Gries
   2003   Collostructions: Investigating the interaction of words and constructions. *International Journal of Corpus Linguistics* 8: 209–243.

Sweetser, Eve
   1990   *From Etymology to Pragmatics*. Cambridge: Cambridge University Press.

Tao, Hongyin
   2001   Discovering the usual with corpora: The case of *remember*. In: Rita C. Simpson and John M. Swales (eds.), *Corpus Linguistics in North America: Selections from the 1999 Symposium*, 116–144. Ann Arbor: University of Michigan Press.
   2003   A usage-based approach to argument structure. *International Journal of Corpus Linguistics* 8: 75–95.

Thompson, Sandra A. and Paul J. Hopper
   2001   Transitivity, clause structure, and argument structure: Evidence from conversation. In: Joan Bybee and Paul Hopper (eds.), *Frequency and the Emergence of Linguistic Structure*, 27–60. Amsterdam/Philadelphia: John Benjamins

Tomasello, Michael
   1992   *First Verbs: A Case Study of Early Grammatical Development*. Cambridge: Cambridge University Press.

Van Valin, Jr., Robert D. and Randy J. LaPolla
   1997   *Syntax: Structure, Meaning and Function*. Cambridge: Cambridge University Press.

Wierzbicka, Anna
   1988   Why you can have a drink when you can't have an eat. In: Anna Wierzbicka, *The Semantics of Grammar*, 293–357. Amsterdam/Philadelphia: John Benjamins.

Caused posture: Experiential patterns emerging from corpus research

Maarten Lemmens

Abstract

The main goal of the article is to map out the semantics of the four basic placement verbs in Dutch: *zetten* 'set', *leggen* 'lay' and *steken/stoppen* 'stick (into)'. They are the causative counterparts of the three cardinal posture verbs (CPVs) *zitten* 'sit', *liggen* 'lie', and *staan* 'staan'. The study also briefly considers the verb *doen* 'do' that can be used in some contexts as a placement verb. The use of an extensive corpus reveals some experientially based patterns underlying the use of cardinal causative posture verbs (CCPV) in Dutch, as aligned with the uses of the non-causative posture verbs in their postural, locational, and metaphorical uses. At the same time, the data also show how the causative posture verbs no longer center around the sitting, lying and standing postures that make up the prototypes for the non-causatives posture verbs. The data further allow us to suggest an explanation for the semantic expansion that has occurred with one of the causative verbs, *zetten* that has shifted from the causative equivalent of *zitten* ('sit') to that of *staan* ('stand'). The (smaller scale) study of *doen* 'do' as a placement verb reveals that its use centers around the notion of containment. Finally, the data suggest that regional factors (Netherlandic versus Belgian Dutch) affect the usage of these verbs as well.

Keywords: placement verbs; posture verbs; corpus-based lexical semantics; Dutch.

1. Introduction

The main goal of the present article is to map out the semantics of the four basic placement verbs in Dutch: *zetten* 'set', *leggen* 'lay' and *steken/stoppen* 'stick (into)'. They are the causative counterparts of the three cardinal posture verbs (CPVs) *zitten* 'sit', *liggen* 'lie', and *staan* 'staan'. All Germanic languages display this systematic vowel alternation between the causative and non-causative verbs as presented in Table 1 that goes back to an umlaut under influence of the Old-Germanic causative suffix *-jan*.[1]

Table 1. Causative and non-causative cardinal posture verb alternation in Gmc. languages

Swedish		German		Dutch		English	
CPV	**CCPV**	**CPV**	**CCPV**	**CPV**	**CCPV**	**CPV**	**CCPV**
sitta	*sätta*	*sitzen*	*setzen*	*zitten*	*zetten*	*sit*	*set/put*
stå	*ställa*	*stehen*	*stellen*	*staan*	*(stellen)*	*stand*	*put/(stall)*
ligga	*lägga*	*liegen*	*stehen*	*liggen*	*leggen*	*lie*	*lay/put*

For the contemporary Dutch causatives, the original paradigm has only been partially preserved. In a nutshell, the changes that have occurred are the following.

(i) *Stellen* has been lost as the causative of *staan*, except in some relics, mostly metaphorical uses, e.g., *in werking stellen* 'set into operation', *ter discussie stellen* lit. 'set to discussion', (= 'make s.th. subject to discussion'), *tentoonstellen* 'put on display'.

(ii) *Zetten* fills the gap left by *stellen*, a change that may appear strange at first sight (especially to non-Germanophones) since what once meant 'MAKE-SIT' now means 'MAKE-STAND'.

(iii) Some other verbs, originally external to the paradigm, take over some of the meanings of *zetten*, i.e., *steken* lit. 'stick (into)', *stoppen* lit. 'stop, fill', and *doen* lit. 'do'.

In Dutch, as in the other Germanic languages, both the non-causatives and the causatives have generally become the obligatory coding for expressing the location of any entity in space (there are some exceptions, but they need not concern us here). The verbs' uses can grossly be divided into three groups: *postural* (referring to human posture), *locational* (referring to the location of any entity in space) and *metaphorical* (referring to location in abstract space). The obligatory use of both causative and non-causative CPVs is weakest in English, as the verb *put* functions as a kind of catch-all verb and many of the earlier uses of *sit*, *lie*, and *stand* have been lost and the verb *be* is now commonly used in locational contexts, e.g., *My keys are on the table* (see Lemmens, submitted).

On the basis of extensive corpus analysis, this article aims at extending Van Tol's (2002) preliminary analysis by revealing the experientially based patterns underlying the use of the causative posture verbs in Dutch, as aligned with the postural, locational, and metaphorical uses of the non-causative CPVs. Secondly, we suggest an explanation for the semantic expansion that has occurred with *zetten*. It should be stressed that, while our analysis is based on a large data set (7,550 sentences in total), our analysis is still more qualitative than (purely) quantitative in nature. As such, it probably will not conform to what corpus hard-liners may expect; actually, it is not the ambition of this paper to present a purely quantitative account. What it does set out to do is to lay out the semantic network of causative posture verbs in Dutch, and reveal their motivation, as they have emerged from analysing extensive data which has revealed patterns that would otherwise have been left unobserved.

The article is structured as follows. After a brief description of the corpus, we present a basic analysis of the causative and non-causative CPVs (Section 3). The description will be in three parts, corresponding to the threefold distinction represented by the rows in Table 1, which will be followed by a short summary (Section 3.4). In Section 4, we show that the causative CPVs have in fact shifted to a different, more generally locational, prototype. Section 5, finally, presents a selective discussion of the most important metaphor schemata.

2. The corpus

The attestations analysed are drawn from the largest of computerized Dutch corpus, available at the *Instituut voor Nederlandse Lexicologie*, Leiden.[2] The corpus contains 38 million words, and includes a variety of texts, exclusively non-fictional. The texts essentially belong to the written register; the spoken data in the corpus are actually all "monologual" and written-to-be-spoken, such as news bulletins or the Queen's speeches for parliament. Given the marked register of the latter, they have been excluded from our analysis. For the same reason, the collection of legal texts (1814–1989) and the reports of community council meetings have also been excluded. What has been retained for analysis (some 24.9 million words) can be divided into two large subgroups: (1) a VARIED corpus including books and magazines of different type and register and (2) a NEWS corpus consisting of newspapers and spoken news bulletins. In short, the present analysis is restricted to the written register.

Unfortunately, in addition to the predominance of the written register, the INL corpus is also regionally biased, as it is predominantly Northern Dutch (89%). The small section of Belgian Dutch data is moreover restricted to two months of the quality newspaper *De Standaard*, and thus represents only one type of written prose for the Belgian variant. Regional variation is important for at least one issue in the present study, the use of the verbs *steken, stoppen* and *doen* to express caused containment (see Section 3.3). It is at present uncertain if – and if so, to what degree – regional differences are also important for other issues related to posture verbs.

While the non-balanced character of the INL-corpus is to be regretted, it does not invalidate the overall lines of the present analysis. It does however imply that it not all patterns observed may be equally typical for all the varieties of Dutch at large. In fact, we plan a follow-up study using the *Corpus Gesproken Nederlands* [Corpus of Spoken Dutch] that has recently become commercially available. A frequency count of the lemmas *zitten, zetten, staan, liggen,* and *leggen* in this corpus, which can be done freely from their website,[3] shows that, at least for spoken language, the quantitative difference between Northern Dutch and Belgian Dutch is non-significant (18,129 vs. 18,005 respectively).[4] Since this is a mere lemma count, it does not say anything about qualitative differences.

The INL corpus is a POS-tagged corpus; consequently, we have been able to limit our extractions to verb forms. The extractions have subsequently been checked manually, since the INL POS-tagging is not without occasional errors. Furthermore, homonyms had to weeded out manually as well (e.g., *stoppen* also has the meaning 'stop, halt a movement', cases instantiating this meaning were not retained) and particle verbs (that often have very specific meanings only vaguely related to the verbs' locational semantics) were not included either (except for some exceptions for reasons that will be explained below). Of the 13,814 original extractions only 7,550 (54.7%) were kept. For *leggen* and *zetten*, about 32% of the extracted attestations were weeded out, for *steken* en *stoppen* this was as high as 70% and 84%.

The remaining extractions have subsequently been analysed one by one, assigning codes that specify, among other things, the actual verb form used, its use (postural, locational, metaphorical), the type of Figure, the type of Ground, the preposition used to introduce the Ground, etc.[5]

For the study of the verb *doen* 'do', which can be used as a placement verb in one particular context (that of caused containment), it has not been possible to use the INL-corpus due to practical limitations.[6] In this particular case, we have drawn on data obtained via Google searches. This will be further elaborated at the end of Section 3.3. Unless marked differently, all examples cited in this paper will come from either the INL or the Internet data set. Some occasional editing may have been done to simplify the structure to what is essential to the discussion (cf. Table 2).

Table 2. Frequency of CPVs and CCPVs in the corpus

CPV			
liggen	staan	zitten	Total
2,668	5,180	2,296	10,144
26.3%	51.1%	22.6%	100%

CCPV				
leggen	zetten	steken	stoppen	Total
3,077	3,551	621	301	7,550
40.8%	47.0%	8.2%	4.0%	100%

The wide range of uses of the causative posture verbs is not without complexities; before looking into some individual usages as they emerge from the corpus, we must therefore sketch some of the basic semantic extension mechanisms which, as can be expected, also apply to the non-causative posture verbs *liggen*, *zitten*, and *staan*. The following section presents such a semantic analysis relating the two types of verbs. There are three subsections, following the three main oppositions: (i) *staan* and *zetten*, (ii) *liggen* and *leggen*, and (iii) *zitten* and *zetten/steken/stoppen/doen*, after which there will be a short summary.

Once again, the discussion is a blend of a qualitative analysis – necessary to understand the basic motivations for the verbs' usages – and quantitative analyses based on our corpus sample. Occasional quantitative references pertaining to the uses of the intransitive verbs (*liggen*, *zitten*, *staan*) are based on corpus samples used in earlier work (see Lemmens 2002a).

3. Towards an experiential account of causative posture verbs

In line with the basic assumptions of Cognitive Grammar, the Dutch posture verbs *liggen*, *zitten*, and *staan* can be safely said to be structured around a prototype, the representation of the three basic human positions. (For this reason *hangen* 'hang' that is often mentioned as the fourth cardinal posture verb has been excluded.) As Newman (2002) correctly observes, these prototypes are "experiential clusters" of attributes, as summarized in Table 3.[7]

Table 3. Experiential Prototype Clusters for CPVs

	staan	**liggen**	**zitten**
(i)	canonical position	non-canonical position	non-canonical position
(ii)	maximally vertical	maximally horizontal	[–max. vertic.] & [–max horiz.]
(iii)	resting on feet ("stand-side")	resting on back ("side-side")	resting on buttocks ("sit-side")
(iv)	physical effort to sustain	no physical effort to sustain	some physical effort to sustain
(v)	(start)position for walking	position for resting and sleeping	position for deskwork and active rest
(vi)	associations: power and control	associations: rest, weakness, illness, death	associations: active rest, stability, fixed

It should be clear that these prototypes are not necessarily reflected in being the most frequent in the corpus. In fact, in the Belgian (non-fiction) corpus that served as a basis for our earlier analyses, only 10–15% of the CPVs concerned humans in one of the three positions; most other cases involve a-postural uses with human subjects, the location of inanimate entities or idiomatic uses.[8] For the causative verbs, the percentage of prototypes in the corpus is even lower (0.8%; see Section 4 for some discussion). The extended uses can be explained drawing on the notion of *image schemata* based on our everyday experience of lying, standing, sitting. As we will show in the following descriptions, the real dimensions of horizontality and verticality, often mentioned in school grammars, are actually only secondary factors.

3.1. STAAN and ZETTEN

The most important image schemata that motivate the locational uses of *staan/zetten* can be summarized as in the schema below. Points (1) to (4) are notions associated with the prototype that give rise to extended uses (represented by the arrows) in which the prototype specifications are loosened and become more widely applicable to different type of entities.

(1)   BE ON ONE'S FEET
      ⇨ BE ON ONE'S BASE

(2)   EXTEND UPWARD FROM FEET
      ⇨ EXTEND UPWARD FROM FEET ⇨ EXTEND FROM ORIGIN IN ANY DIRECTION

(3)   EXTEND MAXIMALLY ALONG ONE'S LONGEST AXIS
      ⇨ EXTEND MAXIMALLY ALONG ALL OF ONE'S AXES

(4)   HAVE A VERTICAL ORIENTATION

The image of an object on its base, a logical extension of the prototype configuration of a human being on its feet, is undoubtedly the most productive one within the locational domain: it accounts for 59.7% of the locational uses. Its salience is further reflected in the fact that the real dimensions of the object do not play a role anymore: for any object resting on its base a coding with *staan/zetten* becomes the most likely candidate, even if it is more vertical than horizontal, as is the case for cars, plates or laptops, which are said to be standing when on their base. Notice that English has similar uses of *stand* (e.g., *the car stood in the dealer's yard*; *the laptop stands on a separate table*), albeit that they are clearly less frequent and more stilted than their Dutch counterparts and often a coding with *sit* is preferred.[9]

Considering cognitive processing, one could argue, as does Serra Borneto (1996), that the conceptualisation of a base triggers a mental verticality, i.e., the mental image of upward extension of an object taking the base as its origin.[10] Typically, the situation involves a vertical extension (e.g., trees or grass growing upwards from their roots and thus "standing"), but through image schematic transformation (rotation), the verbs can also be applied in contexts where non-vertical direction is at issue (image schema 2). This motivates the use of *staan/zetten* in examples like the following (own examples).

(1) a. *Er **staan** geen takken meer aan deze boom.*
 'There stand no branches to this tree anymore'[11]
 b. *Ik **zet** even dit oortje terug (vast) aan het kopje.*
 'I set this handle fixed back to the cup' (= 'fix it to the cup again')

In these examples, the semantics of *staan/zetten* is not about verticality but rather a (moderate) form of perpendicularity.[12]

A similar mental operation underlies uses of *staan/zetten* for situations where the object in question maintains a maximal and rigid extension along its longest axis, an image that is also drawn directly from the prototype. This motivates uses such as *De kabel staat strak (gespannen)* 'The cable stands tight' and *Zet de lijn flink strak* 'Set the line quite tight'. From such examples one easily extends to situations where an object takes its maximal spatial expansion along all its axes, as in *De zeil gingen bol staan.* 'The sail went to stand round' (= 'The sails bulged [out]') or *De wind zet de zeilen bol* 'The winds sets the sails round' (= 'The wind bulged out the sails'). In all of these cases, once again, the real orientation of the object is not pertinent.

The vertical dimension only comes in as a determinative factor in the absence of a base, as in (2), or when the object is not resting upon its base and verticality is needed to identify its orientation, as in (3) (own examples).

(2) *Het boek **staat** in het rek. / **Zet** het boek in het rek.*
 'The book stands on the shelf / Set the book on the shelf'

(3) *De borden **staan** in de afwasmachine / **Zet** de borden in de afwasmachine.*
 'The dishes stand in the dish washer / Set the dishes in the dish washer'

It is particularly in this case that *staan* and *zetten* provide a maximal opposition with *liggen* and *leggen*, discussed next.

3.2. LIGGEN and LEGGEN

Here's an overview of the most important uses of *liggen/leggen* that will be briefly discussed here:

(1) BE ON ONE'S SIDES (human posture)
   ↳ NOT BE ON BASE WITH HORIZONTAL ORIENTATION (inanimate entities)
   (↳ NOT BE ON ONE'S BASE)
(2) LOCATION OF DIMENSION-LESS ENTITIES
(3) GEOTOPOGRAPHICAL LOCATION (cities, buildings, etc.)
(4) LOCATION OF ABSTRACT ENTITIES

The notion of horizontality is much more important for *liggen* and *leggen* than that of verticality is for *staan/zetten*. This horizontality manifests itself in different types (see Figure 1 Section 3.4 for a simplified diagram). Two large categories of horizontal objects can be distinguished, LINE types and SHEET types, which are maximally distinct in their prototypes but share a transitional zone (small boards, for example, are conceivable as wide lines yet also as small elongated sheets). Within the SHEET category are also included different kinds of tissues (e.g., clothes, towels, etc.) and substances (e.g., liquids, sand, etc.), since they are non-rigid objects that naturally take a horizontal expansion under their own gravitational weight. The difference between **Leg** *het zout op tafel* and **Zet** *het zout op tafel* 'lay/set the salt on the table' is thus metonymic: in the first case, *leggen* refers to the salt as substance which, uncontained by any boundaries, will flatten out on the table (it will thus "lie" on the table); in the second case, *zetten* shifts the focus from the substance itself to the saltshaker (itself left implicit however), which will be posited on its base, and thus be (put) in a standing position.

One of the particularities of Dutch (but something one finds in other languages as well) is that it has conventionalized the verbs *liggen* and *leggen* to encode the location of symmetrical entities (balls, cubes, wads, etc.). These can be characterized by a "lack of dimensional salience" as Serra Borneto (1996) correctly observes for German *liegen*, perfectly similar to Dutch in this context (see also Fagan [1991] for an account on German *liegen/legen*, *sitzen/setzen* and *stehen/stellen* that is quite compatible with ours). He points out how in the absence of dimensional differentiation there is no mental tracing away from the origin as one has with vertical objects or objects resting on their base.

The "dimension-less use" of *liggen/leggen* motivates a number of metaphorical extensions. We are not referring here to the cases where these abstract issues are saliently associated with a particular horizontal form, as may be the case for example with frontiers conceived as lines or foundations as horizontal supports. The abstract uses that we are concerned with here are those entities that seem to lack such imagery, as for example in *De verantwoordelijkheid ligt bij jou* 'The responsibility lies with you' and *Ik leg de verantwoordelijkheid bij jou* 'I lay the responsibility with you'. In our corpus, among the abstract figures occurring with causative *leggen*, the most frequent ones are *verantwoordelijkheid* 'responsibility' (26 cases on 135 or 19.2%), *schuld* 'blame, guilt' (27 cases or 20%). Other typical examples in our corpus are *gevoel* 'emotion' (12.6%), *prioriteit* 'priority' (7 cases or 5.1%), *last* 'burden' (5 cases or 3.7%), *oorzaak* 'cause' (4 cases or 3%), *claim* 'claim' (4 cases or 3%), *macht, bevoegdheid* 'power, authority', (4 cases or 3%). Less frequent ones in our sample are *druk* 'pressure', *hypotheek* 'mortgage', or *initiatief* 'initiative', to name but a few. What motivates the use of *liggen/leggen* in these cases, for which it is much harder to argue that the located entity has a particular shape?[13]

Several motivations can in fact be adduced for the abundance of examples. A plausible explanation is that these "shapeless" abstract entities trigger a default location event for which, as Talmy (2000, I: 186) has pointed out, a point location predominates, i.e., in the absence of indications to the contrary we are dealing here with point-like Figures. Talmy advances this hypothesis for closed class items (i.e., prepositions), but in the absence of shape specification as we have here, this hypothesis may very well hold. As said, points are typically conceptualized as round objects, triggering a coding with *liggen/leggen*. Another motivation may be that abstract entities are generally not attributed the power to sustain themselves and thus would be more like non-rigid entities (Sally Rice, personal communication). A third factor that may contribute to the appropriateness of the coding is that in many cases these (shapeless) abstract entities are a "burden" (mortgage, responsibility, burden, etc.) which can be thought of as covering and pressing down the Ground. The triple motivation contributes to the appropriateness of the coding, at least within the powerful "postural logic" conventionalized in Dutch and routinely applied by its speakers.

3.3. ZITTEN and ZETTEN/STOPPEN/STEKEN/DOEN

If *staan* and *liggen* generally still find a direct equivalent in *zetten* and *leggen*, the situation is considerably more complicated for *zitten* that takes a number of causative equivalents. Let us first consider the basic uses of *zitten* and then discuss their causative counterparts. (Figure 1 may once again serve as a diagrammatic summary.)

Oversimplifying things, we could say that *zitten* encodes all that *staan* and *liggen* do not. The latter two encode a maximal contrast in the postural domain (as well as in their extended uses); *zitten* is often used to express the location of people without any trace of posture (or orientation), as in the following examples (all our own).

(4) a. *Zij **zit** in New York voor zaken.*
 'She sits (= is) in New York for business'
 b. ***Zitten** hier olifanten?*
 'Sit (= Are) there elephants here?'
 c. *Hij **zit** in de gevangenis.*
 'He sits (= is) in prison'

In English, as in many other languages, one would generally use the verb *to be*.[14]

In earlier analyses, we have argued that the a-postural character of *zitten* is probably a logical outcome of its greater variability in the postural domain where the verb encodes a number of quite different positions (i.e., on your buttocks, yoga-posture, on your knees, on all fours, squatting, sitting half upright). It also explains why the verb has come to encode the canonical position lower animals (e.g., mice, frogs, etc.) and birds whose posture is judged similar to that of squatting or of being on all fours. For these usages, *zetten* 'make-sit' continues as the causative counterpart: *Ik zet het kind op de stoel* 'I set the child on the chair', *Zet de vogel op de grond* 'Set the bird on the ground'. For humans bringing themselves in a sitting posture, reflexive *zetten* is possible, but only occurs in Belgian Dutch (*Ik zette me naast Joanna* 'I set me next to Joanna' = 'I sat down next to Joanna'); in the Netherlandic variant one generally resorts to the periphrastic construction *Ik ging naast Joanna zitten* 'I went next to Joanna (to) sit' (= 'I sat down next to Joanna').

For the locational uses, two important subgroups can be distinguished that revolve around two attributes derived from the prototype: (1) CLOSE CONTACT (when sitting, there is considerably close contact between body and chair/ground) and (2) CONTAINMENT (when sitting one can be partially contained by the chair). Together they account for almost 45% of the uses of *zitten*. The following sentences (all own examples) illustrate these locational uses that also productively find metaphorical extensions, cf. the c-sentences.

(5) a. *De poot **zit** (vast) aan de tafel.*
 'The leg sit (fixed) to the table'
 b. *Er **zit** een sticker op de voorruit.*
 'There sits a sticker to the windshield'
 c. *Ik **zit** met een probleem.*
 'I sit with a problem'

(6) a. *De wijn **zit** in de fles.*
 'The wine sits in the bottle'
 b. *Het geld **zit** in mijn zak.*
 'The money sits in my pocket'
 c. *De idee **zit** in de tekst.*
 'The idea sits in the text'

What about the causative equivalents for these uses? It is here that the picture becomes more complicated.

For CONTACT-*zitten*, illustrated in (5), the verb *zetten* can sometimes function as the causative equivalent, as in *Zet de poot (vast) aan de tafel* 'Set the leg [fixed] to the table' but such coding is not the most typical nor is it always acceptable, e.g., **Zet de sticker (vast) op de voorruit* 'Set the sticker on the windshield' vs. (5b). In these cases (as for the first set as well) a more specific verb is generally used, referring (1) to the method of fastening, e.g., *plakken* 'stick, glue', *nagelen* 'nail', *schroeven* 'screw' etc. or (2) to its suspended position, leading to verbs such as *hangen* 'hang', which can be used in non-causative as well as causative constructions.

CONTAINMENT-*zitten*, illustrated in (6), does not take *zetten* as its causative, but three other verbs are typically used, i.e., *steken*, *stoppen* and *doen*. Within the scope of the present article, we cannot do justice to the semantic richness of these verbs, yet two issues deserve more elaborate description: (i) the opposition between the near-synonyms *steken* en *stoppen*, and (ii) the emergence of the (action) verb *doen* as a possible coding to express caused containment. These two issues will be taken up in turn in the next part.

STEKEN and *STOPPEN*: Even though there is some degree of overlap, *steken* and *stoppen* have different prototypes related to their different etymological origins. The origin of *steken* is 'to insert a sharp pointed object into something' (related to English *stick*); *stoppen* has as its original meaning 'insert a stopper/plug into an opening'. These verbs have intransitive uses too, e.g., *de paal steekt in de grond* 'the pole sticks in the ground', and they have other non-locative meanings as well (e.g., 'halt a movement' for *stoppen*). While these uses can be related to the causative ones, they will not be discussed here. The differences between the two verbs can be summarized as in Table 4.

Table 4. Prototype clusters for *steken* and *stoppen*

		steken	stoppen
(i)	**figure**	stick-shape, elongated	round, symmetrical, mass or "shapeless"
(ii)	**containment**	partial or weak (large container)	full
(iii)	**ground**	forced open by action	container or object with hole in it

These differences are clearly valid for Netherlandic Dutch; for the Belgian variant, the opposition seem to be less polar (but still applicable) since *steken* has taken over (some of) the meanings of *stoppen* in this domain; actually Flemish people often feel *stoppen* to be typically Netherlandic. Since our corpus does not allow a well-balanced comparison, the extent of the regional variation cannot be measured with full accuracy. So as not to bias our description with regional differences (which seem to be more pertinent here than elsewhere in the domain), we have restricted the data for the present discussion to the Netherlandic data. A further restriction has been to consider locational uses only, so as to avoid skewed results under influence of idioms or productive metaphors (although they generally follow the same patterns). The frequency of the two verbs in locational use in our Netherlandic subcorpus is remarkably similar (*steken* 136; *stoppen* 138) and these uses clearly reflect the distinctions drawn up in Table 4 which we will take up in turn.

First, the two verbs take different types of figures: *steken* shows a preference for elongated objects, like sticks, knifes, extending body parts, etc. (68% vs. only 11% for *stoppen*). Conversely, the types of Figure occurring with *stoppen* is less focused on one particular type and mostly the shape specifications do no really matter. Nevertheless, there is higher number of mass types (20%) and symmetrical types (7%) then with *steken* (2.4% and

0% respectively). Statistical tests show the differences in the type of Figure for *steken* and *stoppen* to be highly significant. (The Freeman-Halton test yields p<0.0001; the Haldane-Dawson test yields the values z=32.36 and p<0.0001; the deviation of the obs./exp. ration is particularly strong: observed: 93:15 vs. expected 53.6:54.4).[15]

Secondly, *steken* typically refers to partial containment and *stoppen*, to full containment, a difference that logically follows from the different Figures. Consequently, alternative encodings such as *een stokje in de grond stoppen/steken* 'stick/stop a little stick into the ground' are semantically non-identical: *steken* means that the stick will be brought into the ground (more or less vertically) and only partially so, whereas with *stoppen* its orientation will be more horizontal and the object will be fully buried in the ground. This explains its link with the prefixed form *verstoppen* 'hide'. Or consider the idiomatic expression *Je kop in het zand steken* 'stick your head into the sand' meaning 'pretend not to see the problems at hand' drawn from the behaviour of ostriches when in danger. A head here is seen as the protruding end of the body, and thus leading to partial containment even if the whole head is contained in the sand. The coding *Je kop in het zand* **stoppen** would express a much more painful situation, since it has the strong implication that the head is severed from the body and subsequently put into the ground (full containment).

The different type of containment is also reflected in the different prepositional phrases expressing the container (the Ground). There is obviously some overlap given that they both refer to some from of containment: the preposition *in* 'in' is most common with both, yet its frequency differs: 72% with *steken* vs. 91% for *stoppen*. In line with the semantics of full containment profiled by the latter verb, the preposition *onder* 'under' is also a logical choice (5.8%); the remaining cases are a miscellaneous collection of single occurrences (*achter* 'behind', *aan* 'at', *bij* 'at/with', *tussen* 'between'). The remaining group occurring with *steken* is quite different, and these prepositions can all be grossly characterized as involving the image of a linear extension (in accordance with the elongated Figure) expressing meanings as 'through', '(a)round', 'across', 'above' (dynamic), etc.

Thirdly, the verbs typically differ in the type of Ground they take, once again in accordance with the different type of containment they encode. *Stoppen* typically occurs with 'pre-existing' containers as Ground, e.g., bag, box, pocket, trunk, mouth, throat, etc. (85% vs. only 20% for *steken*). With *steken*, the containment relationship is typically created by the (forceful) insertion of the Figure into the Ground that previous to the action did not exist as a container as such.[16] Logically, then, the Ground is often a mass or a narrow or tight space. The difference is clear in alternations like *Ze staken/stopten het mes in de rubberboot* 'They stuck/stopped the knife in the inflatable boat': in the case of *stoppen*, one puts the knife into the boat as "container" (or a smaller container within it, of course); *steken* implies that the knife is inserted into the boat's surface, not a good idea if you are in mid-ocean.

There are, however, two contexts where the Ground occurring with *steken* can be argued to be pre-defined as a type of container. The first one concerns the case of openings like windows, hatches, or loops (27 occurrences or 19.8% vs 1 occurrence [0.7%] for *stoppen*). Note, however, that this fits the verb's semantics very well, as these frame-like structures are no real containers but are so in the 2D plane only, partially containing (or rather, framing) the (elongated) Figure "sticking through". The second case where the Ground can be said to be a pre-existing container is that of clothes, e.g.,

(7) *Meer dan 100 mensen hadden zich in ouderwetse kleren **gestoken**.*
    'More then 100 people had stuck themselves in(to) oldfashioned clothes'

Stoppen is unacceptable in this context, unless perhaps when you mean to say that the people were completely contained by (hidden in) the clothes. Generally, however, one is only partially contained by the clothes one wears and, moreover, when envisaging moving into them, we probably attribute considerable salience to the elongated limbs.

As already said, the verbs *steken* and *stoppen* seem to be further characterized by a regional difference: in the Belgian variant, *steken* has become much more general and applicable to situations where one has full containment and non-elongated Figures, uses to which speakers of the Northern variant strongly object. For example, in her preliminary study, Van Tol (a native speaker of Northern Dutch) categorically rejects constructions with *steken* such as for example *Ik steek de bal in de tas* 'I stick the ball into the bag' that are perfectly acceptable to me, native speaker of the Belgian variant.[17] Unfortunately, the INL corpus does not allow a systematic regional analysis, yet a comparison between two comparable subsets (2 months of the Belgian quality newspaper *De Standaard* and 2 months of the Dutch quality newspaper *NRC Handelsblad*) show for example that in the Belgian data, the Figure is less committed to taking an elongated type (50%) than in the Dutch set (62%), as shown in Table 5. The data sets are too small (and not sufficiently representative) to allow any further significance testing, yet encourage further pursuit of the hypothesis.

Table 5. Differences for *steken* and *stoppen* in two regionally differentiated subcorpora

Type of figure in locational use	*De Standaard* (Belgian)		NRC (Netherlandic)	
	steken	*stoppen*	*steken*	*stoppen*
unspecified shape or whole entity	8	10	13	10
	27%	32%	25%	26%
elongated	15	6	33	5
	50%	19%	62%	13%
sheet/flat	1	12	5	6
	3%	39%	9%	16%
mass	3	3	1	6
	10%	10%	2%	16%
symmetrical				4
				11%
indeterminate	3		1	7
	10%		2%	18%
Total N	**30**	**31**	**53**	**38**
Total Pct	**100%**	**100%**	**100%**	**100%**

DOEN: Another possibility to express caused containment is by using the general activity verb *doen* 'do'. It is typically used when the Figure is a substance, as in the following examples (our own).

(8) a. *Hij **deed** de soep in een doos.*
    'He did (= put) the soup in a box'
   b. *Zij **deed** teveel suiker in de pudding.*
    'She did (= put) too much sugar in the pudding'

Nevertheless, the verb does occur in other contexts of containment as well, where one would generally expect *stoppen* (Netherlandic variant) or *steken* (Belgian variant), cf. *Hij deed de brief in de enveloppe* 'He did the letter in an envelope'.[18] The verb *doen* has even extended (and perhaps continues to extend) to contexts where *zetten* 'set' and *leggen* 'lay' would be more common, as shown by the following (Internet-based) examples.

(9) a. Hij **deed/zette** de tas in de kast.
 'He did/set the bag in the wardrobe'
 b. Ik **deed/legde** de CD in de speler.
 'I did/laid the CD in the player'

Unfortunately, the INL corpus does not allow a systematic analysis for practical reasons: the verb is highly frequent, and the INL imposes restrictions on the amount of data one may extract, which in this case were hard to overcome. In order to have some corpus data for further analysis, we did some (admittedly limited) queries on Google using as search string "<DOEN> de * in de *" ('<DO> the * in the *'), with <DOEN> representing the different verbs forms possible in this particular construction.[19] Despite the specific search strings, the retrieval error rate was still high (90.8%): of the 9,892 hits, only 902 refer to placement into a container. A (relatively rudimentary) analysis of the data reveals quite relevant tendencies, worthy of further exploration.

The first of these is that the use of *doen* as a placement verb (at least in these constructions) differs significantly across the regional variety. By taking into account the domain names of the sites from which the examples are drawn (*.be* for Belgium and *.nl* for the Netherlands) the distribution of the use is 90 for the Belgian variant and 658 for the Netherlandic variant, or a ratio of 12% to 88%, a significant difference ($\chi^2=431.316$, p=0, df=1).[20] But there are other register related issues that emerge, since this use of *doen* is mostly found on web pages of more informal type, such as weblogs, personal diaries or recounts, or own creative prose or fantasies (mostly horror or erotic). This suggests that it is typical of informal and non-standardized register, which may even be related to educational standards.[21]

There is another particularly frequent context in which this usage of *doen* occurs, viz. that of cooking, which accounts for 579 of the cases (64.1%). Of these, 92.9% (538 cases) occur in the imperative, as is common in recipes. Here are two typical examples from our Internet data set.

(10) a. ... *doe de garnalen in de hete wok*
 'do (= put) the shrimp in the hot wok'
 b. *We deden de confituur in de taart.*
 'We did (= put) the marmalade in the pie'

The motivation for this should be clear: mostly, when cooking, one is dealing with substances (liquids, chopped up food, etc.) that are being mixed or put in recipients. Now, this usage seems to have established itself sufficiently firmly in this particular domain so that whenever cooking is at issue, *doen* becomes the most prominent candidate to express caused containment, even when non-substance entities are at issue. So, one also regularly finds cases like (in English paraphrase) "do the buns in the oven" or "do the sandwiches in the microwave" or "do the dish in the oven". Once again, these extensions to non-substance entities is more typical of Netherlandic Dutch, as in the Belgian variant *zetten* would be preferred.

Another context where containment-*doen* seems to be typical (93 cases or 10.3%) is that where some kind of "technical tight-fitting" is at issue, such as putting a tape in a video-camera, a CD in a CD-player, a memory stick in its USB-slot, or a plug in the electricity outlet. While the frequency drops sharply for other contexts, the following are nevertheless somewhat more recurrent: putting cards or letters in envelopes or putting letters in mailboxes (27 cases), putting laundry in the laundry machine (14), putting things in the trunk of a car (12), or putting dishes in the dish washer (4).

While more elaborate data analysis is necessary, what these contexts all suggest is that use of *doen* is still strongly tied to substances put into containers, yet also that it is gradually expanding its usage to express *putting things in recipients designed to receive just these things*. That the domain of cooking may have played an influential here comes as no surprise, since it typically involves putting (substance-like) entities in all kinds of recipients designed for this (bowls, pots, pans, skillets, etc.). The other contexts mentioned above (putting letters in envelopes, CDs/tapes in players, laundry in laundry machine, etc.) all fit this tendency.

On the basis of all these findings, the tentative hypothesis that we would like to suggest is that, unlike what might have been expected in view of the verb's "light" semantics, *doen* has not (yet) become a general placement verb, since it is essentially restricted to caused containment. In general, the verb cannot be used for other types of placement events, as shown by the unacceptability of a sentence like **Ik doe het boek op de tafel* 'I do the book on the table'. In such contexts, the "regular" placement verbs apply (*leggen* 'lay' or *zetten* 'set', depending on the orientation of the book). However, running the same Google searches but this time with the preposition *op* instead of *in* does return some contexts of non-containment, e.g., *Doe de stop op de fles* 'Do (= put) the cap on the bottle' or *Je doet de deksel op de pan* 'You do (= put) the lid on the pan', but also in these contexts we see that the placement follows the "locational predestination" of the configuration, which lies in line with the tendency observed for containment. In short, these findings possibly suggest an area of ongoing change in the domain of informal discourse. This still needs to be further elaborated, however.

3.4. Summary

Figure 1 summarizes the correspondences discussed in the three subsections above, which can be recapitulated as follows. *Liggen* and *leggen* correspond in a relatively straightforward manner for basically horizontal or symmetrical entities. For *staan*, the situation is a bit less straightforward, as in a few metaphorical usages the older *stellen* is still possible, whereas for locational uses (pertaining to entities on their base, in the diagram represented by the upward arrow[s] on a base) and the majority of the metaphorical usages, *zetten* has taken on the causative functions. The latter verb's original relation to *zitten* has only been partially preserved and the verbs *steken*, *stoppen* and *doen* have entered the paradigm to expressed different types of caused containment.

The semantics of the causative posture verbs cannot be fully understood without looking at what the non-causative do. However, the above description may have created the impression that, despite the paradigm shifts described above, there is a direct link between the causatives and the non-causatives, in the sense that one can always recast one in terms of the other (with of course the obvious variation pertaining to causativity). This is not the case. There are many complications that we cannot afford to discuss here in detail for limitations of space. Suffice it to mention a few cases by way of illustration.

First, there are many cases where a causative verb does not find a non-causative posture verb equivalent. For example, whereas one can say *contacten leggen* 'lay (= make) contacts', one cannot talk about their existence in terms of *liggen*, for which one resorts to the verbs *zijn* 'be' or *bestaan* 'exist'. In yet other cases, there may be a different intransitive verb than the one predicted by the paradigm. For instance, in Dutch, some abstract entities are often "laid", but they do not "lie". For example, while one can say of a singer *Hij legt veel gevoel in zijn liedjes* 'He lays a lot of emotion in his songs', the sensitivity will not be said to be 'lying' in the songs ($^{??}$*Er ligt veel gevoel in zijn liedjes* 'There lies a lot of emotion in his songs');

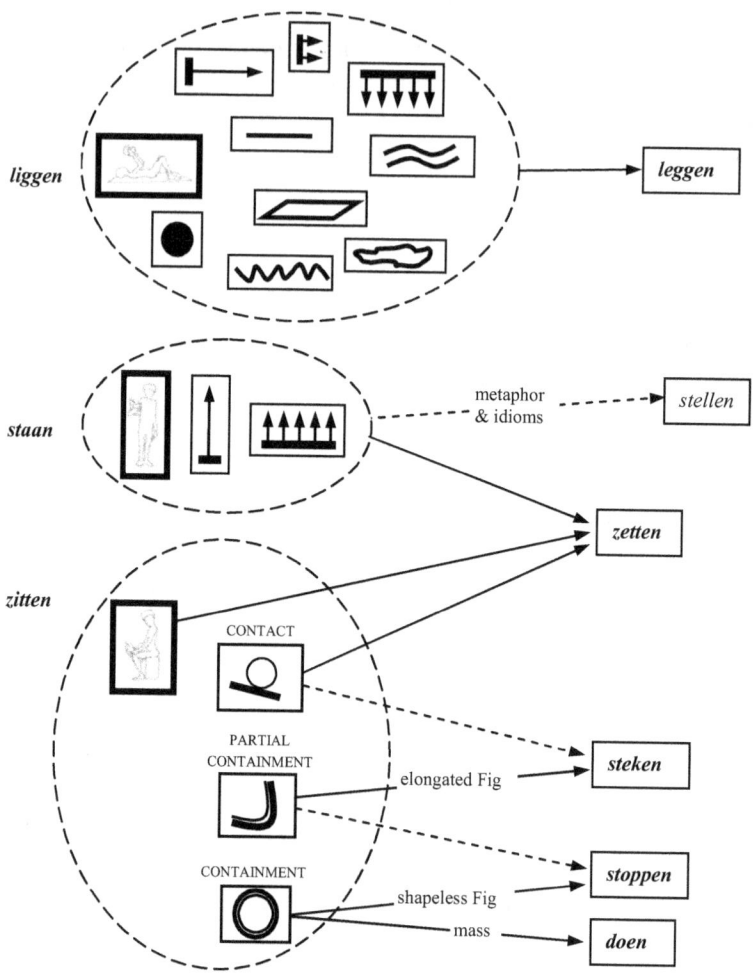

Figure 1. Simplified representation of CPV and CCPV correspondences

rather one will use the verb *zitten* to express containment (*Er zit veel gevoel in zijn liedjes* 'There sits a lot of emotion in his songs'). As a final illustration, many idiomatic expressions with these causative verbs, there simply is no non-causative equivalent. For instance, when ignoring a piece of advice, you can say that you 'lay it down next to you' (*naast zich neerleggen*), but it is quite awkward to try to phrase this non-causatively: **Het advies ligt/is naast me neer* 'The advice lies/is next to me (down)'.

These "mismatches" can be quite substantial. For example, if we look more closely at individual usages of *leggen*, we can see that it does take the non-causative equivalent *liggen* in the majority of the cases (69%), but 18% has no equivalent, 9% takes *zijn* 'be', some (2.4%) take *zitten* or *staan*, others are indeterminate.[22]

Most of these mismatches can be easily explained, but we will not pursue these here (a more detailed discussion will be offered in Lemmens, in prep.). What we will consider in more detail in the next section, is how *zetten* has become the default placement verb in Dutch (all things being equal). This will not take the form of a detailed diachronic study which also is beyond the scope of the present paper. Interestingly, however, the contemporary data reveal clear tendencies as well, which allows us to suggest a plausible hypothesis for this shift.

4. The emergence of a different prototype

Only a very small number of the attested examples for *leggen* and *zetten* (0.8%) involve a postural usage, i.e., where they refer to someone bringing someone else in any of the three postures that were argued to be crucial to the prototypes of the non-causative posture verbs. Clearly, high frequency need not (and often indeed does not) coincide with prototypicality, since (bare) frequency is determined by a host of factors, such as register, idiomatic usage (almost 40% of the attestations for the four causative verbs are idioms), the topic, etc. Nevertheless, the extremely low number of postural uses (43 on 3,077 [1.4%] for *leggen* and 14 on 3,551 [0.4%] for *zetten*, cf. Table 6) do suggest that the conceptual centre of the categories lies elsewhere.

Table 6. Postural and locational usages (Figure = human)

		leggen	*zetten*	*steken*	*stoppen*	Total
postural	N	43	14			57
	% on verb total	1.4%	0.4%			**0.8%**
locational	N		192	35	23	250
	% on verb total		5.4%	5.6%	7.6%	**4.1%**
Total N	N	43	206	35	23	307
Total %	% on verb total	1.4%	5.8%	5.6%	7.6%	**4.1%**
		(3,077)	(3,551)	(621)	(301)	(7,550)

Table 6 also nicely shows that all uses of *leggen* with a human figure are postural and that all uses of *steken* and *stoppen* are locational, as they cannot be postural. The latter point supports the general claim, suggested by Van Tol (2002), that the four causatives are locational rather than postural verbs. The motivation for this, Van Tol correctly reasons, is that human beings are in principle sufficiently capable of controlling their own bodily posture; being brought into a certain posture by someone (or something) else is thus out of the ordinary. In other words, human beings are generally less 'manipulatable' when it comes to their posture. This is confirmed by a more careful analysis of the human Figures that occur in a construction with postural or locational reading (cf. Table 7).

Table 7. Type of human figure for postural and locational uses

	leggen	*zetten*	*steken*	*stoppen*	Total	
general	4	166	35	8	216	70.4%
baby/child	19	2		5	26	8.5%
captured	2	31		10	43	14.0%
dead	6				6	2.0%
ill or injured	5	1			6	2.0%
reflexive	4	3			7	2.3%
tackle	3				3	1.0%
Total	**43**	**206**	**35**	**23**	**307**	**100%**

There is a small subset of reflexive uses, where people bring themselves in a certain posture and one with uses where people are being brought into a lying posture by a tackle. More relevant to our purpose is that a large subgroup (81 cases, or 26.4%) involves people who are indeed not capable of controlling their posture: babies, people who are ill, dead or being tortured, or who have been deprived of their spatial freedom by being put in prison. For the latter *zetten* is most common (31 cases), but also *stoppen* is nicely represented (10 cases), as follows logically from the verb's focus on (forceful) containment (people in prison are supposed to be well-contained there). The use of *zetten* in this context is in fact quite similar to its high frequency in the "general" category (166 cases), where the majority of cases concerns people whose location, rather than posture, we typically conceive of as controllable. These 'transplantable' people are generally those felt to be dispensable with: apart from putting them in prison, we put them on trains, boats or airplanes or out of the country (fugitives), on the street, or out of the house (cf. Table 8, which further specifies the 166 cases of *zetten* in the "general" category in Table 7).

Table 8. Contexts for human Figure with *zetten*

zetten		Total	
expell from country	out of the country	31	18.7%
	put on plane, train, boat, bus	61	36.7%
	out of the city	1	0.6%
	place somewhere isolated	2	1.2%
expell from house	put on the street	18	10.8%
	put out of a room	5	3.0%
	out of one's house	8	4.8%
put player in position in game		3	1.8%
put in sitting position (on chair, etc.)		9	5.4%
miscellaneous		28	16.9%
Total		166	100%

In short, the use of a large corpus has revealed two clear patterns that might otherwise have gone unnoticed: (1) postural readings are applicable to situations where people no longer control their own posture, which mostly involves lying down, and (2) the other contexts, usually involving *zetten* (less frequently *stoppen* and *steken* when one wants to profile containment), concern people that we can "manipulate" or "put somewhere". This usually has negative associations to it, which lies in line with the idea that humans control their own posture and location and are generally not easily conceived of as "transplantable". If one does "transplant" others, this is in contexts where one has the authority to do so (e.g., players placed on the field by their coach or soldiers stationed by their superiors) or where one claims this power regardless of its legitimacy (hence the common negative connotation) and wants to get the others "out of the way". In addition to the contexts in Table 8, we can mention the following idiomatic expressions referring to some other equally non-altruistic situations:

(11) a. *iemand voor schut zetten*
'set s.o. for the pillory' (= 'to make a fool of someone')
  b. *iemand voor {aap/gek} zetten*
'set s.o. for monkey/fool' (= 'to make a fool of someone')

c. *iemand {opzij/aan de kant} zetten*
   'set someone aside' (= 'put someone out')
d. *iemand overboord zetten*
   'set s.o. overboard' (literal and metaphorical usage)

But why is it that *zetten*, formally the causative of *zitten*, has become so productive in the latter case? Of course, careful diachronic analysis is required to fully understand different stages in the paradigmatic shift, yet synchronic data such as these do provide some indications as well. As can be expected, the change is hardly attributable to a single feature, but rather seems to have occurred under a 'conspiracy' of a number of factors.

In some uses, *zetten* is ambiguous between MAKE-SIT versus MAKE-STAND, as for example in *Zet het kind op de stoel* 'Set the child on the stoel'. Admittedly, a sitting posture will probably be most likely, given the context of the chair and the "controllable" nature of the child. This ambiguity confirms that *zetten* is in fact less committed to posture and that the latter can be derived from the context. Recall that a-postural uses with human Figures also commonly occur with *zitten*, especially when close contact or containment is at issue, cf. example (4c), where prisoners were said to "sit" in prison. Prisoners do not constantly sit, of course, and the latter example clearly does not activate any postural reading anymore. In fact, our usual mental image of a human being, even when in a larger container (like a room or a building), is often that of a standing figure, this being the canonical posture (cf. Van Oosten 1986). In other words, while in the above examples *zitten* highlights the fact that one is being stuck or contained, the imagined posture of the Figures, if any, will be a standing one.[23]

The prototypical representation of a placement event as putting an entity somewhere so that it stays there (related to the CONTACT and CONTAINMENT reading strongly associated with *zitten* and originally with *zetten*) means that you place it "properly". The idea of being correctly positioned is what motivates the metaphorical use of *rechtzetten* 'set straight' which, similar to its English equivalent, refers to correcting what is "crooked". Now, for inanimate entities, being correctly positioned usually means being placed on their base, which is once again closely linked to *staan*.

Another factor that may have contributed to the semantic shift is that the canonical position for lower animals (rabbits, frogs, etc. and 0-peds) and birds is precisely expressed by *zitten*, which thus for *zetten* also gives rise to a merger of MAKE-SIT and PUT IN ITS CANONICAL POSITION.

In short, *zetten* has generalized to the meaning 'put an entity in its canonical position', which often involves a standing posture (humans and inanimates) but in other contexts clearly a sitting posture (lower animals, birds, 0-peds). This also provides the reason for *steken* and *stoppen* entering the paradigm, since the semantic generalisation caused *zetten* to lose the associations CONTAINMENT and CLOSE CONTACT, now more appropriately profiled by *stoppen* and *steken*. None of the three verbs are postural verbs any longer, but have become general location verbs and the same is true for *leggen*, although it is still the most postural of the set.

Further evidence that *zetten* has become the 'default' causative verb (much like English *put* although this verb is even more general, see David [2003] for a more elaborate analysis) can be found in the collocational range for idiomatic uses that occur with the causative CPVs as shown in Table 9.

Table 9. Idiomatic collocation power of CCPVs

	leggen	zetten	steken	stoppen	Total
# of different idioms	69	148	23	2	242
	28.5%	61.2%	9.5%	0.8%	100%

As mentioned above, almost 40% (some 3,000 of 7,550) of the causative posture verbs are idioms (a similarly high frequency can be observed with the non-causatives for that matter), yet the widest range occurs with *zetten* confirming its general applicability.

5. Some image schemata associated with causative posture verbs

The following section presents a brief and selective discussion of the experiential patterns that underlie some common metaphorical usages. The main associations that will be discussed are (IN)ACTIVITY, FUNCTIONALITY, and CONTROL and RESISTANCE. The last section considers one additional (productive) pattern pertaining to the domain of printed text.

5.1. (IN)ACTIVITY

Lying is commonly the posture for rest, inactivity, illness and death; standing, on the other hand, is the onset position for walking, the proto-movement for humans (walking upright is one of the striking physical features that distinguish us from other species). These associations give rise to two different types of uses that both hinge on the notion of (IN)ACTIVITY.

The first builds on the idea of standing as the start position for walking, which has been extended to the onset of whichever activity. One is thus not surprised to find constructions with *zetten* that have an inchoative value, such as *iemand/zich aan het V/N zetten* 'set someone/oneself to V/N'. Interestingly, most of the activities expressed by the verb or the noun in this construction are typically carried out when seated (28 out of 72, or 40%), e.g., *lezen* 'read', *schrijven* 'write', *tikken* 'type', *denken* 'think', which testifies once more to the split nature of *zetten*.

Some other expressions are related to these ingressives, e.g., *in gang zetten* 'set in motion', *in beweging zetten* 'set in motion', *in werking zetten/stellen* 'set in operation'. For the latter, there is a possible alternation with *stellen*, but it is at this point unclear what factors influence the choice. Other related constructions are the two ingressive constructions possible with *staan*: *staat te gebeuren* 'stands to happen' (= 'is about to happen') and *staat op V*-nom. 'stands on V-ing' (= 'is on the verge of V-ing'). Finally, there is also a relation with auxiliated CPV usage in progressive constructions (*liggen/zitten/staan te V*) where the choice of colateral action expressed by V appears all but random. Significantly, the *staan te V* construction has the widest range of "complement" verbs as well as the most "active" set.

The second group of metaphorical extensions concerns the different degree to which (IN)ACTIVITY is implied by various particle verb formations. One is the combination with the separable prefix *stil*: *stilzetten* lit. 'put still' (= 'halt'), comparable to the English expression *bring to a standstill*, versus *stilleggen* lit. 'lay still' (= 'halt'), which find their non-causative equivalents in *stilstaan* versus *stilleggen* respectively. In line with the experiential associations, the combinations with *liggen/leggen* imply a higher degree of inactivity or an inactivity of more extensive scope. This is clearly reflected in the distribution (cf. Table 10).

As to be expected, inactivity most commonly expressed with *stilleggen*, 44 attestations, vs. 11 for *stilzetten*. Yet there is another factor distinguishing the two verbs: *stilzetten* profiles the mover (the counterpart to the entity that "stands"); *stilleggen* profiles the larger situation/location (e.g., traffic/factory). This distribution is parallel to other particle forms like *lamleggen* lit. 'lay lame' or *platleggen* lit. 'lay flat', which – in line with the semantics of *lam* and *plat* – only occur with movement and/or location as

Table 10. Type of Figure for *stilleggen* and *stilzetten*

FIGURE	*stilleggen*	*stilzetten*	Total
movement/action	25	1	26
mover/actor	9	10	19
location	9		9
organisation	1		1
Total	44	11	55

Figure, but not with the mover (cf. Table 11). A construction like *De stakers legden tram 44 plat* 'The strikers laid tram 44 flat' (= 'paralyzed tram 44') is unacceptable, except when *tram 44* no longer refers to the individual tram but metonymically extends to refer to the tram's entire operation (i.e., the whole system or network associated with tram 44 went down).

Table 11. Type of Figure for *lamleggen* and *platleggen*

FIGURE	*lamleggen*	*platleggen*	Total
movement/action	21	1	22
all		1	1
location	9	5	14
organisation	2	2	4
Total	32	9	41

Finally, a comparable difference underlies the combinations with the separable prefix *vast* 'fixed', in literal and metaphorical usage: in contexts where both are possible, *vastliggen/vastleggen* imply more than *vaststaan/vastzetten* the idea of being stable or of being fixed or stuck, and thus a higher degree of inactivity.

For all the particle formations discussed here it holds that *staan/zetten* imply that it will be much easier to restart the activity than for the situation expressed by the *liggen/leggen* combinations. This is in line with our ordinary experience that standing is the onset position for activity; if one wants to engage in some activity when lying, one often has to get into a standing posture first. Standing is, in other words, our most functional posture.

5.2. FUNCTIONALITY

Standing is, indeed, commonly associated with maximal FUNCTIONALITY. As said, the experiential basis is that humans are optimally functional when standing, whereas the number of activities one can perform when lying is rather restricted. The association particularly holds for inanimate objects having a base: when in their canonical position (i.e., resting on their base), they are in their functional position. A plate upside down, for example, no longer functions what it was designed for and this position will be described with *liggen/leggen* (which shows once again that the real dimensions of the object are secondary to the image of a base). There are some other interesting uses of *zetten* that build on this notion of functional position as illustrated by the following examples, adapted from our corpus:

(12) a. *Het mes **ligt** op tafel/**staat** in het bakje.*
 'The knife lies on the table/stands in the box'
 b. *Ik **leg** het mes op tafel/**zet** het in het bakje.*
 'I lay the knife on the table/set it in the box'
 c. *Hij **zet** het mes in de taart/op mijn keel.*
 'He sets the knife in the cake/on my throat'

(13) a. *Zijn geweer **lag** op tafel/**stond** tegen de muur.*
 'His gun lay on the table/stood against the wall'
 b. *Hij **legde** zijn geweer op tafel/**zette** hem tegen de muur.*
 'He lay his gun on the table/set it against the wall'
 c. *Hij **zette** het geweer aan zijn schouder.*
 'He set the gun at his shoulder'

The coding in the (a) and (b) sentences is determined by the real orientation of the knife and a gun. In the (c) sentences, however, the use of *zetten* denotes 'bring into a functional position', i.e., put the object in its onset position for carrying out the activity for which it was designed. In these contexts, the real orientation of the knife and the gun is probably more horizontal than vertical. An interesting metaphorical counterpart is found in the expression *de wapens neeerleggen* 'lay down the weapons' and thus stop fighting. English, too, can still use *set* in similar contexts, e.g., *Still smiling, he set the gun against his head* (Internet data), although *put* is probably more common here as well.

Interestingly, while not impossible, these "functional position" uses with inanimate objects are less likely to find a non-causative coding with *staan*

(?*Het mes staat op de taart* 'The knife stands on the cake'). This is because the objects at issue (in contrast to objects resting on their base) are instruments that cannot retain this functional position all by themselves but need to be manipulated by some Agent.

5.3. CONTROL and RESISTANCE

A standing posture is often associated with the image of CONTROL and RESISTANCE (cf. also Gibbs et al. 1994, Gibbs 2002). The experiential basis for this is that humans in standing position have full control over their bodily posture and are thus also in the best position to resist forces that disturb their balance and/or location. Standing humans also have a better control over their environment, as they are physically stronger in that posture and have a better overview of the situation. Logically, then, one finds *zetten* in contexts referring to resistance, mostly in combination with words such as *schrap* 'braced' (10 attestations) or *scherp* 'sharp'; *leggen*, when there is no (more) resistance (mostly in combination with the particle *neer* 'down'; 73 attestations). Consider the following examples from our corpus:

(14) a. *Zij **zette** zich **schrap** voor de aanval.*
'She put herself braced for the attack' (= 'braced herself')
b. *Hij **legt** zich **neer** bij dit besluit.*
'He lays himself down at this decision' (= 'accepts this decision')

Not incidentally, the normal Dutch word for "resist" is the reflexive *zich verzetten* (with the semantically complex and to most speakers opaque inseparable prefix *ver-*); similar to the Latin verb on which the English word *resist* is based, the semantic core of the word is derived from the verb expressing STAND.

Related to these are usages in the context of comparing/opposing entities:

(15) a. *Als we deze resultaten naast elkaar **leggen** ...*
'If we lay these results next to one another ...'
b. *Ik **zet** daar graag een andere visie tegenover.*
'I would like to put another view against that'

The different pre- or postpositions of course contribute to the imagery: *naast* 'next to' vs. *tegenover* 'against'. The appropriateness of *leggen* may be further enforced by the things to be compared often being on paper, which you then 'lay' side by side for better comparison.

5.4. STANDING TEXT

While the description of metaphorical patterns offered here is not exhaustive, most of the attested uses can be seamlessly integrated into the semantic network sketched here, either as logical extensions of the locational uses or as further specifications of the metaphorical patterns described in the preceding paragraphs. One idiomatic usage that stands somewhat apart should be considered, however, as it quite productively extends to new uses (it functions as a "local prototype", so to speak).

The usage in question relates to text being positioned on a carrier. In the non-causative domain, the verb *staan* is used, for which I suggest a multiple motivation: (1) the letters have an inherent orientation and rest on their base on the line; (2) the letters "stand out" in relief vis-à-vis the carrier (a motivation suggested by Van Oosten [1984]); and (3) the written word will last much longer than the spoken word (activating the notion of resistance).[24]

To place a letter or text is then logically expressed by *zetten*, e.g., *Kan je dat op papier zetten?* 'Can you set that on paper?'. A printing mistake is called *zetfout* 'set mistake' (cf. English *typesetting*), although this may also be related to the older printing practice of placing lead letter stamps on the print.[25] By extension, both *staan* and *zetten* can be used to refer to the placement of other imprints on various kinds of carriers (e.g., a picture on a page, an icon on the screen, a song on a CD, etc.) and all kinds of metaphorical extensions thereof.

The use of *zetten* in reference to text being written, or further extensions thereof, is quite frequent, it underlies 585 attestations in the corpus sample, which amounts to 10.4% of all metaphorical and idiomatic uses. There are some interesting idioms that deserve to be mentioned here, cf. (16). (The number of attestations in our corpus is added between square brackets.)

(16) a. *een punt zetten achter iets*
 'set a full stop behind something' (= 'round off') [37]
 b. *de puntjes op de i zetten*
 'set de points on the i' (= 'dot the i's and cross the t's') [15]

c. *vraagtekens zetten/plaasten bij*
'set/place question marks with' (= 'query s.th., cast doubt on something') [59]

6. Conclusions

Our analysis of the three main Dutch placement verbs, in relation to their non-causative equivalent, has revealed the productive power of the semantic network that underlies all of these verbs. Clearly, native speakers may not be consciously aware of this system, yet the productive patterns and the semantically significant oppositions analysed here demonstrate how speakers tacitly yet creatively exploit these linguistic and conceptual subtleties. Even if our description is not fully exhaustive, especially in the realm of idiomatic expressions and particle verbs, it is believed that the vast majority of these additional uses can easily be accounted for within the present account.

The use of extensive corpus material has been essential to unravel this postural logic and to show how the uses of these verbs are not randomly distributed but how their uses are motivated by our experience of the world, at least as it has been translated into specific linguistic structures. Some of the issues discussed here require further analysis on the basis of differently constructed corpus material. Three areas of future research can be mentioned here explicitly. First, a diachronic analysis is desirable to lay out the precise stages in the paradigmatic shift to which *zetten* has been subjected. Secondly, the regional variation for *steken*, *stoppen* and *doen* should be investigated more elaborately on the basis of a regionally well-balanced corpus. Finally, the data used for our study should be complemented with an analysis of spoken data.

In a larger, typological perspective the above account may shed more light onto how languages encode spatial relationships and how these linguistics structures condition speakers to differ as to what aspects of reality they pay attention to, an issue that has been proven relevant in the domain of motion verbs. On-going research (see Lemmens 2005a) shows indeed that causative and non-causative posture verbs, but also other types of location verbs, confirm the larger typological opposition between verb-framed and satellite-framed languages as it has been set forth by Talmy (2000), yet they do add some further nuances as well.

Notes

1. It is to be noted that this alternation is not restricted to these posture verbs, cf. Dutch *drinken-drenken* (parallels English *drink-drench* and Swedish *dricka-dränka*) or *vallen-vellen* (parallels English *fall-fell* or Swedish *falla-fälla*). There is some discussion as to whether the causative forms *stellen/ställa/stellen/stall*, going back to Germ. **stallion*, have not arisen via a derivation from the noun *stall* (cf. e.g., Helqvist 1922). Given that they have been incorporated into the paradigm as "full" members, except perhaps for English *stall*, the true etymological reconstruction will not be pursued here.
2. Use of the INL corpora is herewith gratefully acknowledged. They can be accessed at ⟨http://www.inl.nl⟩.
3. See ⟨http://www.tst.inl.nl/cgn.htm⟩, last accessed June 29, 2005.
4. The design of the *Corpus Gesproken Nederlands* is such that it has twice as much data for Netherlandic Dutch as for Belgian Dutch, given the larger number of speakers for the former. As such, the frequencies obtained in our lemma searches for Netherlandic Dutch have been divided in half.
5. The term *Figure* (cf. Talmy's 2000: 25) will be used here to refer to the entity located in the causative event as well, even though from a strictly constructional point of view, it is a secondary Figure subject to the manipulation by an Agent (Agent places Figure with respect to Ground).
6. The INL interface limits the retrieval of attestations to 1,000 which, unfortunately, are not selected at random. The frequency of all verbs exceeded this limit, but we worked around this by doing individual queries for the different verb forms. This was, however, not possible for *doen* for which there are over 30,000 occurrences in the INL subcorpus, with all verb forms each having well over 1,000 occurrences. This made retrieval quite unfeasible. The INL policy is to be regretted, but according to the institute, it cannot be changed because of copyright legislation.
7. The term experiential prototype clusters is Newman's, not the table which reflects mostly my own groupings. Standing being the canonical posture for humans is a point also made by Van Oosten (1984); see Lemmens (submitted) for some further arguments.
8. See Lemmens (2002a) for arguments for postulating these prototypes even if they are not necessarily the most frequent in a given corpus.
9. The opposition between Dutch *staan* and English *sit* is nicely illustrated by Rice's (2002: 61) observation that any English speaker, when confronted with the test sentence *I thought I left my coffee cup ____ here. Have you seen it?* and forced to choose between the three verbs, would not hesitate to supply *sitting* here. Any Dutch speaker would immediately supply a form of *staan*. It would be interesting to see how much this carries over in EFL since for many Dutch speakers this use of *sit* is quite unusual.

10. This kind of scanning is probably similar to the cognitive simulation in the domain of fictive motion as in *The road runs along the coast line*. The cognitive simulation consist in tracing dynamically all the points that define the spatial extension of the object. (cf. Talmy 2000; Matlock 2002).
11. The English glosses are but literal translations of the Dutch originals using as much as possible the English equivalents *set*, *lay*, *stick* and *stop*; while sometimes a bit awkward, they are hoped to be sufficiently transparent. Since syntactic details (word order, tenses, etc.) are usually irrelevant to our purposes, no attempt is made to render these explicitly (unless warranted, of course).
12. Dutch is not isolated in this. Perpendicularity is a notion also important for example to a language as Trumai, a genetic isolate spoken in Brazil (cf. Guirardello-Damian 2002).
13. We have excluded from the counts here the idiomatic usages *nadruk/ klemtoon/accent leggen op* 'put the emphasis/accent on' which have a higher unit status (little if any formal variation, something which still occurs in the other cases mentioned here); they account for 326 occurrences or 27.4% of all metaphorical and idiomatic usages taken together (1,191).
14. The verb *sit* can still be used in the context of being in prison, e.g., *He continues to sit in prison serving his life sentence* ⟨www.findcarrieculberson.com/quickfacts.html⟩ or *Men and women are sitting in prison learning how to be a smoother criminal* ⟨http://journalism.emerson.edu/jr610/spring03/cit/roxbury/main.html⟩.
15. Thanks to Stefan Gries for help with these statistics.
16. This is not an unusual case. An even more rigid restriction holds for the Russian verb *sidet'* 'sit' that, when referring to a containment relation, can only be used in situations where there is no pre-existing hole that can function as a container. So, in Russian nails can be said to 'sit' in the table, but this cannot be said of bolts, since they are inserted in clearly defined pre-existing holes (cf. Lemmens and Rakhilina 2003).
17. In a non-systematic enquiry, we have asked some 10 native speakers of either variant for an acceptability judgment for this sentence. Invariably, speakers of the Netherlandic variant rejected it or felt it was quite marked whereas the speakers of the Belgian variant all thought there was nothing wrong with it.
18. Thanks go to Liesbeth Degand (personal communication) for pointing out that this usage of *doen* may be more important than our earlier analysis suggested. It can be added that *doen* is indeed also expanding in metaphorical domains, e.g., *ik doe de motor in de neutraal* ⟨www.roofvisforum.nl/forum/viewtopic.php?t=5601⟩ 'I do the engine in (the) neutral' (= 'I put the engine in idle'), a context where one usually expects *zetten* 'set'. The verb is also encroaching upon other domains, such that of verbs of giving, cf. *Doe mij maar een broodje kaas* 'Do me just a cheese sandwich' (= I'd rather you gave me a cheese sandwhich').

19. The specific search strings thus were : *doe de * in de ** (1st pers. sing. and imperative), *doet de * in de *** (present, 2nd and 3rd pers. sing.), *doen de * in de *** (present plural), *deed de * in de *** (past sing.) and *deden de * in de *** (past plural). Clearly, these do not capture all possibilities; for instance, constructions with subject inversion are excluded, e.g., *Dan doe je de * in de *** 'Then do you (= you do) the * in the *', as are constructions where *doen* is in final position (e.g., *Ik wou de * in de * doen*, lit. 'I wanted the * in the * do'). The data retrieved is, however, judged to be sufficiently indicative for the purpose at hand.
20. For 154 examples, no regional distinction can be traced. Even if these are added up with the Belgian ones, the difference remains significant (χ^2 = 190.018, p = 0, df = 1).
21. Similarly, in a recent study of Swedish location verbs (based on exclusively spoken material), Hellerstedt (2005) has suggested that the use of the "neutral" location verb *finnas* 'be found' in contexts where one generally expects a posture verb may be due to the educational level of the speaker. For less frequent location verbs this may have been an expected result, but we did not expect it to show up for basic posture verbs as well. This is certainly an issue to be explored further.
22. These percentages are based on the possible non-causative equivalents that have been added manually to each attestation. The specification of these has been arrived at in three ways: (i) what is intuitively judged acceptable, (ii) what has been attested in the INL-corpus and (iii) what has been attested through a Google search. For instance, for the idiomatic expression *zoden aan de dijk zetten* lit. 'set sodes to the dyke' = 'be of any use', the first 1,000 hits of a Google search on the string "*zoden aan de dijk*" (yielding in total ca. 21,000 hits) have been checked for non-causative verbs and none were found.
23. Similar "fusion" can occur with English *sit* as illustrated in *What's this cop still sitting outside the shop*, said in reference to a police officer who was actually standing next to a wrongly parked car he was writing a ticket for (cited from the film *It can happen to you*). Such "fusion" of the image of a standing posture with the semantics of *zitten* is also at issue in aspectual constructions with movement verbs, as in *We hebben heel de middag zitten rondlopen* 'We sat to walk around all afternoon' = 'we have been walking around'; these are discussed in Lemmens (2005b).
24. The use of *stand* is also still possible in English (possibly mostly in professional jargon), e.g., *This made for low-contrast letters with slab serifs (serifs are those little feet that the letters* stand *on)* (Internet data) or *I strap my pieces down onto a steel block with masking tape, use a pencil to mark the line the letters* stand *on* (idem).
25. This may also be a motivating factor for *staan*, yet this verb was also used before printing had been invented.

References

David, Caroline
    2003   Les "verbs of putting": Typologie, schéma syntaxique et organisation sémantique des construction prépositionnelles en anglais contemporain. Doctoral dissertation, Université de Poitiers, France.

Fagan, Sarah
    1991   The semantics of the positional predicates *liegen/legen, sitzen/setzen*, and *stehen/stellen. Die Unterrichtpraxis* 24: 136–145.

Guirardello-Damian, Raquel
    2002   The syntax and semantics of posture verbs in Trumai. In: John Newman (ed.), *The Linguistics of Sitting, Standing, and Lying*, 142–177. Amsterdam/Philadelphia: John Benjamins.

Gibbs, Raymond W., Dinara A. Beitel, Michael Harrington, and Paul. E. Sanders
    1994   Taking a stand on the meanings of *stand*: Bodily experience as motivation for polysemy. *Journal of Semantics* 11: 231–251.

Hellerstedt, Maria
    2005   De la position à la localisation: Étude sur l'expression de l'emplacement en suédois. MA-thesis, Etudes Langues Germaniques, Université Lille3, France.

Hellqvist, Elof
    1922   *Svenk Etymologisk Ordbok.* Lund: Gleerups förlag.

Lemmens, Maarten
    2002a   The semantic network of Dutch posture verbs. In: J. Newman (ed.), *The Linguistics of Sitting, Standing, and Lying.* 103–139. Amsterdam/Philadelphia: John Benjamins.
    2002b   On the motivated omnipresence of *liggen, zitten*, and *staan*: Linguistic and didactic perspectives [in Dutch]. In: Philippe Hiligsmann (ed.), *Le néerlandais en France et en Belgique francophone: approches scientifiques, approches didactiques.* [Collection UL3 Travaux et recherches], 91–114. Lille: Université Lille3.
    2002c   Tracing referent location in oral picture descriptions. In: Andrew Wilson, Paul Rayson, and Tony McEnery (eds.), *A Rainbow of Corpora – Corpus Linguistics and the Languages of the World*, 73–85. München: Lincom Europa.
    2005a   Motion and location: Toward a cognitive typology. In: Geneviève Girard (ed.), *Parcours linguistique.* [Travaux 122 du Cierec], 223–244. Publications de l'Université St Etienne.
    2005b   Aspectual posture verb constructions in Dutch. *Journal of Germanic Linguistics* 17: 183–217.
    subm.   Métaphor, image schématique et grammaticalisation: Une étude diachronique cognitive de *stand*.

in prep. Posture verbs in Dutch: Semantic and typological perspectives. Manuscript in preparation for publication in the series *Cognitive Linguistics Research*. Berlin/New York: Mouton de Gruyter.

Lemmens, Maarten and Ekatarina Rakhilina
- 2003 Semantika russkogo *sidet'* na fone niderlandskogo *zitten*. [The semantics of the Russian verb *sidet'* compared to Dutch *zitten*]. *Russian Linguistics* 27: 313–327.

Newman, John (ed.)
- 2002 A cross-linguistic overview of the posture verbs 'sit', 'stand', and 'lie'. In: John Newman (ed.), *The Linguistics of Sitting, Standing, and Lying*, 1–24. Amsterdam/Philadelphia: John Benjamins.

Rice, Sally
- 2002 Posture and existence predicates in Dene Suline (Chipewyan). In: John Newman (ed.), *The Linguistics of Sitting, Standing, and Lying*, 61–78. Amsterdam/Philadelphia: John Benjamins.

Serra Borneto, Carlo
- 1996 *Liegen* and *stehen* in German: A study in horizontality and verticality. In: Eugene Casad, (ed.), *Cognitive Linguistics in the Redwoods*, 458–505. Berlin/New York: Mouton de Gruyter.

Talmy, Leonard
- 2000 *Toward a Cognitive Semantics*. Cambridge, MA: MIT Press.

Van Oosten, Jeanne
- 1984 Sitting, standing and lying in Dutch: A cognitive approach to the distribution of the verbs *zitten*, *staan*, and *liggen*. In: Jeanne Van Oosten and John Snapper (eds.), *Dutch linguistics at Berkeley*, 137–160. Berkeley, CA: UCB.

Van Tol, Eveline
- 2002 De causatieven op een rijtje gezet. Een cognitief-semantische analyse van de causatieve werkwoorden *zetten*, *leggen*, *stoppen* en *steken*. Student term paper, University of Leiden.

From conceptualization to linguistic expression: Where languages diversify

Doris Schönefeld

Abstract

The study presented here reports on a corpus-based analysis of English, German and Russian expressions of posture scenes focussing on the conceptualizations they reflect. With the focus being on the verbal elements habitually and regularly realizing the trajector of a posture scene and the location at which a person or object is positioned, it can be shown that even for the verbalization of such commonly experienced scenes as posture scenes, different speech communities may conventionalize different routes or diverging construals, and thus cause language-specific "idiosyncrasies" in the form of particular collocations. The languages at issue are found to exhibit such differences for scenes in which the trajectory of a posture scene is construed relative to a location that is independent of the posture, and they turn out to be mainly due to the variation in the salience attributed to image-schematic aspects involved in the construal of the respective scenes.

Keywords: corpus analysis; cross-linguistic; collocations; construal; image-schemas.

1. Introduction

Collocations are language-specific to a considerable extent.[1] How can this be explained against the background assumption that – apart from culture-specific aspects – many of the scenarios which human beings are concerned with and hence also talk about are identical or at least very similar? Obviously, there must be points at which speakers can understand and structure these scenarios differently. The structure they give to them, to their experience – though it is basically determined or "set" by the human biological make-up, e.g. our perceptual apparatus – appears to leave room for considerable choice. Indeed, the choices we have in the conceptualization, in particular in the "framing", of a scene are manifold and they can vary from speaker to speaker. This variability becomes tangible in language, since the conceptualization of scenes leaves traces in their verbalization. That means that from habitual, i.e., typical and frequent, expressions of a language we can infer a speech community's habitual ways of conceptualization. However, that there is some choice in the conceptualization becomes explicit only when the language under analysis uses more than one option to verbalize a particular scene. Looking at collocations from a cross-linguistic perspective will broaden the database in this respect, since – due to their (potentially) language-specific (i.e., diverging) forms – they can be taken to contain explicit hints at differences in the underlying conceptualizations. Note in this respect that collocations may show strongly "idiosyncratic" aspects even when they refer to situations that are quasi-universal in that they belong to some of the most basic experiences human beings are exposed to. We thus take their cross-linguistic comparison to increase the potential for disclosing some of the options people employ in the ways they "see" the world.

In my investigation, I will analyse a number of collocations for the clues they give to the conceptualization of the scenes they verbalize. From the many processes and phenomena involved in conceptualization (for a summarizing discussion see Croft and Cruse [2004: 40–46]), I focus on construal operations that are related to (predominantly visual) image schemas. This also determined the type of collocations I have selected as the database of my investigation, namely, collocations that the posture verbs SIT, STAND and LIE enter into.[2] More specifically, the analysis is based on a cross-linguistic, corpus-based comparison of English, Russian and German collocations of this kind, and aims at presenting evidence for the influence image schemas have on the construal of posture scenarios by uncovering image-schematic motivations for the differences that can be tracked down.

2. Theoretical prerequisites

Image-schemas are commonly defined as pre-conceptual representations of human bodily experience. They represent abstractions from repeated particular experiences of the same kind, reflecting recurring patterns present in human bodily movement, manipulation of objects, and perceptual interactions. As such they can also be understood to construe our experience (cf. Croft and Cruse 2004: 45). Johnson motivates the term by pointing out that "they [image schemas] function primarily as abstract structures of images"

(Johnson 1987: xix). Having to do with perception, movement, and object manipulation, they primarily fall into two groups: sensory-motor and visual schemas (PATH, BALANCE, COMPULSION, CONTAINER, PART-WHOLE, CONTACT, VERTICALITY, SUPPORT etc.).[3] It has, however, been argued that also non-visual image schemas are to be included here: Lakoff (1987: 444) points out that, apart from visual images, we also have auditory and olfactory images and those of force dynamics. Palmer (1996: 46) opts for a definition of image that "should allow for imagery that arises from all the sensory modes" and lists auditory, olfactory, temperature and affective imagery/images along with visual, and kinesthetic imagery. Ergo, image schemas in all sensory modes can be assumed to be involved in the structuring of what we perceive and experience. Given that human perception is subject to our biological make-up, the image schemas people have should also be (more or less) identical for all of them. However, though we assume to have the same schemas, we can (and do) employ them differently, e.g. in different combinations or with different salience attributed to the one or the other schema involved, in the perspectivization(s) we give to an identical scene, in its construal.

Construal is Langacker's term to refer to "our ability to construe a conceived situation in alternate ways – by means of alternate images – for purposes of thought or expression" (Langacker 1987: 110). Sentences (1) and (2) are meant to illustrate this point.

(1) *My aunt is sitting to the left of Tom.*

(2) *Tom is sitting to the right of my aunt.*

One and the same situation or scene can be understood from different perspectives, i.e., we are able to "see" or understand the same content in alternative ways. We – as conceptualizers – have an array of possibilities from which to view a scene, possibilities of how we can think about a scene and how we would like to represent it. The perspective we choose, in examples (1) and (2) the alignment of figure and ground, leaves traces in the wording of the resulting expressions, thus also serving as a clue for the understander to construct the respective scene in a similar way in the comprehension process. Langacker (e.g. 1999: 5–8) elaborates on construal and lists as the potential dimensions being employed in conceptualization those of specificity, background, perspective, scope, and prominence (profiling and choice of focal element). Taylor (2002: 11) exemplifies as construal resources different figure-ground organizations, varying amounts of detail in a scene's specification, or perceiving a situation from different perspectives.[4]

It is perhaps not accidental that another term used to denote the ability of variously structuring one and the same scene is *imagery* (Langacker 1987: 110–113, 1995: 5–12), and that also the definition (given above) mentions *alternate images* as underlying alternate construals. This makes explicit some similarity in the relationship between an image schema and the associated sensational experiences on the one hand, and construal, the structure imposed on a scene by adopting a particular perspective or view, and the scene as such on the other. In both cases, for sensations and scenes to be understood and communicated, we must put some order on them. Moreover – and more importantly from the perspective of my investigation – construal and image schemas are interrelated in that some construal mechanisms operate on the basis of image schemas, giving particular kinds of image-schematic structuring to particular scenes.

3. Construal and posture verbs

I will now turn to the question whether (image-schematic) construal can indeed be assumed to be causally related to the kind of linguistic diversity that shows in a language's repertoire of collocations, and if so, how.

Starting out from Johnson's (1987: 29) claim that in order for us to make sense of the world around us, we must be cognitively equipped with ordering patterns, or image schemas, we would have to think that these patterns for human actions, perceptions and conceptions are mental constructs available to human cognition in general and in an identical form. We could further conclude that these schemas are employed similarly for the conceptualization of phenomena, the experience of which are associated with such patterns. This being the case, we should also find some hints at that in language, and it can be assumed that also image schemas should leave traces in the verbalizations of the respective phenomena. In order to find such traces, one of the potential things to do is to consider verbal expressions that have a straightforward connection to (visual and kinesthetic) image schemas in that the concepts they denote are closely and inseparably linked with such schematic representations. This is why the following considerations will be made with regard to verbal expressions employing verbs of (human) posture: SIT, STAND and LIE, which can be shown to be associated with combinations of image schemas (see Section 4 below).

It is not surprising to find in almost any language verbal forms (possibly simple verbs) expressing the ideas of SITTING, STANDING or LYING, the most salient postures that humans can adopt (for more details on that see Newman [2002: 3–4] and Newman [ed. 2002]). They seem to reflect the same image schemas for the very reason that they are intimately related with our posture experience, i.e., that of bodily perception and movement, or rather rest from movement.

Extending our perspective to larger linguistic units that speakers regularly build around these (more basic) forms, we will notice that there is considerable diversity in what speakers associate with these common and very general notions of SITTING, STANDING and LYING. That means that people do not only use the respective verbs to denote their own posture, but they extend the concepts to the 'posture' of things other than themselves, e.g. when talking about their locations:

(3) *continued the Headmaster, opening a thick **book lying on** the table*

(4) ***Salt and pepper sit on** the tables in old jam-jars.*

For English, Rice (2002: 61) notes that "even when functioning as locational or existence predicates, the cardinal English posture verbs impose a powerful yet covert semantics on their themes". Assuming that this semantic constraint should be effective in language in general, it seems to be counter-intuitive that people do not always end up with identical extensions. Still, as Rice (2002: 62) puts it, "languages partition their posture lexicons differently subject to contrasting motivations and expressive need", and usage data from various languages show that different mechanisms must be at work. So, German has, for example,

(5) ***Salz und Pfeffer stehen** auf dem Tisch*
     'salt and pepper stand on the table'

Does that follow from different image schemas associated with the posture verbs, or is it a consequence of particular objects (the things positioned) not cueing the same schema(s) in individual languages? The affirmative answer lies more plausibly with the second question. From this it follows that there is no predictable link as to what people understand to SIT, STAND or LIE, though, post-hoc, there will almost certainly be found motivations for the respective uses once the latter have been identified.[5] One might assume that this is the point where languages diversify: Different speech communities have agreed on different conventionalized ways of understanding and talking about the scenes at issue. That means they have (community-)specific expressions signalling how they understand and perspectivize a particular situation. At a very general level, these expressions are a consequence of different construals of comparable situations. At a more specific level, the diversification in the construal may be shown to follow from two different strategies: the observable differences in a language's wording can be explained as following from the perception of one and the same scene by employing radically distinct image schemas – if that is conceivable at all, especially in the prototypical sense of literal posture/position of things –, or as following from the fact that speakers give different weight to the partaking schemas and/or combine them differently.

4. Image schemas and SIT, STAND, LIE[6]

Posture scenes represent stative events, but at the same time they can be understood as situations associated with movement in that they usually precede or follow processes of motion. Though – at first thought – it looks as if the perceptual (esp. visual/spatial) representations were almost exclusive vis-à-vis those of kinesthetic experience (sensory-motor patterns), also the latter can be expected to be involved in the conceptualization of these states, since postures are taken by moving into them, i.e., stopping movement, or are positions from which movement begins. Moreover, also maintaining the postures – where we are exposed to the forces of gravitational pull – will involve sensory-motor experience, e.g. that of keeping one's balance and resisting gravitational pull.

Assuming that the meanings of the three posture verbs in isolation are the same in the languages under consideration, I first (and as a preliminary step) try to connect the individual posture meanings with (variations in) image schema combinations employed in the understanding of the respective postures. Thus, a prominent difference between the postures can be attributed to the fact that – though identical schemas (VERTICALITY, BALANCE, SUPPORT) are involved – they are so with a difference in their importance or salience.

Elaborating on the embodied experience of standing, Gibbs et al. (1994) and Gibbs (2002: 392–393) find a number of image schemas that "best reflect people's recurring bodily experience of standing ... [t]he five most salient schemas associated with physical standing [being] BALANCE, VERTICALITY, CENTER-PERIPHERY, RESISTANCE, and LINKAGE". When we extend our perspective to include the other two postures, it is suggested that we add (from Johnson's [1987: 126], Grady's [2001: 1][7], and Croft and Cruse's [2004: 45] lists) further salient schemas associated with them, namely: CONTACT, COMPULSION, SUPPORT, SURFACE, FORCE, COUNTERFORCE, OBJECT, ENABLEMENT, COMPLEXITY.[8] The arrangement in which they combine in the three postures, the *image-schema profile* (IS profile) as Gibbs (2002: 394) puts it, is a matter of weighting them: some are more salient, some are backgrounded, and the following profiles can be plausibly hypothesized. It turns out that the postures as such must be associated with two different profiles each, since it makes a difference whether the posture is considered from the point of view of the object or thing in a particular posture, prototypically a person sitting, standing, or lying, or the perception of a thing's posture by a potential viewer.

From the perspective of the person standing, literal STAND will be associated with the following IS profile (adapted from Gibbs et al. 1994: 237ff): BALANCE, CENTRE-PERIPHERY (CENTRE is associated with balance: for STAND it is the lowest part of the person's vertical axis, his/her legs and feet, the base where "forces" are kept balanced), COMPULSION, (COUNTER)FORCE (gravitational pull), RESISTANCE (against gravitational pull), CONTACT, LINKAGE (to the ground one is standing on – again due to gravitational pull), SUPPORT (by the ground), VERTICALITY. The latter schema would have to be rated more or even most prominent when taking the viewer's perspective.

For literal SIT – from the perspective of the person sitting – the following IS profile is suggested: ENABLEMENT, SUPPORT, CONTACT, LINKAGE (by/with/to the object one is sitting on), CONTAINER (the "sitter" may be more or less enclosed in the seat), CENTRE-PERIPHERY (the centre being the person's buttocks), BALANCE, and COMPLEXITY/COMPACTNESS, the latter of which is again more prominent from the viewer's perspective.

Literal LIE exhibits the following IS profile (from the perspective of the person lying): SUPPORT, CONTACT, LINKAGE, (by/with/to the "thing" one is lying on), CONTAINER (which can be seen as a substitute [or even compensation] for BALANCE in the other two postures), ENABLEMENT and HORIZONTALITY, the latter ranking first from the viewer's experience of LIE.

The IS profiles just listed are not solely based on introspection, but they can be traced in dictionary descriptions of the meanings of the basic posture verbs, and they can be isolated from people's descriptions of typical posture scenes (cf. also Newman [2002: 2] on the central meanings of English *sit, stand* and *lie*; Rice [2002: 63f] on conceptual and kinesthetic correlates of a posture continuum; Lemmens [same volume] on experiential prototype clusters for cardinal posture verbs in Dutch).

As for the part they play in a language's wording of posture scenes, two things must be kept apart: the verbs denoting these postures in the three languages at issue will most likely draw on the same image schema combinations if considered in isolation, for – in their default reading – they are related to the same types of (bodily) experience: human posture. Since, however, the same verbs are more often than not associated with the posture of things other than people – Lemmens (same volume) finds a low frequency of the prototype meanings in a Dutch non-fiction corpus of 10 to 15 % of the occurrences extracted –, the profiles may turn out to be variously employed in providing the basis for the extensions from the prototype to be found. Thus, we will have to look at the way these verbs occur in language use, more specifically, at the trajectors and landmarks speakers link with posture and location:[9] (SOMEONE/SOMETHING) A THING SITS/STANDS/LIES (SOMEWHERE) AT SOME LOCATION. This is the level at which conceptualization and communication most often operates, i.e., we do not usually contemplate or talk about a particular posture abstracted away from what is posted and where, but much more typically, we are concerned with the posture of a particular thing at a particular location.

5. Posture verbs in English, German and Russian: Usage data

If we assume that there is some correspondence between what is frequent in language use and what is there as a unit, as a cognitive routine, in our minds, the close cognitive link of some posture with particular trajectors (things) and landmarks (locations) should become obvious in corpus data. It should become evident in concordance lines in which the respective verbs are the node words and co-occur with particular subject phrases (NP) and adverbial phrases (AvP and PP) more often than chance would predict.[10] The expressions extracted from usage data are at a fairly specific level: posture verbs are associated with particular things and with particular locations, such as English *a person lying in bed; a house standing on a hill; a person sitting on the sofa.* Both the specified trajectors *person, house* and the specified locations *bed, field, sofa* can be shown to take an influence on the way we see a thing positioned with regard to the very location: *someone is lying in bed* vs. *clothes are lying on the floor.* Note that these linguistic expressions reflect the construal of the scene: The trajectors, the landmarks and the relations construed between the trajector and the landmark (cued by the prepositions) highlight particular image schemas of the verbs' IS profiles, namely CONTAINER and SUPPORT respectively. This will be shown in the following sections.

5.1. Posture verbs and their trajectors

The choice of the posture verb for the communication of a posture scene (in a predication) is a matter of the "internal" spatial arrangement of the thing the posture of which is being talked about, the trajector. It is triggered by salient spatial parameters of the trajector itself. If the thing is not a human being – from the postures of which we have the posture concepts of SITTING, STANDING and LYING – we project a human being's posture to these other entities.[11] These projections or extensions operate on the basis of particular (foregrounded) schemas of the verb's IS profile and – as also shown by the data – different languages may follow different strategies when extending posture verbs to one and the same trajector in an identical scene (cf. examples [37] to [41] below).[12] In order to track down expressions exhibiting such differences, I had a close look at the usage patterns the verbs occur in. The patterns were extracted from parts of the BNC (for English), from parts of the COSMAS corpus from the IDS Mannheim (for German) and from a number of Russian corpora accessible on the Internet (for Russian). Since these corpora are of a quite distinct character with regard to both size and composition, I tried to make up for that by selecting three comparable subcorpora: for the simple reason that all the corpora contained newspaper text corpora, I concentrated on this text type and – for reasons of feasibility of the task – I selected an amount of roughly 3 million words of running text from the respective corpora to be searched for occurrences of the posture verbs SIT, STAND and LIE.[13] Table 1 gives a numerical overview of the data extracted from the corpora:

Table 1. Posture verbs in English, Russian and German corpora

verb	total number of occurrences (English)	total number of occurrences (German)	total number of occurrences (Russian)
SIT	354	467	619
STAND	706	3.413	258
LIE	247	1.614	301

The totals of the verbs' occurrences differ widely. In order to find out in what way these differences (as well as all the other differences in the observed frequencies to be discussed in the following) can actually be claimed to be significant and not just a product of chance, I had to test the respective numbers for their significance. Since for my data a number of factors were observed for the potential influence they might exert on the usage of a posture verb, I opted for a multifactorial test method, the so-called hierarchical configural frequency analysis.[14] The significance values for the numbers in Table 1 can be read off from Table 1 in the Appendix: The German (G) data contain conspicuously, i.e. highly significantly, more occurrences of *stehen* (stand) and *liegen* (lie) than both the Russian (R) and English (E) data, which seems due to a highly frequent usage of these verbs in extended (i.e., non-literal) senses. In contrast, the Russian and English usage of LIE is comparatively small, but though the frequencies are similar, it is what chance would predict for Russian, whereas it is an "anti-type" (i.e. significantly less frequent than expected, or highly significantly dispreferred) in the English data.. The frequencies of STAND show an inverse contrast: whereas Russian *stojat'* (stand) turns out to be an "antitype", English *stand* is as frequent as expected on the basis of chance. As for SIT, GERMAN *sitzen* is the "antitype", Russian and English usage is significantly more frequent than expected. All these intra- and interlingual "imbalances" have to do with the extensions of posture concepts to things other than human beings that speakers of a language habitually and conventionally make. These extensions can be read off the trajectors the verbs take in a predication. Table 2 provides a list of examples classified into groups of human trajectors, trajectors denoting concrete and abstract objects, trajectors denoting personified objects and those denoting animals.[15, 16] The results of the hierarchical configural frequency analysis reaching significance are given in the Appendix (Table 2).

Table 2. Posture verbs and their trajectors

verb	trajectors/subjects		%	examples
Sit	Human beings	308	87.0	men, people, proper nouns
	Concrete objects	14	3.9	house, journal, book, plant, building
	Abstract objects	8	2.3	music, superstructure
	Personified objects	20	5.6	government, court, Pentagon
	Animals	4	1.1	fox, mouse, owl
Sitzen	Human beings	346	74.0	*Mann* 'man', *Leute* 'people'
	Abstract objects	33	7.1	*Schock* 'shock', *Mißtrauen* 'distrust'
	Concrete objects	16	3.2	*Modell* 'model', *Brille* 'glasses'
	Personified objects	23	4.9	*Land* 'country', *Institut* 'institute'
	Animals	8	1.7	*Hund* 'dog', *Rabe* 'raven'
Sidet'	Human beings	575	92.9	*ljudi* 'people', *devuška* 'girl'
	Concrete objects	7	1.1	*frak* 'tail coat', *ion* 'ion'
	Abstract objects	7	1.1	*citata* 'quotation', *bolezn'* 'disease'
	Personified objects	12	1.9	*narod* 'people(s)', *kompanija* 'society'
	Animals	8	1.3	*kot* 'cat', *sobaka* 'dog', *orël* 'eagle'
Stand	Human beings	421	59.6	proper noun, people, deputy, candidate
	Abstract objects	135	19.1	case, deal, things, directive, conditions
	Concrete objects	62	8.8	car, machine, book, tanks, temple
	Personified objects	62	8.8	pronoun, world, Britain, army, firm
	Animals	10	1.4	sheep, gelding, cat
Stehen	Abstract objects	1350	39.5	*Ergebnis* 'result', *Chance* 'chance'
	Concrete objects	468	13.7	*Baum* 'tree', *Haus* 'house'
	Human beings	900	26.4	*Frau* 'woman), *Kind* 'child'
	Personified objects	247	7.2	*Klub* '(sports) club', *Team* 'team'
	Animals	12	0.4	*Kuh* 'cow', *Tier* 'animal', *Reh* 'roe'
Stojat'	Concrete objects	80	31.0	*dom* 'house', *pamjatnik* 'monument'
	Abstract objects	43	16.7	*vopros* 'question', *zadača* 'task'
	Human beings	97	37.6	*pron, čelovek* 'people', *mužik* 'man'
	Personified objects	11	4.3	*narod* 'people'
	Animals	1	0.4	*lošad'* 'horse'
Lie	Abstract objects	104	42.1	blame, responsibility, problem, task
	Concrete objects	73	29.5	village, ship, coal, clothes, boat
	Human beings	65	26.3	proper, people, man, child, girl
	Personified objects	4	1.7	(sports) club, talent
	Animals	1	0.4	dog
Liegen	Abstract objects	775	48.0	*Problem* 'problem', *Grund* 'reason'
	Concrete objects	361	22.4	*Fotos* 'photos', *Transparent* 'poster'
	Human beings	163	10.1	*Frau* 'woman', *Mann* 'man'
	Personified objects	69	4.3	*Klub* 'sports club', *Grüne* 'the Greens'
	Animals	6	0.4	*Katze* 'cat', *Tier* 'animal'
Ležat'	Concrete objects	69	22.9	*kniga* 'book'; *sapogi* 'boots'
	Abstract objects	60	19.9	*princip* 'principle', *interesy* 'interests', *proekty* 'projects'
	Human beings	115	38.2	*čelovek* 'people', *starik* 'old man'
	Personified objects	10	3.3	*trupy* 'troops', *gosudarstvo* 'state'
	Animals	4	1.3	*bul'dog* 'bulldog', *olen'* '(red) deer'

For SIT, human trajectors and animals significantly predominate in general, with the former being highly significantly preferred and the latter only significantly so. This makes human trajectors appear as the canonical case, whereas its usage with animal trajectors is very significant in the Russian data only, which is why it reaches overall significance. This is plausible when we consider that there is only a relatively small number of animals whose postures we (can) conceptualize as sufficiently close to the human posture of sitting, with various aspects being extended: E *dogs, cats, bird* / G *Hund* 'dog', *Vogel* 'bird', *Panda* 'panda' / R *kot* 'cat' *sobaka* 'dog'. It does not appear unnatural – if we take animacy to play a role here – that personified objects, which gain this feature only via metonymic extension, occur just as frequently as chance would predict (E, R) or are even highly significant antitypes, i.e. strongly dispreferred (G).

The group of personified objects represents, strictly speaking, a hybrid of those of human beings and abstract objects, because they can refer to both persons and objects. It contains expressions which, for example, represent common metonymies, such as INSTITUTION FOR ITS REPRESENTATIVES, or PART FOR WHOLE.[17] Their use with a posture verb selects the person reference, which is an entrenched meaning in the respective language's lexicon. In contrast to that, the co-occurrence with posture verbs of expressions referring to abstract trajectors (listed as abstract objects) do not refer to persons but are conceptualized metaphorically as if being persons (see examples [11]–[16]).

As the remaining values for SIT show, it is significantly dispreferred for inanimate trajectors (listed as concrete and abstract objects) to be associated with the posture of sitting, though a few examples can be found. We assume these extensions to also be motivated by similarities speakers are willing to perceive or construct between the "target" trajector and the posture of a human being:

(6) *that prevented Cale from screaming at a potted **plant sitting** on his piano*

(7) *oil-fired electric **power station** that **sits** on Bankside next to the site of*

(8) G: ***Haselnussmakronen sitzen*** *schon auf dem Blech und werden*
'hazelnut biscuits sit on the baking tray and will'

(9) G: *auf deren edler Nase eine **Porzellanbrille sitzt***
   'on whose noble nose a pair of china glasses sits'

(10) R: *Ved' v rastvore – vodnoj srede, kotoraja očen' poljarna, každyj **ion**, kak ljubjat pisat' populjarizatory, "**sidit** v glubokoj potencial'noj jame"*
   'In the solution – in a moist environment, which is very cold, every ion, as the popular writers like to write, "sits in a deep potential hollow"'

The unexpected (since strongly dispreferred) usage of SIT with a trajector denoting an abstract object is due to a metaphorical mapping in which the mapping of the human trajector from the source domain of posture to the trajectors in the abstract scenarios results in their (ad-hoc) personification, giving them a human touch:

(11) ***Songs*** *about relationships, growing older and social issues **sat** alongside primitive rock'n'roll revelry*

(12) ***music*** *that would **sit** well in the Palm Court or the pier pavilion*

(13) G: *denen der **Schalk** im Nacken **sitzt***
   'Puck sitting in their necks [...]' (= 'they're in a devilish mood')

(14) G: *den Leuten [...] sitzt der **Schreck** noch in den Knochen.*
   'fright sits in their bones' (= 'their knees are still like jelly')

(15) R: *Vo mne davno **sidit** citat: "[...]"*
   'In me has sat a quotation for long: "[...]"'

(16) R: *Znamenitoe (nadeemsja) **buduščee** i velikoe **prošloe** sovetsko-rossijskogo kino **sideli** v odnom rjadu.*
   'The famous (as we hope) future and the great past of the Russian-Soviet cinema sat in one row.'

For STAND and LIE we can report mixed results. STAND attracts human trajectors very frequently in English (highly significantly preferred), but rejects them in the Russian and German data (highly significantly dispreferred). The association of STAND with animals is at chance level, i.e. not significant, in all three languages. Inanimate trajectors, especially personified objects and abstract objects, are also interesting to look at for potential parallels with what has been observed for SIT: with the exception of the German data, the combination of STAND and an inanimate trajector is comparable to SIT: it is highly significantly dispreferred for abstract objects in English and Russian, and for concrete objects in English, and is as chance would predict for concrete objects in Russian. The German data, however, exhibit a highly significant attraction between STAND and abstract objects, thus reflecting the verb's non-literal usage, which was already hypothesized to be the reason for the surprisingly large number of overall occurrences of this posture verb in German (cf. above). The following examples illustrate animate and inanimate trajectors of STAND:

(17) E: *Bombay, where* **you** *can* **stand** *on the roof-top of the small pavilion and watch*

(18) E: *the Lord Chief Justice:* **Oppression** *doesn't* **stand** *on the doorstep with a toothbrush moustache swastika*

(19) G: *Mehr als anderthalb Stunden* **steht er** *allein auf seiner Bühne und*
'For more than an hour and a half he has been standing alone on his stage'

(20) G: *Hinter jedem Sozialhilfefall* **steht** *ein* **Schicksal***. Mit Manfred T*
'Behind any hardship case there stands a fate'

(21) R: *Vidit,* **devuška stoit** *u kolonny i na časy posmatrivaet.*
'(S/He) sees, a girl is standing at the queue and looks at the watch'

(22) R: *V golove posle takogo omovenija ešče dolgo* **stoit strannyj šum** *i vatnyj tuman*
'In the head – after such an ablution – for a long time stands a strange noise and a cotton-wool like mist'

In a similar way, LIE is significantly frequently associated with inanimate trajectors in German. Moreover, also the Russian data reflect a highly significant association between LIE and concrete objects. The opposite is true for abstract objects, which are strongly dispreferred in the Russian data. Human/animate trajectors can be tracked down with a moderate frequency, though their attraction to LIE is clearly negative. Examples (23)–(28) illustrate the co-occurrence of LIE with objects and human beings:

(23) E: **vases** had been **lying** in deep salt water

(24) E: the **man** himself **lay** in a nearby hospital

(25) G: das **Hauptquartier** des Unternehmens **liegt** in Australien
'the **headquarters** of the enterprise **lie** in Australia'

(26) G: bevor er das überprüfen konnte, **lag er** schon auf der Seite am Boden.
'before he could check this, **he lay** on the floor on his side'

(27) R: Uvažaja te **objazannosti**, kotorye na ètom čeloveke **ležat**
'Considering the **duties** which on this man **lie**'

(28) R: I **ja**, na samom dele **ležal** na polu s zakrytymi glazami
'And **I** really **lay** on the floor with closed eyes'

On the basis of the data for LIE, it might be asked whether the canonical case can really be associated with the human posture of lying, which is the posture that humans take when they are tired, or sick, or when they sleep or are dead (cf. Newman 2002: 2), and whose "typical socio-cultural value" is low (Rice 2002: 64). More plausibly, horizontally elongated (lying or spread) things in general (inclusive of human beings) can be assumed to be the classic or prime examples of the scene, so that the dominant factor for the association of verb and trajector seems to be (the image schema) HORIZONTALITY rather than human posture as a more concrete image.

Turning our attention to STAND and LIE and inanimate trajectors (the object group), we can summarize that the respective verbs in all three languages show a strongly dispreferred co-occurrence with concrete and abstract objects, with the exception of STAND in the German data. If they do co-occur, we can tentatively assume that for SIT and (less so) for STAND, human posture serves as the source domain in metaphorical mappings to other concrete and particularly abstract domains, whereas in the case of LIE (and less so for STAND), the extensions seem to start out from the more abstract, though still concrete spatial concept of a horizontally elongated object. The extended uses of STAND do also not exclude the assumption of a vertically erected object as a potential source domain of the mapping. This suggests that in all the extensions various image schemas of the respective verb's IS profile are more prominent in the mapping than more concrete images of human postures. We will further illustrate this point in Section 6.2.

What can already be stated at this stage is that the extensions found in the three languages exhibit a difference in the frequencies with which they are encountered in language use rather than differences in kind. The data do, however, support the general assumption that – in a cross-linguistic comparison – one and the same trajector may attract different posture verbs. Such divergences are elaborated in Section 6.2. Since it is natural to assume that the association between posture and trajector may also be influenced by the latter's location, I will turn to the locations against which the posture of things is portrayed before.

5.2. Posture verbs and prepositions

In a first step, the most frequent co-occurring prepositions of posture verbs are reported in abstraction from their objects. They alone suffice to give us an idea of the orientation which we understand a trajector to have with respect to an unspecified ground.

Frequency counts of the prepositions co-occurring with posture verbs in the languages at issue yield the associations illustrated in Table 3. In order to be able to discuss the significance of these data, I will again refer to the results of a configural frequency analysis given in the Appendix in Table 3. In another corpus-based analysis of these posture verbs in English (Bank of English: brspoke) Newman (2001: 209) found that "[f]or all three posture verbs, locating a figure on top of the ground is preferred ... The high frequency of *on* is highly suggestive of this". My data, drawn from a corpus of written language, show a preference of IN (high significance), no matter which of the three posture verbs occurs. However, also ON is highly significantly co-occurrent with these verbs, though slightly less so, followed by AT. Prepositions such as NEXT TO, BEYOND, BY, FOR, BEHIND etc are significant antitypes of posture verbs. The data for the individual posture verbs reveal distinct preferences: for SIT, IN, BEHIND and ON reach high significance, STAND attracts highly significantly the prepositions TO, IN FRONT OF, and UNDER, FOR and BY are attracted significantly, the verb LIE highly significantly associates with AT, WITH and OVER. These results are interesting in that they may serve as a basis for a cross-linguistic comparison between English, Russian and German. Table 4 gives the preposition types and the antitypes for the respective verbs in the respective languages.

Table 3. Verbs and prepositions[a]

Verb	English		%	German		%	Russian		%
SIT	total	354	100.0	total	467	100.0	total	619	100.0
	in	82	23.1	in/m	127	27.2	v	195	31.5
	on	72	20.3	auf	57	12.2	na	121	19.5
	at	28	7.9	an/m	31	6.6	za	50	8.1
	with	16	4.5	mit	14	3.0	u	23	3.7
	by	4	1.1	vor	14	3.0	pered	17	2.7
	next to	4	1.1	hinter	6	1.3	pod	3	0.5
STAND	total	706	100.0	total	3413	100.0	total	258	100.0
	in	61	8.6	in/m	580	17.0	na	66	25.6
	for	51	7.2	auf	453	13.3	v	32	12.4
	at	50	7.1	zu/r	255	7.5	za	27	10.5
	on	46	6.5	vor	199	5.8	u	21	8.1
	by	45	6.4	an/m	134	3.9	pered	11	4.3
	as	19	2.7	unter	113	3.3	nad	2	0.8
LIE	total	247	100.0	total	1614	100.0	total	301	100.0
	in	70	28.3	in/m	270	16.7	na	98	32.6
	on	27	10.9	bei	176	10.9	v	97	32.2
	at	12	4.9	auf	121	7.5	pod	9	2.9
	behind	12	4.9	an/m	121	7.5	u	7	2.3
	with	11	4.4	mit	75	4.6	čerez	5	1.7
	beyond	5	2.0	über	39	2.4	pered	5	1.7

[a] Legend: German prepositions: *in/m* 'in'; *auf* 'on'; *an/m* 'at', *mit* 'with'; *vor* 'in front of'; *hinter* 'behind'; *zu/r* 'to'; *unter* 'under'; *bei* 'at/by'; *über* 'above/over'. Russian prepositions: *na* 'on'; *za* 'behind'; *u* 'at'; *pered* 'in front of'; *pod* 'under'; *v* 'in'; *nad* 'above/over'; *čerez* 'over'. (The polysemous senses of the prepositions are not distinguished here, i.e., the literal [spatial] senses are not isolated from the extended senses.)

Table 4. Preferred and dispreferred prepositions of posture verbs in English, Russian and German[a]

	preferred prepositions	dispreferred prepositions
SIT		
English	ON, IN, WITH, NEXT TO	TO, IN FRONT OF
Russian	IN, BEHIND, ON, IN FRONT	Ø
German	Ø	TO, **ON**, AT, UNDER, **IN**, IN FRONT OF
STAND		
English	FOR, BY, AS	IN, TO, **IN FRONT OF**, ON, **UNDER**, WITH, BEHIND
Russian	BEHIND	IN, **TO**, AT, **UNDER**, WITH
German	TO, IN FRONT OF, UNDER	WITH, BEHIND, AT, **FOR**, **BY**, OVER
LIE		
English	BEYOND	TO, IN FRONT OF
Russian	ON, IN	TO, AT
German	AT, WITH, OVER	TO, IN FRONT OF, UNDER, ON, BEHIND, FOR, BY

[a] The prepositions in bold face are the ones that generally turned out to be "types" and "antitypes" of the three posture verbs.

With regard to SIT, German is special in that it has the generally significant prepositions ON and IN as "antitypes". As for STAND and LIE, however, German seems to be the language closest to the values calculated for the posture verbs in general. A further noticeable aspect is that the preferred prepositions for these two verbs do not seem to be those that we would associate with the respective posture on an intuitive basis, such as ON or IN. The prepositions listed as types suggest that the respective verbs are often used in an extended, i.e., non-literal, sense. And indeed, if we consider the literal posture readings only (i.e., the spatial senses the verbs express), the results are different.[18]

Table 5. Literally used verbs and prepositions

Verb	English		%	German		%	Russian		%
SIT	in	65	79.3	in/m	58	45.7	v	164	84.0
	on	49	68.0	auf	30	52.6	na	101	83.5
	at	26	92.9	an/m	18	58.0	za	44	88.0
STAND	on	29	63.0	in/m	117	20.1	na	43	65.1
	in	29	47.5	auf	92	20.3	v	22	68.8
	at	11	22.0	vor	72	36.2	za	6	22.2
LIE	on	26	96.3	in/m	95	35.2	na	75	76.5
	in	22	31.4	auf	60	49.6	v	72	74.2
	at	5	41.7	an	30	24.8	pod	7	77.8

The significance of these findings is again discussed on the basis of the results of a hierarchical configural frequency analysis. The complete list of results is given in the Appendix, Table 4.

There is no change in the ranks of the prepositions co-occurring with the posture verbs in general, the top-ranking preposition being IN, followed by ON. However, taken separately, the verbs show different preferences: SIT prefers BEHIND, STAND – IN FRONT OF, and LIE does not attract a single preposition at all to a degree reaching significance. From the perspective of the individual languages, the posture verbs attract (and repel) most the prepositions given in Table 6.

As can be seen from the data, the separate calculation of the posture verbs' literal uses even more strongly deviates from Newman's finding (and my own expectations given above as based on intuition) as to what the posture verbs suggest for the orientation of a thing with respect to its location: ON is preferred by German STAND only and is repelled by German SIT, IN shows exactly the same distribution and is additionally attracted by Russian SIT and repelled by Russian STAND. All the remaining prepositions indicate that speakers construe posture scenes significantly frequently from an anthropocentric perspective: rather than locating an object on top of its ground, they, firstly, exploit their body-based orientation in space: their experience of gravity gives them the reason for locating objects on a vertical axis (cf. UNDER); their experience of the directionality of vision motivates the location of objects on the horizontal axis of FRONT and BACK (cf. BEHIND and IN FRONT OF). Such a strategy shows up in such phrases as *X stands behind Z*.

Table 6. Preferred and dispreferred prepositions of literally used posture verbs[a]

	preferred prepositions	dispreferred prepositions
SIT		
English	AT	Ø
Russian	BEHIND, **IN**	AT, IN FRONT OF
German	Ø	ON, IN, IN FRONT OF, BEHIND
STAND		
English	Ø	Ø
Russian	Ø	IN, AT, IN FRONT OF
German	IN FRONT OF, IN, **ON**	AT
LIE		
English	Ø	Ø
Russian	**UNDER**	AT, IN FRONT OF
German	AT	IN FRONT OF

[a] The prepositions in bold face are the ones that generally turned out to be "types" and "antitypes" of the three posture verbs.

Usage events with the prepositions IN FRONT OF and BEHIND suggest furthermore that speakers also exploit "inherent features" of the "landmark objects", as in *in front of the house*. At a closer look, these intrinsic coordinates, too, turn out to be related to anthropocentric coordinates for they result from the projection of our own bodily orientation (UP-DOWN, FRONT-BACK, LEFT-RIGHT) onto such concrete objects around us. This is the reason why such intrinsic coordinates (as found in verbal expressions of English, Russian and German, for example) can more exactly be qualified as metaphorical projections of the anthropocentric perspective onto inanimate objects and artefacts (for a discussion of human orientation in space, see Schönefeld 2005). In addition to such orientations, speakers may also refer to an object's posture by locating it simply with reference to a second object, which is more salient in the respective scene, using AT. This is a significant construal for English SIT and German LIE.

Still, the data elicited here neither completely contradict Newman's finding of a preference of *on*, nor are they incompatible with the intuitive associations specified above: they show that both IN and ON are significantly preferred ways of giving an orientation to a thing positioned (the trajectory or figure) with respect to the landmark (the ground) in the case of German STAND and Russian SIT and STAND. The two prepositions do, however, not behave analogously in the usage events identified: a closer inspection of the respective data reveals different construals associated with them.[19] Speakers using ON construe the scene of a figure on top of some sort of ground calling up or rather employing the image schemas: UP-DOWN, SURFACE, SUPPORT, CONTACT, LINKAGE, (COUNTER)FORCE. These schemas structure the same elements of the scene as the respective schemas also associated with the posture verbs. Speakers using IN construe a different scene: the figure's location is conceived of as in a room (a CONTAINER), with the posture not depending on this location. That means that the image schema of CONTAINER, as part of the preposition's IS profile, does not structure the same element of the scene as the CONTAINER schema associated with the postures of sitting (and lying). As a consequence, the element related to the scene via IN (the ground or landmark) is not directly, i.e., not causally, associated with the posture itself in that it does not represent the base of the posture on which the thing rests. Though the attraction of IN is not significant in our data for the postures of LYING, for which also the idea of enclosure (and thus the CONTAINER schema) was suggested (cf. Section 4), it is nevertheless interesting to consider the construal a combination of LIE and IN may signal: actually we can identify a second construal: using the preposition IN, the speaker may also project the CONTAINER schema to the same element of the scene as the schema originating from the posture verb. This results in a scenario in which the figure is enclosed by a container that also holds and supports it in this particular posture, serving as a base of the posture (which is why we assume the CONTAINER schema in the IS profile of LIE to be "made up for" by the BALANCE schema in the other two posture verbs). In a particular expression, the ground related to the figure via IN, i.e., the prepositional object, signals which of the construals is actually relevant in the respective scene. Example (29) gives a scene of the latter type, i.e., the CONTAINER profiled by IN is also the base on which the figure rests, example (30) gives a scene in which the figure is to be found in some room (CONTAINER), with the posture being independent of this CON-

TAINER. That means that the CONTAINER is of no importance for the posture of LYING. From the perspective of LYING, an expression like (30) would also be valid for a scene in which the person talked about (the thing) is not actually lying (in [a] bed), but is merely an in-patient in a hospital.

(29)   *to another room where a man was **lying in bed** watched by his wife*

(30)   *the man himself **lay in a** nearby **hospital*** (same example as [24])

If the preposition IN co-occurs with SIT, the speaker may also signal the same two types of construal, which again depends on the ground against which the posture is perspectivized (examples [31] and [32]).

(31)   *The deceased, at that time, was **sitting in the** front passenger **seat**.*

(32)   *Officers **sat in booths** in a side chapel for people wanting*

As in the case of LIE (example [29]), in example (31), the CONTAINER schemas as parts of the posture verb's and the preposition's IS profile "collapse" on the same object, whereas in (32) they structure two different elements in the respective scene: the location where the sitting takes place is given explicitly by the prepositional phrase *in booths*, the element the officers sat on/in, the base of SITTING, is merely implied. It follows naturally that both types of construal can also co-occur, as shown for LIE in example (33):

(33)   *Mr Delmo Vigna, who was **lying in bed in** his first-floor **flat** when the bomb went off*[20]

To sum up here, we can conclude from our data (of all three languages) that posture scenes are mainly construed in three ways: firstly, people locate an object as being close to other, more salient, objects. This is indicated by the usage of AT and is independent of this object's posture. Secondly, posture verbs may be used to locate an object by projecting the speaker's body-based spatial orientation (verticality and front-back) onto the visual field. This results in using such prepositions as IN FRONT OF, BEHIND and UNDER. Thirdly, and this is in line with Newman's observations, speakers may use the prepositions ON and IN, indicating the employment of a construal in which (part of) the verb's and the preposition's IS profiles are projected to or taken from one and the same landmark, resulting in an expression that construes the posture of a thing relative to the base on which it rests. Thus, it becomes obvious that the choice of the prepositions reflects the image-schematic (spatial) arrangement of posture and location. The choice is determined by the spatial relation that speakers perceive to exist between the thing (figure) and the location (ground), the landmark of the preposition.

In other words, at least in the cases of literal posture description when the location of the thing positioned is added, the spatial configuration between this thing and its locational specification, the ground against which the figure is placed, is what guides verbalization. The aspect that sets the preposition ON apart from all the "other" prepositions is that the former selects as ground the basis on which the object (the trajector) rests, whereas the latter highlight other "posture-independent" parts of the spatial configuration of a thing's posture and its location (cf. [34a], [35a], [36a]). This is also why both types of specifications can easily and naturally co-occur in one predication, as is shown in the respective (b)-examples.

(34) a. E: *the wizened, worn-out figure of the 87-year-old woman* **sitting beside** *him*
  b. E: *the wizened, worn-out figure of the 87-year-old woman* **sitting beside** *him* in an easy-chair

(35) a. D: **vor** *einer zweiten Kamera* **steht** *der frierende SFB Reporter*
   'in front of a second camera, there stands the SFB-reporter shivering with cold'
  b. D: **vor** *einer zweiten Kamera,* auf einem Stuhl, **steht** *der frierende SFB-Reporter*
   'in front of a second camera, on a chair, there stands the SFB-reporter'

(36) a. R: *I tak on uže polgoda tupo* **ležit** *pered televizorom.*
   'And he's already been lying in front of the TV set for half a year'
  b. R: *I tak on uže polgoda tupo* **ležit** *pered televizorom* na poly.
   'And he's already been lying on the floor in front of the TV set for half a year'

IN is special in that it may represent an instance of the "other" group specifying the trajector's location as inside a container, and, for SIT and LIE, additionally allow for a construal parallel to that of ON. For this reason both

IN and ON can be considered to be conceptually closer to the posture verbs than the other prepositions.

From what has been said about the usage of ON and IN it follows that no dramatic differences should be expected to surface in verb-preposition collocations across the three languages at issue, when a thing's posture is construed relative to the base on which it rests. It is in the more "unconstrained" uses of prepositions of the "other" group that the three languages show diverging conventionalized expressions (hence, also conceptualizations). They will be discussed in Section 6.1.

Before turning to the discussion it should be mentioned that posture verbs are also found to be used for the communication of scenes without hinting at the location of the thing. In such (intransitive) uses, the SUPPORT- and CONTAINER-related parts of the posture verbs' IS profiles are backgrounded, so that the expressions are understood to denote the ability of an animate or inanimate thing to enter into and maintain the respective posture. The prominent image schema then is BALANCE – which makes it only too obvious that the verb LIE is usually not used in this way.

6. Discussion

The analysis of the (collocational) usage of the three posture verbs in the three languages is revealing: despite the assumed sameness of their (posture) meanings, they do not "automatically" enter into the same kinds of collocations: although there is considerable overlap, there is also noticeable dissimilarity in the patterns in which they occur, and a number of diverging collocations (and patterns) could be extracted from the corpora. In these diverging collocations, a certain degree of subjectivity can be detected in the selection of such aspects of a particular posture scene that the speakers of a language take to be salient enough to be used as the vantage point in its conceptualization and verbalization. That means that the differences found in the wording of the three languages at issue signal and result from differences in the construal of the scenes conceptualized and communicated. It is differences in the perspective and the prominence given to (parts of) the scenes that show up in the respective expressions, with the former being the spatial vantage point employed by the speaker and the latter – the relative salience given to such factors as relational participants and elements explicitly mentioned (cf. Langacker 1991: 9, 12). Differences in both the spatial vantage point and the salience attributed to individual aspects of a scene are associated with a scene's particular image-schematic structuring of thing, posture, location and orientation. That means that a scene may be conceptualized by foregrounding particular image schemas at the expense of others, as will be exemplified in this section.

In the following, I will comment on (cross-linguistically) diverging collocations where the wording indicates that an identical (or at least very similar) experiential scene is conceptualized differently, especially focusing on expressions that make the exploitation of different image-schema combinations in the respective languages obvious. The collocations presented here all encode a thing, its posture, its location and its orientation relative to the location. That is why they typically have a trajector phrase (NP-subject), a posture verb, a preposition (rendering the orientation) and a landmark (NP – prepositional object). Differences show up at the level of the realisations of these (functionally specified) constituents. They can be categorized into three groups, which I will present sequentially.

6.1. One scenario – one posture verb – different prepositions

In a number of expressions for particular scenes, expressions of group 1, the three languages – or at least two of them – use different prepositions, though the same posture verb:

(37) E: *(people)* **sit over** *the books*
G: *über den Büchern* **sitzen**
'sit over the books'
R: **sidet'** *za knigami*
'sit behind the books'
R: *sideli za matematičeskoj zadačej*
'sit behind a mathematical task'
sideli za kakoj-to rabotoj
'sit behind some kind of work'

(38) E: *(books)* **stand on** *the shelf*
G: *im Regal* **stehen**
'stand in the shelf'
R: **stojat'** *na polkach*
'stand on the shelves'

(39) E: *(people)* **sit on** *the train*
      G: **im** *Zug* **sitzen**
          'sit in the train'
      R: **sidet'**/**exat' na** *poezde*
          'sit/go on the train'

(40) R: *(ljudi)* **sidjat na** *telefone*
          'sit on the phone'
      G: **am** *Telefon* **sitzen**
          'sit at the phone'
      E: **sit on** *the phone*

(41) R: *(ženščina)* **sidela na** *drugix obsuždenijax*
          'a woman sat on other meetings'
      G: *in anderen Besprechungen* **sitzen**
          'sit in other meetings'
      E: **sit in** *other meetings*

As the examples show, the respective scenarios are construed differently in some part. The different prepositions employed signal a different image-schematic structuring of such parts of the verbalized scenes that more exactly specify the location of the thing positioned and its orientation relative to the ground (the ground against which the trajector is perspectivized). This is why, from a cross-linguistic perspective, the respective collocations differ notably, though not totally, or, emphasizing the "common ground", they are notably similar, but not identical.

Let me elaborate on some examples. In (37), the scene of doing some "mental" work, i.e., sitting at a desk with books to read, notes to be taken etc. is structured identically in English and German: the books are lying on the table, the reader sits at the desk with his head bent over them, turning pages, reading, taking notes etc. In Russian, however, the scene is portrayed slightly differently: there is also someone sitting at his desk with books to be used in the working process, but the books are seen or construed as being put in front of the reader's nose, i.e., they "stand" on the table vertically, so that the reader's head or face is hidden behind the books' covers. Thus, the verbalization of the whole scenario can be explained as a compound structure with four composite structures (the image-schemas called upon are given in brackets):

1. the figure/trajector – the person about whom the predication is being made (OBJECT),

2. the state in which the trajector is found – the posture of the trajector (COMPLEXITY/COMPACTNESS), i.e., a state of rest denoting a temporal relation, supported by something to sit on (ENABLEMENT, SUPPORT, CONTACT, LINKAGE),

3. the ground/landmark against which the posture is portrayed – here the location in the (interlocutors') visual field rather than giving the base at which the trajector rests (OBJECT), and

4. the orientation of the trajector relative to the ground (variable image schemas possible).

The difference as it surfaces in Russian is due to the fourth composite structure: the spatial arrangement of the trajector and the landmark, in this case, the person denoted by the subject and the thing denoted by the nominal *kniga* (book): the Russian expression has *sb sits* behind *books*, whereas the English and German expressions have *over*. The image-schematic content of *over* (UP-DOWN) and *behind* (FRONT-BACK, NEAR-FAR) respectively reflect how the landmark is (typically) thought or seen to be arranged with respect to the trajector (whose posture and location is determined in the scenario). The selection of the respective prepositions signals that the scenario is structured by foregrounding two distinct image schemas for the specification of the trajector's location: that of UP-DOWN or those of FRONT-BACK and NEAR-FAR, both of which employ body-based orientation in space rather than specifying the base at which the trajector rests.

The scene would be construed more "simply" if a copular verb (En: *be*, G: *sein*, R: zero) were used instead, which does not denote a posture but simply associates a trajector with an attribute or a location. If a copula is used, the temporal relation between trajector and landmark does not include any image-schematic information yet, the hint at the trajector's orientation is given by the prepositions alone and is encoded as an atemporal relation. The prepositions' semantic import in this case can be considered an instantiation of the schema UP-DOWN (in English and German) and FRONT-BACK and NEAR-FAR (in Russian) in combination with others such as OBJECT. The function of the copular verb is merely to incorporate the relation's second element and to make the relation between trajector and landmark temporal, whereas a posture verb itself already contains specific information on the trajector's own "spatial extension", its posture, by contributing image-schematic structure on its own. In our example of SIT, the image-schematic content of the posture verb does not overlap with that contributed by the preposition, which is why there is a wider choice in the construal of the scene as compared with scenes in which the orientation of the trajector relative to the ground takes up, and thus emphasizes, image-schematic content that is already implied in the posture verb. From the latter it follows naturally that the choice a speaker has in the construal of the respective scene is limited, and also cross-linguistic differences must be expected to be less pronounced.

Example (38) is about books and their whereabouts, i.e., the book is the trajector whose posture and location are being predicated. In this case, German is the odd one out in that it differs from Russian and English: the book's posture is identical in all three expressions: it STANDS, reflecting its vertical extension and thus foregrounding the image schema of VERTICALITY. The location of the book is also the same, but again, the expressions signal a difference in the image-schematic structuring of the complete scene: in German, the preposition *im* (in) triggers the image schema of a CONTAINER, whereas in Russian and English the prepositions *na/on* trigger the image schema of an OBJECT resting on the surface of and being SUPPORTed by another OBJECT, so that, as a result, German conceptualizes the book as being in a particularly organized container, the other two languages – as resting on the surface of a board. Thus the latter construal picks as landmark the base on which the trajector rests, whereas German construes the trajector as being in an upright position in a container with the supportive base left unspecified. As just shown for example (37), the posture verbs add information on the trajectors' orientation lacking in a comparable expression employing a copular verb: they are vertically oriented, the typical orientation we associate with books on a shelf.

6.2. One scenario – different posture verbs

The second (cross-linguistic) overall difference in the verbalization patterns, categorized as group 2, is the following: the three languages – or at least two of them – exploit different posture verbs for the verbalization of one scenario. Potentially, also different prepositions may be employed, the choice of which is not necessarily linked with the selected posture verb:

(42) G: *ein Schiff **liegt vor** Anker*
'a ship lies before anchor'
R: *korabl' **stoit na** jaroke*
'ship stands on anchor'
E: *a ship **lies/rides/is at** anchor*

(43) G: *etwas **liegt im** Magen*
'sth lies in the stomach'
R: *čto-l. **sidit v** pečenkach*
'sth sits in the liver'
E: *(food) **sits** heavy **on** the stomach*

(44) E: *Salt and pepper **sit on** the tables in old jam-jars*
R: *sol' i perec (solonka i perečnica) **stojat na** stole*
'salt and pepper (salt and pepper shaker) stand on the table'
G: *Salz und Pfeffer **stehen auf** dem Tisch*
'salt and pepper stand on the table'

The examples of this group make it obvious that the scenes are construed more radically differently in the respective languages than examples of group 1 and hence, the verbalizations have a more pronounced language-specific flavour. The individual expressions signal a different image-schematic structure of the respective scenes, this time reflecting the speakers' variable (perceptual) perspective on the trajector's posture itself, and – indicated by the occurrence of non-identical prepositions – also a diverging construal of its orientation relative to the ground.

In example (42), English and German construe the scene giving prominence to the horizontal extension of the verb's trajector (the ship LIES). As for the orientation between the trajector and the landmark (*anchor/Anker*), both languages go different ways. In English, this orientation is simply depicted as one of (spatial) closeness so that interaction between the two elements involved in the relation is construed as generally possible (NEAR(-FAR), LINKAGE). In German – though most speakers will no longer be aware of it – the trajector's orientation relative to the ground is (construed and) expressed as "position on the FRONT-BACK axis", with no indication of potential interaction. This use seems motivated by the fact that a ship is not in the harbour when literally at anchor – it is "in front of" the coast.

Russian construes the same scene from a noticeably different perspective taken on the trajector's posture. The use of *stojat'* (stand) backgrounds its horizontal extension and triggers the IS profile of STAND instead, selecting as the trajector's active zone the part that it normally rests on: the ship stands on its base in an upright position (a perspective linked with VERTICALITY), as against malfunctionally lying on one of its sides. This is in line with Rakhilina's (1997) finding for Russian that *stojat'* 'stand' often foregrounds its trajector's functionality. The Russian expression signals a further difference in the construal of the scene by the preposition *na* (on): being associated with the image schemas of SURFACE, LINKAGE, CONTACT and SUPPORT, it imports into the scene the idea that the anchor holds, i.e., supports, the ship in its position, an idea that is triggered neither by the English nor by the German expression.

In example (43), German has *liegen im* (lie in), employing the schemas of LIE, with a special emphasis given to HORIZONTALITY and CONTAINER (by the preposition *im* [in]). English, however, has *sit* triggering the schemas of SIT and *on* emphasizing the schemas of CONTACT, SUPPORT, and (COUNTER)FORCE. The Russian expression reflects a "mixed" construal: *sidet' v* (sit in), with the IS profiles of SIT and IN. Thus, abstracting away from the particular meanings of the lexicalizations of both trajectors and landmarks, the verbs and prepositions alone depict different scenes. The German verb encodes a posture different from that in the Russian and English expression, and only the English expression verbalizes a scene in which forces are actually on stage, because *on* alone makes prominent the idea of the landmark supporting the trajector in that it counteracts the trajector's weight. This aspect of the trajector exerting pressure (weight) is made up for in German and Russian by the posture verbs themselves: they signal non-movement/non-action in the source domain of digestion, which gives the target-domain reading of feeling not at ease.

6.3. One scenario – different verbs

In a third group of cases, we find that one or two of the three languages considered go about the verbalization of the same scene using verbs other than posture verbs.

(45) R: *na vašej sovesti budet **ležat'** pjatno*
 'on your conscience will lie a stain'
 G: *etwas **lastet auf** jemandes Gewissen*
 'something weighs heavily on someone's conscience'

G: *etwas liegt jemandem auf der Seele*
'something lies on someone's soul'
E: *something* **pricks** *someone's conscience,* **have** *something* **on** *one's conscience*

(46) R: *Put' v Gollivud ... ležal čerez Brodvej*
'the way to Hollywood lay through the Broadway'
G: *der Weg nach H* **führt über** *den Broadway*
'the way to H leads via the Broadway'
E: *the road to arms control* **lay through** *the process of negotiation*
(an actual corpus example)

(47) R: *no-vidimo, ona krepko* **sidela na** *igre*
'as noticeable, she strongly sat on the needle'
G: *jemand* **hängt an** *der Nadel*
'someone hangs at the needle'
E: *someone is* **hooked on** *(a drug) heroin*

As is suggested by the corpus data that fall under group three, this type of diversification is largely confined to (metaphoric) extensions of the posture senses of the respective verbs. Here we have the most obvious cross-linguistic differences: what is conceptualized as an extended sense of a posture verb in one language, can – in other languages – be understood radically differently in that no posture sense at all is employed.

In example (45), all three languages express a comparable situation – that we have something on our conscience – differently: Russian uses the posture verb *lezat'* (lie) with an inanimate abstract trajector, which is described as resting on someone's conscience. As already specified for example (43) the preposition *na* (on) verbalizes the IS profile of CONTACT, SUPPORT, and (COUNTER)FORCE, thus emphasizing the respective parts of the verb's IS profile. If one turns one's perspective to the landmark, the schema COUNTERFORCE accounts for the idea that the trajector burdens one's conscience (BURDENS ARE WEIGHTS). In German, we have the same image – something burdening us by lying heavily on us, but the scene is triggered by a more obvious cue, as it is lexically encoded in the verb stem: the verb *lasten* (weigh heavily) is derived from the noun *Last*, which means 'heavy weight' and as such makes the source domain of the mapping (WEIGHTS) explicit. The English expression goes back to a different scene: *something pricks somebody's conscience* describes the way in which one's conscience is affected by something irritating rather than a burden.

Example (46) is the last illustration I will give here. The scene or situation to be verbalized is that one can get to a particular location by using or travelling a particular route, both literally and metaphorically (STATES ARE LOCATIONS, ACTION IS MOTION). As the expressions show, English and Russian may employ the same type of construal: the way to some destination lies somewhere – as on a map. Despite the posture verb's static sense, the way is construed dynamically – as if following it with one's eyes or fingers on the virtual map. This construal is cued by the use of the directional preposition *čerez* (through) and *through* respectively, with the complete prepositional phrase verbalizing an area or place we traverse on our way to the final destination. German expressions of a comparable scene signal a different conceptualization, namely "fictive motion": the verb *führen* (lead) encodes a dynamic event and thus more easily and naturally combines with a directional preposition. The conceptualization of ways or roads as 'lying' also surfaces in German expressions, though in combination with a locational adverbial rather than a directional one: *ein schwieriger Weg liegt vor uns* (a difficult road lies ahead of us).

7. Conclusions

Cross-linguistic differences in a language's repertoire of collocations make it obvious that some ways of structuring a scene, or construing it, are preferred over others, and that individual languages do not necessarily conventionalize the same construals for a particular scene for both making sense of it and communicating it to others.

If posture verbs are employed literally in order to refer to a thing's posture and location, the choice of the particular posture verb depends on such image-schematic aspects that are perceived as salient in the posture of this thing, the trajector in such a scene. Secondly, also the (spatial) relation of the trajector to the ground against which its posture is specified contributes to the overall structuring of the scene and shows up in the respective expressions in the form of particular prepositions.

In non-literal uses, the extensions are constrained by the (image-schematic) similarities speakers recognize or construe between a posture scene and the "other" (more abstract) scenes to be verbalized: Posture verbs are extended to non-human concrete trajectors due to similarities people perceive in their postures, they are extended to abstract trajectors on the basis of whether speakers see any reason for understanding the target domains of the (metaphoric) mapping in a way compatible with an actual posture relation between a human trajector and some ground, which then allows for the mapping to be made. Examples (42)–(47) above were meant to show in what way both sensory-motor and perceptual experiences related to the human postures guide the choice of a particular posture or other verb. It must be kept in mind here that the motivations found are of a post-hoc nature, so that they cannot be understood to predict the conceptualization of the respective scenes. This is also why speakers of different speech communities may have conventionalized slightly or even totally different construals of the same scene, which accounts for the respective language-specific divergencies found in the data.

In nearly all scenes encoded by posture verbs, speakers construe the trajector as being involved in two kinds of relation, a posture and a location, namely the trajector – a thing – has a particular posture and is located at a particular place. In more technical terms, the scenes comprise

1. a temporal relation of a static event in which a posture is assigned to the trajector – cued by the verb, and
2. an atemporal relation between the trajector and the ground against which its posture is portrayed – cued by a preposition.

As for the contribution of the two relations to the construal of the overall scene, there is a ranking noticeable which, in the default case, puts the location of the trajector over its posture. This shows in the typical thematic organisation of the utterance (thematic progression) as well as in the potential substitution of the posture verb by a simple copular verb, without dramatically changing the content of the expression. What is missing in the latter case is the trajector's posture, which – in the default case – is not the focus of such an expression, i.e., does not represent rhematic information. If it is, the substitution does – of course – not work. In contrast to that, leaving out the trajector's location is a (more) marked change, reducing the expression's content to that of a trajector's posture. Such an expression is usually understood as an expression of the trajector's ability to take the posture named. Additionally, the resulting expression can be understood to follow from a contextual deletion of the location, where a number of readings have become entrenched, such as G: *Er sitzt. Sie liegt.* 'He sits/is sitting.' 'She lies/is lying', which mean that he is imprisoned (G: *Er sitzt im Gefängnis*) and that she is ill (G: *Sie liegt [krank] im Bett*).

In its complete form, a posture verb expression contains the composite structures already specified in Section 6.1. The posture verb – versus a potentially used copular verb – gives information on the trajector's own spatial "lay-out", the preposition specifies the orientation of the trajector relative to the ground. As for the preposition to be chosen, there are two different constellations. Firstly, if the trajector's orientation is construed against a location that is also involved in the posture, i.e., when an element is profiled as landmark that is causally related to the posture (because it enables that posture), the verb's and the preposition's IS profiles structure the same element of the respective scenario, namely this landmark. As a consequence, the choice of the preposition in such cases is constrained in that its IS profile must – at least in parts – match that of the verb: we *sit on* or *in* an object that enables sitting, we *lie in* or *on* or *stand on* an object that can hold us. This holds for all three languages, so that this kind of a posture scenario does not exhibit language-specific features. Secondly, if the trajector's orientation is construed relative to a location that is independent of the posture, the choice of preposition is not constrained by the IS profile of the posture verb. In such cases, it is selected solely on the basis of the trajector's location as the speaker perceives it relative to the ground. That means that selection here follows from a more general way of applying an anthropocentric perspective to spatial orientation in the (interlocutors') visual field. The preposition adds to the posture scene from its own IS profile information on the trajector's spatial orientation with regard to a landmark that is unrelated to the posture verb, which implies that the preposition's image-schematic structure is also unrelated to that of the verb. This holds for any such conceptualization that employs posture verbs. It is in the construals of such scenes that languages may have conventionalized different routes, which explains language-specific features of collocations with respect to the prepositions employed.

To sum up on the language-specific features of collocations found in the data, we can draw up the following list:

1. The collocations in the languages at issue show differences in the extensions of posture verb scenes to non-human trajectors, which results in a number of language-specific associations of the posture verbs and particular things/objects that this posture is ascribed to.

2. They show differences in the orientation of the trajector relative to the (same) landmark, which results in different prepositions being associated with identical scenarios.

3. They exhibit differences in the selection of a particular posture verb for one and the same trajector in an identical scenario, which results in collocations around different posture verbs.

4. They show completely different ways of construing a comparable scenario, which results in collocations that have a posture verb in one language, but not in another.

In all these cases, the differences in the wording are due to differences in the construal of the scenes to be verbalized. More particularly, whenever posture verbs and/or prepositions turn out to be different, this signals a divergence in the image-schematic structuring of the scenario. Hence, I find my claim corroborated that diversification between languages – the emergence of language-specific ways of verbalization – may be the result of diverging construals by drawing on different image-schema combinations in the conceptualizations of the phenomena to be expressed. In particular, it has been demonstrated that image schemas are centrally employed – in different combinations – in the conceptualization and verbalization of identical/comparable (posture) scenes, and that different speech communities can construe these scenes differently by highlighting particular image schemas at the expense of others. It has also been shown that the differences revealed are gradual: the scenes to be expressed can be "understood" from different perspectives, though on the basis of the same posture concepts, they can be construed on the basis of different posture concepts, or they can be conceptualized on the basis of totally different concepts.

Appendix

Table 1. Posture verbs in the English, Russian and German corpora (configural frequency analysis)

LANGUAGE	POSTURE	TRAJECTOR	Freq	Exp	Cont.chisq	Obs-exp	P.adj.Holm	Dec	Q
ENGLISH	Sit		354	235.8792	59.1511	∧	9.615553e-04	***	0.015
RUSSIAN	Sit		619	212.5981	776.8767	∧	7.038142e-71	***	0.052
GERMAN	Sit		467	991.5227	277.4763	∨	9.849649e-85	***	0.075
ENGLISH	Stand		706	716.9744	0.1680	∨	3.425276e-01	ns	0.002
RUSSIAN	Stand		258	646.2096	233.2164	∨	2.231333e-71	***	0.053
GERMAN	Stand		3413	3013.8160	52.8725	∧	1.932758e-19	***	0.080
ENGLISH	Lie		247	354.1464	32.4170	∨	2.013599e-09	***	0.014
RUSSIAN	Lie		301	319.1924	1.0369	∨	3.120082e-01	ns	0.002
GERMAN	Lie		1614	1488.6612	10.5530	∧	5.707485e-04	***	0.019

Table 2. Posture verbs and their trajectors in the English, Russian and German corpora

LANGUAGE	POSTURE	TRAJECTOR	Freq	Exp	Cont.chisq	Obs-exp	P.adj.Holm	Dec	Q
ENGLISH	Sit	Human_beings	308	104.3818	397.1992	∧	3.69E-58	***	0.029
ENGLISH	Sit	Abstract_objects	8	87.7994	72.5283	∨	1.64E-26	***	0.011
ENGLISH	Sit	Concrete_objects	14	40.1469	17.029	∨	4.10E-05	***	0.004
GERMAN	Sit	Abstract_objects	33	324.8783	262.2303	∨	7.55E-97	***	0.043
GERMAN	Sit	Concrete_objects	16	148.5527	118.276	∨	1.00E-42	***	0.019
GERMAN	Sit	Personified_objects	23	59.1627	22.1041	∨	1.77E-06	***	0.005
RUSSIAN	Sit	Human_beings	575	88.858	2659.6822	∧	2.28E-263	***	0.069
RUSSIAN	Sit	Abstract_objects	7	74.7417	61.3973	∨	2.43E-22	***	0.01

Table 2 continued

LANGUAGE	POSTURE	TRAJECTOR	Freq	Exp	Cont.chisq	Obs-exp	P.adj.Holm	Dec	Q
RUSSIAN	Sit	Concrete_objects	7	34.1761	21.6099	v	5.15E-07	***	0.004
RUSSIAN	Sit	Animals	8	1.6048	25.4852	∧	5.56E-03	**	0.001
ENGLISH	Stand	Abstract_objects	135	246.4579	50.4056	v	7.71E-14	***	0.016
ENGLISH	Stand	Human_beings	421	293.0056	55.9121	∧	1.21E-11	***	0.019
ENGLISH	Stand	Concrete_objects	62	112.6944	22.8043	v	2.81E-06	***	0.007
GERMAN	Stand	Abstract_objects	1350	911.9513	210.4133	∧	3.48E-47	***	0.07
GERMAN	Stand	Human_beings	900	1084.1886	31.2911	v	8.27E-09	***	0.03
GERMAN	Stand	Personified_objects	247	166.073	39.4355	∧	5.00E-08	***	0.012
RUSSIAN	Stand	Abstract_objects	43	209.8042	132.6172	v	5.85E-44	***	0.024
RUSSIAN	Stand	Human_beings	97	249.4292	93.1513	v	1.77E-27	***	0.022
RUSSIAN	Stand	Personified_objects	11	38.2069	19.3739	v	5.32E-06	***	0.004
ENGLISH	Lie	Human_beings	65	141.2048	41.1259	v	1.22E-11	***	0.011
ENGLISH	Lie	Personified_objects	4	21.6294	14.3691	v	1.01E-04	***	0.002
GERMAN	Lie	Human_beings	163	522.4905	247.3412	v	2.96E-78	***	0.054
GERMAN	Lie	Abstract_objects	775	439.4862	256.1389	∧	1.65E-49	***	0.05
GERMAN	Lie	Concrete_objects	361	200.9579	127.4569	∧	1.19E-23	***	0.023
RUSSIAN	Lie	Abstract_objects	60	101.1085	16.7138	v	1.33E-04	***	0.006
RUSSIAN	Lie	Concrete_objects	69	46.2325	11.212	∧	2.02E-02	*	0.003
	Sit		1389	2389	418.5852	v	8.40E-152	***	0.209
	Sit	Abstract_objects	48	487.4194	396.1463	v	2.08E-149	***	0.066
	Sit	Human_beings	1229	579.4768	728.0367	∧	7.79E-135	***	0.099
	Sit	Concrete_objects	37	222.8757	155.0181	v	1.08E-53	***	0.027
	Sit	Personified_objects	55	88.7627	12.8423	v	4.40E-04	***	0.005

Table 2 continued

LANGUAGE	POSTURE	TRAJECTOR	Freq	Exp	Cont.chisq	Obs-exp	P.adj.Holm	Dec	Q
	Sit	Animals	20	10.4655	8.6863	>	2.22E-02	*	0.001
	Stand		3899	2389	954.4161	>	2.14E-292	***	0.316
	Stand	Human_beings	1418	1626.6234	26.7571	<	1.13E-08	***	0.038
	Stand	Abstract_objects	1528	1368.2133	18.6607	>	9.29E-06	***	0.028
	Stand	Personified_objects	320	249.1617	20.1398	>	4.54E-05	***	0.01
	Lie	Human_beings	343	783.8998	247.9815	<	7.33E-76	***	0.069
	Lie		1879	2389	108.874	<	4.12E-39	***	0.107
	Lie	Concrete_objects	503	301.4999	134.6677	>	1.23E-26	***	0.029
	Lie	Abstract_objects	939	659.3672	118.5902	>	1.78E-26	***	0.043
	Lie	Personified_objects	83	120.0756	11.4478	<	9.84E-04	***	0.005
	Lie	Concrete_objects	1150	1433.4	56.0315	<	4.78E-18	***	0.049

Table 3. Posture verbs and co-occurring prepositions in the English, Russian, and German corpora

LANGUAGE	POSTURE	PREPOSITION	Freq	Exp	Cont.chisq	Obs-exp	P.adj.Holm	Dec	Q
		in	1514	531.9333	1813.1127	>	4.54E-292	***	0.132
		next_to	4	531.9333	523.9634	<	4.82E-229	***	0.071
		beyond	5	531.9333	521.9803	<	5.08E-227	***	0.071
		as	19	531.9333	494.612	<	1.76E-203	***	0.069
		over	46	531.9333	443.9112	<	8.53E-170	***	0.065
		by	49	531.9333	438.447	<	1.27E-166	***	0.065
		for	51	531.9333	434.823	<	1.43E-164	***	0.065

Table 3 continued

LANGUAGE	POSTURE	PREPOSITION	Freq	Exp	Cont.chisq	Obs-exp	P.adj.Holm	Dec	Q
		behind	95	531.9333	358.8997	<	2.47E-125	***	0.059
		with	116	531.9333	325.2297	<	3.82E-110	***	0.056
		under	125	531.9333	311.3073	<	3.24E-104	***	0.055
		on	1061	531.9333	526.2155	>	1.78E-98	***	0.071
		in_front	246	531.9333	153.6994	<	1.00E-45	***	0.038
		to	255	531.9333	144.1761	<	8.31E-43	***	0.037
		at	603	531.9333	9.4946	>	9.30E-04	***	0.01
	sit	to	0	46.0208	46.0208	<	3.70E-19	***	0.006
	sit	in	404	273.2372	62.579	>	1.08E-12	***	0.017
	sit	behind	56	17.145	88.0555	>	3.05E-12	***	0.005
	sit	under	3	22.5592	16.9582	<	1.06E-05	***	0.002
	sit	on	250	191.4826	17.883	>	5.91E-04	***	0.008
	sit	for	0	9.2042	9.2042	<	2.20E-03	**	0.001
	sit	over	0	8.3018	8.3018	<	5.19E-03	**	0.001
	stand	with	0	63.6335	63.6335	<	7.89E-27	***	0.008
	stand	to	255	139.8841	94.7332	>	2.94E-17	***	0.015
	stand	at	205	330.7847	47.8311	<	9.05E-13	***	0.016
	stand	in_front	210	134.947	41.742	>	3.26E-08	***	0.01
	stand	in	673	830.5274	29.8785	<	5.10E-08	***	0.022
	stand	over	2	25.234	21.3925	<	1.17E-07	***	0.003
	stand	under	113	68.5706	28.7874	>	1.43E-05	***	0.006
	stand	for	51	27.9768	18.9467	>	1.37E-03	**	0.003
	stand	behind	27	52.1137	12.1023	<	2.15E-03	**	0.003

Table 3 continued

LANGUAGE	POSTURE	PREPOSITION	Freq	Exp	Cont.chisq	Obs-exp	P.adj.Holm	Dec	Q
	stand	by	45	26.8797	12.2154	>	1.62E-02	*	0.002
	lie	to	0	69.0951	69.0951	<	3.27E-29	***	0.009
	lie	at	316	163.3896	142.5423	>	2.52E-25	***	0.02
	lie	in_front	5	66.6565	57.0316	<	4.40E-21	***	0.008
	lie	with	86	31.4315	94.7368	>	2.77E-14	***	0.007
	lie	over	44	12.4642	79.7891	>	1.07E-10	***	0.004
	lie	under	9	33.8702	18.2617	<	1.22E-05	***	0.003
	lie	for	0	13.819	13.819	<	2.76E-05	***	0.002
	lie	by	0	13.2771	13.2771	<	4.57E-05	***	0.002
	lie	behind	12	25.7413	7.3354	<	3.70E-02	*	0.002
ENGLISH	sit	on	72	31.3658	52.6414	>	3.57E-08	***	0.005
ENGLISH	sit	in	82	44.7576	30.9891	>	3.32E-05	***	0.005
ENGLISH	sit	with	16	3.4292	46.0822	>	6.45E-05	***	0.002
ENGLISH	sit	next to	4	0.1182	127.482	>	6.44E-04	***	0
ENGLISH	sit	to	0	7.5384	7.5384	<	3.82E-02	*	0.001
ENGLISH	sit	other	148	112.0419	11.5402	>	4.35E-02	*	0.005
ENGLISH	sit	in_front	0	7.2724	7.2724	<	4.78E-02	*	0.001
ENGLISH	stand	for	51	4.5827	470.152	>	4.23E-33	***	0.006
ENGLISH	stand	by	45	4.403	374.3167	>	1.21E-27	***	0.005
ENGLISH	stand	as	19	1.7073	175.1523	>	4.77E-12	***	0.002
ENGLISH	stand	in	61	136.0445	41.3958	<	3.25E-11	***	0.01
ENGLISH	stand	to	0	22.9137	22.9137	<	1.16E-08	***	0.003
ENGLISH	stand	in_front	0	22.105	22.105	<	2.58E-08	***	0.003

Table 3 continued

LANGUAGE	POSTURE	PREPOSITION	Freq	Exp	Cont.chisq	Obs-exp	P.adj.Holm	Dec	Q
ENGLISH	stand	on	46	95.339	25.5335	∨	1.28E-06	***	0.006
ENGLISH	stand	other	434	340.5606	25.6369	∧	3.38E-05	***	0.012
ENGLISH	stand	under	0	11.2322	11.2322	∨	1.10E-03	**	0.001
ENGLISH	stand	with	0	10.4235	10.4235	∨	2.39E-03	**	0.001
ENGLISH	stand	behind	0	8.5365	8.5365	∨	1.45E-02	*	0.001
ENGLISH	lie	other	110	168.2184	20.1487	∨	7.93E-05	***	0.007
ENGLISH	lie	beyond	5	0.2219	102.8853	∧	3.32E-04	***	0.001
ENGLISH	lie	to	0	11.3181	11.3181	∨	1.02E-03	**	0.001
ENGLISH	lie	in front	0	10.9187	10.9187	∨	1.49E-03	**	0.001
RUSSIAN	sit	in	195	40.3401	592.9506	∧	5.76E-67	***	0.019
RUSSIAN	sit	behind	50	2.5312	890.205	∧	4.68E-44	***	0.006
RUSSIAN	sit	on	121	28.27	304.1688	∧	2.60E-36	***	0.012
RUSSIAN	sit	other	210	100.9834	117.6888	∧	1.14E-19	***	0.014
RUSSIAN	sit	in front	17	6.5546	16.6458	∧	3.42E-02	*	0.001
RUSSIAN	stand	other	99	306.9475	140.878	∨	1.04E-42	***	0.027
RUSSIAN	stand	in	32	122.617	66.9682	∨	1.46E-20	***	0.012
RUSSIAN	stand	to	0	20.6521	20.6521	∨	1.09E-07	***	0.003
RUSSIAN	stand	behind	27	7.6939	48.4443	∧	4.55E-06	***	0.002
RUSSIAN	stand	at	21	48.8362	15.8664	∨	5.04E-04	***	0.004
RUSSIAN	stand	under	0	10.1236	10.1236	∨	3.15E-03	**	0.001
RUSSIAN	stand	with	0	9.3947	9.3947	∨	6.29E-03	**	0.001
RUSSIAN	lie	on	98	42.4443	72.7173	∧	2.13E-11	***	0.007
RUSSIAN	lie	other	80	151.6154	33.8275	∨	9.29E-09	***	0.009

Table 3 continued

LANGUAGE	POSTURE	PREPOSITION	Freq	Exp	Cont.chisq	Obs-exp	P.adj.Holm	Dec	Q
RUSSIAN	lie	in	97	60.5661	21.917	>	7.85E-04	***	0.005
RUSSIAN	lie	to	0	10.201	10.201	<	2.95E-03	**	0.001
RUSSIAN	lie	at	7	24.1224	12.1537	<	3.33E-03	**	0.002
GERMAN	sit	other	218	470.9702	135.8768	<	1.10E-38	***	0.034
GERMAN	sit	to	0	31.688	31.688	<	1.90E-12	***	0.004
GERMAN	sit	on	57	131.8468	42.489	<	1.31E-11	***	0.01
GERMAN	sit	at	31	74.9327	25.7575	<	6.81E-07	***	0.006
GERMAN	sit	under	0	15.5333	15.5333	<	1.68E-05	***	0.002
GERMAN	sit	in	127	188.1395	19.8684	<	9.86E-05	***	0.008
GERMAN	sit	in_front	14	30.5696	8.9812	<	4.60E-02	*	0.002
GERMAN	stand	to	255	96.3182	261.4243	>	1.30E-39	***	0.02
GERMAN	stand	in_front	199	92.9188	121.1081	>	5.73E-20	***	0.013
GERMAN	stand	with	0	43.8153	43.8153	<	1.00E-17	***	0.006
GERMAN	stand	behind	0	35.8833	35.8833	<	2.86E-14	***	0.005
GERMAN	stand	under	113	47.2148	91.6597	>	3.17E-14	***	0.008
GERMAN	stand	other	1679	1431.5532	42.7717	>	9.37E-11	***	0.038
GERMAN	stand	at	134	227.7643	38.6002	<	7.22E-10	***	0.012
GERMAN	stand	for	0	19.2636	19.2636	<	4.29E-07	***	0.002
GERMAN	stand	by	0	18.5082	18.5082	<	8.97E-07	***	0.002
GERMAN	stand	over	0	17.3751	17.3751	<	2.71E-06	***	0.002
GERMAN	lie	at	297	112.5032	302.5609	>	4.63E-46	***	0.023
GERMAN	lie	to	0	47.576	47.576	<	2.32E-19	***	0.006
GERMAN	lie	in_front	0	45.8968	45.8968	<	1.25E-18	***	0.006

Table 3 continued

LANGUAGE	POSTURE	PREPOSITION	Freq	Exp	Cont.chisq	Obs-exp	P.adj.Holm	Dec	Q
GERMAN	lie	with	75	21.6424	131.5489	>	3.17E-17	***	0.007
GERMAN	lie	over	39	8.5823	107.8075	>	3.29E-12	***	0.004
GERMAN	lie	under	0	23.3216	23.3216	<	7.84E-09	***	0.003
GERMAN	lie	on	121	197.9533	29.9152	<	1.79E-07	***	0.01
GERMAN	lie	behind	0	17.7244	17.7244	<	1.93E-06	***	0.002
GERMAN	lie	other	812	707.1094	15.5592	>	2.27E-03	**	0.014
GERMAN	lie	for	0	9.5152	9.5152	<	5.64E-03	**	0.001
GERMAN	lie	by	0	9.142	9.142	<	7.99E-03	**	0.001

Table 4. Literally used posture verbs and prepositions in the English, Russian and German corpora

LANGUAGE	POSTURE	PREPOSITION	Freq	Exp	Cont.chisq	Obs-exp	P.adj.Holm	Dec	Q
		in	644	228	759.0175	>	3.62E-149	***	0.365
		under	7	228	214.2149	<	5.51E-95	***	0.194
		on	505	228	336.5307	>	1.14E-71	***	0.243
		behind	50	228	138.9649	<	1.69E-51	***	0.156
		in_front	72	228	106.7368	<	9.57E-38	***	0.137
		at	90	228	83.5263	<	5.44E-29	***	0.121
	sit	in_front	0	29.2105	29.2105	<	2.55E-12	***	0.022
	sit	behind	44	20.2851	27.7246	>	3.91E-05	***	0.018
	stand	in_front	72	22.1579	112.1151	>	3.01E-16	***	0.037
	stand	at	11	27.6974	10.066	<	3.23E-03	**	0.012
	lie	in_front	0	20.6316	20.6316	<	1.50E-08	***	0.015

Table 4 continued

LANGUAGE	POSTURE	PREPOSITION	Freq	Exp	Cont.chisq	Obs-exp	P.adj.Holm	Dec	Q
ENGLISH	lie	behind	0	14.3275	14.3275	v	8.34E-06	***	0.011
RUSSIAN	sit	at	26	6.993	51.6611	∧	1.18E-06	***	0.014
RUSSIAN	sit	behind	44	7.9183	164.4152	∧	1.90E-17	***	0.027
RUSSIAN	sit	in	164	101.9877	37.7058	∧	1.07E-07	***	0.049
RUSSIAN	sit	at	0	14.2529	14.2529	v	2.82E-05	***	0.011
RUSSIAN	sit	in_front	0	11.4024	11.4024	v	4.58E-04	***	0.008
RUSSIAN	stand	in	22	77.3637	39.6199	v	1.76E-12	***	0.043
RUSSIAN	stand	at	0	10.8117	10.8117	v	7.92E-04	***	0.008
RUSSIAN	stand	in_front	0	8.6494	8.6494	v	6.48E-03	**	0.006
RUSSIAN	stand	under	7	0.783	49.3628	∧	7.52E-04	***	0.005
RUSSIAN	lie	at	0	10.0669	10.0669	v	1.64E-03	**	0.007
RUSSIAN	lie	in_front	0	8.0536	8.0536	v	1.09E-02	*	0.006
GERMAN	sit	on	30	85.6659	36.1718	v	5.31E-11	***	0.043
GERMAN	sit	in	58	109.2453	24.0384	v	9.25E-07	***	0.041
GERMAN	sit	in_front	0	12.2138	12.2138	v	2.11E-04	***	0.009
GERMAN	sit	behind	0	8.4818	8.4818	v	7.27E-03	**	0.006
GERMAN	stand	in_front	72	9.2649	424.796	∧	9.18E-38	***	0.046
GERMAN	stand	at	0	11.5811	11.5811	v	3.91E-04	***	0.009
GERMAN	stand	in	117	82.8689	14.0575	∧	5.74E-03	**	0.027
GERMAN	stand	on	92	64.9826	11.2329	∧	2.32E-02	*	0.021
GERMAN	lie	at	30	10.7833	34.2457	∧	4.60E-05	***	0.014
GERMAN	lie	in_front	0	8.6267	8.6267	v	6.45E-03	**	0.006

Notes

1. I use the term – as is usual in Corpus Linguistics – to refer to phrases or fragments in a sentence in which the selection of words is not free, that is, in which all or some lexico-syntactic choices are pre-empted. This gives room to subsume habitually co-occurring words of various degrees of stability, ranging from idioms at the one extreme to fragments with variable items at the other, with the proviso that the latter co-occur more often than chance would predict (cf. Schönefeld, to appear).
2. I use small capitals when referring to the posture concepts as against their verbal expressions, which are given in italics.
3. I follow here, and throughout this paper, the practice commonly applied in cognitive linguistics of giving image schemas in small capitals.
4. For a concise and comprehensive survey of linguistic construal operations and elaborations on them see Croft and Cruse (2004: 41–73).
5. For details and examples see Newmann (2002: 7–20), Lemmens (2002: 103–105), Lemmens (this volume).
6. The sequential arrangement of the three verbs is not just arbitrary, it is the "natural" iconically motivated arrangement (phonesthetic phonological constraints [cf. Birdsong 1995, among others]). Re-arrangement according to the "activity" or rather "control" involved would result in "stand, sit, lie", which is so rare that it does not seem to play a role as a motive.
7. Grady distinguishes two types of image schemas – according to the type of content: a) schematic representations of the perceptual world (such as PART-WHOLE, CENTRE-PERIPHERY, LINK etc) and b) those which lack perceptual content, i.e., representations of other aspects (such as ENABLEMENT, CYCLE, SCALE etc) (cf. 2001: 1).
8. All the image schemas posited and discussed in this paper have been suggested in (at least one of) these lists.
9. The distinction between trajector and landmark is a manifestation of the figure-ground distinction that guides our sensory perception as one type of construal operation: we focus our attention on some element or aspect (of a scene) as against other aspects which are thus backgrounded. In the three languages analysed, the trajector of a state-of-affairs (as when we state the posture/location of some entity) is typically associated with the grammatical subject at the level of syntactic organisation, the landmark – with the object of the preposition.
10. It is true that frequency of occurrence is only one potential indicator of an expression's status as a unit. Experiments, such as association tests, would be another source of inquiry.

From conceptualization to linguistic expression 341

11. For a detailed description of these projections see Newman (2002: 7–21), who also notes in this respect that "languages differ in the extent to which posture verbs can be extended to non-human referents". (Newman 2002: 7).
12. Although at first sight such diverging mappings seem to contradict the Invariance Hypothesis (posited as a constraint to hold in metaphorical mappings [cf. Lakoff 1990: 54]), the image-schematic structure of the source domain (human posture) is preserved in the mapping, though with different schemas (of the whole profile) being prominent.
13. For the analysis of English posture verbs, I chose a 3 million newspaper subcorpus of the BNC, comprising texts from the Independent (October 1989, 1.06 million words), the Guardian (November and December 1989, almost 900,000 words) and the Daily Telegraph (April 1992, 1.2 million words). For the analysis of German posture verbs, I selected a subcorpus comparable to the English one, both in size and register, comprising texts from the Mannheimer Morgen (December 2002, 1.9 million words), the Frankfurter Allgemeine (1989 and 1990, ca. 800,000 words), the Rheinische Merkur (1989 and 1990, ca. 200,000 words) and Die Zeit (1989 and 1990, ca. 100,000 words). Russian posture verbs were analysed on the basis of the corpora provided by Tübingen University (19th and 20th Century literature, press texts and the Uppsala Corpus). To keep the data comparable to the other two corpora I randomly selected 1/6 of the press texts (with a total of 18.4 million tokens), so that the analyses of Russian are also based on about 3 million words of running text.
14. I am very much indebted to Stefan Th. Gries, who suggested this kind of test to me and also did the respective calculations. I would, however, like to emphasize that I retain responsibility for any and all the shortcomings in the interpretation of the results.
15. I owe special thanks to Silke Höche for substantial help in the analysis of the Russian data, and to Klaus Heimeroth for compiling the German and Russian newspaper subcorpora and for (equally substantial) help in the analysis of the German data.
16. The data contain numerous examples with pronominal trajectors. Occasionally, these turned out to be difficult to categorize, since in German and Russian pronouns reflect the grammatical gender of the nouns they substitute. That means that in examples lacking sufficiently large contexts in the concordance line to find their antecedents, they could not always be classified unambiguously. Still, in the majority of cases we were able to distinguish between human and inanimate reference.
17. For the specification of metonymic and metaphoric mappings I use small capitals, following the practice commonly applied in Cognitive Linguistics.
18. The percentages of the literal uses of the verbs (Table 5) are calculated with respect to the total number of the respective preposition. The results of this

literal – non-literal comparison indicate a larger proportion of literal uses of these verb-preposition combinations in Russian.
19. Just as the posture verbs are understood to be linked with image-schema profiles, I claim that also prepositions are associated with such image-schema combinations or profiles.
20. Illustrations are given for English only, analogous examples can also be found in German and Russian.

References

Barlow, Michael
    2000   Usage, blends and grammar. In: Michael Barlow and Suzanne Kemmer (eds.), *Usage-Based Models of Language*, 315–346. Stanford, CA: CSLI Publications.

Birdsong, David
    1995   Iconicity, markedness and processing constraints in frozen locutions. In: Marge E. Landsberg (ed.), *Syntactic Iconicity and Linguistic Freezes*, 31–46. Berlin/New York: Mouton de Gruyter.

Croft, William and D. Alan Cruse
    2004   *Cognitive Linguistics*. Cambridge: Cambridge University Press.

Enfield, Nick J.
    2002   Semantics and combinatorics of "sit", "stand" and "lie". In: John Newman (ed.), *The Linguistics of Sitting, Standing, and Lying*, 25–41. Amsterdam/Philadelphia: John Benjamins.

Gibbs, Raymond W.
    2002   Embodied standing and the psychological semantics of *stand*. In: John Newman (ed.), *The Linguistics of Sitting, Standing, and Lying*, 387–400. Amsterdam/Philadelphia: John Benjamins.

Gibbs, Raymond W., Dinara A. Beitel, Michael Harrington, and Paul E. Sanders
    1994   Taking a stand on the meanings of *stand*: Bodily experience as motivation for polysemy. *Journal of Semantics* 11: 231–251.

Grady, Joseph
    2001   Image schemas and perception: refining a definition. Handout presented at the 7th ICLC, University of California at Santa Barbara.

Guirardello-Damian, Raquel
    2002   The syntax and semantics of posture forms in Trumai. In: John Newman (ed.), *The Linguistics of Sitting, Standing, and Lying*, 141–177. Amsterdam/Philadelphia: John Benjamins.

Langacker, Ronald W.
    1991   *Concept, Image, and Symbol*. Berlin/New York: Mouton de Gruyter.
    1999   *Grammar and Conceptualization*. Berlin/New York: Mouton de Gruyter.

Lemmens, Maarten
    2002   The semantic network of Dutch posture verbs. In: John Newman (ed.), *The Linguistics of Sitting, Standing, and Lying*, 103–139. Amsterdam/Philadelphia: John Benjamins.

Newman, John
    2001   A corpus-based study of the figure and ground in *sitting, standing, and lying* constructions *Studia Anglica Posnaniensia* 36: 203–216.
    2002   A crosslinguistic overview of the posture verbs "sit", "stand", and "lie". In: John Newman (ed.), *The Linguistics of Sitting, Standing, and Lying*, 1–24. Amsterdam/Philadelphia: John Benjamins.

Newman, John and Sally Rice
    2001   English SIT, STAND, and LIE in small and large corpora. *ICAME Journal* 25:109–133.

Newman, John and Toshiko Yamaguchi
    2002   Action and state interpretations of "sit" in Japanese and English. In: John Newman (ed.), *The Linguistics of Sitting, Standing, and Lying*, 43–59. Amsterdam/Philadelphia: John Benjamins.

Rakhilina, Ekaterina V.
    1997   Semantics and combinability (how concrete nouns reveal non-locative semantics of locative predicates in Russian). Paper presented at the 5th ICLC Amsterdam, The Netherlands.

Reid, Nicholas
    2002   Sit right down the back. In: John Newman (ed.), *The Linguistics of Sitting, Standing, and Lying*, 238–276. Amsterdam/Philadelphia: John Benjamins.

Rice, Sally
    2002   Posture and existence predicate in Dene Suliné (Chipewyan). In: John Newman (ed.), *The Linguistics of Sitting, Standing, and Lying*, 61–78. Amsterdam/Philadelphia: John Benjamins.

Schönefeld, Doris
    1999   Corpus linguistics and cognitivism. *International Journal of Corpus Linguistics* 4 (1): 137–169.
    2005   Frozen locutions – frozen dimensions: Left and right in English, German and Russian. In: Costantino Maeder, Olga Fischer, and William J. Herlofsky, (eds.), *Inside-Out and Outside-In. Iconicity in Language and Literature 4*, 241–265. Amsterdam/Philadelphia: John Benjamins.

to appear *Hot, heiss*, and *gorjachij*: A case study of collocations in English, German, and Russian. In: Paul Skandera, *Idiom(s) and culture(s) in English*, Berlin/New York: Mouton de Gruyter.

Taylor, John R.
   2002   *Cognitive Grammar*. Oxford: Oxford University Press.

Name index

Adamson, 217
Aikhenvald, 202
Alm-Arvius, 227
Apresjan, 20, 22, 23, 25, 27, 31–35, 37, 43, 46
Armstrong, 162
Atkins, 5, 8, 20, 32, 34, 61–63

Barlow, 6
Bartsch, 73, 91
Bencini, 3, 152
Berglund, 5
Biber, 5, 61, 80, 245
Birdsong, 340
Boas, 6, 152
Broccias, 152
Brugman, 59
Bybee, 6

Caffray, 181
Carden, 103
Casanova, 174
Čermák, 167
Chodorow, 91
Chuquet, 174
Church, 119
Cooper, 236
Cristofaro, 23, 28, 206
Croft, 1, 2, 19, 21, 26, 47, 58, 60, 78, 79, 135, 199, 203–205, 217, 298, 303, 340
Cruse, 1, 2, 21, 32, 58, 298, 303, 340

Dabrowska, 91
David, 285
Davidse, 6
de Haan, 5

Degand, 182, 293
Denison, 217
Divjak, 6, 8, 12, 14, 23, 33, 36, 37, 50, 73, 90
Dixon, 26, 197, 198, 202, 207, 218
Dowty, 203
Duffley, 206, 209

Eastwood, 102
Edmonds, 33
Elman, 88
Evans, 59, 75, 77
Everitt, 36
Evgen'eva, 32, 37, 43

Fagan, 269
Fauconnier, 130
Faure, 174
Fehr, 162
Fillmore, 61, 63, 161, 206, 207
Fischer, 152, 206, 209
Fisher, 20, 47
Flank, 31
Fodor, 182, 206
Fries, 3

Geeraerts, 58, 159, 168, 169
Gibbs, 3, 13, 60, 63, 73, 86, 87, 289, 303
Gildea, 62, 88
Gilquin, 7, 10, 11, 159, 174, 195, 196
Givón, 3, 26, 28, 29, 32, 45, 160, 176, 206, 209, 219
Goldberg, 3, 19, 20, 102, 105, 113, 127, 129, 150–152
Goldsmith, 165
Goodenough, 22

Grady, 303, 340
Gries, 1, 3, 5, 7–9, 12, 20, 33, 39, 47, 57, 61, 73, 77, 105, 109, 110, 119, 122, 128, 131, 132, 153, 181, 217, 254, 293, 342
Guirardello-Damian, 293

Haiman, 162
Hampe, 7, 10, 127, 131, 132, 151
Hampton, 179
Hanks, 5, 8, 21, 34, 61, 62, 75
Hare, 3, 88
Hay, 203
Hellerstedt, 294
Hirst, 33
Hollmann, 7, 11, 12, 198, 199, 204, 213, 218
Hopper, 103, 105, 113, 161, 193, 197, 199, 200, 202, 204, 209, 219, 231, 232, 238, 241, 253, 254
Huddleston, 102, 228, 232, 238, 246
Hudson, 217
Hutchinson, 181

Ide, 91
Inoue, 198
Itkonen, 164

Jackendoff, 152, 206, 207
Janda, 49
Johnson, 164, 166, 300, 303
Jorgensen, 3
Jurafsky, 62, 88

Käding, 3
Katz, 209
Keenan, 197
Kegl, 5
Kemmer, 6, 50, 167, 220

Kennedy, 203
Kilgarriff, 58, 61, 237
Kishner, 60, 63, 73, 86, 87
Klein, 60
Krauth, 89

Lakoff, 1, 38, 59, 75, 105, 113, 164–166, 183, 227
Langacker, 2, 23, 24, 27, 29, 38, 50, 150, 162, 182, 253, 255, 319, 299
LaPolla, 229, 230, 257
Leacock, 91
Lehrer, 92
Lemmens, 7, 12, 20, 29, 182, 261, 291–294, 340
Levin, 5, 9, 20, 32, 49, 67, 69, 108, 117, 121, 123, 203, 239
Levontina, 22, 31, 37
Lichtenberk, 227
Lorge, 3

MacLennan, 166
Mair, 167
Matlock, 60, 293
McDonald, 80
McRae, 88
Mervis, 3
Meyer, 5
Miller, 91, 94
Moens, 107
Mukherjee, 6
Murphy, 60

Nedjalkov, 194
Newman, 7, 12, 86, 225, 227, 236, 237, 254, 255, 265, 304, 340, 341
Niemeier, 181
Norvig, 59, 75, 227
Nunberg, 72

Oh, 5
Oostdijk, 5

Paillard, 174
Pall, 25, 27
Palmer, 299
Pesetzky, 103
Plungjan, 32
Posner, 182
Poutsma, 225
Pullum, 102, 228, 232, 238, 246
Pustejovsky, 23

Quirk, 102

Radden, 168, 227
Rakhilina, 293
Raukko, 3
Raxilina, 32, 37, 48
Reed, 182
Renouf, 253
Rice, 3, 7, 11, 12, 59, 75, 86, 193, 197, 209, 220, 225, 227, 236, 237, 239, 254, 255, 292, 301, 304
Roland, 88
Rosch, 3, 160, 168, 182
Ross, 236
Rubenstein, 22
Russell, 162

Sag, 72
Sandra, 3, 59
Scheibman, 6, 254
Schmid, 182
Schönefeld, 7, 10, 13, 127, 132, 151, 297, 340
Schütze, 218
Serra Borneto, 227, 267, 269
Shannon, 209
Shen, 227
Shopen, 103, 104, 120

Shortall, 159
Sinclair, 167, 169, 253
Šmelev, 50
Smessaert, 24, 49
Stedman, 107
Stefanowitsch, 5, 9, 20, 105, 106, 110, 113, 114, 119, 121, 122, 131, 132, 153, 167, 181, 183, 196, 197, 206, 209, 216–219, 254
Stubbs, 5, 159, 197
Sugamoto, 167
Sweetser, 227

Talmy, 20, 23, 204, 205, 217, 270, 291–293
Tao, 254
Taylor, 20, 33, 135, 161, 299
Teubert, 167
Theakston, 76, 86
Thompson, 161, 193, 197, 199, 200, 202, 204, 209, 219, 220, 231, 232, 238, 241, 253, 254
Thorndike, 3
Tomasello, 148, 255
Toops, 217
Tsohatzidis, 161, 180
Tuggy, 58
Turner, 130
Tyler, 59, 75, 77

Ungerer, 128, 182

Van Oosten, 284, 292
Van Tol, 262, 282
Van Valin, 182, 229, 230, 257
Vanden Eynde, 6
Vendler, 36
Verhagen, 50, 220
Véronis, 91
Veryzer, 181
von Eye, 89

Wasow, 72
Werner, 174
Wierzbicka, 20, 27, 159, 181, 206, 227
Williams, 91

Wulff, 3, 7, 9, 91, 101

Yamamoto, 167

Zaliznjak, 50

Subject index

affectedness, 35, 205, 243
affective, 205, 211, 214
  –, causation, 210
Amsterdam corpus, 34, 50
animacy, 35, 75, 90, 167, 174, 175, 204, 205
argument
  –, slot, 141, 149
  –, structure, 23, 24, 28, 30–32, 35, 46, 127–132, 134, 135, 137, 140, 142, 145, 146, 150–152, 229, 253, 254
attributive, 135, 136, 149, 152
  –, construction, 147, 148

bare stem, 255
  –, condition, 103
behavioral profile, 19, 34, 36, 44, 47, 57, 62, 63, 73, 75, 76, 78, 79, 81, 83, 84, 88, 90, 91
billiard-ball model, 163, 164, 166, 167, 170, 172–174, 179
blending, 128–131, 146, 149–151
  –, morphological, 128
  –, syntactic, 127, 128, 130, 151
BNC, *see* British National Corpus
British National Corpus (BNC), 102, 106, 110, 122, 127, 129, 133, 136, 137, 140, 146, 147, 160, 169, 193, 195, 199, 225, 226, 232, 238
Brown Corpus of American English, 57, 63

causality, 180, 201, 202, 210, 212
causation, 73, 134, 138, 140, 160, 162, 164, 165, 167, 169, 172, 179, 180, 198, 204–207, 209–214, 216, *see also* billiard-ball model
  –, of motion, 164
  –, prototypical, 159, 160, 163–167, 169-171, 174, 175, 177–179, 181
  –, volitional, 210
causative, 50, 81, 127, 134, 148, 149, 153, 159, 163, 169, 170, 173, 183, 184, 193, 194, 196–201, 203–206, 209, 210, 213, 215, 261, 262, 266, 279
  –, construction, 160, 162, 165, 167, 174, 177–180, 182, 184, 193, 196
  –, extension, 69–71
  –, posture verb, *see* posture verb
caused-motion, 140, 144, 153
  –, construction, 136, 142
  –, pattern, 137, 138, 152
  –, uses, 139, 142, 143, 148, 149
causee, 208
causer, 207, 208
cluster analysis, 19, 21, 36, 51, 52, 80, 81, 83, 93
collexeme, 102, 119, 120, 131, 133, 135, 149, *see also* collostructional analysis
collocational overlap, 102
collostruction, *see* collostructional analysis
collostructional analysis, 101, 102, 110, 111, 113, 114, 116, 119–121, 123, 131–133, 134, 135
complex-transitive, 127, 254

configural frequency analysis, 89, 310
construal, 27, 138, 140, 143, 144, 299, 300, 302
construction, 20–22, 24–29, 30–33, 35, 37, 38, 42, 46, 47, 49, 50, 58, 60, 72, 88, 101–114, 116, 117, 119, 121, 130–132, 139, 149, 161, 228, 253
–, prototypical, 30, 162
–, transitive, 66, 68, 250
constructional synonymy, 122
Construction Grammar, 101, 102, 105, 106, 108, 112, 122, 129, 134, 253
construction-specificity, 253, 255
contrastivity, 21
corpus, 4, 19, 47, 49, 57, 58, 60, 61, 75, 76, 78, 80, 81, 83, 87, 90, 102, 121, 122, 131, 132, 150, 159, 160, 167–169, 184, 211, 217, 257, 304, *see also* Amsterdam, BNC, Brown, COSMAS, ICE, NRC Handelsblad, Russian
–, data, 77, 176
–, linguistics, 4, 57, 78, 80, 159, 167, 178
corpus-based, 49, 57, 79, 167
COSMAS corpus, 305
counter-intuitive, 46
creativity, 127, 130, 131, 136, 137, 141, 147–150

De Standaard, 263, 275
direct manipulation, 163, 164, 166, 170, 172, 175–179, 183, 184
distribution, 22, 32, 33, 36, 46, 47, 49, 50, 78, 80, 83, 87, 90, 111, 115, 117, 123, 172
distribution-based, 19, 46
doen, 272, 276–279

double verb, 101, 102, 105

elicitation, 19, 21, 22, 37, 46, 48–50, 75, 169, 178, 180
Estimation of Significant Collocate Overlap (ESCO), 108–110, 115, 120, 121
event structure, 28, 30–32, 46
extension, 58, 64, 68, 70, 72, 83, 87–91, 107, 127, 250, 305

Fake-*and* Deletion, 103, 121
Fisher-Yates exact test, 111, 116, 119, 123, 132, 133
frequency, 21, 33, 39, 49, 60–62, 76, 84, 85, 89, 91, 110, 111, 113, 115, 117, 119, 123, 132, 133, 136, 137, 159, 160, 167–170, 177, 178, 180–182, 184, 236, 243, 254, 340
–, high, 159, 281
–, linguistic, 159, 168, 169
–, of passivization, 195
–, referential, 168

go-and-V construction, 101, 113, 114, 117
go-V construction, 101

H-CFA, *see* configural frequency analysis

ICE, *see* International Corpus of English
ID tag, 34, 36, 37, 47, 57, 62, 73, 75, 76, 80, 81, 83–86, 88–90, 93, 94
image schema, 60, 67, 81, 89, 266, 267, 285, 298, 300–303, 305, 322, 323
inanimacy, 35, 146, 167, 174, 175, 204, 205, 210, 213, 250, 311

Subject index 351

individuation, 241, 243
inflection, 103, 253–255, 257
inflectional island, 225, 255
inheritance, 120, 129, 131, 146, 149
International Corpus of English (ICE-GB), 57, 63, 76, 131, 135, 151, 184
intuition, 30, 43, 46, 49, 59, 77, 78, 80, 87, 128–131, 178, 181, 316

landmark, 340
leggen, 268–270, 279, 282
lexical manipulation, 148, 150
lie, 255, 262, 266, 301–303, 309–311, 314, 315, 317
liggen, 266, 268–270, 279, 280
links between constructions, 129
literalness, 64, 66, 81, 90, 137, 138, 140, 141, 147, 318, 327
lower level, 127, 147, 150

morphological blending, *see* blending
M-transitivity, 229, 230

near-synonymy, 19
network, 19, 30, 38, 44, 47, 48, 57, 59, 60, 68, 75, 79, 80, 83, 86, 88
–, information, 20
–, of construction, 19, 20, 22, 30, 46, 47
non-animate, *see* inanimacy
non-elicited, 50
non-literal, 147, 327
non-prototypical, 175
non-volitional, 175
NRC Handelsblad, 275

passive, 86, 146, 147, 194, 196, 199, 200, 208, 211, 212

passivizability, 86, 193, 195–197, 213, 214, 216, 217
passivization, 147, 194, 196, 199, 213–216, 218
polysemy, 37, 39, 48, 57–60, 63, 73, 75, 77, 78, 81, 83, 86, 87, 108, 114, 117, 122, 135
posture, 254, 262, 281, 282, 301, 305, 323
posture verb, 300, 305, 307, 312, 322, 323
–, causative, 262, 263, 285
–, non-causative, 261, 262, 281
preposition, 312
Principle of No Synonymy, 102, 105, 106, 121
prototype, 32, 37, 57, 75, 77, 159–161, 167–169, 176, 180–184, 265–267, 281
prototypicality, 30, 47, 63, 68, 69, 75–79, 81, 83, 88, 92, 114, 117, 159–163, 165, 167–170, 175–181, 183, 184, 206, 213–215, 217, 281, 302
–, and corpus linguistics, 167

radial network, 36, 38, 44, 59
resultative, 26, 130, 134, 144–146, 149, 152
–, construction, 134, 136, 142, 151
run, 57, 58, 60, 63–65
Russian corpora, 305

salience, 38, 90, 135, 159, 160, 168, 169, 178, 181, 184, 196, 205, 235, 236, 267, 299, 301–303, 317
sit, 255, 262, 266, 292, 301–303, 308–311, 314, 315, 317
situation type, 31, 107, 111, 113, 115–117

352 *Subject index*

staan, 262, 266–269, 279, 280, 292
stand, 255, 262, 266, 267, 301–303, 309–311, 314, 315
steken, 262, 272–276, 279, 282
stellen, 262, 279
stoppen, 262, 272–276, 279, 282
synonymy, 19, 21, 22, 31–34, 38, 39, 43, 44, 46–48, 49, 51, 71, 90, 102, 105, 108, 121, *see also* near synonymy, Principle of No Synonymy
syntactic
    –, blending, *see* blending
    –, creativity, 127, 129, 146, 148

trajector, 143, 144, 304, 305, 307, 322, 340
transitivity, 68–73, 81, 86, 91, 94, 135–137, 140, 142, 145–147, 151, 152, 161, 179, 193, 197–201, 203–219, 225–232, 237–239, 243, 250, 253, 257
typology, 202, 206

unusual argument structure, 128

verb
    –, class, 20, 46, 108, 111, 116–118, 123, 127, 129, 131, 135, 146, 150, 149
    –, island, 148, 255
verticality, 269
volition, 37, 39–41, 171, 175, 179, 204, 205, 214, 243

zetten, 262, 263, 267–269, 271, 272, 279, 284, 285
zitten, 266, 270–272, 279, 280, 284

www.ingramcontent.com/pod-product-compliance
Lightning Source LLC
Chambersburg PA
CBHW071359300426
44114CB00016B/2114